# Learn Ethereum

Build your own decentralized applications with Ethereum and smart contracts

**Xun (Brian) Wu**
**Zhihong Zou**
**Dongying Song**

**BIRMINGHAM - MUMBAI**

# Learn Ethereum

**Commissioning Editor:** Pravin Dhandre
**Acquisition Editor:** Joshua Nadar
**Content Development Editor:** Nazia Shaikh
**Senior Editor:** Ayaan Hoda
**Technical Editor:** Joseph Sunil
**Copy Editor:** Safis Editing
**Project Coordinator:** Kirti Pisat
**Proofreader:** Safis Editing
**Indexer:** Manju Arasan
**Production Designer:** Joshua Misquitta

First published: September 2019

Production reference: 1200919

Published by Packt Publishing Ltd.
Livery Place
35 Livery Street
Birmingham
B3 2PB, UK.

ISBN 978-1-78995-411-1

www.packt.com

Packt.com

Subscribe to our online digital library for full access to over 7,000 books and videos, as well as industry leading tools to help you plan your personal development and advance your career. For more information, please visit our website.

## Why subscribe?

- Spend less time learning and more time coding with practical eBooks and Videos from over 4,000 industry professionals

- Improve your learning with Skill Plans built especially for you

- Get a free eBook or video every month

- Fully searchable for easy access to vital information

- Copy and paste, print, and bookmark content

Did you know that Packt offers eBook versions of every book published, with PDF and ePub files available? You can upgrade to the eBook version at www.packt.com and as a print book customer, you are entitled to a discount on the eBook copy. Get in touch with us at customercare@packtpub.com for more details.

At www.packt.com, you can also read a collection of free technical articles, sign up for a range of free newsletters, and receive exclusive discounts and offers on Packt books and eBooks.

# Contributors

## About the authors

**Xun (Brian) Wu** has over 17 years of extensive hands-on experience in design and development with blockchain, big data, the cloud, UIs, and system infrastructure. Brian is a co-author of *Blockchain Quick Start Guide, Hyperledger Cookbook, Security Tokens and Stablecoins Quick Start Guide, Blockchain By Example,* and *Seven NoSQL Databases in a Week,* and is a technical reviewer for more than 50 books for Packt. He owns several patents in the blockchain area. He holds a master's degree in computer science from NJIT. He lives in New Jersey with his two beautiful daughters, Bridget and Charlotte.

> *I would like to thank my parents, wife, and children for their patience and support throughout this endeavor.*

**Zhihong Zou** has more than 20 years of software architecture, design, and development experience in the telecommunication and healthcare industries. As a seasoned enterprise and solution architect, and a thought leader in blockchain, business process management, big data, AI, and machine learning, he has leveraged emerging technologies to solve complex real-world business problems. He holds a master's degree in computational mathematics and a master's degree in computer science. He has published several papers on numerical computation in renowned academic journals.

> *I would like to thank my wife Yufang and my son Kevin for their understanding, encouragement, support, and patience throughout this journey. I appreciate all the sacrifices you made so that I could complete the book.*

**Dongying Song** has more than four years of extensive hands-on experience in blockchain, Ethereum, big data, machine learning, and data science. As an experienced software engineer and data scientist, she has worked for a top-tier bank and pharmaceutical companies. Dongying holds a master's degree in statistics from Columbia University and majored in mathematics during her undergraduate years. Her recent activities have focused on blockchain, Ethereum, and smart contract developments.

# About the reviewers

**Voith Mascarenhas** is a software engineer by profession who is skilled in the Python programming language. He discovered Ethereum in early 2017 through his colleagues. Fascinated by the complexity of Ethereum and its promise for decentralized governance, he has made it his new hobby project. He has been contributing to Ethereum's Python ecosystem ever since discovering it and can also be found helping beginners in public chat groups. He recommends this book to any software engineer planning to dive deep into Ethereum.

> *I would like to thank Christoph Burgdorf for recommending to Packt that I review this book.*
> *I would also like to thank Packt for giving me this wonderful opportunity. Not only was it a pleasure reading this book, but it was also a great learning opportunity.*

**Christoph Burgdorf** works as a software engineer at Ethereum. He is part of a team that develops and maintains many different projects of the Python Ethereum ecosystem. His main focus is on the Trinity client, a Python node for Ethereum 1 and 2. Before joining Ethereum, Christoph spent several years traveling the world as the co-founder of thoughtram to perform training on Angular, a web framework by Google to which he also contributed. When he's not writing code, Christoph likes spending time with his family, going camping, cycling, and traveling the world.

**Sumit Chauhan** is a speaker, advisor, and a CEO with more than 19 years of experience in delivering enterprise solutions focused on global growth and digital transformations with emerging technologies such as blockchain and AI. He has worked in various technical roles for different technology companies across the globe. He is currently a co-founder of Datopic Technologies, which works on building decentralized white label products with big data, machine learning, and blockchain technologies for cybersecurity, Internet of Things, and FinTech companies.

**Nikola Tchouparov** is a co-founder and CEO at Moneyfold Ltd in the UK, which is the world's first regulation-compliant stablecoin provider. He has been engaged in the blockchain and cryptocurrency space since 2013. In his previous career, Nikola implemented trading and risk management systems at banks around the world.

# Packt is searching for authors like you

If you're interested in becoming an author for Packt, please visit `authors.packtpub.com` and apply today. We have worked with thousands of developers and tech professionals, just like you, to help them share their insight with the global tech community. You can make a general application, apply for a specific hot topic that we are recruiting an author for, or submit your own idea.

# Table of Contents

# Section 2: Blockchain Development Cycle

# Preface

Ethereum is a blockchain and decentralized computing platform that allows the execution of smart contracts.

This book provides a basic overview of the Ethereum ecosystem, the concept behind Ethereum, and the mechanism of Ethereum, and demonstrates a step-by-step approach in building decentralized applications. It offers a quick guide, allows a reader who does not have in-depth or systematic knowledge on the topic to master the following skills.

This book begins with the very basics of Ethereum, blockchain, the Solidity language, and cryptocurrency. The book will simplify cryptography for you and then demonstrate how it can be used to secure ether, cryptographic data structures, **advanced encryption standard (AES)**, hashes, private keys, and more. The book will then demonstrate how mining works and how miners make their profits. After this, the book will cover concepts such as proof of work, proof of stake, and smart contracts. The book will cover smart contracts in details, including concepts such as the Solidity programming language, token standards, and more. The book will cover how to build UIs for applications in Node.js and web3.js, explore Ethereum wallets, and look at building real-time scalable Ethereum applications. In addition, the book covers use cases highlighting the potential applications of Ethereum across sectors such as banking, financial services, healthcare, insurance, and real estate. By reviewing various Ethereum tools and frameworks with examples, readers will learn Truffle, Remix, MetaMask, IPFS, SWARM, Infura, Whisper, OpenZeppelin, and many other Ethereum technologies.

By the end of this book, you will learn about Ethereum decentralized application development, testing, deployment, developer tools, frameworks, more advanced blockchain concepts.

## Who this book is for

This book appeals to all those developers who want to go beyond the theory and possibilities of cryptocurrencies, blockchain, and Ethereum. Those who wish to build secure, transactional, and third-party independent applications will benefit from the practical examples in the book.

# What this book covers

Chapter 1, *Blockchain and Cryptocurrency*, covers the basics of blockchain, discusses how blockchain is disrupting existing technology, how cryptocurrency came into the picture, and how the Ethereum consensus mechanism works. We will also learn how cryptography makes the Ethereum blockchain secure. By the end of the chapter, you should understand Ethereum accounts, forks, and the concept of mining.

Chapter 2, *Ethereum Architecture and Ecosystem*, describes the architecture of Ethereum and helps you to understand the **Ethereum Virtual Machine (EVM)**, Gas, accounts, and more. It also covers the basic concepts of Ether mining. We look at **initial coin offerings (ICOs)** and the Ethereum token economy. We will also explore various tools and technologies in the Ethereum ecosystem.

Chapter 3, *Deep Research on Ethereum*, teaches you about ongoing research on the Ethereum platform in the field of ICOs, sharding EVM improvements, economics, low-level protocol improvements, and decentralized storage.

Chapter 4, *Solidity Fundamentals*, deals with the basic features of the Solidity programing language. We cover Solidity's development tools and learn about various Solidity language fundamentals, including the structure of contracts, contract patterns, and exception handling. We cover smart contract security and best practices.

Chapter 5, *Developing Your Own Cryptocurrency*, teaches you how to write your own cryptocurrency using smart contracts. We look at smart contract open source libraries and review the ERC 20 token standard. Finally, we develop our first cryptocurrency token.

Chapter 6, *Smart Contract Development and Test Fundamentals*, shows you how to use Remix to develop and debug smart contracts. We explore various options for the Truffle suite tool. We cover smart contract unit tests by using these development tools.

Chapter 7, *Writing UIs for DApps*, shows you various methods to deploy smart contracts. There will be examples to demonstrate everything. We look at the web3.js API and write client-side Node.js code to call smart contracts.

Chapter 8, *Ethereum Tools and Frameworks*, covers the tracking of data inside smart contracts.

Chapter 9, *Creating an Ethereum Private Chain*, explains the difference between public and private blockchains. It covers how to set up private blockchains on Ethereum, including the options flags we can use with new chains. It also presents private blockchains in production usages.

Chapter 10, *Deployment of Your Smart Contract*, shows you how to deploy smart contracts to various blockchain environments.

Chapter 11, *Building Ethereum Wallets*, looks at the concepts of Ethereum wallets. Then, we create a **hierarchical deterministic (HD)** wallet. We also discuss popular third-party Ethereum wallets.

Chapter 12, *Conclusion*, is a summary of the entire book and the Ethereum blockchain technologies covered therein.

# To get the most out of this book

You need to have some basic knowledge of Ethereum frameworks such as Truffle. Knowledge of JavaScript will also be useful.

# Download the example code files

You can download the example code files for this book from your account at www.packt.com. If you purchased this book elsewhere, you can visit www.packtpub.com/support and register to have the files emailed directly to you.

You can download the code files by following these steps:

1. Log in or register at www.packt.com.
2. Select the **Support** tab.
3. Click on **Code Downloads**.
4. Enter the name of the book in the **Search** box and follow the onscreen instructions.

Once the file is downloaded, please make sure that you unzip or extract the folder using the latest version of:

- WinRAR/7-Zip for Windows
- Zipeg/iZip/UnRarX for Mac
- 7-Zip/PeaZip for Linux

The code bundle for the book is also hosted on GitHub at https://github.com/PacktPublishing/Learn-Ethereum. In case there's an update to the code, it will be updated on the existing GitHub repository.

We also have other code bundles from our rich catalog of books and videos available at https://github.com/PacktPublishing/. Check them out!

# Download the color images

We also provide a PDF file that has color images of the screenshots/diagrams used in this book. You can download it here: http://www.packtpub.com/sites/default/files/downloads/9781789954111_ColorImages.pdf.

# Conventions used

There are a number of text conventions used throughout this book.

CodeInText: Indicates code words in text, database table names, folder names, filenames, file extensions, pathnames, dummy URLs, user input, and Twitter handles. Here is an example: "With web3.js installed, to instantiate web3, here is some typical JavaScript code:"

A block of code is set as follows:

```
componentDidMount = async () => {
        const web3 = await getWeb3();
        const contractInstance = await getInstance(web3);
...
        this.setState({ contractInstance: contractInstance });
    }
```

Any command-line input or output is written as follows:

```
npm install -g create-react-app
```

**Bold**: Indicates a new term, an important word, or words that you see onscreen. For example, words in menus or dialog boxes appear in the text like this. Here is an example: "As we discussed earlier, the **PUBLISH YOUR ARTS** page is the place for the art owner to do the following:"

Warnings or important notes appear like this.

Tips and tricks appear like this.

# Get in touch

Feedback from our readers is always welcome.

**General feedback**: If you have questions about any aspect of this book, mention the book title in the subject of your message and email us at `customercare@packtpub.com`.

**Errata**: Although we have taken every care to ensure the accuracy of our content, mistakes do happen. If you have found a mistake in this book, we would be grateful if you would report this to us. Please visit `www.packtpub.com/support/errata`, selecting your book, clicking on the Errata Submission Form link, and entering the details.

**Piracy**: If you come across any illegal copies of our works in any form on the Internet, we would be grateful if you would provide us with the location address or website name. Please contact us at `copyright@packt.com` with a link to the material.

**If you are interested in becoming an author**: If there is a topic that you have expertise in and you are interested in either writing or contributing to a book, please visit `authors.packtpub.com`.

# Reviews

Please leave a review. Once you have read and used this book, why not leave a review on the site that you purchased it from? Potential readers can then see and use your unbiased opinion to make purchase decisions, we at Packt can understand what you think about our products, and our authors can see your feedback on their book. Thank you!

For more information about Packt, please visit `packt.com`.

# Section 1: Blockchain and Ethereum Basics

Since its inception, blockchain has fundamentally changed how people can transfer values such as ether and establish trust between parties without any intermediary. In this section, we will learn all about blockchain. We will also learn about the architecture and ecosystem that Ethereum functions on.

This section comprises of the following chapters:

# 1
# Blockchain and Cryptocurrency

It is a common belief that the bankruptcy filed by Lehman Brothers, a Wall Street banking giant, on September 15, 2008, triggered the global financial crisis in 2008-2009. Excessive risk exposure in subprime mortgage and financial derivatives by large banks almost brought down global financial systems. The crisis was the ultimate consequence of a fundamental breakdown of trust in the relationship between customers and the financial institutions that should have been serving them.

Shortly after that, Satoshi Nakamoto, a mysterious and anonymous entity, published a whitepaper on October 31, 2008, called *Bitcoin: A Peer-to-Peer Electronic Cash System*, which is considered the origin of Bitcoin and all cryptocurrencies. Satoshi proposed a completely decentralized approach for **Peer-to-Peer (P2P)** payment without central banks or intermediaries. He outlined the principles and functions of what would be developed and introduced as Bitcoin in the following year.

The technologies behind his invention are called blockchain and have since evolved well beyond Bitcoin and digital payment. It is now a suite of technologies, forming the foundation of distributed ledgers and cryptocurrency. No one knows who or what Satoshi is, if it is one individual or a group, but its paper is profoundly changing money, digital- and cryptocurrencies, business, and the world.

The purpose of this book is to help you to understand blockchain technologies, introduce you to the tools and technologies in the Ethereum ecosystem, and get you started with developing smart contracts and end-to-end decentralized applications. We will start with basic concepts in Bitcoin, Ethereum, cryptocurrency, and blockchain. In this chapter, we will cover the following topics:

- Introducing blockchain technology
- Rehashing cryptography
- Anatomizing the blockchain consensus mechanism
- Understanding Bitcoin and cryptocurrency
- Ushering in the world of Ethereum

# Technical Requirements

For all the source code of this book, please refer the following GitHub link:
`github.com/Packt-Publishing/Learn-Ethereum`.

# Introducing blockchain technology

You might have heard the parable of the blind men and an elephant. It is a folk tale about each of six blind men's individual descriptions of the same elephant based on their own touch and feel of the animal. It highlights the fact that different perspectives may lead to distinct viewpoints, emphasizing the limits of perception and the importance of a complete context.

When Satoshi invented Bitcoin, the fundamental concept in its vision was to build a **blockchain**, a shared public ledger (longest **proof-of-work** (**PoW**) chain), that verifies and records immutably all transactions through a decentralized computer network (**P2P network**) and a **consensus mechanism** with computational proof. Satoshi came up with an elegant solution solving the double-spend problem of electronic monies. A **double-spend** is an attack when someone tries to spend money through a transaction that isn't actually available anymore as the money was already spent before.

Blockchain is a new elephant in the digital world. To most of the public, blockchain is nothing but an obscure pseudonym for all cryptocurrencies, including Bitcoin, Ethereum, and more. So, what is blockchain? What does a blockchain look like? How does it work? Where can we use blockchain? Do you need a blockchain? Although there are many ways to describe a blockchain, mainly from different perspectives, there is no universal definition of a blockchain.

On the contrary, there are prevalent debates over the essential attributes or qualities of a blockchain. It is perceived as a new architecture with existing technologies, the next generation of the internet and web, a future database and distributed shared ledger, the new Napster (a P2P file-sharing system used in the 90s) with a pure decentralized P2P network, a cryptocurrency, or a trustless secure transaction system, and so on. It is all of them. Only by combining all of them can we understand the whole picture of blockchain technologies and get a sense of the true potential of blockchain.

The following diagram illustrates different viewpoints of blockchain technology:

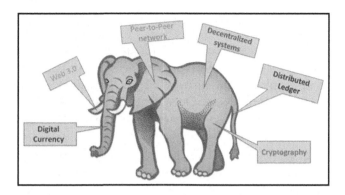

So, what is a blockchain anyway? Think of blockchain as a new architecture paradigm and a new trust protocol. It is a computer science primitive forming the foundation of most cryptocurrencies and decentralized applications. It is a P2P transaction model that can enable two parties to transact in a way that is tamper-resistant and cryptographically proven. As the technology behind Bitcoin and other cryptocurrencies, blockchain is an open, distributed ledger that can be simultaneously used and shared within a large decentralized, publicly accessible network.

In essence, blockchain is a distributed shared ledger technology supported by three pillars, as shown in the following screenshot; these are P2P networks, cryptography, and a consensus mechanism:

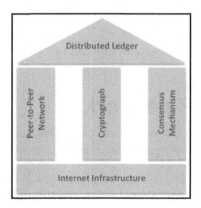

To understand how blockchain works, let's start with the fundamental concepts and key building blocks of blockchain technologies. Then, we'll discuss the key differences between centralized, distributed, and decentralized systems. We will then dive into the blockchain data structure and discuss how transactions, blocks, and chains are maintained and how the network reaches a consensus on the state of the chain, as well as how to secure the blockchain with cryptographic technologies.

Following is a list of the key building blocks of blockchain technologies:

- **Transactions**: A transaction is a value transfer between two parties. It could be a transfer of money, tangible assets, or cryptocurrency. Transactions are broadcasted to the blockchain network. They are validated and verified by all nodes and collected into blocks. Once the block reaches a certain depth—in Bitcoin, this is 6 blocks—those transactions in the block can be considered irreversible.
- **Block**: All verified transaction records are collected into a data structure called a block. It has a header and body part, where the header contains a cryptographic hash of the previous block, a timestamp, and a Merkle tree root hash of all transactions in the block. The body is the container of transaction data.
- **The chain of block (blockchain)**: A blockchain is a linked list of a chain of blocks. Blocks are linked together using a cryptography hash as the pointer to the previous block.
- **Decentralized P2P network**: It is a P2P network in which interconnected nodes share resources amongst each other without the use of a central authority or some sort of intermediary.
- **Consensus protocol**: The consensus protocol in blockchain is a set of rules that all network nodes will enforce when considering the validity of a block and its transactions. The consensus mechanism is the process used by the network nodes to achieve agreement on the network state. It is a fault-tolerant mechanism to ensure the reliability and integrity of the network.
- **Mining**: Mining is the process by which network nodes in blockchain systems add new blocks to the blockchain and get rewarded with crypto-incentives.

# Decentralized P2P network

To explain how blockchain works, let's look at what steps are involved with the existing business model for completing a simple payment transaction.

A customer, Alice, needs to pay $10 to Bob, who happens to have an account in the same bank as Alice. She can make the payment either by visiting a bank branch or using the web. Let's say she tries to do that online through the bank's web portal. She will need to authenticate herself using her username and password and then put the transfer order in and wait for the bank system to confirm whether the transaction is completed.

As shown in the following diagram, in order to support such online banking activities in the traditional world, the bank has to establish an identity and access management system and authenticate Alice's login credentials. Behind the scenes, the bank needs to develop a bank web portal and a backend system to verify whether Alice has the right account with the bank and has enough money to pay Bob to transfer $10 out of Alice's account, and put $10 in Bob's account. The bank has to maintain a ledger to record the details of the transaction in a database and show the balance each person has.

The following diagram shows a centralized bank system model:

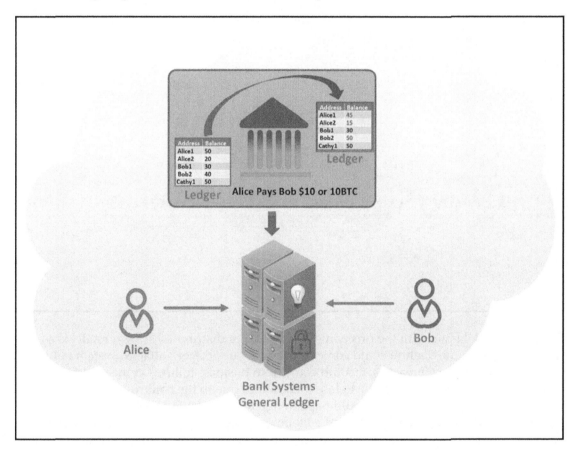

As the business grows, customers' needs change too. The traditional brick and mortar business model is being replaced by the digital banking and commerce model. This requires technology changes in the bank system too. Banks nowadays deploy a distributed system model to serve the ever-growing needs of their customers.

The following diagram shows the distributed bank system model:

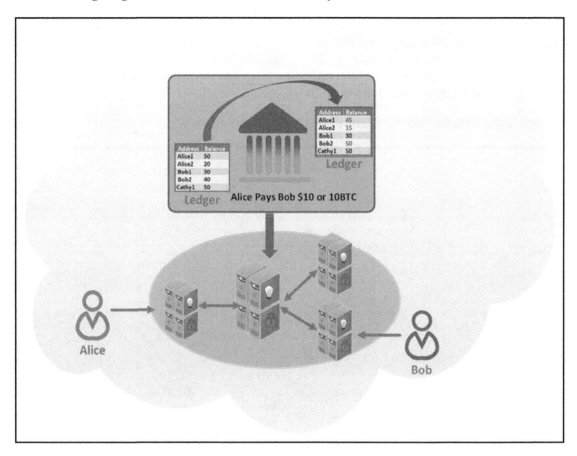

The fundamental issue with the preceding centralized or distributed system model is a single point of failure. Failure could come from malicious network attacks, system failures, or security and privacy breaches; it could come from business failures in the bank itself, which can cause millions of people to lose their homes due to the bankruptcy of big banks during a global financial crisis. It could happen due to currency failure itself, such as the currency collapse in Venezuela, where the lifetime savings of average citizens suddenly became worthless overnight. Also, the payment may be blocked due to government censorship.

Satoshi Nakamoto believed that the root problem with traditional fiat currency is all the trust required to make it work. Citizens have to trust the central bank not to devalue the currency. Consumers have to trust the bank to manage their money. But history has shown again and again that trust is often breached.

Satoshi designed an elegant decentralized P2P electronic cash system, and the technology behind that, blockchain, is the solution, where transactions are maintained in a distributed shared ledger and replicated across a global P2P network; security and privacy are ensured with cryptographic technologies, and transaction integrity is achieved through a consensus mechanism.

The following diagram shows a decentralized bank system model:

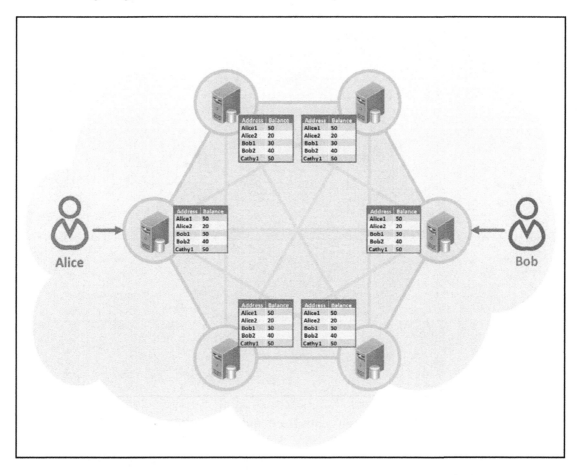

As new transactions are made, they are broadcasted to all network nodes, and over time all transactions that have occurred are sequenced together in the public ledger and made available in all replicated network nodes, as shown in the following diagram:

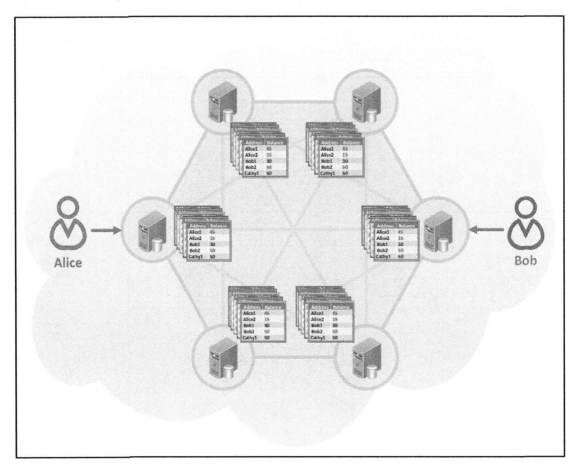

Now that we understand the between centralized and decentralized models, let's how blockchain works.

# How does blockchain work?

Using the previous example, as shown in the following diagram, let's assume Alice wants to buy something from Bob and she agrees to pay Bob $10 or 10 Bitcoins (BTC):

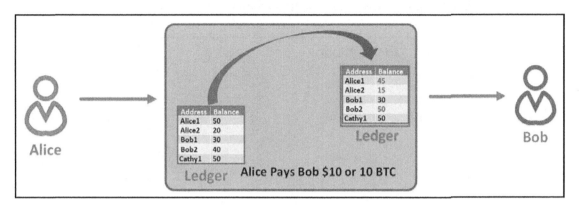

Let's walk through the high-level processes step-by-step, demonstrating how the blockchain works:

1. **Create blockchain transactions:** A transaction is a value transfer between two parties. When Alice sends $10 or 10 BTC to Bob, it will create a transaction with one or more inputs and two or more outputs, where the inputs reflect Alice's account, and the outputs reflect which account(s) Alice intends to transfer to. The transaction is then digitally signed with Alice's private key and broadcasted to the P2P network. The receiver will use the digital signature to verify the ownership of Alice's funds. We will discuss digital signatures and cryptographic hash functions in detail in later sections.

2. **Validate the transactions and add to the transaction pool:** Once the transaction is submitted to the blockchain network, the bookkeeper node (usually a full node in a P2P network that receives the transactions) will validate it according to the business and technical rules defined by the blockchain network. If the transaction is valid, the bookkeeper will add it to the transaction pool and relay the transaction to the peers in the network.

3. **Create the candidate blocks:** Transactions in the transaction pool are collected into the block periodically. In a Bitcoin network, every 10 minutes, a subset of network nodes, called **mining nodes** or miners, will collect all valid transactions from the transaction pool and create the candidate blocks. The following diagram shows the structure of a candidate block:

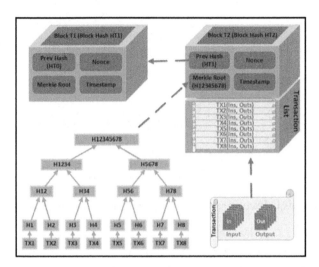

As illustrated in the preceding diagram, the high-level processes are as follows:

- The candidate block packages recent valid transactions into the block structure based on block specifications.
- For each transaction in the package, it creates a cryptographic hash of the transaction data, recursively calculates the hash out of existing hashes, and creates a Merkle root of all transactions, as depicted in the following diagram:

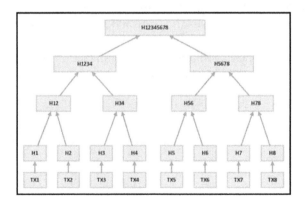

The miner node looks for the latest block on the blockchain and adds its hash to the block header of the candidate block as the reference from the candidate block it intends to link to.

4. **Mine the new block:** Once the candidate block is created, the race starts for the chance to add new blocks and win the rewards. The process for such a race is called **mining**. The winning of the race is determined by the consensus mechanism. We will discuss different consensus mechanisms in later sections. In blockchain systems such as Bitcoin or Ethereum, the PoW consensus mechanism is applied to mining. Miners will keep trying to find a random number, the nonce in the block header structure, until the hash meets certain challenging conditions. For example, one such challenging condition is, *the resulting block hash is smaller than a target number*, or in some cases, *the hash has a few leading zeros*. In practice, every random number has the same chance to win the race, so practically, you can just start a loop through from 1 to $2^{32}$ until it finds such a nonce. It requires huge CPU hashing power to find such a nonce. The challenging condition, called **difficulty**, can be adjusted based on the target number or bits in the block header structure. The difficulty in winning the race grows exponentially the smaller the target number is or the fewer bits are in the block header structure.

5. **Add a new block to the blockchain**: The first winning node will announce the new block to the rest of the network for verification. Once the block is verified and approved by the majority of the network miners, it will be accepted and becomes the new tip of the chain. Since all blocks are chained together by linking the hash to the previous block, any tampering with the ledger becomes impossible since it will require PoW on all previous transitions.

All miners have the chance to solve the puzzle, but only the winning miner has the authority to add the block to the chains and claim the bounty. Once the new block is added to the blockchain, all **in-progress** miners will stop their mining efforts on the newly added block and start the race again on a new block.

The following diagram summarizes the step-by-step process when new transactions are submitted to the blockchain network:

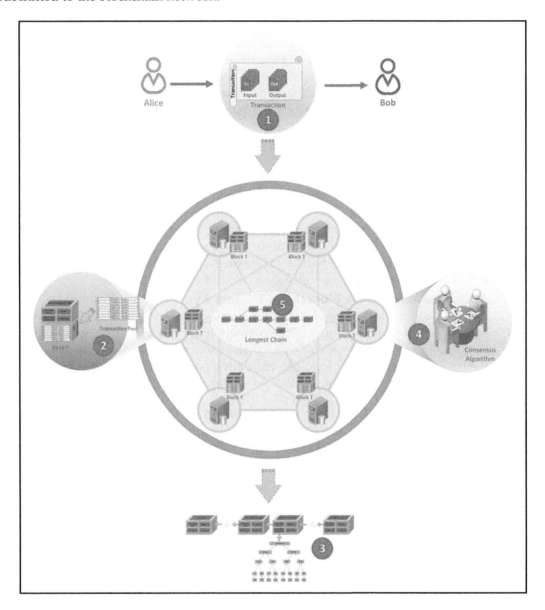

Now you know how works. Cryptography plays a critical role in maintaining the transaction state in the blockchain and ensuring immutability. Cryptography is not new. In the next section, we will go over some key concepts in cryptography.

# Rehashing cryptography

Cryptography is the study of secure communication techniques that prevent third parties or the public from reading private messages and allow only the intended recipient of a message to view its contents. It is the cornerstone of information security, which serves as the basis for delivering secure business applications and services. Modern cryptography concerns itself with the following five objectives of information security:

- **Confidentiality**: This is the concept of preventing sensitive data from being accessible by any unauthorized entities.
- **Integrity**: This means protecting sensitive data from unauthorized changes during transit from one party to another party.
- **Authentication**: This is the process of ensuring that user identity is truly what the user claims it to be, whether the user is human or a system.
- **Authorization**: This is the concept of determining what actions an authenticated user is allowed to perform.
- **Non-repudiation**: When a user performs an action on data, the action must be bound with the user so that it can't deny performing such actions.

Cryptography deals with the design of algorithms for encryption and decryption, which are intended to ensure the secrecy and the authenticity of the messages or transactions. Let's start with some key elements in modern cryptography:

- **Encryption**: This is the process of converting plain text or data into an unintelligent form, typically using a mathematical algorithm.
- **Decryption**: This is the process of reversing encryption—converting an encrypted message back into its original text and data.
- **Hash**: This is the process of converting any data block (arbitrary size or message) into a fixed-length hash code. A cryptographic hash function is a deterministic mathematical function performing such a conversion using cryptography, and it always maps to the same result for a given data block.

Cryptography is a key cornerstone of blockchain technology, along with the consensus mechanism and decentralization. It is used in many different forms, including, for example, wallets (for proof of cryptocurrency ownership), transactions (for PoW consensus), and P2P communication. In this section, we will go over key blockchain-related cryptography topics, including public-key cryptography, digital signatures, cryptographic hashing, and Merkle trees.

# Public key cryptography

Public-key cryptography is a form of cryptographic function in which encryption and decryption are performed using two different keys—one public and one private key. They are generated in pairs. It is also called **asymmetric cryptography**. The public key can be shared with the public, but the private key is meant to be a secret code only known by its owner.

The keys are used in tandem too. Either of the two keys can be used in encryption, with the other one used for decryption. It is computationally improbable to determine the private key given only knowledge of the cryptographic algorithm and the public key.

Public key cryptography is most used in three ways, to:

- Secure the message transmission between two parties and ensure the confidentiality of messages or data.
- Authenticate the sender and ensure the message is indeed sent from the sender.
- Combine with the cryptographic hashing function and provide a digital signature on a document before sending it to the receiver.

We will go over the first two here and discuss digital signatures in the following section:

- **Public key cryptography for confidentiality:** In this case, as depicted in the following diagram, the digital signature is used to encipher messages between two parties during transmission. The sender (**Alice**) uses the receiver's public key to encrypt a message, and the receiver (**Bob**), who holds their own private key in secrecy, can decrypt the messages using their private key:

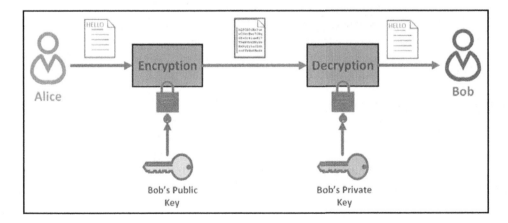

- **Public key cryptography for authentication:** In this case, as shown in the following diagram, the signature is used to authenticate the sender's message. The sender uses its own private key to encrypt a message before sending it to the intended parties. The receiver can use the sender's public key to confirm the message's authenticity and decrypt it. The combination of this approach with the message's cryptographic hashing function provides a digital signature, which we will discuss in the next section:

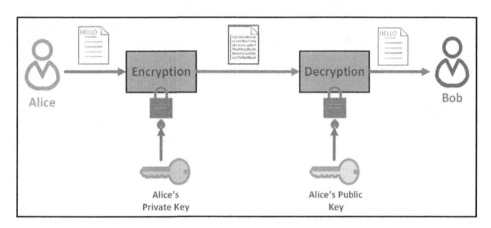

Public key cryptography is an essential technology underpinning wallets and transactions in the blockchain. We will discuss the Bitcoin wallet in the *Understanding Bitcoin and cryptocurrency* section.

# Cryptographic hash function

A cryptographic hash function is an algorithm used to randomly convert a string of binary data into a condensed representation of a message—a **message digest**. Its output is called a **hash value**, **digital fingerprint**, **digest**, or **checksum**. It is deterministic and always results in the same hash value for a given message. It is capable of taking any size of data block and producing a fixed-size hash value that uniquely identifies the original data block. It is a one-way, irreversible function; the only way to recreate the input data is to try a brute-force approach with all possible values to see whether there is a match, which is almost computationally infeasible.

Cryptographic functions have been widely used in blockchain technology, including the following:

- **Merkle trees**: As we showed earlier, when a miner node pulls transactions from the transaction pool, it packages them in a block, where the block header has a field referencing the Merkle root of all transactions.
- **Block chaining**: Blocks in the blockchain are chained together with a reference to the previous block using a cryptographic hash.
- **PoW**: The PoW consensus algorithm itself is a game in solving a cryptographic hash function. We will discuss it in more detail in the *Understanding the blockchain consensus mechanism* section.

# Digital signature

A **digital signature** is a set of algorithms for determining the authenticity and integrity of digital messages or documents. It assures the recipient that the message was indeed created by the expected sender and that the message was not altered during transmission. The sender cannot deny having sent the message.

When **Alice** sends a document to **Bob**, she will follow certain steps to digitally sign the document, as shown in the following diagram:

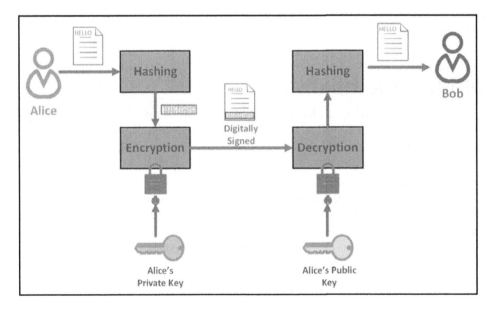

These steps are as follows:

1. Calculate the message digest of the document Alice wants to send to Bob with a cryptographic hash function, usually MD5 or any SHA algorithm.
2. Encrypt the message digest with Alice's private key, append the encrypted message digest to the original document, and send the combined message out.
3. Once Bob receives the combined message from Alice, he will separate the encrypted message digest from the document itself. Bob will use Alice's public key to decrypt the encrypted message digest.
4. At the same time, Bob will calculate the message digest of the received document and compare the resulting message digest with the decrypted message digest to see whether there is a match. If yes, Bob is assured that the document originated from Alice without any tampering.

In blockchain, a digital signature is a way to prove ownership of the underlying cryptocurrency or electronic coin. When Alice needs to pay Bob 10 BTC, she will digitally sign a hash of the previous transaction, which can prove that Alice has ownership of the 10 BTC.

In summary, cryptography is one of three foundational pillars in blockchain technology. Public key cryptography is the basis for blockchain wallets and transactions, and the cryptographic hash function is a key element underpinning the PoW consensus mechanism. A digital signature is used as proof of ownership of the underline electronic coins or cryptocurrency.

In the next section, we will introduce and look at a blockchain consensus mechanism in detail and discuss how cryptography technologies are leveraged to reach consensus among decentralized parties.

# Anatomizing a blockchain consensus mechanism

A fundamental problem in large-scale distributed systems is how to achieve overall system reliability in the presence of failures. Systems need to be fault-tolerant. This requires a process for distributed, often heterogeneous systems to reach a consensus and agree on the network state, whether it is a database commit or an action to take. In this section, we will discuss two types of consensus algorithms, PoW and **proof-of-stake (PoS)**.

# What is consensus?

Consensus in a blockchain is the process by which a network of mutually distrusted nodes reaches an agreement on the global state of the chain of blocks. In blockchain, transactions or data are shared and distributed across the network. Every node has the same copy of the blockchain data. Consensus allows all of the network nodes to follow the same rules to validate transactions and add new blocks to the chain, and therefore allows it to maintain uniformity in all of the copies of a blockchain.

Sometimes, it is also called a consensus mechanism or consensus algorithm. A consensus mechanism focuses on the process and approach of how to reach an agreement. A consensus algorithm is a formal procedure or computer program for solving a consensus problem, based on conducting a sequence of specified actions. It is designed to achieve reliability in a network involving multiple nodes. Consensus algorithms ensure that the next block in a blockchain is fully validated and secured. Multiple kinds of consensus algorithms currently exist, each with different fundamental processes. Different blockchain platforms may implement different consensus mechanism. In this section, we will focus on the following two popular algorithms, show how they work, and discuss the pros and cons of each mechanism:

- **PoW**: This consensus algorithm was introduced by Satoshi and commonly adopted by many other blockchains, including Ethereum. The **PoW** is the mining process with the purpose of finding an answer to a cryptographic hashing problem. To do so, the miner has to follow the block selection rules to locate the previous block and use the hash from the previous block header, together with the Merkle root of current transactions in the new block, to solve the hashing problem. It requires considerable computations and hashing power. In Bitcoin, block selection rules that specify the longest chain wins.
- **PoS**: This consensus algorithm aims to select miners based on the various combinations of random selection based on the miners' wealth or age (the stake). Instead of miners competing to solve energy consuming cryptographic hash functions, the network will instead use a pool of **validators**. Validators are nodes that are willing to *stake* their cryptocurrency on the blocks of transactions that they claim should be added to the public blockchain.

# Proof-of-work

Proof-of-work, also referred to as PoW, is the most popular consensus algorithm used by blockchain and cryptocurrencies such as Bitcoin and Ethereum, each one with its own differences. We will talk about the specific implementation of PoW in Bitcoin and Ethereum in later sections.

## How PoW works

In general, PoW is like a race between miners to solve a cryptographic puzzle; upon solving the puzzle, they win the chance to add the block to the chain and get rewarded. As shown in the following screenshot, miners collect all pending transactions from the decentralized network and compete with each other to solve the puzzle. Whoever solves the puzzle will generate a block and push that block into the network for verification from other nodes, after which, the other nodes can add that block to their own copy of the blockchain:

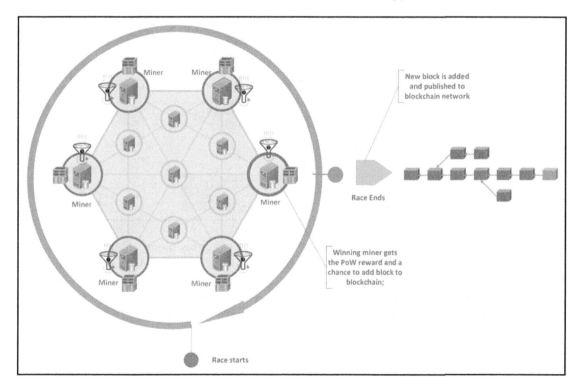

The cryptographic puzzle that miners race to solve is identifying the value of the nonce. A nonce is an attribute in the block header structure. In the beginning, each miner guesses a number to start with, checking whether the resulting hash value is less than the blockchain specific target. Bitcoin uses the SHA-256 algorithm for this. SHA-256 outputs a fixed-length number. Every number between 0 to $2^{32}$ has the same chance to solve the puzzle, therefore a practical approach is to loop through from 0 to $2^{32}$ until a number can meet the criteria, as shown in the following diagram:

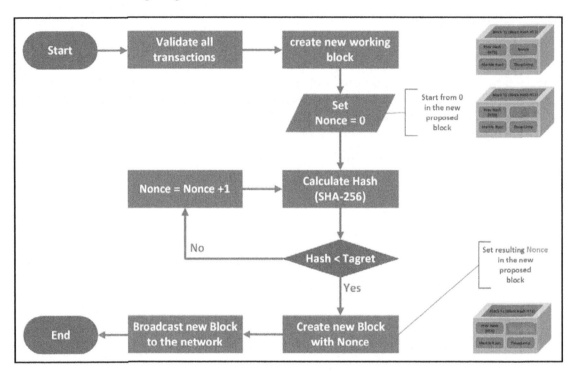

Once a miner finds the nonce, the results, including the previous block's hash value; the collection of transactions; the Merkle root of all transactions in the block; and the nonce are broadcasted to the network for verification. Upon being notified, the other nodes from the network automatically check whether the results are valid. If the results are valid, they add the block to their copies of the blockchain, stop the mining work in hand, and move on to the next block.

# Targets and difficulty

A target is a blockchain-specific 256-bit number that the network sets up for all miners. The SHA-256 hash of a block's header—the nonce plus the rest of the block header—must be lower than or equal to the current target for the block to be accepted by the network.

The difficulty of a cryptographic puzzle depends on the number of leading zeros in the target. The lower the target, the more difficult it is to generate a block. Adding leading zeros in the target number will increase the difficulty of finding such a nonce exponentially. As you can imagine, the higher the difficulty setting, the more difficult it will be to evaluate the nonce. Adding one leading zero in the target will reduce by 50% the chance of finding the nonce. The difficulty is decided by the blockchain network itself. The basic rule of thumb is to set the difficulty proportionally to the total effort on the network. If the number of miner nodes doubles, the difficulty will also double. The difficulty is periodically adjusted to keep the block time around the target time. In Bitcoin, it is 10 minutes.

# Incentives and rewards

The winner of the cryptographic puzzle needs to expend huge energy and crucial CPU time to find the nonce and win the chance to create new blocks in the blockchain. The reward for such actions depends on the blockchain itself. In a Bitcoin blockchain, the winner will be rewarded with Bitcoin, the cryptocurrency in the Bitcoin blockchain.

The PoW consensus is a simple and yet reliable mechanism to maintain the state of the blockchain. It is simple to implement. It is a democratic lottery-based system that lets you participate in the game of mining and get the rewards, where every node can join and higher CPU power may not translate into higher rewards. Currently, the winning miner is rewarded with 12.5 BTC for each block created in the Bitcoin blockchain.

# Double-spend issues

Satoshi's original intention in using a PoW mechanism is to solve double-spend issues and ensure the integrity of the global state of the Bitcoin blockchain network. Let's say Alice sends 10 BTC to Bob, and at the same time or later on she pays Catherine the same 10 BTC. We could end up with the following three situations:

- The first transaction goes through the PoW and is added to the blockchain when the second transaction is submitted. In this case, the second one will be rejected when miners pull it from the transaction pool and validate it against all parent blocks.

- Both transactions are submitted simultaneously and both go into the unconfirmed pool of transactions. In this case, only the first transaction gets a confirmation and will be added in the next block. Her second transaction will not be confirmed as per validation rules.
- Both get confirmed and are added into competing blocks. This happens when miners take both transactions from the pool and put them into competing blocks. The competing blocks form a temporary fork on the blockchain. Whichever transaction gets into the longest chain will be considered valid and spent, and the other one within the block on the short chain will be recycled. When it is reprocessed, it will be rejected since it is already spent. In this case, it may take a few blocks to get the other one recognized as the double-spent one.

# Advantages and disadvantages

However, there are a few drawbacks with the PoW algorithm, thanks to the economic cost of maintaining the blockchain network safety:

- **Energy consumption:** PoW consensus, which uses a network of powerful computers to secure the network, is extremely expensive and energy-intensive. Miners need to use specialized hardware with high computing capacity in order to perform mining and get rewards. A large amount of electricity is required to run these mining nodes continuously. Some people also claim these cryptographic hash calculations are useless as they can't produce any business value. At the end of 2018, the Bitcoin network across the Globe used more power than Denmark.
- **Vulnerability:** PoW consensus is vulnerable to 51% attacks, which means, in theory, dishonest miners could gain a majority of hashing power and manipulate the blockchain to their advantage.
- **Centralization:** Winning a mining game requires specified and expensive hardware, typically an ASIC type of machine. Expenses grow unmanageable, and mining becomes possible only for a small number of sophisticated miners. The consequence of this is a gradual increase in the centralization of the system, as it becomes a game of riches.

On the flip side, it requires huge computing power and electricity to take over the PoW-based blockchain. Therefore, PoW is perceived as an effective way to prevent **Denial-of-Service (DoS)** and **Distributed Denial-of-Service (DDoS)** attacks on the blockchain.

# Proof-of-stake

As opposed to PoW consensus, where miners are rewarded for solving cryptographic puzzles, in the PoS consensus algorithm, a pool of selected validators take turns proposing new blocks. The validator is chosen in a deterministic way, depending on its wealth, also defined as a stake. Anyone who deposits their coins as a stake can become a validator. The chance to participate may be proportional to the stakes they put in. Let's say, Alice, Bob, Catherine, and David put in 40 Ether, 30 Ether, 20 Ether, and 10 Ether stakes to participate respectively; they will get a 40%, 30%, 20%, and 10% chance of being selected as the block creator.

The following is how it works in the PoS consensus mechanism. As shown in the following diagram, the blockchain keeps track of a set of validators, sometimes also called block creators or forgers. At any time, whenever new blocks need to be created, the blockchain randomly selects a validator. The selected validator verifies the transactions and proposes new blocks for all validators to agree on. New blocks are then voted on by all current validators. Voting power is based on the stake the validator puts in. Whoever proposes invalid transactions or blocks or votes maliciously, which means they intentionally compromise the integrity of the chain, may lose their stakes. Upon the new blocks being accepted, the block creator can collect the transaction fee as the reward for the work of creating new blocks:

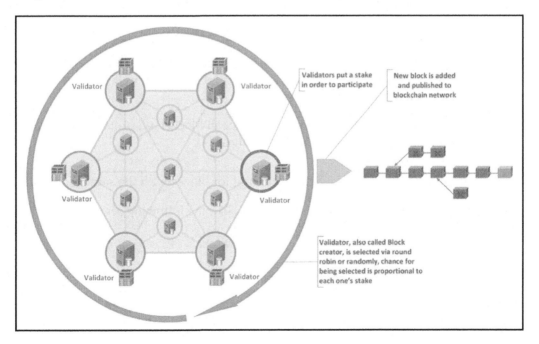

PoS is considered more energy-efficient and environment-friendly compared with the PoW mechanism. It is also perceived as more secure too. It essentially reduces the threat of a 51% attack since malicious validators would need to accumulate more than 50% of the total stakes in order to take over the blockchain network.

Similar to PoW, total decentralization may not be fully possible in the PoS-based public blockchain. This is because a few wealthy nodes can monopolize the stakes in the network. Those who put in more stakes can effectively control most of the voting. Both algorithms are subject to the social and economic issue that it makes the rich richer.

# Forking

Earlier, we spoke about the temporary fork that occurs when two competing blocks are added to the blockchain. As shown in the following screenshot, this can continue until the majority of the nodes see the longest chain. Newer blocks will be appended to the longest chain. Blocks added to the shortleaf of the forked chain will be discarded, and those transactions will go back to the transaction pool and will be picked again for reprocessing. Eventually, the blockchain will comprise all conforming blocks, chained together using cryptographic hashes pointing to its ancestor:

Just like software development, forking is a common practice in blockchain. Forking takes place when a blockchain bifurcates into two separate paths. The following events, intentionally or accidentally, can trigger a blockchain fork:

- New features are added, requiring a change in blockchain protocol, such as block size, mining algorithm, and consensus rules.
- Hacking or software bugs.
- A temporary fork occurs when competing for blocks with the same block height.

A general forking scenario in a blockchain may look like the following screenshot:

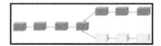

Depending on the nature of such events, the actions to fix the issues could be a hard fork or a soft fork or, in the case of a temporary fork, doing nothing and allowing the network to self-heal.

# Hard fork

A **hard fork** happens when radical changes in the blockchain protocol are introduced and it makes historical blocks non-conformant with new protocols or rules. Some are planned. Developers and operators agree with protocol changes and upgrades to new software. Blocks following the old protocol will be rejected, and blocks following the new protocol will become the longest chain moving forward.

But, in some cases, this is controversial and heavily debated in the blockchain community, as was the case with the Bitcoin fork on 6 August 2010 or the fork between Ethereum and Ethereum Classic. In such contentious hard fork cases, as long as there are miners maintaining the old and new software, the blocks created by the old and new software will diverge into separate blockchains.

The following screenshot illustrates both planned and contentious hard forks:

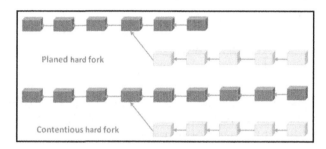

During a contentious hard fork of blockchain, a new cryptocurrency will be created to fuel the new blockchain. The owner of the existing crypto-assets may stay in the current network or move to the new network. When moving to the new network, they will receive a proportional amount of new cryptocurrency in the new network. Hard forks often create pricing volatility. The conversion rate between the old and new fork may be determined by the market. It is important to know the context and details of a hard fork, and understand the crypto-economic impacts of such a fork to both cryptocurrencies in order to take advantage of such sudden and drastic changes.

Once forked, nodes will start with separate paths moving forward. Nodes would need to decide which blockchain network they want to stay in. For example, Bitcoin Cash diverged from Bitcoin due to a disagreement within the Bitcoin community as to how to handle the scalability problem. As a result, Bitcoin Cash became its own chain and shares the transaction history from the genesis block up to the forking point. As of September 2 2019, Bitcoin Cash's market cap is around $5 billion, ranking fourth, versus Bitcoin's $215 billion.

# Soft fork

**A soft fork**, by contrast, is any change of rules that is backward-compatible between two versions of the software and the blocks. It goes both ways. In the soft fork case, existing historical blocks are still considered valid blocks by the new software. At the same time, the new blocks created through new software can still be recognized as valid ones by the old software. In the decentralized network, not all nodes upgrade their software at the same time. Nodes staying with an older version of the blockchain software continue creating new blocks using the older software. Nodes upgraded to the newer version of blockchain software will create new blocks using new software. Eventually, when the majority of the network hashing capacity upgrades to a newer version of the software, in theory more blocks will be created with the newer version and make it the longest chain. Nodes with older software can still create new blocks. Since it is not in the longest chain, as illustrated in the following screenshot, similar to the temporary fork case, these blocks will soon be overtaken by the new chain:

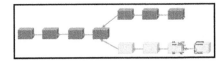

Where more nodes are stuck on the older version, as illustrated in the following screenshot, new blocks created from an older version of blockchain software may become longer and longer; it will take a while for the new software to be effective:

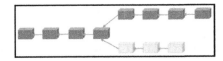

So far, you have learned how PoW and PoS work. We have analyzed the advantages and disadvantages of different consensus mechanisms. In the next section, we will help you to understand what Bitcoin and cryptocurrency are and discuss how blockchain technology applies to Bitcoin.

# Understanding Bitcoin and cryptocurrency

Blockchain is the technology behind Bitcoin, which is considered the origin of all cryptocurrencies. In this section, we will introduce the basics of Bitcoin and discuss the digital payment mechanism with Bitcoin.

# Bitcoin basics

Bitcoin is a decentralized electronic cash system that makes peer-to-peer payment possible without going through an intermediary. The original Bitcoin software was developed by Satoshi Nakamoto, released under the MIT license in 2009, following the Bitcoin whitepaper, *Bitcoin: A Peer-to-Peer Electronic Cash System*. Bitcoin is the first successful implementation of a distributed cryptocurrency. Ten years after Bitcoin was born, as of February 16, 2019, it has about 17.5 million Bitcoins in circulation and it has reached about a 64 billion market cap (`https://coinmarketcap.com/currencies/bitcoin/`):

| Market Cap | Volume (24h) | Circulating Supply | Max Supply |
|---|---|---|---|
| $63,975,604,310 USD | $5,956,337,934 USD | 17,540,837 BTC | 21,000,000 BTC |
| 17,540,837 BTC | 1,632,658 BTC | | |

Like any fiat currencies or tangible assets, the price of Bitcoins can fluctuate over time and its valuation is determined by the open market. Several factors can influence the price, including supply and demand on the market, competing cryptocurrencies and altcoins, and governance and regulations. The following screenshot shows the Bitcoin market cap, daily transaction volume, and price movement since its inception up to February 2019:

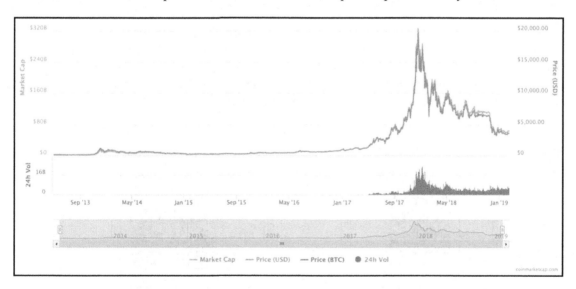

In this section, we will present key concepts in Bitcoin, including the wallet, transaction and account balances, Bitcoin supply, and bootstrap. We will demonstrate how Bitcoin payment works with blockchain. We will also discuss major challenges in Bitcoin and the Bitcoin blockchain. In the end, we also briefly talk about various altcoins, a different type of cryptocurrency on the market.

# What is a wallet?

Bitcoin is a cryptocurrency, digital cash, or virtual money. Unlike a fiat currency, you can't touch or feel it. You can't stash Bitcoins under your bed. So, where do you store your Bitcoins? How do you prove ownership of the Bitcoins? Technically, Bitcoins aren't stored anywhere. They don't exist in any physical form. They are a set of software objects circulating around the Bitcoin network, where ownership of the Bitcoin is proved with a cryptographic key. Payment records, with money transferred in or out, are recorded as a chain of private keys showing ownership transfer in the blockchain. If you own the private keys, you own that Bitcoin. If you lose your keys, you lose everything you have on the Bitcoin network.

A Bitcoin wallet is an application where the cryptographic keys, pairs of a public and private key, are stored. There are many forms of Bitcoin wallets in use, but broadly, they are categorized into the following four types; desktop, mobile, web, and hardware wallets. The private key is used for you to digitally sign the transaction when you spend the Bitcoin. Anyone who knows your public key can verify your signature of the payment you make to them. The public key—more accurately, a wallet address associated with your public key—is used for anyone to pay you with Bitcoin. You can have as many pairs of public and private keys as you want in your wallet.

In Bitcoin, a private key is a 256-bit-long hash and a public key is 512 bits long. They can be converted into shorter lengths in a hexadecimal representation. A Bitcoin address is generated based on the public key, using multiple rounds of mixed use of the following cryptographic hash functions: SHA-256 and RIPEMD-160. You can have as many addresses as you need, and each address can be used once for each Bitcoin transaction.

The following screenshot gives an example of a Bitcoin wallet generated from the `bitaddress.org` website:

The QR code on the left side is the Bitcoin address you can share with your trading partners. The secret one, the QR code on the right, is your private key when you sign your transaction.

# Transactions, UTXO, and account balances

Whenever you check your bank account, you always see a balance associated with your checking or savings accounts. Your bank keeps track of all of your transactions, and accumulates them and updates your balances following each and every transaction. A Bitcoin wallet provides you with a balance too. However, the balance in Bitcoin is not that straightforward. Instead of keeping track of every transaction, Bitcoin keeps track of unspent coins, also called UTXO.

**UTXO** stands for **Unspent Transaction Output**. In Bitcoin, a transaction is a collection of inputs and outputs transferring the ownership of Bitcoins between payer and payee. Inputs instruct the network which coin or coins the payment will draw from. Those coins in the input have to be unspent, which means they have not been used to pay someone else. Outputs provide the spendable amounts of Bitcoins that the payer agrees to pay to the payees. Once the transaction is made, the outputs become the unspent amounts to the payee; they remain unspent until the current payee pays someone else with the coin.

Taking the earlier example where Alice needs to pay Bob 10 BTCs, let's assume, prior to this transaction, that Alice has two UTXOs in her wallet, one with 5 BTCs and another with 8 BTCs. Bob has one UTXO of 30 BTCs in his wallet from other transactions. Let's also ignore the transaction fee for now. When Alice uses both UTXOs as the input to pay 10 BTCs to Bob, both will be the inputs of the transaction. One 10 BTC UTXO will be created as output to Bob, and one 3 BTC UTXO will be returned to Alice. After the transaction, Alice will have one 3 BTC UTXO in her account, and Bob will have two UTXOs in his account. They remain as UTXO until they are used to pay for other transactions:

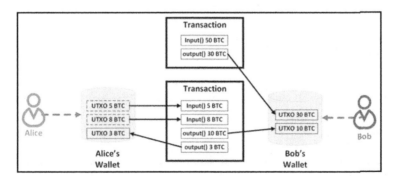

When either Alice or Bob pays someone with the remaining UTXOs, the unspent output from the previous transaction becomes an input to the new transaction. Since all transactions are digitally signed, essentially a Bitcoin becomes a chain of digital signature on the Bitcoin blockchain network.

# Genesis block and coin supply

In Bitcoin, there is no central authority issuing the cryptocurrency and controlling the money supply. Instead, Bitcoin is created by the Bitcoin blockchain network through the discovery of new blocks. As shown in the following screenshot, the first block is also called the genesis block, or block #0, which was mined on June 3, 2009, with an output of 50 BTC. The first 50 BTC is unspendable.

The following screenshot shows the genesis block in the Bitcoin blockchain:

| Block #0 | | | | |
|---|---|---|---|---|
| **Summary** | | | **Hashes** | |
| Number Of Transactions | 1 | | Hash | 00000000019d6689c085ae165831e934ff763ae46a2a6c172b3f1b60a8ce26f |
| Output Total | 50 BTC | | Previous Block | 0000000000000000000000000000000000000000000000000000000000000000 |
| Estimated Transaction Volume | 0 BTC | | Next Block(s) | 00000000839a8e6886ab5951d76f411475428afc90947ee320161bbf18eb6048 |
| Transaction Fees | 0 BTC | | Merkle Root | 4a5e1e4baab89f3a32518a88c31bc87f618f76673e2cc77ab2127b7afdeda33b |
| Height | 0 (Main Chain) | | | |
| Timestamp | 2009-01-03 18:15:05 | | | |
| Received Time | 2009-01-03 18:15:05 | | | |
| Relayed By | Unknown | | | |
| Difficulty | 1 | | | |
| Bits | 486604799 | | | |
| Size | 0.285 kB | | | |
| Weight | 0.896 kWU | | | |
| Version | 1 | | | |
| Nonce | 2083236893 | | | |
| Block Reward | 50 BTC | | | |

**Transactions**

| 4a5e1e4baab89f3a32518a88c31bc87f618f76673e2cc77ab2127b7afdeda33b | | (Size: 204 bytes) 2009-01-03 18:15:05 |
|---|---|---|
| No Inputs (Newly Generated Coins) | ➡ 1A1zP1eP5QGe... (Genesis of Bitcoin 🌐) - (Unspent) | 50 BTC |
| | | 50 BTC |

Source: https://www.blockchain.com/btc/block/
000000000019d6689c085ae165831e934ff763ae46a2a6c172b3f1b60a8ce26f

Bitcoin uses a Bitcoin generation algorithm to control how many coins will be minted and at what rate. It is a function of the Bitcoin block height and its block reward. It started with a block reward of 50 BTC. The block reward will be cut in half for every 210,000 blocks, or approximately, every four years. The rate of block creation is adjusted based on mining difficulty. The maximum capacity of Bitcoins in the system is 21 million, which can be reached when 6,929,999 blocks have been mined.

> For more information, the curious reader should check out the Bitcoin wiki site: `https://en.Bitcoin.it/wiki/Controlled_supply`.

# How does Bitcoin payment work?

Take the earlier example, when Alice needs to pay Bob 10 BTC. Alice opens her Bitcoin wallet, and scans or copies Bob's transaction address and creates a transaction with a 10 BTC payment to Bob. Once the transaction is digitally signed and submitted, it is sent to the Bitcoin blockchain network:

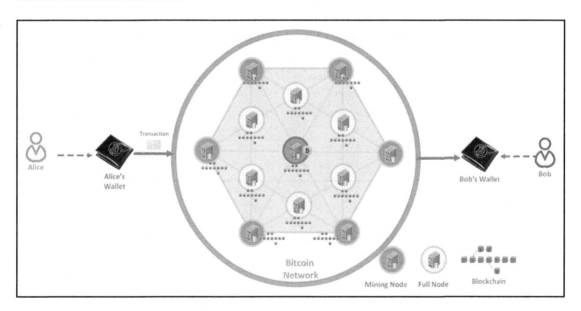

Once the transaction is broadcasted to the Bitcoin network, the bookkeeper node, usually a full node in a P2P network that receives the transactions, will validate it according to Bitcoin protocol rules. If the transaction is valid, the bookkeeper will add it to the transaction pool and relay the transaction to the peers in the network. In a Bitcoin network, every 10 minutes, a subset of network nodes, called "mining nodes" or miners, will collect all valid transactions from the transaction pool and create the candidate blocks. They also create a Coinbase transaction for themselves to get rewarded and collect transaction fees, in the event they win the mining race and add the block to the chain. All nodes will verify the new block and add it to their own copy of the blockchain. Magically, Bob will be able to see the payment from Alice and 10 BTC in his wallet.

# Bitcoin transaction and block structure

When creating a Bitcoin transaction, the wallet application has to follow the Bitcoin protocol rules and creates the transaction data structure in line with the Bitcoin specification. Invalid transactions will be rejected by the network. For details of the Bitcoin transaction and block structure, please refer to `https://en.Bitcoin.it/wiki/`.

- **Bitcoin block structure**:

  The following table shows the data structure within a Bitcoin block:

| Field | Description | Size |
|---|---|---|
| Magic no | value always 0xD9B4BEF9 | 4 bytes |
| Blocksize | number of bytes following up to end of block | 4 bytes |
| Blockheader | consists of 6 items | 80 bytes |
| Transaction counter | positive integer VI = VarInt | 1 - 9 bytes |
| transactions | the (non empty) list of transactions | <Transaction counter>-many transactions |

- **Block header structure**:

  The following table shows the data structure for a block header:

| Field | Purpose | Updated when... | Size (Bytes) |
|---|---|---|---|
| Version | Block version number | You upgrade the software and it specifies a new version | 4 |
| hashPrevBlock | 256-bit hash of the previous block header | A new block comes in | 32 |
| hashMerkleRoot | 256-bit hash based on all of the transactions in the block | A transaction is accepted | 32 |
| Time | Current timestamp as seconds since 1970-01-01T00:00 UTC | Every few seconds | 4 |
| Bits | Current target in compact format | The difficulty is adjusted | 4 |
| Nonce | 32-bit number (starts at 0) | A hash is tried (increments) | 4 |

In particular, `hashPrevBlock` references the 256-bit hash value of the previous block, and `hashMerkleRoot` is the hash Merkle root of all transactions in the block, including coinbase transactions. And the nonce is the magic number that miners need to find so that the SHA-256 hash value of the block header is smaller than or equal to the blockchain-defined specific target.

- **Transaction structure in Bitcoin**:

  The following screenshot shows the general data structure of a Bitcoin transaction:

| Field | Description | Size |
|---|---|---|
| Version no | currently 1 | 4 bytes |
| Flag | If present, always 0001, and indicates the presence of witness data | optional 2 byte array |
| In-counter | positive integer VI = VarInt | 1 - 9 bytes |
| list of inputs | the first input of the first transaction is also called "coinbase" (its content was ignored in earlier versions) | <in-counter>-many inputs |
| Out-counter | positive integer VI = VarInt | 1 - 9 bytes |
| list of outputs | the outputs of the first transaction spend the mined bitcoins for the block | <out-counter>-many outputs |
| Witnesses | A list of witnesses, 1 for each input, omitted if flag above is missing | variable, see Segregated_Witness |
| lock_time | if non-zero and sequence numbers are < 0xFFFFFFFF: block height or timestamp when transaction is final | 4 bytes |

A transaction can have many inputs and outputs, as specified in the field of **list of inputs** and **list of outputs** fields. The input structure is shown as follows:

| Field | Description | Size |
|---|---|---|
| Previous Transaction hash | doubled SHA256-hashed of a (previous) to-be-used transaction | 32 bytes |
| Previous Txout-index | non negative integer indexing an output of the to-be-used transaction | 4 bytes |
| Txin-script length | non negative integer VI = VarInt | 1 - 9 bytes |
| Txin-script / scriptSig | Script | <in-script length>-many bytes |
| sequence_no | normally 0xFFFFFFFF; irrelevant unless transaction's lock_time is > 0 | 4 bytes |

The following table shows the structure for the output:

| Field | Description | Size |
|---|---|---|
| value | non negative integer giving the number of Satoshis(BTC/10^8) to be transfered | 8 bytes |
| Txout-script length | non negative integer | 1 - 9 bytes VI = VarInt |
| Txout-script / scriptPubKey | Script | <out-script length>-many bytes |

# Transaction validation and block verification

Bitcoin protocol rules define a set of validation rules, including syntactic rules and valid values. Bookkeepers, or miner nodes, need to validate transactions according to those rules before the transaction is added to the pool. It also checks the following (`https://en.Bitcoin.it/wiki/Protocol_rules`):

- **Transaction duplication**: This is to see whether we have matching transactions in the transaction pool or in a block in the main branch.
- **Double spend**: This is to check whether the input is used to pay concurrently in any other transactions in the pool or in the main branch.
- **Orphan transaction**: For each input, this checks whether we can find the reference output transaction in the main branch and the transaction pool.
- **Coinbase maturity**: This is to make sure coins from the coinbase transaction are mature enough to be spent.
- **Overdraft**: This checks the inputs and outputs to make sure there is enough to make the payment and be able to make a reasonable transaction fee.

Once a miner completes a new block with the mining, the new block will be broadcasted to the Bitcoin network for verification. Each full node, including mining nodes, will verify the new block and all transactions within the block. The same set of transaction validation rules will be applied. For block verification, all nodes check whether the block has the right cryptographic hash and the nonce makes the hash smaller than the target. The miner will add the block to the longest chain. As we discussed earlier, temporary forking may happen; a Bitcoin block tends to self-heal and only the blocks in the longest chain will stay.

# Limitations in Bitcoin

Thanks to Bitcoin, blockchain technology has attracted worldwide attention. Like any new technology, it has its limitations. Notable limitations include the following:

- **Scalability and throughput:** Scalability is the major concern in the Bitcoin network, or in general, any PoW-based blockchain. By design, every transaction has to be verified by all nodes, and it takes about an average of 10 minutes to create a new block with the block size limited to 1 MB. Block size and frequency limitations further constrain the network's throughput.

- **Transaction processing cost:** Mining in the Bitcoin network is costly and energy-intensive. The miners who add new blocks to the blockchain are rewarded with Bitcoins. As Bitcoin supply is close to the maximum capacity of 21 M Bitcoins, mining becomes less profitable. Miners will more and more rely on transaction fees to offset the mining cost and make a profit. It will drastically increase the transaction cost in Bitcoin. Please refer to `https://Bitcoinfees.info` for real-time transaction fees in the Bitcoin network.

- **Security and privacy:** Bitcoin has the 51% attack issue, at least in theory, if the majority of CPU hashing power is controlled by dishonest miners. It may not be economically feasible to launch such an attack on the main Bitcoin network. But recently, at least five cryptocurrencies with much smaller networks have been hit with an attack like this. By design, all transactions are permanently stored in the Bitcoin network and can be traced to the involving parties. They are made public. This greatly improves transparency, however, unfortunately, also raises privacy concerns.

- **Usability:** Bitcoin uses a stack-based scripting system for transaction processing. It supports very rudimental operations and lacks the functionalities of modern programming languages. It is Turing-incomplete and inhibits the ability to build more sophisticated real-world business and payment applications.

# Altcoins

Altcoins are cryptocurrencies other than Bitcoin. Many altcoins are variations of Bitcoin with changes and improvements created to address some particular limitations we talked in an earlier section. Some, like Ethereum and EOS, are intended as a new blockchain platform for building decentralized applications. According to `http://coinmarketcap.com`, the following are the top ten altcoins based on the market cap, as of Feb 17, 2019:

### Top 100 Coins by Market Capitalization

(Not including tokens)

Cryptocurrencies ▾    Exchanges ▾    Watchlist                                 USD ▾    Next 100 →    View All

| # | Name | Market Cap | Price | Volume (24h) | Circulating Supply | Change (24h) | Price Graph (7d) |
|---|------|-----------|-------|--------------|-------------------|--------------|------------------|
| 1 | Bitcoin | $63,670,593,306 | $3,629.38 | $6,436,070,783 | 17,543,112 BTC | -0.36% | |
| 2 | Ethereum | $13,244,365,335 | $126.26 | $3,397,218,965 | 104,896,058 ETH | 2.11% | |
| 3 | XRP | $12,385,711,770 | $0.300565 | $406,977,249 | 41,208,093,050 XRP * | -0.65% | |
| 4 | Litecoin | $2,618,586,217 | $43.28 | $1,032,719,008 | 60,509,525 LTC | -1.52% | |
| 5 | EOS | $2,555,061,174 | $2.82 | $822,153,867 | 906,245,118 EOS * | -0.66% | |
| 6 | Bitcoin Cash | $2,142,848,180 | $121.57 | $204,987,947 | 17,626,950 BCH | -1.17% | |
| 7 | TRON | $1,584,110,656 | $0.023756 | $115,698,563 | 66,682,072,191 TRX | -0.84% | |
| 8 | Stellar | $1,494,795,818 | $0.077956 | $137,201,896 | 19,174,868,660 XLM * | -0.81% | |
| 9 | Bitcoin SV | $1,093,438,428 | $62.04 | $76,560,033 | 17,625,798 BSV | -0.64% | |
| 10 | Cardano | $1,055,325,942 | $0.040704 | $12,661,947 | 25,927,070,538 ADA | -0.64% | |

**Ethereum**: It is one of the best known smart contract platforms that enables **Decentralized Applications (DApps)**. It was invented by Vitalik Buterin in 2013. Ether is the native currency in Ethereum platform. It goes with the symbol "ETH". We will dive into Ethereum details in the rest of this book.

**XRP**: Ripple (XRP) is a digital asset that enables value transfer in the Ripple network. Unlike most of the altcoins, Ripple doesn't have a blockchain. It is a **Distributed Ledger Technology (DLT)** based on the Ripple Consensus ledger.

**Litecoin**: This is almost identical to Bitcoin except that the time for adding a new block was reduced from 10 minutes to 2 minutes.

**EOS**: Similar to Ethereum, EOS is a blockchain platform intended to bring together the best features from different blockchain platforms and make it easy for developing DApps. It introduces some sort of centralization components into the network, as a means of addressing scalability and throughput issues.

**Bitcoin Cash**: This is a hard fork of the Bitcoin chain that was created because of a group of Bitcoin core developers that wanted to use a different way of addressing the scalability issue.

# Ushering in the world of Ethereum

Vitalik Buterin, the founder of Ethereum, addressed the limitations of Bitcoin quite differently. While working on Bitcoin, he recognized that Bitcoin's stack-based scripting is very limited and lacks the functionality and capability for application development beyond the transfer of cryptocurrency ownership. He saw it as a huge opportunity and began writing his own whitepaper in 2013.

In his famous Ethereum whitepaper (`https://github.com/ethereum/wiki/wiki/White-Paper`), Vitalik laid out his vision and intent to build a blockchain that includes the following:

- It has a built-in Turing-complete programming language.
- It establishes a smart contract and decentralized application platform allowing anyone to define, create, and trade all types of cryptocurrencies and crypto-assets.

Similar to Bitcoin, Ethereum is built on blockchain technology. It has all of the critical characteristics of a blockchain. It is a shared distributed ledger on top of a decentralized P2P network. It works in a similar way to what we discussed in the *Bitcoin and cryptocurrency* section. Unlike Bitcoin, which is a decentralized state transition system with limited decentralized computing capability via Bitcoin scripting, Ethereum is a decentralized computing and data platform featuring Turing-complete smart contract functionality.

Ethereum introduced a few new and critical concepts, including a smart contract, an **Ethereum Virtual Machine (EVM)**, and an account. We will cover them in detail in the rest of this book.

# Smart contract

A smart contract is programming code that is stored and executed on the blockchain. Ethereum now has a Turing-complete language, Solidity, which enables developers to develop and deploy smart contracts. In addition to moving ether, the cryptocurrency in Ethereum network, between accounts, Ethereum smart contract code can support more modern program language constructs such as loops and perform much more complex computations, including data access, cryptographic algorithms, and function calls. Each such operation has a gas price associated with it. That is how Ethereum calculates the transaction cost of the smart contract and, through a gas limit, protects a smart contract from infinite loops or programming errors.

A smart contract is like a scripted agreement between interacting parties; the code built into the contract is stored on the Ethereum blockchain and cannot be tampered with or removed. This greatly increases the credibility of the legal document.

# Ethereum Virtual Machine

The EVM is the runtime environment for smart contracts in Ethereum. It is a virtual operating system deployed as an Ethereum client to all network nodes across the Globe. Similar to the JVM in the Java world, the contract code is compiled into the bytecode, which is loaded into EVM as part of contract creation.

# Account

There is no account concept in Bitcoin. Instead, Bitcoin uses the concept of UTXO to keep track of money transfers and account balances. Ethereum introduces the concept of the world state and account. The world state comprises a mapping of all accounts and their public addresses. To facilitate both state transactions and decentralized computing, Ethereum introduces two types of account: **Externally Owned Accounts (EOAs)**, controlled by private keys, and contract accounts, controlled by their contract code.

# Summary

In this chapter, we explained key blockchain components and elements and the different characteristics of blockchain, and we discussed how blockchain works. We reviewed cryptography technologies and how they were leveraged in the blockchain. We illustrated how PoW and PoS consensus mechanisms work. We went over key concepts in Bitcoin, as well as some Bitcoin limitations. We provided a short overview of cryptocurrencies and altcoins. We also briefly introduced Ethereum, as well as the key difference between Bitcoin and Ethereum.

We will delve into the Ethereum architecture and ecosystem in greater depth in the next two chapters. We will show you, step-by-step, how to develop and deploy decentralized applications in Sections 2 and 3 of this book. Stay tuned.

# Ethereum Architecture and Ecosystem

2

In this chapter, you will be able to learn the internals of Ethereum architecture, get a deep understanding of how the **Ethereum Virtual Machine (EVM)** works and how smart contract code is executed within the EVM. In the end, we will touch base on various tools, technologies, and frameworks in the Ethereum ecosystem and get you ready to learn smart contracts and develop the first decentralized application.

We will cover the following topics:

- Introducing Ethereum architecture
- Diving deep into Ethereum
- Understanding mining in Ethereum
- Working with tools and technologies in Ethereum ecosystem

## Technical Requirements

For all the source code of this book, please refer the following GitHub link :

```
https://github.com/PacktPublishing/Learn-Ethereum
```

# Introducing Ethereum architecture

Vitalik Buterin, the creator of Ethereum and co-founder of the Ethereum Foundation, envisioned Ethereum as a decentralized computing platform that enables anyone to create, store, and run smart contract-based **Decentralized Applications**, or **DApps**.

As the following diagram shows, an Ethereum blockchain network is a decentralized **Peer-to-Peer (P2P)** network of Ethereum clients, representing network nodes. An Ethereum client refers to any node that can verify the new transaction, execute the smart contract, and process new blocks of the chain. It is a kind of enclave, residing in thousands of computers or devices on the internet, and connected through the Ethereum P2P network. What is enclaved is the EVM and the runtime environment in the P2P network for smart contract execution. The following diagram shows the P2P network:

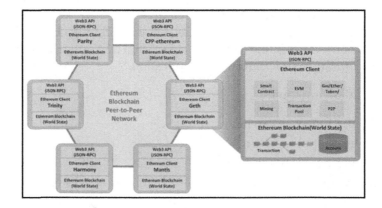

Ethereum clients run the EVM and can technically be written in any popular programming language. There are many different implementations of Ethereum clients. Ethereum makes it possible for such a variety of different client implementations since every implementation has to conform to the protocol specification defined in the **Ethereum Yellow Paper** (https://github.com/ethereum/yellowpaper). There are many advantages with such a variety of Ethereum client implementations, including the following:

- It makes the network more resilient against bugs.
- It prevents the centralization of developer resources.
- In general, competitions between teams help to find the best solutions to common and challenging issues.
- Each client may have a different focus, strength, and weakness in mining, prototyping, DApp development, and more. DApp developers or private Ethereum blockchain operators may choose the ones fitting their own special needs.

Notable Ethereum clients include the following:

| Client | Language | Developers | Where to download? |
|---|---|---|---|
| Geth | Go | Ethereum Foundation | https://geth.ethereum.org/downloads/ |
| Parity | Rust | Parity | https://www.parity.io |
| cpp-ethereum | C++ | Ethereum Foundation | https://github.com/ethereum/aleth |
| Trinity | Python | Ethereum Foundation | https://github.com/ethereum/trinity |
| Harmony | Java | Ether Camp | https://github.com/ether-camp/ethereum-harmony |
| Mantis | Scala | IOHK's Team Grothendieck | https://mantis.readthedocs.io/en/latest/ |

Ethereum clients provide a set of web3 APIs over JSON-RPC for DApps interacting with an Ethereum blockchain. From your web or wallet application, you can use the web3 object provided by the web3.js library to communicate with the Ethereum network. It works with any Ethereum client. Behind the scenes, it connects to a local or remote Ethereum node and makes RPC calls. In some sense, this is like the old client-server model, where DApps are the client, and the entire Ethereum network as a whole, acts as a server. To DApps, the Ethereum network is just like a giant world computer, assembled together with thousands of computing devices throughout the internet. Once you connect to the network, you could connect to any node in the decentralized network, as shown in the following diagram:

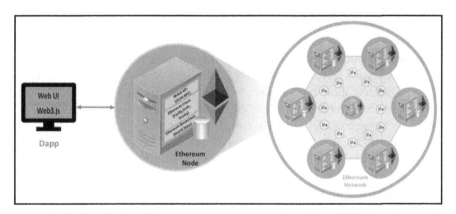

Beyond smart contracts and the EVM, an Ethereum client provides all blockchain components to maintain world state and state transitions in the blockchain network, including the following:

- Managing transaction and state transition with the Ethereum blockchain
- Maintaining world state and account state
- Managing P2P communication
- Block finalization with mining
- Managing transaction pool
- Managing cryptoassets, gas, ether, and tokens

We will discuss more details in the next section when we dive deep into Ethereum and the EVM.

The design behind Ethereum, based on the whitepaper, is intended to build a simple, efficient and extensible blockchain platform, and have a Turing-complete program language to support more sophisticated and complex computations. It not only has all of the benefits of a blockchain but can serve as the framework for supporting all types of digital assets and value transfers as well.

# Ethereum – the world computer

Ethereum is often pegged as the world computer in the decentralized world. What does that mean? How does Ethereum fulfill the tall order of the humongous computation needed in the digital world? Let's start with the history of the internet and web and discuss the potentials of Ethereum.

## The world of decentralization

The World Wide Web started as the decentralized content network in the early '90s. It is designed for people to publish and share content without going through any central authority or intermediary. But from the early 2000s, with the advent of e-commerce, social and mobile, collectively called Web 2.0, we began to communicate, interact, and transact with each other and share information through centralized services provided by big companies such as Google, Facebook, Microsoft, and Amazon. Thanks to the power of platforms, platform businesses such as Uber, Airbnb, and Facebook managed to disrupt traditional business models and dominate vast traditional industries within just a few years of their own launch and outcompeted the traditional companies with a tiny fraction of the number of employees and resources. The direct consequence of such platform success is all that user data concentrated in the hands of a few, creating risks that our data will be misused or even hacked. It also makes it easier for governments to conduct surveillance and impose censorship.

Blockchain is on the way to become the new internet, Web 3.0. Bitcoin laid a foundation of decentralization with its shared public ledger, a digital cryptocurrency payment model, and P2P technology. Ethereum took this model further beyond finance and P2P payment, which propelled the creation of a new business model called DApps.

A DApp is an application or service that runs on a blockchain network and enables direct interaction between consumers and providers, for example, connecting buyers and sellers in a decentralized marketplace. Similar to the centralized application architecture, a DApp usually involves a decentralized backend that runs on the blockchain network and a centralized frontend that allows end users to access their wallets and make a transaction. The following diagram shows the differentiation between centralized and decentralized applications:

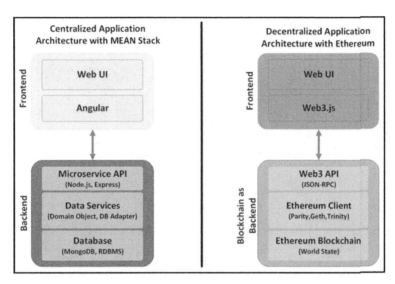

Although there are many different viewpoints, it is a common belief that a DApp must be completely decentralized and open source. It must run on a blockchain network and use and generate cryptographic tokens. Most DApps often start with a whitepaper and a working prototype. If garnering enough attention from the investors, it may involve a token sale and an **Initial Coin Offering (ICO)**.

Instead, as a DApp, Ethereum provides a platform for anyone to write smart contracts and decentralized applications based on your business needs and value propositions. It is intended as the world computer for the decentralized world. As such, Ethereum provides four decentralized computing facilities, along with a large list of development and testing tools, which make it very easy to develop and deploy DApps on to the Ethereum blockchain. The four decentralized computing facilities are as follows:

- Ethereum blockchain for decentralized state
- Smart contracts for decentralized computing
- Swarm and IPFS for decentralized storage
- Whispers for P2P messaging

The following diagram shows the decentralized computing facilities:

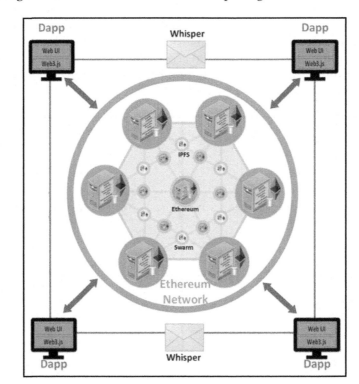

Many types of DApps are being created. According to State of the DApps (stateofthedapps.com), as of February 2019, there are over 2,500 DApps and about 6,000 smart contracts listed, and over 90% of them are running on the Ethereum network.

In the next section, we will discuss how Ethereum works, and go into details of the Ethereum architecture. We will discuss IPFS, swarm, and whisper in more detail in Chapter 3, *Deep Research on Ethereum.*

# Diving deep into Ethereum

In this section, we will get into the details of Ethereum architecture, including the following:

- Basic concepts of account, contract, transaction, and messages
- EVM internals and how EVM works

# Account

As we discussed earlier, instead of the UTXO model, Ethereum manages accounts and transactions differently than Bitcoin. In Ethereum, it introduces the **world state** concept, the collection of all accounts on the blockchain network. World state presents the global state of the Ethereum network, which is constantly updated following any transaction execution. It is a kind of a global database, which is replicated to all Ethereum nodes behind the scene. Like your bank account, an Ethereum account is used for holding ethers and transacting with each other. It has a 20-byte cryptographic address, an account balance, and state transitions between accounts. The address identifies the owner of the account.

In addition to the address, an Ethereum account contains four fields:

- **Nonce**: A counter used to identify distinct transactions
- **Balance**: The account's current ether balance
- **Contract code**: Optional cryptographic hash code pointing to smart code associated with the contract creation
- **Storage**: Optional cryptographic hash code pointing to the account's storage

The following diagram further illustrates the structure of an Ethereum account:

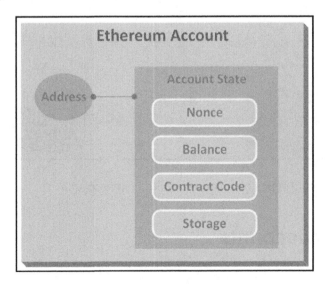

In Ethereum, a transaction is a state transition of account from one state to another, which is initiated by an external entity. All transactions, whether it is ether movement from one account to another or smart contract code execution, will be collated into a block. Also, the resulting account states and transaction receipts are added to the block too. The new block will be mined by the blockchain network and added to the blockchain. Data in the blockchain is stored in supporting storage, usually a database. Depending on the Ethereum client implementation, it may be stored into a different type of database. For example, the Geth implementation uses Google LevelDB as the underlying database implementation for the global state, as shown here:

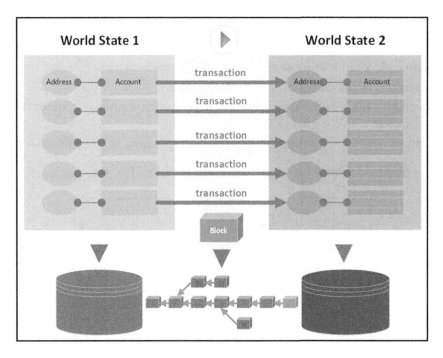

We will get into different types of accounts in the next section.

# Two types of accounts

Accounts play an essential role in Ethereum. Ethereum introduces two types of accounts:

- One is the **Externally Owned Account (EOA)**, which is used for ether transfer and is controlled by private keys. There is no code associated with EOA.

- Another one is a **Contract Account (CA)**, which is used for contract creation and smart code execution. The EVM activates and executes the smart contract code logic whenever the contract account receives a message. Beyond normal operations, it may read from and write to internal storage or invoke smart contracts on the other contracts.

They are both state objects; an EOA has a balance, and a CA has both a balance and storage. Without CAs, Ethereum would be limited to the mere transfer of value between accounts, as with Bitcoin.

# Externally owned account

Just like your personal or business account in a financial institute, an EOA is associated with an external entity as an owner who has an interest in the account or has ownership of the underlying cryptoassets. Every EOA has a pair of cryptographic keys. It is controlled by the owner's private key. The owner uses its private key to digitally sign all transactions so that the EVM can securely validate the identity of the senders. In the world state, the account is linked to a public address, which is generated based on the owner's public key. We will talk about the address in detail in the *Address and wallet* section, as part of the discussion about the Ethereum wallet.

The following diagram shows the structure of the EOA:

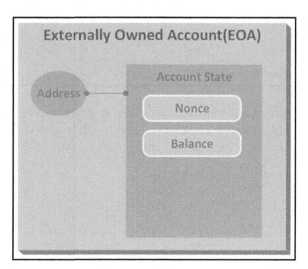

As shown here, EOA has a balance associated the address, mainly used for ether transfer.

# Contract account

A CA, or a contract, has an ether balance and associated code, which is linked to the smart contract code in an EVM. It may have optional storage, which is pointing to EVM storage. A state change in a contract account may involve an update of the ether balance, the associated data in the storage, or both. A contract account has an associated address too, which is calculated using the Keccak-256 hash function, based on the address of its creator (sender) and the nonce:

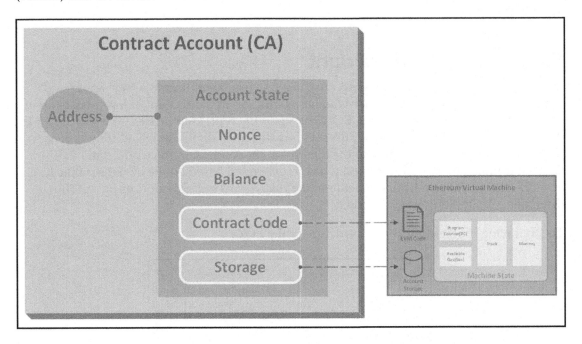

The associated smart contract code is executed when it is triggered by transactions or messages received from other contracts. Once a new block is added to the blockchain, all participating nodes will execute the contract code again as part of the block verification process.

# Transactions and messages

Transactions and messages in Ethereum are a little bit confusing, largely because they are often discussed together. There are some subtle differences. The following diagram will give some clarity about the differences and commonalities between these two terms:

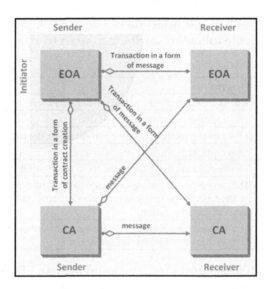

In Ethereum, the term transaction represents the signed data package of a message that is sent from an EOA to another account. The message itself instructs what action to take on the blockchain. They all require the initiator of the transaction to digitally sign the messages, and transactions will be recorded into the blockchain. Three types of transactions can happen:

- **CA creation**: In this case, an EOA acts as the initiator or creator of the new contract account.
- **A transaction between two EOAs**: In this case, one EOA initiates an ether movement transaction by sending a message to the receiving EOA.
- **A transaction between EOA and CA**: In this case, the EOA initiates a message call transaction, and the CA will react with the referenced smart contract code execution.

The CA can send messages to other CAs or EOAs. Unlike the transaction, messages are virtual objects during the execution and will not be recorded into the blockchain. If an EOA is the recipient, the recipient's account state will be updated and recorded in the world state. If a CA is the message recipient, they are accepted as function calls and the associated contract code will be executed.

From a data structure perspective, a transaction is a digitally signed message. According to web3.js, a message contains the following attributes. Apart from attribute, all others are optional:

| Attribute | Data type | Length | Description |
| --- | --- | --- | --- |
| from | DATA | 20 | This is a required field as the sender's address. |
| to | DATA | 20 | This represents the receiver's address. |
| gas | QUANTITY | | This represents the gas value provided for the transaction execution. |
| GasPrice | QUANTITY | | This represents the unit gas price used for each paid gas. |
| value | QUANTITY | | This represents the ether value to be sent with this transaction. |
| data | DATA | | This represents the compiled code of a contract when creating a contract account or the hash of the invoked method signature and encoded parameters during the contract invocation. |
| nonce | QUANTITY | | This represents a nonce. This allows you to overwrite your own pending transactions that use the same nonce. |

Transactions will have additional attributes. Ethereum uses an **Elliptic Curve Digital Signature Algorithm (ECDSA)** signature for digital signatures; $r$ and $s$ are outputs of an ECDSA signature, and $v$ is the recovery ID.

# Smart contract

A smart contract is an executable code that is digitally signed by the contract creator as part of contract account creation. It is like a scripted agreement between transacting parties; the code built into the contract is stored on the Ethereum blockchain and cannot be tampered with or removed. This greatly increases the credibility of the legal document.

Typically, DApp developers write smart contracts in some high-level programming language and then compile them into the bytecode. It is the bytecode living on the blockchain and executed within the EVM. There are not a lot of choices in determining which programming languages to use. The following are a couple of options that the developers may consider:

- **Solidity**: Solidity is the most popular one in the market for developing smart contracts. It is a JavaScript type language and is Turing complete.
- **Vyper**: Vyper is a general-purpose, experimental programming language that compiles down to the EVM bytecode, as does Solidity. It is a contract-oriented, Pythonic programming language that targets smart contract development language. Vyper aims to be auditable, secure, and human-readable. Being simple to read is more important than being simple to write.
- **Serpent**: Serpent is another pythonic programming language for smart contract development. It is largely deprecated. Serpent is compiled using LLL, a Lisp-like low-level language similar to Assembly.

Folks may wonder which one to use, Solidity or Vyper? For the majority of use cases, this is a personal preference. Solidity is the most popular one and has all tools and utilities in place for developing end-to-end decentralized applications. Vyper is still in the earlier experimental stage. On purpose, it omitted several programming constructs for being more secure, auditable, and human-readable. If your use case requires these, use Solidity instead of Vyper.

We will focus on the Solidity programming language in this book. In `Chapter 4`, *Solidity Fundamentals*, we will provide a comprehensive introduction of various Solidity language fundamentals including the structure of a contract, contract pattern, and exception handling. In *Chapter 5* through to *Chapter 11*, we will show you, step-by-step, how to design and develop, test and debug, and deploy and monitor decentralized applications using Solidity, Ethereum, and various tools and utilities in Ethereum ecosystems.

# Ether and gas

The Bitcoin network uses Bitcoin as the cryptocurrency to bootstrap the network and has a sophisticated algorithm to control the coin supply. The miner, by providing computing capacity for costly mining processes, gets rewarded with new-minted coins and transaction fees in Bitcoin.

Ether is the cryptocurrency powering the Ethereum blockchain network. **ETH** is the officially listed symbol for **ether**. Gas is the energy fueling smart contract execution in EVM and can be purchased with ether. To obtain ether, you either need to trade for ether from the crypto market or sign up as the miner. In Ethereum, the supply side will be lowered with the move to PoS, simply because there is no expensive mining anymore that we need to compensate for. Ether will be issued at a constant linear rate during the block mining process. Interested readers can check out online discussions and blogs here, `http://ethdocs.org/en/latest/ether.html`, for more information about the pros and cons of supply limitations.

Wei is the smallest denomination of ether in Ethereum. One ether is one quintillion or $10^{18}$ weis. The following table is a list of the named denominations and their value in wei:

| Unit | Wei Value | Wei |
|---|---|---|
| wei | 1 wei | 1 |
| Kwei (babbage) | $10^3$ wei | 1,000 |
| Mwei (lovelace) | $10^6$ wei | 1,000,000 |
| Gwei (shannon) | $10^9$ wei | 1,000,000,000 |
| microether (szabo) | $10^{12}$ wei | 1,000,000,000,000 |
| milliether (finney) | $10^{15}$ wei | 1,000,000,000,000,000 |
| ether | $10^{18}$ wei | 1,000,000,000,000,000,000 |

Ethereum is a general-purpose decentralized computing platform powered by ether. In addition to mining, all Ethereum nodes need to perform all computational steps as defined in the smart contract as part of the transaction and block verification process. The Ethereum protocol charges a fee per computational step in exchange for the computing resources supplied by the network nodes for the contract execution.

The execution fee is dynamically determined based on the total gas needed for the execution, and the gas price within the network. Gas in Ethereum is an internal virtual machine token to identify relative cost between operations (calculations, storage, and memory access) of contract execution. The gas price per ether is determined by the miners and generally fluctuates as a result of supply and demand on the network. The sender can purchase the gas from the miners using ether. The sender creating a transaction needs to set both a gas limit and price per gas-unit, which together becomes the price in ether that is paid.

When a smart contract is compiled into bytecode, it is actually assembled as encoded opcode and loaded into the EVM. Each opcode is identified as specific operations. The total gas cost of those operations will be the cost of your transaction. Every time the sender sends a transaction to a contract, the following two inputs need to be provided:

- `gas`: The gas limit the sender allows for processing a transaction
- `gasPrice`: The unit gas price the sender is willing to pay

The execution fee the sender offers for the transaction will be calculated as follows:

$$gas * gasPrice \text{ (in eth/g)} = ether$$

It is recommended to set a large enough gas limit since all unused gas is returned to the sender. If there is not enough gas, the miner still collects the fee even though the transaction execution will be rolled back. In the next section about the EVM, we will talk more about these computational steps and the gas associated with each step.

# The Ethereum Virtual Machine

In the Java world, developers write Java code in any Java IDE and compile it into bytecodes, which in turn are loaded into a virtual machine called the **Java Virtual Machine**, or **JVM**, behind the scenes through a Java class loader, and executed in the JVM. The JVM specification describes what is required of a JVM implementation and ensures the interoperability of Java programs across different implementations and underlying hardware platforms.

Similarly, in Ethereum, smart contracts and DApp developers code smart contracts in an Ethereum high-level language such as Solidity, compile them into bytecodes, and upload them on blockchain for invocation and execution. The EVM is the runtime execution environment for smart contracts in Ethereum. It comes with a different implementation of Ethereum clients, as we discussed earlier. Each implementation follows the EVM specification defined in the **Ethereum Yellow Paper**: `https://ethereum.github.io/yellowpaper/paper.pdf`.

Now, let's delve deeper to understand what the EVM is and how it executes a smart contract.

The EVM is a simple stack-based architecture. When executing a smart contract, it performs all operations, or in technical terms, opcodes, as defined in the EVM code, or bytecode. Ethereum provides three types of space in the EVM for the operations to access and store data:

- **Stack**: This is a last-in, first-out container with a fixed size and maximum depth of 1,024 items to which values can be pushed and popped. Each stack item is 256 bits long. This was chosen to facilitate the Keccak- 256 hash scheme and elliptic-curve computations.
- **Memory**: This is a volatile and expandable word-addressed byte array.
- Key/value store: This is a word-addressable word array. It is meant to be used as the long term account storage for the smart contract. Depending on whether you use account storage, your smart contract may be considered stateful or stateless.

During smart contract execution, the EVM has access to the incoming message, as well as block header data. Additionally, the EVM keeps track of the available gas and a **Program Counter (PC)** during execution. The following diagram shows the EVM:

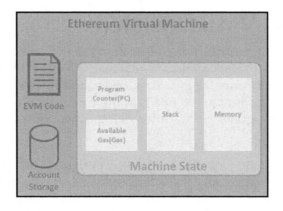

Unlike Java, Ethereum smart contract bytecode is uploaded through contract creation transactions, instead of some class loader within the virtual machine. As we discussed earlier, all transactions are digitally signed by the EOA. As shown in the following diagram, when a new smart contract needs to be created, the developer typically follows these steps to get a smart contract deployed into the EVM:

1. The developer writes the smart contract in Solidity and compiles it into bytecodes.
2. They use their own Ethereum account to sign the account creation transaction with the bytecode.
3. They send an account creation transaction to the Ethereum network.

*Steps* 2 and 3 allow Ethereum to upload the code on the blockchain and the creation of the accounts in the world state through the Ethereum mining process:

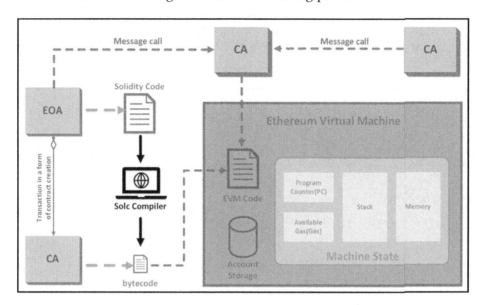

Depending on the tools you use, you will likely invoke a JSON-RPC call such as web3.eth_sendTransaction to create a new contract on the blockchain, with parameters as follows:

```
params: [{

"from": "< EOA Address >",

"to": "",

 "gas": "<gas>",

"gasPrice": "<gasPrice>",

"value": "<value>",

"data": "0x <compiled smart contract code>"
}]
```

Once the contract account is created through the mining process, you can invoke a JSON-RPC call such as web3.eth_getTransactionReciept to find out the contract address. You can always go to the Etherscan site to view and search your contract code using the contract address.

The following screenshot was taken on March 9, 2019 and shows the latest 1,000 verified Solidity contracts on the Ethereum blockchain (`https://etherscan.io/ contractsVerified?filter=solc`). A verified smart contract means the ownership of the Ethereum address used to create the smart contract has been verified, and the owner has an Etherscan account. You can click any address and further view the smart contract source code:

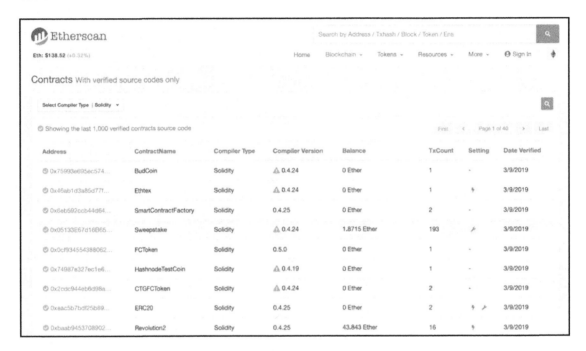

As we discussed earlier, the contract can be invoked by an externally owned account via a transaction or a contract account via a function call from another smart contract.

Check out the following diagram:

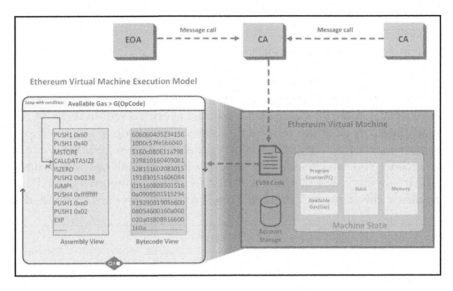

As shown in the preceding diagram, we can see the following:

1. Once invoked, the EVM will load contract bytecodes into memory, loop through opcodes while checking the available gas, and perform all operations on the EVM stack.
2. During the execution, if there is not enough gas or an error occurs, the execution will abend.
3. The transaction will not go through, but the sender will not get the spent gas back.

EVM executes around 140 operations or opcodes that are divided into the following 11 categories. All of the opcodes and their complete descriptions are available in the Ethereum Yellow Paper (`https://github.com/ethereum/yellowpaper`):

- Stop and arithmetic operations (0x00 – 0x0b)
- Comparison and bitwise logic operation (0x10 – 0x1a)
- SHA3 (0x20)
- Environmental information (0x30 – 0x3e)
- Block information (0x40 – 0x45)
- Stack, memory, storage, and flow operations (0x50 – 0x5b)
- Push operations (0x60 – 0x7f)

- Duplication operations (0x80 – 0x8f)
- Exchange operations (0x90 – 0x9f)
- Logging operations (0xa0 – 0xa4)
- System operations (0xf0 – 0xff)

You may remember the relationship between transaction fees, gas, and gas prices from our earlier discussion. In fact, the winning node adding the new block to the blockchain gets paid with the transaction fee for every smart contract executed within its EVM. The payment is calculated for all of the computations the miner made to store, compute, and execute the smart contract. The EVM specification defines a fee schedule for every operation or opcode. You can check the Ethereum wiki site for all opcodes supported by Ethereum. The following is a screenshot captured from the Ethereum Yellow Paper. For more details, please check out the complete Paper from the previously provided link:

### APPENDIX G. FEE SCHEDULE

The fee schedule $G$ is a tuple of 31 scalar values corresponding to the relative costs, in gas, of a number of abstract operations that a transaction may effect.

| Name | Value | Description* |
|---|---|---|
| $G_{zero}$ | 0 | Nothing paid for operations of the set $W_{zero}$. |
| $G_{base}$ | 2 | Amount of gas to pay for operations of the set $W_{base}$. |
| $G_{verylow}$ | 3 | Amount of gas to pay for operations of the set $W_{verylow}$. |
| $G_{low}$ | 5 | Amount of gas to pay for operations of the set $W_{low}$. |
| $G_{mid}$ | 8 | Amount of gas to pay for operations of the set $W_{mid}$. |
| $G_{high}$ | 10 | Amount of gas to pay for operations of the set $W_{high}$. |
| $G_{extcode}$ | 700 | Amount of gas to pay for operations of the set $W_{extcode}$. |
| $G_{balance}$ | 400 | Amount of gas to pay for a BALANCE operation. |
| $G_{sload}$ | 200 | Paid for a SLOAD operation. |
| $G_{jumpdest}$ | 1 | Paid for a JUMPDEST operation. |
| $G_{sset}$ | 20000 | Paid for an SSTORE operation when the storage value is set to non-zero from zero. |
| $G_{sreset}$ | 5000 | Paid for an SSTORE operation when the storage value's zeroness remains unchanged or is set to zero. |
| $R_{sclear}$ | 15000 | Refund given (added into refund counter) when the storage value is set to zero from non-zero. |
| $R_{suicide}$ | 24000 | Refund given (added into refund counter) for suiciding an account. |
| $G_{suicide}$ | 5000 | Amount of gas to pay for a SUICIDE operation. |
| $G_{create}$ | 32000 | Paid for a CREATE operation. |
| $G_{codedeposit}$ | 200 | Paid per byte for a CREATE operation to succeed in placing code into state. |
| $G_{call}$ | 700 | Paid for a CALL operation. |
| $G_{callvalue}$ | 9000 | Paid for a non-zero value transfer as part of the CALL operation. |
| $G_{callstipend}$ | 2300 | A stipend for the called contract subtracted from $G_{callvalue}$ for a non-zero value transfer. |
| $G_{newaccount}$ | 25000 | Paid for a CALL or SUICIDE operation which creates an account. |
| $G_{exp}$ | 10 | Partial payment for an EXP operation. |
| $G_{expbyte}$ | 10 | Partial payment when multiplied by $\lceil log_{256}(exponent) \rceil$ for the EXP operation. |
| $G_{memory}$ | 3 | Paid for every additional word when expanding memory. |
| $G_{txcreate}$ | 32000 | Paid by all contract-creating transactions after the *Homestead transition*. |
| $G_{txdatazero}$ | 4 | Paid for every zero byte of data or code for a transaction. |
| $G_{txdatanonzero}$ | 68 | Paid for every non-zero byte of data or code for a transaction. |
| $G_{transaction}$ | 21000 | Paid for every transaction. |
| $G_{log}$ | 375 | Partial payment for a LOG operation. |
| $G_{logdata}$ | 8 | Paid for each byte in a LOG operation's data. |
| $G_{logtopic}$ | 375 | Paid for each topic of a LOG operation. |
| $G_{sha3}$ | 30 | Paid for each SHA3 operation. |
| $G_{sha3word}$ | 6 | Paid for each word (rounded up) for input data to a SHA3 operation. |
| $G_{copy}$ | 3 | Partial payment for *COPY operations, multiplied by words copied, rounded up. |
| $G_{blockhash}$ | 20 | Payment for BLOCKHASH operation. |

In addition to smart contract execution, the EVM also performs transactions between two EOAs to transfer ethers from one to another account. In all cases, whenever there is a transaction submitted to the Ethereum network, as the Ethereum mining node, the EVM and Ethereum client perform the mining operations and add new transactions to the blockchain. We will talk about mining in the next section.

If you come from a Java development background, you may remember the Java **Just-In-Time (JIT)** compiler and its advantage in Java runtime. It is a feature that compiles the bytecode into the machine code instructions of the running machine. This makes sense since, from the bottom line machine execution view, it was machine code being executed, not the bytecode. By doing the initial compilation, it avoids instant interpretation from bytecode to machine code at execution time, hence improving the performance of Java applications.

Some newer EVM implementations support a JIT compiler too, including Parity and Geth. Similar to Java JIT, EVM JIT is a library for the just-in-time compilation of EVM bytecode. Before the EVM can run any code, it must first compile the bytecode into components that can be understood by the JIT-enabled EVM. By compiling the bytecode into logical pieces, the JIT can analyze the code more precisely and optimize where and whenever necessary. It may seem slower at the beginning since it needs to check whether the JIT-compiled code is in the library and compile the bytecodes if it is not. Interested readers can check out both the Go Ethereum and Parity sites for more details.

# Address and wallet

Earlier, we introduced Ethereum accounts, transactions, and smart contracts. They are all linked to an address, which refers to the owners of both types of accounts or the senders of messages and transactions. Like Bitcoin, Ethereum has the concept of the Ethereum wallet too. It is a tool that allows you to easily share your public keys and securely keep private keys. In this section, we will discuss the details about the Ethereum address and wallet. We will also provide a brief introduction to different wallet tools.

# Addresses in Ethereum

As we discussed earlier, an EOA has a pair of public and private keys. The private key is used to digitally sign any transactions. The public key is used to generate the account address, which is linked to account state in the world state. An Ethereum address is described as follows in the Yellow Paper:

> For a given private key, $p_r$, the Ethereum address $A(p_r)$ (a 160-bit value) to which it corresponds is defined as the right most 160-bits of the Keccak hash of the corresponding ECDSA public key:
>
> (213) $$A(p_r) = \mathcal{B}_{96..255}(\text{KEC}(\text{ECDSAPUBKEY}(p_r)))$$

In other words, to generate an Ethereum address, take the Keccak-256 hash of the public key. The rightmost 20 bytes of the hash, with a prefix of 0x as the hexadecimal identifier, is your Ethereum address.

The CA has an account address too. Traditionally, it is generated based on the sender's public key and the transaction nonce. A newer address creation schema based on EIP 1014, `Skinny CREATE2`, was implemented as part of the system-wide upgrade release of Constantinople. It allows the developer to create an address for future smart contract deployment. Interested readers can check out the EIP link at `https://eips.ethereum.org/EIPS/eip-1014`. Once the transaction is processed, the CA will be linked to the account address in the world state.

# Ethereum wallet

Before you can trade ether, you need a place to store it. Ether, just like every other cryptocurrency, doesn't exist in any tangible shape or form. All that exists are records on the Ethereum blockchain. In the same way as Bitcoin, the Ethereum wallet allows you to interact with the blockchain to enable cryptocurrency transactions.

An Ethereum wallet stores the public and private keys, where the private key is used for paying or spending ethers and the public key for receiving ethers. A wallet can contain multiple public and private key pairs. An Ethereum address, derived from public keys, is used as the public address for you to receive the ethers. However, every piece of cryptocurrency has a private key. You will need the private keys from your wallet to unlock the funds to spend the coins.

# Wallet tools

There are many wallet implementations to choose from. You may have to decide for yourself which wallet is best for you. You have options to choose between hot and cold wallets—in other words, online and offline wallets. Or you can choose between hardware, software, or even paper wallets. There are a lot of mobile wallets available too.

For Ethereum, you may want to choose an ERC-20 compatible wallet. ERC-20 is an Ethereum token standard that defines standards, smart contract interfaces, and rules for issuing crypto-tokens on the Ethereum network. The following are a few known to be compatible with ERC-20 token standards:

- MyEtherWallet (`https://www.myetherwallet.com/`)
- MetaMask (`https://metamask.io/`)
- Mist (`https://github.com/ethereum/mist/releases`)
- Parity (`https://ethcore.io/parity.html`)

We will discuss more in `Chapter 3`, *Deep Research on Ethereum*, about Ethereum tokens, including ERC-20, ERC-223, ERC-721, and ERC-777 tokens. We will further demonstrate how to build Ethereum wallets in `Chapter 11`, *Build Ethereum Wallets*.

# Understanding mining in Ethereum

In this section, we will explain how mining works in Ethereum, and briefly discuss Ethereum's plan for the PoS consensus mechanism.

The mining process in Ethereum is largely the same as the one we discussed in Bitcoin. For each block of transactions to be added to the Ethereum blockchain and the world state to be updated, consensus must be reached among all network nodes that the new blocks proposed by the miners, including the nonce found with the PoW, must be verified by all nodes.

However, there are quite a few notable differences between Ethereum mining and Bitcoin mining. Most of them are driven by the protocol and architecture difference in the blockchain. As we discussed earlier, Ethereum maintains both the transaction list and the world state on the blockchain. We will discuss those differences in detail here.

# Mining and consensus protocol

Bitcoin uses a general-purpose cryptographic hash function SHA-256 as the PoW algorithm. With advances in specialized mining equipment such as ASIC, miners have been building large mining pools to compete with each other for the rewards of the bitcoin. It puts small miners at a disadvantage and leads to more mining centralization.

To avoid such concerns, Ethereum uses a memory-hard hash function called Ethash, a modified version of the Dagger-Hashimoto algorithm, as the PoW algorithm and targets GPUs as the primary mining equipment.

As with other PoW algorithms, Ethash involves finding a nonce that makes the resulting hash value fall under a protocol defined target. The design idea for a new hash algorithm is twofold. First, it is that it is hard enough for miners to mine but it is trivial for the validators to verify. Also, the hash results are uniformly distributed for easy control at the time of finding a new block. In Ethereum, new blocks are created every 12 seconds, instead of the 10 minutes of the Bitcoin network. The difficulty is dynamically adjusted to ensure the much fast block creation speed.

Overall, the Ethash algorithm in Ethereum involves two stages. The first stage is to generate a dataset of a **Directed Acyclic Graph**, referenced as **DAG**. This is usually calculated for each epoch—or every 30,000 blocks. The second stage is to repeatedly hash the dataset, the proposed header, and a random nonce using Keccak-256, until the resulting hash value meets the difficulty target. DAG generation is composed of the following three steps:

1. A seed is created from the blockchain by hashing the headers of each block together with the current epoch using Keccak-256.
2. Once the seed is found, a 16 MB pseudorandom cache is generated from the seed using Keccak-256.
3. A DAG is generated using the **Fowler–Noll–Vo (FNV)** hash function. It consists of many chunks of 64-byte elements; each of them depends on a part of the cache.

Each Ethereum client may implement DAG differently. It is typically generated in advance and cached for performance improvement. Geth implements automatic DAG generation and maintains two DAGS at a time for smooth epoch transitions.

# Ethereum transaction and block structure

Due to blockchain architecture and mining difference in Ethereum implementations, Ethereum defines quite different transaction and block structures in the Ethereum protocol. Ethereum DApps need to follow Ethereum protocol rules to format and submit transactions to the network. Invalid transactions will be rejected by the network.

The following are the essential data structures in Ethereum, taken from Ethereum's GitHub code:

- **Ethereum block structure**:

  An Ethereum block structure looks similar to the screenshot:

  | Field | Description | Size |
  |-------|-------------|------|
  | header | The block header information | |
  | uncles | The list of uncle block headers | |
  | transactions | List of transactions in the block | |
  | td | The address of the recipient of the ether in the transaction | >= 1 Bytes |
  | receivedAt | Timestamp used for peer to peer relay | 32 Bytes |
  | ReceivedFrom | Transaction data | Any |

- **Block header structure**:

  The following screenshot shows the Ethereum block header structure:

  | Field | Description | Size |
  |-------|-------------|------|
  | parentHash | The Keccak-256 hash of previous block header | 32 bytes |
  | UncleHash | The Keccak-256 hash of uncle block header list | 32 bytes |
  | Coinbase | The coinbase address for sending block reward and transaction fees | 20 bytes |
  | stateRoot | The Keccak-256 root hash of world state trie after all transactions are applied | 32 bytes |
  | transactionsRoot | The Keccak-256 root hash of transactions trie populated with all transactions in the block | 32 bytes |
  | receiptsRoot | The Keccak-256 root hash of transaction receipts trie populated with all receipts in the block | 32 bytes |
  | logsBloom | The bloom filter for the log information during the execution of the transactions in the block | 256 bytes |
  | difficulty | Network specified mining difficulty. | ≥1 byte |
  | number | Number of the ancestor blocks | ≥1 byte |
  | gasLimit | the gas limits | ≥1 byte |
  | gasUsed | The actual gas being used | ≥1 byte |
  | timestamp | timestamp for the block creation | ≤32 bytes |
  | extraData | Reserved for arbitrary data miners may use | ≤32 bytes |
  | mixHash | The Keccak-256 generated from the cache calculations of previous cache elements as defined by Ethash algorithm | 32 bytes |
  | nonce | The resulting nonce from mining based on Ethash algorithm | 8 bytes |

Instead of a Merkle hash root in Bitcoin, Ethereum uses a modified Merkle Patricia Trie notation for the root hash in the block header. More specifically, `stateRoot` in the preceding structure is the Merkle Patricia Trie of account state, `transactionRoot` is the Merkle Patricia Trie of all transactions in the block, and `receiptsRoot` is the Merkle Patricia Trie of all transaction receipts. Interested readers can check out Vitalik's blog about the rationales implementing Merkle Patrica Trie in Ethereum: `https://blog.ethereum.org/2015/11/15/merkling-in-ethereum/`.

Another difference in Ethereum is, when creating new blocks, Ethereum adds the new block to the heaviest branch of the block tree, instead of to the longest chain as we saw in Bitcoin. The header attribute, `difficulty`, is used by the miner to determine which branch is heavier.

- **Transaction structure in Ethereum**:

  Let's have a look at the following table :

| Field | Description | Size |
| --- | --- | --- |
| AccountNonce | The account nonce | 8 Bytes |
| Price | The price of the gas | >= 1 Bytes |
| GasLimit | The gas limit | >= 1 Bytes |
| Recipient | The address of the recipient of the ether in the transaction | 20 Bytes |
| Amount | The amount of ether sending to the recipient | >= 1 Bytes |
| Payload | Transaction data | Any |
| V | V value of v.r.s trie, r and s are outputs of an ECDSA signature, and v is the recovery id. | >= 1 Bytes |
| R | R value of v.r.s trie, r and s are outputs of an ECDSA signature, and v is the recovery id. | >= 1 Bytes |
| S | S value of v.r.s trie, r and s are outputs of an ECDSA signature, and v is the recovery id. | >= 1 Bytes |
| Hash | Used for JSON marshalling | 32 Bytes |

The preceding table shows the general data structure of Ethereum transactions. The following table shows the data structure of transaction receipts:

| Field | Description | Size |
| --- | --- | --- |
| PostState | The state object from the transaction execution | Byte array, any size |
| Status | The statue code of the transaction execution | 8 Bytes |
| CumulativeGasUsed | The total gas used in the block | 8 Bytes |
| Bloom | The bloom filter information based on the logs | 256 Bytes |
| Logs | Log information being logged during contract execution | >= 1 Bytes |
| TxHash | Transaction hash | 32 Bytes |
| ContractAddress | The contract address | 20 Bytes |
| GasUsed | The gas used for the contract execution | 8 Bytes |

A transaction receipt is generated once the blockchain accepts the submitted transaction. The preceding shows the data structure of transaction receipts.

# Transaction validation and block verification

Ethereum maintains all accounts in the underlying world state, which makes the state transition much easier. When the transaction is submitted to the Ethereum blockchain, miners will perform an intrinsic validity check on the transaction. It will be validated according to the consensus rules and heuristic limits of the local node, such as price and size. If the transaction size is over 32KB, it will be rejected for preventing DoS attacks. The transaction needs to be well-formed with **Recursive Length Prefix (RLP)** encoding. They will be checked to ensure that the transaction is properly signed by the sender and has the proper nonce ordering and to make sure the sender should have enough funds to cover the total transition costs—in other words, the amounts being transferred plus the gas cost for the smart contract execution.

Miners add transactions to the transaction pool once they pass the intrinsic validity check. Every 12 seconds, miners take transactions out of the transaction pool and start to propose the new block. They determine ommer or uncle blocks, and the total gas used in the block. They will create the block structure as defined earlier and start mining. Once the nonce is found to meet the ethash target, the new block with newfound nonce is broadcasted to the network for all network nodes to verify and add to their local copy of blockchain.

# Shift to proof-of-stake

The consensus mechanism is the trust protocol for securing the blockchain. Out of more than a dozen consensus protocols, **Proof-of-Work (PoW)** and **Proof-of-Stake (PoS)** are the most popular ones. Ethereum started off based on the PoW protocol, which is now in favor of shifting to PoS.

You may remember that we analyzed both PoW and PoS consensus algorithms in depth in the *Anatomizing blockchain consensus mechanism* section of `Chapter 1`, *Blockchain and Cryptocurrency*. We discussed the advantages and disadvantages of both algorithms. The main issue with PoW is that it is energy-intensive, has a high cost of mining, and is less scalable.

A PoS-PoW hybrid consensus model, with intentions to provide stronger economic finality and security, was originally planned as part of Constantinople but didn't happen. Ethereum 2.0, also known as Serenity, is planned to be the system's final upgrade, as the entire network transitions from a PoW to a PoS consensus algorithm, and tackles fundamental questions such as scalability, economic finality, and security. It plans to fade out the PoW chain overtime via another milestone in the future.

We will discuss more about Casper and advanced scalability topics in `Chapter 3`, *Deep Research in Ethereum*.

# Working with tools and technologies in Ethereum ecosystem

By now, we have introduced blockchain technology, key concepts in Bitcoin, and Ethereum. We delved deeper into detail on how the blockchain is maintained and how a decentralized network of peers reaches the consensus. One key takeaway is that Ethereum is a decentralized computing platform that has the potential to become a disruptor for the years to come. Thanks to the vibrant community and ecosystem, developers around the world can take advantage of the rich set of development tools to jump-start the implementation of decentralized applications. In this section, we will provide some of the key tools, technologies, and utilities to get you started. Some more details regarding some of the tools can be found in the second and third sections of this book.

# Ethereum client

Ethereum clients run the EVM and are written in a programming language. The following are two of the most popular Ethereum clients:

- **Geth**: It is also called the go-ethereum client. It was implemented in Go and was one of the three original implementations (along with C++ and Python) of the Ethereum protocol. It provides the command-line interface for running a full Ethereum node and has a JSON-RPC server interface for DApps to interact with. It can be downloaded from `https://ethereum.github.io/go-ethereum/`.
- **Parity**: Parity Ethereum aims to become the fastest, lightest, and most secure Ethereum client. It is a full Ethereum node implementation developed using the Rust programming language. Parity Ethereum is licensed under the GPLv3 license and can be downloaded from the Ethcore website: `https://ethcore.io/parity.html`.

# The Web3 Server API

All Ethereum clients provide a set of JSON-RPC methods for external DApps to interact with the Ethereum blockchain network. JSON is a lightweight data-interchange format. JSON-RPC is a stateless, lightweight **Remote Procedure Call (RPC)** protocol. The DApp UI layer implemented in the web and JavaScript has the option to use the web3.js JavaScript library to interface with Web3 JSON-RPC methods on the blockchain.

The following is a list of protocol supports among different Ethereum clients:

|  | cpp-ethereum | go-ethereum | Trinity | parity |
|---|---|---|---|---|
| JSON-RPC 1.0 | ✓ |  |  |  |
| JSON-RPC 2.0 | ✓ | ✓ | ✓ | ✓ |
| Batch requests | ✓ | ✓ | ✓ | ✓ |
| HTTP | ✓ | ✓ | ✓ | ✓ |
| IPC | ✓ | ✓ |  | ✓ |
| WS |  | ✓ |  | ✓ |

Most notable, JSON-RPC 2.0 is supported by all listed clients. Interested readers can check the Ethereum wiki site for details of interface and methods: `https://github.com/ethereum/wiki/wiki/JSON-RPC#json-rpc-methods`.

# DApp development tools

You can develop smart contracts in any editor and deploy them on the Ethereum blockchain using rudimental command-line utilities. There are quite a few essential tools, such as the ones mentioned here, which can leverage to speed up DApp development:

- Web UI development with web3.js
- Remix development IDE
- A command-line framework with Truffle and Embark
- Ethereum blockchain with Etherscan

**Web UI Development with web3.js**: The web3.js library is a collection of JavaScript modules that UI and JavaScript developers can leverage to integrate DApps with the Ethereum blockchain network. It provides the following sub-packages:

- `web3-eth`: A package for interacting with Ethereum blockchain and smart contracts
- `web3-shh`: A package to support the Whisper protocol for P2P messaging
- `web3-bzz`: A package to support the Swarm protocol and the decentralized file storage
- `web3-utils`: A package of utility functions for DApp developers

We will introduce whisper and Swarm in `Chapter 3`, *Deep Research in Ethereum.*

**Remix development IDE**: Remix is an open source, browser-based IDE that enables Ethereum developers to develop, compile, test, debug, and deploy smart contracts in Solidity. Developers can use Remix in the browser as well as locally. It also comes with its own code analyzer to check and ensure code quality. Remix communicates with the Ethereum blockchain through Metamask. Metamask is a browser extension for Chrome, Firefox, and Opera and allows developers to run DApps right within the browser.

 The Remix project with all its features is available at `remix.ethereum.org`. The Remix IDE tool can be downloaded from `our GitHub repository`.

**A command-line framework with Truffle and Embark:** Truffle is one of the most popular blockchain frameworks aiming to make developing smart contracts easier. The development environment gives developers a configurable build pipeline allowing for streamlining your DApp coding, testing, deploying process. Ganache CLI, part of the Truffle suite of the Ethereum development tools, is the command-line version of Ganache, your local blockchain for Ethereum development.

Another popular one is Embark. Similar to Truffle, Embark makes it easier for developers to code, test, and deploy smart contracts DApps and provide integration with Ethereum blockchain, decentralized storage platform (IPFS and Swarm) and decentralized messaging (Whisper). We will discuss more about IPFS, Swarm and Whisper in Chapter 3, *Deep Research on Ethereum*.

More information about Truffle can be found on the Truffle website and its GitHub repository: https://truffleframework.com. Information about Embark can be found here: https://embark.status.im.

**Ethereum blockchain with Etherscan**: We have shown several screenshots of Etherscan in the previous sections and chapter. Etherscan is one of the really handy tools a DApp developer could wish for. It allows you to search and view all transactions and smart contracts on the blockchains.

For a more comprehensive list of all Ethereum tools, please visit https://github.com/ConsenSys/ethereum-developer-tools-list.

# Summary

In this chapter, you learned details of Ethereum architecture and how Ethereum works. We went through key Ethereum concepts, including accounts, contracts, transactions, and messages. We discussed how the EVM works and how the smart contract code is executed within the EVM. In the end, we also showed you the tools and technologies that you will need while developing your very first smart contract and decentralized applications.

In the next chapter, we will discuss Ethereum's various initiatives in addressing scalability challenges. We will also get you familiar with the decentralized file system and messaging system so that you have a complete understanding of the Ethereum ecosystem. For folks eager to get their feet wet and develop smart contracts, you can jump to Chapter 4, *Solidity Fundamentals*, and come back to Chapter 3, *Deep Research on Ethereum*, when you need to understand the ongoing deep researches in Ethereum community.

# Deep Research on Ethereum

3

In this chapter, we will delve deeper into the key challenges of the Ethereum blockchain, examine various layer 1 and layer 2 scalability solutions being implemented, or to be implemented, in the current or future Ethereum releases. Then, in the *Introducing cryptoassets and Ethereum token standards* section, we will further discuss various layer 3 application topics, including **initial coin offering (ICO)**, **security token offering (STO)**, and **initial exchange offering (IEO)** funding mechanisms and the Ethereum token standards, and we will scratch the surface of cryptoeconomics. We will explore how the decentralized filesystem works with **InterPlanetary File System (IPFS)**, Swarm, and BigchainDB, and how decentralized messaging works with Whisper. If you have just started learning about Ethereum and plunge into the development of smart contracts, you can jump directly to Chapter 4, *Solidity Fundamentals*, and come back later on to see various deep research topics in the Ethereum community.

The following topics will be covered in this chapter:

- Understanding challenges in distributed systems
- Scaling Ethereum
- Following up on EVM and lower-level protocol improvements
- Implementing the Ethereum 2.0 roadmap
- Introducing cryptoassets and Ethereum token standards
- Working with decentralized data and content storage
- Decentralized messaging with the Whisper protocol

# Technical Requirements

For all the source code of this book, please refer the following GitHub link :

```
https://github.com/PacktPublishing/Learn-Ethereum
```

# Understanding challenges in distributed systems

In today's world, distributed systems are everywhere. A distributed system is a collection of computing resources, including computers, devices, software components or applications, which are physically separated, but linked together to complete certain acts or tasks. Internet, intranet or mobile networks are examples of distributed network systems. More sophisticated ones include a cluster, a grid, and cloud infrastructure. Examples of distributed applications vary from client server applications, SOA-based systems to massive multiplayer online games. Thanks to social, mobile, and cloud applications, large-scale distributed systems have evolved into an indispensable technology platform and are a ubiquitous always-on environment for businesses, consumers, and private citizens around the world.

With the help of advanced technologies, heterogeneity, openness, and transparency are no longer considered to be a major issue. However, guaranteeing availability, security, and scalability, and ensuring data consistency and fault tolerance are still major challenges that business and technology leaders face when developing large-scale distributed systems.

It is no surprise at all, that the decentralized peer-to-peer network is a distributed system at a global scale too. Design choices and trade-offs have to be made by the designers of distributed systems to address those challenges and issues and come up with products that fulfill the design goals and meet real-world business needs. In a distributed database system and NoSQL type of big data platform, the goal is security and scalability of the system. Consistency and availability of data and information, along with fault tolerance in a distributed network, are the trade-offs and design choices.

In the blockchain network, which is a distributed database in a decentralized peer-to-peer network, decentralization and being trustless are the ultimate goals; the blockchain network has to make trade-offs between decentralization, security, and scalability. This leads to more discussions in the next few sections about design trade-offs in distributed systems in general and in the blockchain network in particular. In the following sections, we will look at design trade-offs in distributed systems in general and in the blockchain network in particular.

# The CAP theorem

Proposed by Eric Brewer, a Berkeley computer scientist, the CAP theorem asserts that any distributed system with shared state can only have at most, two desirable properties out of the following three:

- Consistency
- Availability
- Partition tolerance

There is no guarantee that network nodes are free of failure in a distributed heterogeneous environment. Therefore, the CAP theorem suggests that the designer of large distributed systems has to make a trade-off between consistency and availability. Traditional RDBMS is more targeted to ensure consistency and availability in a centralized system.

The following diagram illustrates the three properties of the CAP theorem and the designer's choices in different distributed database systems:

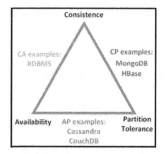

For example, the Cassandra database, a massively scalable open source NoSQL database from the Apache foundation, is the right choice for use cases where scalability, high availability, and performance are the most important design objectives.

Design choices made in Cassandra favor availability and partition tolerance over consistency, although you can eventually make it consistent by tuning the Cassandra database with the replication factor and consistency level. Its linear scalability, together with its strong fault-tolerance on commodity hardware or cloud infrastructure, makes it a perfect option for many mission critical applications. CouchDB falls in the same category.

On the other hand, MongoDB is strongly consistent by default, which also means it compromises **availability**. It employs a single-master system to ensure all writes occur on the primary node, and nothing is written to the secondary node. All reads go to the primary node by default. If the primary goes down, no writes can happen until a secondary takes over as the primary. HBase falls in the same category.

# Horizontal scaling versus vertical scaling

One of the most difficult and most challenging problems in a distributed system is scalability. Scalability refers to the capability that a distributed system can handle a growing amount of workload without degrading the overall system performance, and has the potential to accommodate that growth.

In case of a typical three-tier application, as shown is the following diagram, the web server accepts the requests coming from the users. Depending upon the request, the application server will process the same, and the final state will be updated in the underlying database of the database server. When users increase drastically, let's say 5-10 concurrent users suddenly access the system, how do you scale the multi-tier applications and meet the required service level agreement?

There are two ways to scale the system, and so this means the designer or architect of the multi-tier application needs to ensure each tier can scale independently and, as a whole, it can meet the desired performance when the number of concurrent users increases. One technique is vertical scaling. In this case, you can increase the computing capacity in each layer, by increasing memory, storage, using a more advanced CPU, and so on. Another technique is horizontal scaling, where additional servers can be provisioned and added to the server farm in each layer:

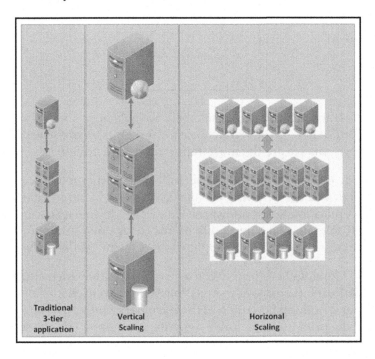

There are trade-offs between these two techniques. Vertical scaling makes the server management straightforward, while horizontal scaling increases the server management complexity. Horizontal scaling is considered to be more advantageous, since with today's cloud and virtualization technology, it is possible to scale the system up and down, based on the user traffic. However, in the vertical scaling case, it is not easy to increase or decrease the system capacity.

In the case of a distributed database, with both an RDBMS and NoSQL type database, a number of different approaches, like partitions and shading, and design trade-offs, enable them to grow to a very large size while being able to scale out, up, and down.

Many of the scaling techniques were applied to solve the scalability challenges in the Ethereum blockchain too. Now it is time for us to go over the different Ethereum salability solutions and proposals, and get an understanding of how the Ethereum community addresses the scalability issues.

# Scaling Ethereum

Like Bitcoin, the main reason for the Ethereum scalability problem is the network protocol that each node in the network has to process each transaction. Ethereum 1.x implements a slightly modified version of the **proof-of-work (PoW)** consensus mechanism. In Ethereum, miners have to race to find the nonce to meet the target difficulty. Every node needs to verify that the miners' work is valid and keep an accurate copy of the current network state. This greatly limits the transaction process capability and throughput of the Ethereum blockchain network. Currently it can only process 12-15 transactions per second.

# Blockchain scalability trilemma

First used by Vitalik Buterin, the **scalability trilemma** is a concept in blockchain regarding its capability to address scalability, decentralization, and security, without compromising any of them. The trilemma claims that it is almost impossible to achieve all three properties in a blockchain system:

- **Decentralization**: This is a core tenet upon which Bitcoin and blockchain were created. Decentralization enables censorship-resistance and permits anyone to participate in a decentralized ecosystem without a central authority or intermediary.
- **Security**: This refers to the integrity and immutability of the public ledger, and the ability to resist 51% or DDoS like network attacks.

- **Scalability**: This concerns the ability to handle a growing amount of transactions in the blockchain network. In order for the Ethereum blockchain to be the world computer as the inventor envisioned, it needs to match the transaction throughput of many centralized systems, like Amazon, Visa, or Mastercard.

The following diagram is an illustration of the scalability trilemma in the blockchain:

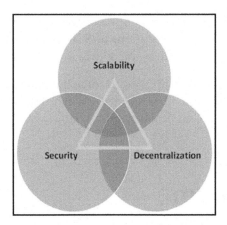

The key challenge of scalability is finding a way to achieve all three at the base layer. The design choices of Bitcoin and Ethereum favor decentralization and security, while making a sacrifice in scalability. Some of the altcoins we discussed in the *Altcoins* section in Chapter 1, *Blockchain and Cryptocurrency*, address Bitcoin scalability issues with a compromise of either decentralization, by introducing some centralized concepts or components, or security, by applying variations to the consensus protocols.

# Ethereum scaling solutions

Ethereum scalability solution is one of most active topics in the Ethereum community. The following are a few areas of concern the community is trying to tackle:

- Transaction processing and block creation time with PoW—how fast can the miners process all transactions and create a new block through mining?
- Transaction finality – how soon can the decentralized network reach consensus that a transaction has happened and can't be reverted? Currently it takes about six blocks in Bitcoin and 3-4 minutes in Ethereum for the network to consider a block is finalized in the main chain. Interested readers should check out Vitalik's block for transaction settlement and block finality probability (https://blog. ethereum.org/2016/05/09/on-settlement-finality/).

Solutions being implemented or proposed, fall into three categories: on-chain solution, off-chain solution, and consensus mechanism protocols. There are some obvious or theoretical ones, like increasing block size or slicing one blockchain into many independent altcoin chains. Due to the nature of peer to peer, a traditional horizontal scaling approach may not work.

Specific to the Ethereum network, some consideration was also given to stateful or stateless smart contracts contributing to scalability issues. We will go over high-level concepts of all those solutions, and then delve deeper into some of the promising ones.

# Block size

This is similar to the vertical scaling approach. Some of the altcoins, like Bitcoin Cash, Ethereum Core, and so on, are implementing a larger block size to gain overall transaction performance. The theory behind this approach is that since PoW mining is the main bottleneck in the entire process, by increasing the block size we can have more transactions processed per mining. It may take a little bit longer to create a **directed acyclic graph (DAG)** for stash-based mining, but the average time to complete the mining may not get any worse, since most of the Ethereum clients cache the DAG anyway.

The following diagram illustrates how this technique works:

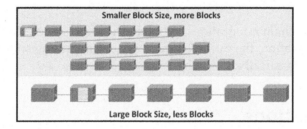

However, like vertical scaling, in general, this solution demands that network nodes have better computing capacity in order to process large sized blocks. This may lead to a scenario where a network is concentrated into a few rich hands and, thus, may ultimately compromise decentralization and security, the main tenets of the blockchain.

# Altcoins

Another solution is not to have one gigantic blockchain, but to have many smaller blockchains and altcoins. This may eventually be the case, since many vertical industries are creating or plan to create industry-specific chains. This will reduce user activity on each individual blockchain and, thus, should allow for a more scalable ecosystem.

The following diagram illustrates how this technique works:

However, there are a few issues with this option. One is security concerns. It is a common belief that the network is more secure if more network nodes participate in the transaction processing in the blockchain. With wider distribution of altcoin chains, fewer nodes will operate on any given blockchain. This may make the blockchain less secure, since a smaller altcoin network may be more vulnerable to network attacks. Let us say, we have about 10,000 nodes on the larger network, it will require at least 5,001 nodes (or called 51%) to be compromised to launch an attack on the network. If we slice 10,000 nodes into 50 smaller chains, each chain comprises 200 nodes, and it only requires 101 nodes to take down any smaller chain, which is what we call a 1% attack problem.

Another issue is cross chain integration. Although there are some solutions for handling cross blockchain integration, the overall complexity of integrating smaller chains and altcoins will increase drastically.

# On-chain solutions

On-chain solutions, sometimes also called layer 1 solutions, are to look for solutions to address scalability and performance issues at the base layer of the Ethereum blockchain network. One such solution is sharding. Sharding is not a new concept as traditional RDBMS and new big data platforms have been using sharding as a way to improve scalability and performance for many years.

With the Ethereum network, the purpose of sharding is to group the network nodes, the blockchain, and global states into different shards, and each shard will reach a consensus on the shard-wide transaction state among those nodes within the group. At the conceptual level, this may not be much different from Plasma, the layer 2 side-chain approach, but the technical difficulty, implications, and network efforts are quite different. We will go into detail about sharding in the *Ethereum sharding and Casper* section.

Another layer 1 or on-chain solution is the shift to a **proof-of-stake (PoS)** consensus mechanism, which is one of the most active research areas addressing scalability and performance issues in Ethereum. There are many debates in terms of advantages and disadvantages of a PoW-based consensus mechanism. It is quite effective in securing the blockchain in the decentralized network, but it is also a major bottleneck in the blockchain performance.

We had much detailed discussion in Chapter 1, *Blockchain and Cryptocurrency*, on how PoS works and how it compares with PoW. In the following sections, we will look at different PoS-related activities and a roadmap to shift Ethereum to PoS.

## Off-chain solutions

Similar to the rationales for an on-chain solution, the Ethereum community is also actively looking for off-chain solutions, sometimes called layer 2 solutions. One is a side-chain solution with Plasma. Instead of putting all transactions in the main chain, Plasma allows anyone to create side chains and bond side chains into the global blockchain. This is similar to the lighting network solution in Bitcoin.

Another one is a state channel solution with Raiden, similar to payment channels in Bitcoin. The hypothesis behind this approach is that many interparty transactions only need to be validated by the parties involved, and there is no need to have all transactions to be validated by the entire network. We will discuss in detail how they work in later sections.

## ZK-SNARK

As we discussed in Chapter 1, *Blockchain and Cryptocurrency*, one of the Bitcoin limitations is the privacy issue. Zcash is the first and perhaps the most popular cryptocurrency to implement **Zero-Knowledge Succinct Non-Interactive Argument of Knowledge**, or abbreviated as **ZK-SNARKs**, as a means of addressing privacy issues in the public blockchain.

It maintains strong privacy by allowing the transaction to be fully encrypted on the blockchain, and encrypted transactions can still be verified as valid with ZK-SNARK proofs. Under ZK-SNARK consensus rules, one, as the prover, can let others, as the verifiers, know that it possesses certain knowledge without revealing the specific knowledge, and without any interaction between them.

Ethereum community is incorporating ZK-SNARK into the Ethereum blockchain implementation too, with an intention to use ZK-SNARK to mass-validate transactions, thus improving the Ethereum scalability dramatically.

You can read Vitalik's proposals on the Ethereum research site, `https://ethresear.ch/t/on-chain-scaling-to-potentially-500-tx-sec-through-mass-tx-validation/3477`.

# State channel with Raiden

Imagine you are taking your family on a cruise ship for a dream vacation. You all will be issued cruise cards at the time you are boarding. Typically the cruise card is linked to your credit card account. It will serve as your ID to get on and off the ship, provide you with access to your cabin, and make it for easy swiping when you decide to have some drinks or buy something.

All onboard purchases are paid for using your cruise card. At the end of the trip when you disembark, you will receive an invoice of all charges charged to your credit card. The cruise card becomes the mutual trust between you and the cruise ship.

The same applies to a digital payment system too. Trusted parties may perform a large number of trivial transactions directly and settle the payment once at some agreed time. That is how Raiden network and state channels work.

State channels are a technique for performing transactions and other state transitions in a second layer built on top of a blockchain. By moving many processes off-chain, the blockchain can be more efficient and scalable, while still retaining transaction integrity and network security. Payment channels are a type of state channel that allow users to make off-chain payments to each other.

The term **state channels** generalizes this approach beyond payments. Raiden network is an off-chain network implementation of state channels which enables near real-time, low cost, and highly scalable ERC-20 compatible payments.

Take the examples, as shown in the following diagram: there are about 10 payment transactions between A, B, and C. Many are trivial and insignificant payments. At the end when all three complete the transactions, A will need to pay B for 60 finney (which is one thousandth of an ether), and pay C for 70 finney, and B will need pay C for 110 finney:

| TX No | Sender | Receiver | Finney | Time |
|-------|--------|----------|--------|---------|
| 1 | A | B | 100 | 11:10am |
| 2 | A | B | 10 | 11:11am |
| 3 | B | A | 40 | 11:12am |
| 4 | B | A | 10 | 11:13am |
| 5 | A | C | 100 | 11:14am |
| 6 | C | A | 10 | 11:15am |
| 7 | C | A | 20 | 11:16am |
| 8 | B | C | 200 | 11:17am |
| 9 | B | C | 10 | 11:18am |
| 10 | C | B | 100 | 11:25am |

| Account | Balance | Time |
|---------|---------|---------|
| A | 1000 | 11:00am |
| B | 2000 | 11:00am |
| C | 1500 | 11:00am |

| TX No | Sender | Receiver | Finney | Time |
|-------|--------|----------|--------|---------|
| 1 | A | B | 60 | 11:30am |
| 2 | A | C | 70 | 11:30am |
| 3 | B | C | 110 | 11:30am |

| Account | Balance | Time |
|---------|---------|---------|
| A | 870 | 11:30am |
| B | 1950 | 11:30am |
| C | 1680 | 11:30am |

With Raiden and State Channels, all three parties would enter an agreement to open the channels, and deposit some coins for payment assurance. All parties can start transactions between parties with their own digital signature; all those micropayment transactions happen in this Raiden network, sometimes called uRaiden. New parties can join or leave the state channel. Any party can check the registered deposits of all parties involved. At the time when any party closes the channel, Raiden network will send a settlement transaction to the main Ethereum blockchain, and the world state will be updated with the new settlement.

As you can see from the following diagram, a settlement transaction with three payments from A to B, A to C, and B to C will be sent to the Ethereum blockchain.

Both open and close channel transactions happen on the blockchain; they are costly. It is not a good idea always opening new state channels between new parties. For this reason, Raiden allows all participants to form a network of channels, and participants can make off-chain micropayment transactions as long as they are transitively connected to each other.

For example, in the case where A, B, and C, are connected in one state channel, and C and D in another channel, there is no need to create a new direct channel between A and D. The payment can still go through C en route between A and D, although there may be some incentives involved:

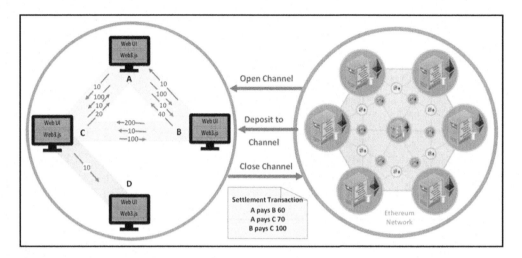

Raiden provides Rest APIs for any party to open and close channels, deposit funds, and make payments.

 You can check out the Raiden site for a more detailed API document (`https://github.com/raiden-network/raiden/blob/master/docs/api_walkthrough.rst#id3`).

# Ethereum side chain with Plasma

As we discussed earlier, one intuitive solution to improve scalability and throughput is to create many small chains. This may sound like a plausible solution, since it may suit business and social needs. Take ourselves for example, as customers or citizens, we buy fruit and vegetables from our local grocery, which might leverage one blockchain to ensure traceability and food safety through the entire supply chain of fresh produce.

At the end of your shopping, you may pay the grocery directly through a P2P payment blockchain. When you apply your mortgage or business loan, you might be able to get your mortgage and loan approved through the mortgage blockchain, and so on. We are more likely to meet all these vertical chains or private chains before we see a gigantic global chain.

However, it creates cross-chain integration and security enforcement issues. This is what Plasma tries to address. It was first proposed in August 2017 by Joseph Poon and Vitalik Buterin. The design idea is to offload transactions to many faster and less crowded side chains, also called Plasma chains. Similar to the state channel approach, a Plasma chain will periodically commit its transactions to the Ethereum root chain.

Security and integrity will be enforced through the root chain. If any suspicion of fraud is detected in the plasma chains, the transactions will be rolled back and Plasma users can exit the plasma chain and move out to the root chain.

The following diagram shows what a Plasma network may look like:

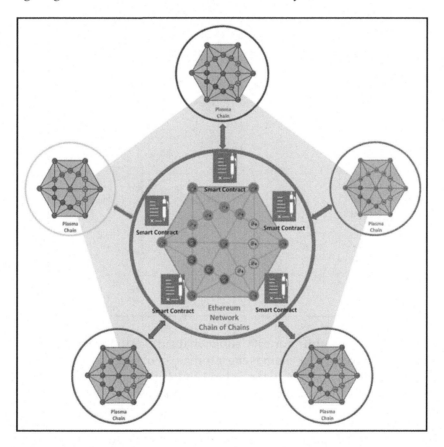

Each plasma chain is a blockchain on its own. They are bonded with an Ethereum root chain through a smart contract. The smart contract essentially connects an entire child chain to the root chain, acting as a bridge. Anyone can create a plasma chain, and write a smart contract binding the plasma chain to the root chain.

As the following diagram shows, at each period, the block headers of each block of the plasma chains are submitted to the root chain and recorded in the blocks of the root chain. Transactions in the plasma chains will stay at each plasma chain. The Merkle proof in the block headers will then be used to verify data on the child chain. This allows for tens and thousands of transactions to be processed in many plasma chains in parallel, and also leaves minimal and enough Merkle header information on the root chain to enforce security:

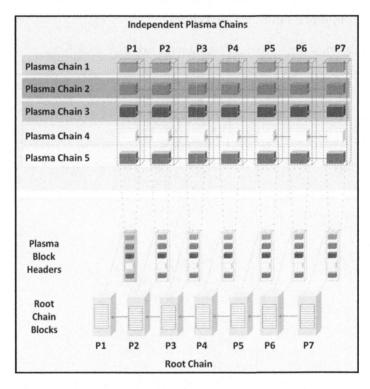

The root chain will play an arbitrator role, somewhat similar to the federal court system in the United States, where the root chain is the supreme court and the plasma chains are the circuit courts, or the district courts. In the federal court system, once the federal district court has decided a case, the case can be appealed to the circuit court or supreme court for an arbitration.

When a fraud occurs in a plasma chain, whether it is a double spend across the chains or you cash out more than you have in all accounts, anyone can provide a fraud proof to prove the transaction is invalid. If proven to the fraud transactions, the transaction will be rolled back.

Plasma users can exit the child plasma chain and transfer ethers back to the main chain. The original proposals introduce a single validator concept, as the operator for the plasma blockchain, to validate and add transactions to the blocks, and manage the state of the child blockchain.

The idea behind this approach is that security and integrity of the blockchain at the global level is enforced by the root chain, using either PoW or, most likely, a hybrid PoW and PoS consensus protocol. In the case where the validator of the plasma chain may hold the fund and commit fraudulent activities, anyone can provide a fraud proof against the validator to the root chain.

Once proven to be fraudulent from the validator, the root chain will allow all accounts at the impacted plasma chain to move out to the root chain. This is called a **mass exit** scenario. In this case, individual accounts will be migrated to the root chain one by one, the invalid transaction will be rolled back, and the validator of the plasma chain will be penalized with the stake it puts in the smart contract. Depending on how many accounts need to be migrated, it may take a while to complete the mass exit.

Although it has been one of the most interesting and active topics in the Ethereum research community, there is no public release of a plasma implementation yet. Instead, a scaled down version of the original proposal, also called a minimal viable plasma, or MVP, was proposed for a simple implementation, which includes a simplified security model and basic operations for exiting plasma chains.

One very interesting aspect of an MVP is the reintroduction of a UTXO model. As we discussed in the last two chapters, one key difference in Ethereum is to move away from Bitcoin's UTXO model to a more defined account model, where account balance is the state object maintained at the world state.

The Ethereum account model makes transaction verifications and money transfer simple, with the sacrifice of parallelism. This may not be a significant drawback, since all transactions need to be verified by all nodes. But with Plasma, as the root chain moves away from transaction processing to security enforcement and arbitration, it becomes important to be able to verify invalid transactions in parallel.

A tree structure of blockchains, hence the tree of UTXOs from all child chains, makes it easy to apply distributed parallel algorithms to verify fraud proofs and enforce security across all plasma chains.

 You can check them out at the Ethereum research site, `https://ethresear.ch/c/plasma`.

The following diagram shows what the potential Plasma may be able to bring into the Ethereum blockchain network when a tree of Ethereum plasma child chains are bonded with the parent plasma chain, and are ultimately connected to, and secured through, the Ethereum root chain:

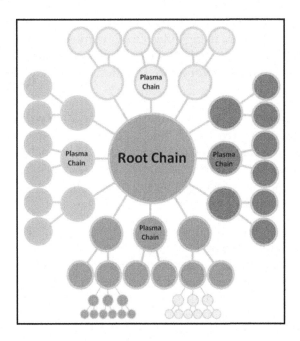

Massive scalability will be achieved through offloading expensive computations to the child chains, and allow the root chain to provide the shared security and arbitration services to the blockchain at a global level. There are a few similar cross chain interoperability solutions, like Cosmos network. Claimed to be the internet of blockchains, Cosmos network provides a hub-spoke integration architecture. Independent blockchains, as the zones or spokes, are attached to the main blockchain as the hub. Its purpose is to facilitate blockchain integration through the IBC (inter-blockchain communications) protocol.

# Ethereum sharding and Casper

As we mentioned earlier, sharding has been implemented in many distributed database systems. Essentially, sharding is a particular method for horizontally partitioning a large dataset within a database. More specifically, the database is broken into little pieces called **shards**. When aggregated together, they form the original database. In the following diagram, one large dataset can be sliced horizontally into two or more partitions, and each partition may be stored in separate database instances:

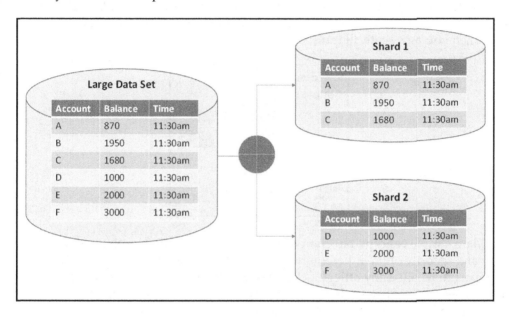

In a decentralized blockchain network, the network consists of a series of nodes connected in a peer-to-peer format, with no central authority. As is the case with current blockchain system, each node stores all states of the network and processes all of the transactions.

In order to match transaction scalability and throughput from Mastercard or Visa, Ethereum will have to process large volumes of transactions much faster. One logical way we discussed earlier is to increase the block size, but this may not be able to fundamentally address the scalability issues, since every node still needs to validate and verify a large block of more transactions. They will need more computing resources to handle the increased load. That is where sharding comes to help.

Not only the large volume of transactions can be sharded, but the entire peer-to-peer network of nodes can be grouped into smaller groups, also called shards. This greatly improves the parallel execution in the network, and scalability.

Imagine at any period, in order to process a large volume of transactions, you would need to have a really large block to be able to hold all the transactions submitted in this period. Instead of creating a larger physical block, what if you slice them into different smaller blocks, as in the following diagram, and have smaller blocks stored in the subset of network nodes? Similar to database sharding, in order to find all transactions and verify any particular transactions, you have to aggregate the transactions from all shards for that period. When you aggregate all transactions, you will have a virtual large block:

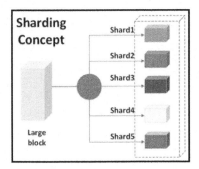

It looks like a simple concept, but complexity arises when dealing with maintaining the integrity and security of the Ethereum world state and transaction ledger across a subset of network partitions. Like any other blockchains, Ethereum maintains transactions and their ordering in the chain of blocks through a consensus mechanism. Furthermore, Ethereum also manages the account as a state object in the work state. A state object makes things much more complicated.

Let us take a look at how the transactions and data work in Ethereum sharding. As depicted in the following diagram, let us say the network is split into multiple groups and each group is an Ethereum shard. Transactions pertaining to each shard will be collected and added to the shard chain. A group of validators in the collator pool, stake their coins and become the validators in the PoS system. Let's take a look at the following diagram:

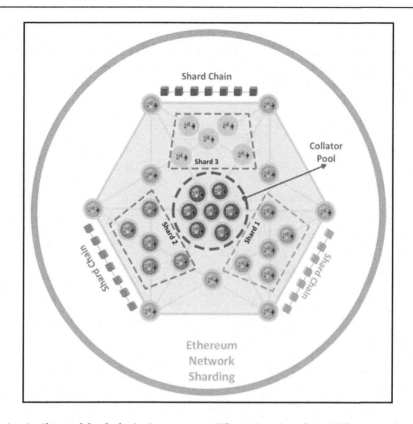

Shard chain is similar to blockchain in concept. The miner's role in Ethereum is split into three separate roles: collation proposer, collator, and executor. A collation is the same as a block in the blockchain. As the following diagram shows, at any time period, a collation proposer collects all transactions, and adds them to a proposed collation. Data blobs from transactions are packaged together into the collation body, a Merkle tree of the data blobs, and other shard identifier information is packaged as the collation header.

The collation proposer proposes the proposed collation to the collator, which is randomly selected from the validator pool. The collator's role in this process is to validate the proposed collations and pass the collation header to smart contracts through the executor on the main chain. The collation headers from all shards will be added to blocks on the main blockchain:

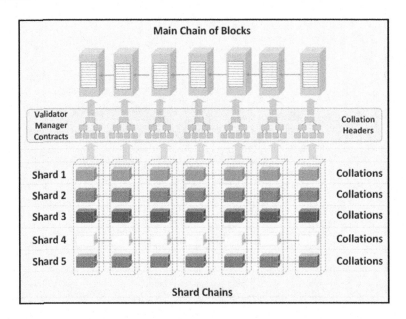

The smart contract is also called a validator manager contract (VMC), as depicted in the preceding diagram. It is a shard-specific smart contract, deployed on the main chain. The VMC main role is to maintain the entire sharding systems and act as the connection between the main chain and the shard chain it links to. Its responsibilities include the following:

- Validate and maintain collation headers from each shard
- Manage a pool of collation proposers
- Manage a pool of collators and hold the collator's stakes to enforce PoS and perform random sampling of collators for each shard
- Shuffle and pseudo-randomly select an eligible collator for each shard
- Process cross-shard transactions and record all cross-shard receipts

Cross-shard transactions, as discussed earlier, are one of the challenges that the sharding system faces. When a transaction happens across different shards, it is typically implemented through the cross-shard communications of transactions and receipts.

For example, suppose Alice from shard 1 needs to pay 100ETH to Bob on shard 2. The single transaction will be broken into two separate transactions: one is a debit transaction to draw 100ETH from Alice's account on shard 1, and another one is the credit transaction of 100ETH made to Bob on shard 2. The following are the steps involved:

1. One debit transaction of 100ETH deducted from Alice's account on shard 1 is submitted to the main chain. A receipt is generated once the transaction is verified.
2. Wait until the debit transaction is finalized.
3. Submit the second credit transaction to deposit 100ETH to Bob's account on shard 2, along with the original receipt from the debit transaction.
4. A second receipt is generated once the debit transaction is processed. The receipt is sent back to Alice on shard 1, so that further account action can be taken.

Sharding, along with the PoS consensus mechanism, has the potential to drastically improve Ethereum's scalability and increase the transaction throughput in Ethereum. There are too many moving parts in combining both layer 1 scalability solutions and creating a solid implementation. It has been handled in multiple phases, we will go over the current Ethereum 2.0 roadmap in later sections to discuss which different components should be implemented and when.

# PoS consensus in Ethereum

As we discussed in Chapter 2, *Ethereum Architecture and Ecosystem*, Ethereum is shifting from a PoW-based consensus mechanism to PoS-based consensus mechanism, which will be implemented as part of the Casper work stream. However, there are two separate approaches proposed, Casper FFG and Casper CBC. Both will facilitate an Ethereum move to PoS, but the design philosophies behind both approaches are quite different.

Casper FFG, also known as Casper the friendly finality gadget, is a hybrid PoW and PoS consensus mechanism proposed by Vitalik. Just like the current implementation, it leverages a Stash-based PoW mechanism to create new blocks. On top of the PoW-based chains, it leverages a pool of PoS validators to check the finality of the blocks periodically, typically every 50 or 100 blocks, called one epoch.

Validators stake their ethers on the network. They get rewarded with new ether if they successfully check the finality, or get penalized otherwise. As depicted here, once one epoch of blocks is created, a validator will be selected out of a validator pool and will start assessing the finality of all blocks in the current epoch on the blockchain:

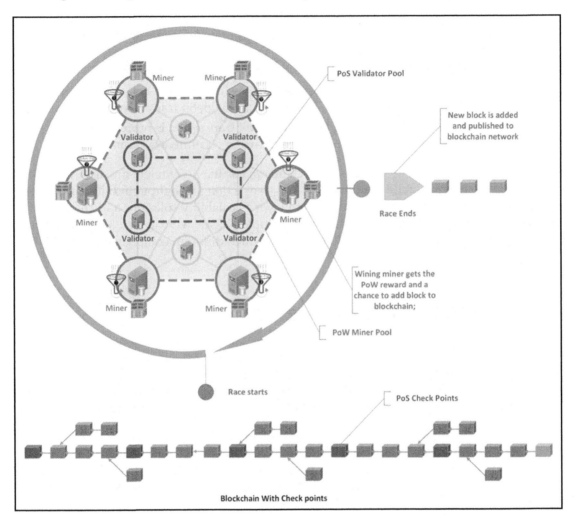

One of issues with PoS consensus, at least theoretically, is that nothing is at stake. The doubt about PoS is that the stake alone won't deter the bad behavior. For example, in the case of a potential temporary fork, validators could potentially build on both sides of the fork, and make the temporary fork forever, since they will collect a transaction fee no matter if they win or lose. This also makes the finality issue even worse.

Casper CBC proposed by Vlad Zamfir, also called the **Friendly GHOST Correct-by-Construction** is a protocol designed to address the finality and nothing-at-stake issue. The theory behind this is that validators can make a decision about which path to build new blocks on, based on the messages they've seen from other nodes:

- The message includes the sender or the validator, the blocks where it arrives, and the justifications.
- It can provide knowledge regarding how other validators reach a decision on the latest blocks.
- If two messages are sent by the same validator with no knowledge links between them, it is considered as invalid, and the validator will be penalized with the stake.

Both Casper FFG and Casper CBC are active work streams in the Ethereum community. The final PoS implementation in Casper may depend on how each one works out. Casper FFG probably is the one to give you a taste of the PoS consensus mechanism in Ethereum, and CBC will give us a pure PoS implementation with a finality safety guarantee. One of the planned phases in the Ethereum 2.0 roadmap, the PoS beacon chain with sharding, will implement the PoS consensus mechanism on the beacon chain as an overlay to the Ethereum main chain and leverage Casper FFG for block finality.

# Following up on EVM and lower-level protocol improvements

At the heart of Ethereum is the EVM, the engine powering the entire Ethereum network. It is the runtime execution environment for smart contracts and blockchain. There are quite a few lower-level protocol improvements proposed, including some at EVM opcode level. There are many discussions about improving the account model, including further account data abstraction.

 You can check out the Ethereum EIP site for more details (`https://github.com/ethereum/EIPs/issues`).

One of the interesting topics worth discussing further is the next generation of the EVM, eWASM. It is an Ethereum version of **WebAssembly (WASM)**.

WebAssembly is a W3C standard, defining the binary instruction set for a stack-based virtual machine. It is intended for compilation of C/C++/Rust and similar high-level programming languages and for deployment on the web, similar to a JavaScript engine inside a web browser. It is supported by all four major browsers, including Safari, Chrome, Firefox, and Edge. The goal is to be able to execute the code next to the metal and to take advantage of general hardware capabilities available on a wide variety of platforms.

Basically, eWASM provides a restricted subset of WASM to be used for smart contracts in Ethereum. It is intended to provide improved EVM performance, and make Ethereum a global computing platform. In theory, developers can write smart contracts in any high-level languages on an ecosystem with a variety of tooling and technologies.

The eWASM specification defines a subset of WASM components to be supported by a newer EVM. Since Blockchain requires deterministic behavior from smart contract execution, non-deterministic features in WASM were restricted. Furthermore, a number of system smart contracts are provided in eWASM to allow access to Ethereum platform features. At this moment, it supports both the WASM and EVM instruction sets, with the intention of being backward compatible with the current EVM version. It also provides a transcompiling tool for translating the EVM instruction set into the eWASM instruction set.

 There have been quite a few eWASM projects developed by the Ethereum community, you can check out the eWASM GitHub site for design rationales and project details (`https://github.com/ewasm/design`).

# Implementing Ethereum 2.0 roadmap

The Ethereum community intends to fundamentally address Ethereum scalability issues with the release of Ethereum 2.0. It is a massive undertaking to incorporate all these scaling techniques into Ethereum.

The following diagram shows the Ethereum's roadmap to the Serenity release, Ethereum 2.0:

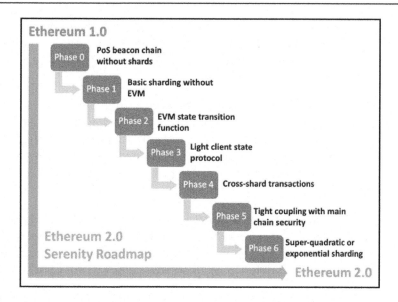

It is going to be a phased approach since there are too many moving parts. Some are foundational capabilities that need to be done early to facilitate the move to sharding and the pure PoS consensus protocol, the Casper CBC. The following list explains each phase:

- **Phase 0, PoS beacon chain without shards**: This is the first step to establish a foundation for moving to the PoS and supporting the shards. Ethereum 2.0 consists of a central beacon chain along with a certain number of shard chains. So, this phase starts to introduce a central system chain called the **beacon chain**. Its main responsibility is to store and manage the registry of validators. The beacon chain is like a side chain to the Ethereum 1.0 main chain, and acts as the bridge to transition from the Ethereum 1.0 PoW chain to the Ethereum 2.0 PoS Chain. It is unclear if the Ethereum 1.0 PoW chain will continue to play the main-chain role or switch to side-chain role for the beacon chain to be the main chain, once the Ethereum 2.0 is fully functional.

  In this phase, someone can be a validator by making a one-way 32 ETH transaction to a deposit contract on Ethereum 1.0. Once the required activation balance is reached, and the deposit receipts are processed by the beacon chain, it will be added to the validator activation queue. Activation as a validator happens after a queuing process. Exit is either voluntary or done forcibly as a penalty for misbehaviors.

The RANDAO contract is included in this phase, which enables validators to create random numbers (RNG) in block proposals, and organize into proposers and attestation committees from the output of the RNG, and creating crosslinks for stubbed shards.

- **Phase 1, Basic sharding without EVM**: Phase 1 will focus on the construction, validity, and consensus of the data of these shard chains. As we discussed earlier, the proposer's role is to package all transaction data as blobs, trunk the blobs into trunks, and create a Merkle tree out of the transaction data. They will be collated in shards without transactions. The proposer notarizes the collations with its own signature.

- **Phase 2, EVM state transition function**: Phase 2 is primarily concerned with various EVM-level improvements in the Ethereum full node, including eWASM as the next generation Ethereum virtual machine. Some other topics, including account abstraction, stateless model, and storage rent, are under evaluation.

- **Phase 3, Light client state protocol**: Phase 3 is primarily concerned with the transaction execution and executor's role in the system, and with the light client protocol for the state-minimized execution model, where the cost of validation is pushed away from on-chain validators onto off-chain executors.

- **Phase 4, Cross-shard transactions**: Phase 4 was intended for supporting cross shard transactions, including synchronous and asynchronous cross shard communication models.

- **Phase 5, Tight coupling with main-chain security**: Phase 5 will address issues and needs with data availability proofs, internally fork-free sharding, and manager shards.

- **Phase 6, Super-quadratic or exponential sharding**: Phase 6 is the one intended to bring everything together and to enable Ethereum transition from PoW and one main chain to PoW and sharding. There are many sharding related researches and ideas, and any of them may come up and influence some of the future phases.

# Introducing cryptoassets and Ethereum token standards

A large percentage of crypto-tokens are Ethereum ICOs running on the Ethereum platform. What makes the Ethereum platform stand out as the platform choice for crypto-tokens and ICOs? In this section, we will compare ICOs, STOs, and IEOs, how the crypto-tokens work, get an understanding of key mechanisms in Ethereum in creating and issuing tokens, and make sense of the economic perspectives of a token-enabled economy.

# Initial coin offerings

Social media giant Facebook announced its own cryptocurrency ambitions in June 2019, and is planning to launch its own cryptocurrency, Libra, next year. Libra is a stablecoin and will be used for purchasing things on Facebook apps and money transfers between facebook users. Since the first crypto-token sale by Mastercoin in July 2013, ICOs have been popular among blockchain, cryptocurrency, and investment communities as one quick and effective way to raise funding in the form of cryptocurrencies.

An ICO is a type of crowdfunding or crowd-sale using a blockchain platform and cryptocurrency. It is similar to an IPO (initial public offering) in the traditional finance market. In the case of an IPO, the company raises millions of funds through the sales of its stocks. In an ICO, the company raises the money, in the form of Bitcoin, ether, or fiat currency through the sales of its coins or tokens to the public, investors, or speculators. Unlike IPO, which is much regulated, ICO is not bound by any legal requirements.

An ICO is intended to fund DApp's implementations, operations, and expansion. Usually, the company raising funds via an ICO will market their ICO plan publicly or privately, and create a whitepaper, explaining their project, the technology behind it, and details about their team members. In most cases, a smart contract is created for prospective investors to participate in the ICO. Once launched, the smart contract will credit the investors with ICO's native crypto assets in exchange for existing cryptocurrencies like Bitcoin or ether.

According to `icostats.com`, the following are the top 10 ERC-20 tokens based on ROI (return on investment) since ICO, as of March 13, 2019. Binance gets a whopping 100 times return on the original investment since its ICO date on Jul 13, 2017.

The following screenshot taken on March 13, 2009 shows the top 10 tokens with the best ROI:

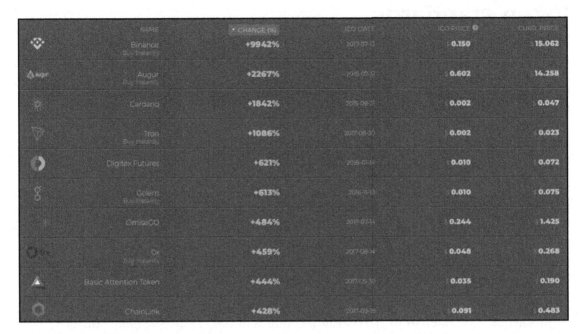

| NAME | CHANGE (%) | ICO DATE | ICO PRICE | CURR. PRICE |
|------|-----------|----------|-----------|-------------|
| Binance | +9942% | 2017-07-13 | 0.150 | 15.062 |
| Augur | +2267% | 2015-07-31 | 0.602 | 14.258 |
| Cardano | +1842% | 2015-08-31 | 0.002 | 0.047 |
| Tron | +1086% | 2017-08-30 | 0.002 | 0.023 |
| Digitex Futures | +621% | 2018-01-14 | 0.010 | 0.072 |
| Golem | +613% | 2016-11-11 | 0.010 | 0.075 |
| OmiseGO | +484% | 2017-07-14 | 0.244 | 1.425 |
| 0x | +459% | 2017-08-14 | 0.048 | 0.268 |
| Basic Attention Token | +444% | 2017-05-30 | 0.035 | 0.190 |
| ChainLink | +428% | 2017-09-19 | 0.091 | 0.483 |

It may not last long for ICOs to be unregulated. The US Security and Exchange Commission is making waves in considering rules and regulations to classify ICOs as security. If it happens, the government will certainly tighten the compliance requirements of ICOs too. As a result of that, compliance with **anti-money laundering** (**AML**) and **know your customer** (**KYC**) laws will become a critical challenge those offering an ICO may have to meet.

# STO and IEO

In addition to an ICO, another common mechanism is to go through an STO as the crowdfunding or crowd-sale type of funding method to fund blockchain and cryptocurrency projects. It is essentially similar to an ICO, in that an investor exchanges their own assets (money and/or other assets) for coins or tokens as investments. It goes through the same process.

But there are some key differences. Most ICOs serve as the utility tokens, and are used to fund the normal operations of the cryptocurrency and blockchain network. STOs have to comply with regulatory governance and have to be offered under the security law. Therefore, the barrier to offering tokens under an ICO is relatively low, while for an STO it is much higher. For the same reason, tokens under an STO are considered less risky compared to ICO coins, since STO tokens are backed by real assets and, in general, are protected under the security laws. You will continue to see both models as the new funding channels for cryptocurrency and blockchain projects. You may continue to hear the debate about ICO versus STO. Depending on individual jurisdictions, the line between ICO and STO may become very murky.

Both ICOs and STOs would be a good way to secure the funding of cryptocurrency, but both, by themselves, lack the liquidity the crypto-market requires. This gives rise to a new and popular crypto-funding vehicle with an IEO. Instead of issuing their own ICOs or STOs, the token issuer will go to an exchange to get their tokens and projects listed under the IEO. In return, the exchange will exercise due diligence on all the requirements for such listing, and market the tokens to the potential investors on behalf of the token issuer. Binance is the perfect example of such an exchange. You can check out the Binance model at https://www.binance.com/en.

# Ethereum token standards

Ethereum started as the world computer and blockchain platform for developing smart contract- based decentralized applications. Quickly, the Ethereum community realized it was the perfect platform for creating unique tokens that exist and operate on the Ethereum blockchain. As such, many token standards were developed to facilitate the creation and launch of a vast variety of crypto-tokens.

# Fungible and non-fungible tokens

There are many ways to categorize an asset and investment. Most well-known ones include stocks, bonds, currency, real estate, commodities, futures, and financial derivatives, and so on. Some financial professionals also include art and collectibles, even cryptocurrency, in the mix. Cryptoassets refers to a new asset class of digital assets arising from cryptocurrency and blockchain technologies, regulated autonomously from the peer-to-peer network, and secured with cryptographic technologies.

Like fiat currency, cryptocurrencies, including Bitcoin, ether, and altcoins, are considered as fungible crypto-assets, which means they can be interchangeable with the same type of assets. A Bitcoin is a Bitcoin. When you exchange a Bitcoin with someone, you are expecting one Bitcoin as an exchange. Only quantity matters. There are other non-fungible digital assets, like digital art works and collectibles, digital rights, digital royalties, and so on. The most popular one is the CryptoKitties, an Ethereum-based video game for breeding, trading, and collecting various types of virtual cats. They are similar to an art work or a collectible. Each one item is considered distinct, and valued differently.

Ethereum defines a platform and standard token interface through a smart contract for ICO companies to implement and launch new coins or tokens. A smart contract is the digital legal contract as a code between the investors and Ethereum token offerers. The ERC-20 standard, and its variations, defines the standard smart contract interface for fungible tokens. The ERC-721 is another official standard for implementing and launching non-fungible tokens.

The following is an illustration of the most popular token standards:

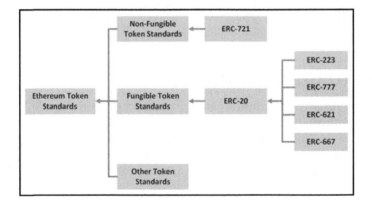

In the further sections, we will discuss the ERC-20 and ERC-721 standards in detail. If you're interested, you can check out the Ethereum EIP site for more details on the various standards listed here and on the new standards being proposed.

# ERC-20

The ERC-20 defines the standard interface to address functionalities needed for issuing money-like fungible tokens, including how tokens can be transferred between accounts, and how users can retrieve data associated with a given ERC-20 token. All the ERC-20 compatible tokens have to implement the ERC-20 interface, as shown in the following screenshot (https://theethereum.wiki/w/index.php/ERC20_Token_Standard):

```
1  // ---------------------------------------------------------------------------
2  // ERC Token Standard #20 Interface
3  // https://github.com/ethereum/EIPs/blob/master/EIPS/eip-20.md
4  // ---------------------------------------------------------------------------
5  contract ERC20Interface {
6      function totalSupply() public view returns (uint);
7      function balanceOf(address tokenOwner) public view returns (uint balance);
8      function allowance(address tokenOwner, address spender) public view returns (uint remaining);
9      function transfer(address to, uint tokens) public returns (bool success);
10     function approve(address spender, uint tokens) public returns (bool success);
11     function transferFrom(address from, address to, uint tokens) public returns (bool success);
12
13     event Transfer(address indexed from, address indexed to, uint tokens);
14     event Approval(address indexed tokenOwner, address indexed spender, uint tokens);
15 }
```

The following six functions are defined in the standard interface:

- The `totalSupply()` function: It allows anyone to call and get the total supply of tokens. The internally smart contract implementation keeps track of the total supply of the tokens.

- The `balanceOf(address tokenOwner)` function: It allows authorized users to retrieve the token balance of account associated with the `tokenOwner` address.

- The `allowance(address tokenOwner, address spender)` function: When executed, it returns the total number of tokens that the account owner specifies for someone from another account to be able to withdraw and spend.

- The `transfer(address to, uint tokens)` function: It allows you to send a certain number of tokens to a given address. The sending account must have enough tokens. When executed, it will fire a `Transfer` event. If there aren't sufficient tokens to be sent, it will throw an exception.

- The `approve(address spender, uint tokens)` function: This function enables a specific account to approve a predefined upper limit for the number of tokens to be withdrawn by the spender. Internally, the smart contract maintains a list of spenders and the allowance for each token owner. The allowance can be reset through this call. On a successful call, it will trigger an `Approval` event.

- The `transferFrom(address from, address to, uint tokens)` function: It allows the smart contract to send a specific number of tokens from one contract address to another contract address.

Optionally, the token issuer may define additional attributes for the token, such as the name, symbol, and decimal. Decimal is the decimal the token is using; by default, it is 18 decimals. It can provide getter methods to query the attributes.

Some other standards are extended from the ERC-20 to specifically address some of the issues with ERC-20. The ERC-223 standard was created to address the **lost tokens** problem from ERC-20, where a transfer transaction mistakenly sends tokens to a wrong or invalid smart contract address. It added security perspective to ensure approve and transferFrom behave as they are supposed to be. It is backward compatible with the ERC-20 standard.

The ERC-777 addresses the same issue differently. It tries to improve the wildly used ERC-20 standard while remaining backward compatible with the ERC-20. It allows both contract accounts, and regular accounts have control over the tokens being transferred. It introduces an operator concept as the mediator for the sender to send the tokens on their behalf. The operator, set up as a verified contract, can act like an exchange and so on, and is able to transfer funds or burn coins on behalf of the token holders. The interface provides methods for the senders to authorize and revoke operators which can send tokens on their behalf.

 You can check out the EIP site for more details about the ERC-777 standard (`https://eips.ethereum.org/EIPS/eip-777`).

# ERC-721

The ERC-721 defines the standard for building non-fungible tokens on the Ethereum blockchain. In this class of crypto-assets, every token is unique, has distinct perspectives, and is valued differently. It is a kind of collectible, like rare stamps, works of art, or exotic cars. The standard interface defined by the ERC-721 enables smart contract implementations to manage, own, and trade the tokens in a unique way, appropriate to the underlying crypto-asset.

The following screenshot shows the functions specified in the ERC-721 interface:

```
/// @title ERC-721 Non-Fungible Token Standard
/// @dev See https://github.com/ethereum/EIPs/blob/master/EIPS/eip-721.md
///  Note: the ERC-165 identifier for this interface is 0x80ac58cd
interface ERC721 /* is ERC165 */ {
        event Transfer(address indexed _from, address indexed _to, uint256 indexed _tokenId);
        event Approval(address indexed _owner, address indexed _approved, uint256 indexed _tokenId);
        event ApprovalForAll(address indexed _owner, address indexed _operator, bool _approved);
        function balanceOf(address _owner) external view returns (uint256);
        function ownerOf(uint256 _tokenId) external view returns (address);
        function safeTransferFrom(address _from, address _to, uint256 _tokenId, bytes data) external payable;
        function safeTransferFrom(address _from, address _to, uint256 _tokenId) external payable;
        function transferFrom(address _from, address _to, uint256 _tokenId) external payable;
        function approve(address _approved, uint256 _tokenId) external payable;
        function setApprovalForAll(address _operator, bool _approved) external;
        function getApproved(uint256 _tokenId) external view returns (address);
        function isApprovedForAll(address _owner, address _operator) external view returns (bool);
}

interface ERC165 {
        function supportsInterface(bytes4 interfaceID) external view returns (bool);
}

interface ERC721TokenReceiver {
        function onERC721Received(address _operator, address _from, uint256 _tokenId, bytes _data) external returns(bytes4);
}
```

Every such token has a unique token identifier, or token ID. The ERC-721 standard does not mandate any standard set of token metadata nor restrict adding supplemental functions. It is up to the developer of non-fungible tokens to define additional metadata or functions suitable for defining the uniqueness of the token. The following list explains some of the functions present here:

- The `balanceOf(address _owner)` function: This function allows the token owner to retrieve the count of all non-fungible tokens the owner was assigned to.
- The `ownerOf(uint256 _tokenId)` function: It returns the token owner's addresss for a given token ID.
- The `safeTransferFrom(address _from, address _to, uint256 _tokenId, bytes data)` function: This function allows the token owner to transfer the ownership of a non-fungible token to another address. It throws an exception if the sender is not the owner of the token or the authorized operator. Some data with no specific format can be passed as part of the transfer function.
- The `safeTransferFrom(address _from, address _to, uint256 _tokenId)` function: It is an overloaded function with no data passed as part of the transfer.
- The `approve(address _approved, uint256 _tokenId)` function: It allows the third-party operator, given by the `_approved` address, the permission to transfer the token on behalf of the token owner.
- The `setApprovalForAll(address _operator, bool _approved)` function: This function gives the token owner the ability to grant or revoke the approval permissions of all operators. When `_approved` is given as true, it sets the approval permissions; otherwise, it revokes all the operator permissions.
- The `getApproved(uint256 _tokenId)` function: It returns the approved operator address for a given non-fungible token ID.
- The `isApprovedForAll(address _owner, address _operator)` function: It is a boolean function which checks if the operator, given by the `_operator` address, is the approved operator for the given token owner, given by the `_owner` address.

# Stablecoin

Imagine on a sunny day you go for a cup of coffee in a busy downtown coffee shop. You are paying for coffee with your ether, and by the time you get your coffee, you have to pay 10% more ethers after 30 minutes of waiting in line. That is as crazy as it can get. Unfortunately, that is the volatility we saw in major cryptocurrencies, like Bitcoin and ether during the crypto-market crash between late 2017 and early 2018. The value of some coins fluctuated as much as 20% on a daily basis.

Stability is a major issue for cryptocurrencies looking to gain mainstream adoption in the mass market. That is where stablecoin comes to help. As the name suggests, it is a type of crypto-coin designed to minimize the volatility of the value of coins and make them more stable in value over a period of time. Typically, they are pegged to fiat currency, commodity, or leading cryptocurrency. There are four types of stablecoins, as shown in the following diagram:

- **Fiat Collateralized Stablecoin**: This is pegged to a fiat currency like the US dollar or the euro. It is backed by a reserve with a certain amount of fiat currencies as the collateral. One of the most popular ones is Tether (USDT), which is pegged to the US dollar with a ratio targeted to be 1:1.
- **Crypto Collateralized Stablecoin**: This is collateralized by a major cryptocurrency, like Bitcoin or ether. This category of stablecoins normally is backed by certain amount of ethers or Bitcoins. One popular one is the Dai created by MakerDAO, which is pegged to the US dollar with a target ratio of 1:1.
- **Commodity Collateralized Stablecoin**: This is pegged to a common commodity like gold. It is backed by a certain value of the commodity as the collateral. One example is Digix Gold(DGX), a ERC-20 coin which is pegged to gold with a ratio targeted to be 1 DGX to 1 gram of gold.
- **Stablecoin with no collateral**, which is not collateralized with any other assets.

It typically relies on complex algorithms to influence the supply and demand, and stabilize the valuation of the coins. One example is basecoin, which was confirmed as shutting down in late 2018.

Stablecoins, backed by the fiat currency or a commodity, introduce the centralized entity overseeing the collateral provisions and managing the reserve. They may require additional transparency and oversight as well as audit and compliance enforcement. Stablecoins backed by cryptocurrency or no collateral stablecoins are supported through the blockchain and secured with the decentralized peer-to-peer network and cryptograph.

# Dai stablecoin

The concept of Dai stablecoin is like a HELOC (home equity line of credit) loan, through which you tap into your home equity on the house as the collateral and get a pool of cash for your own financial purposes. The interest rate of a HELOC loan is normally tied to the prime rate, which is set by the federal reserve. The bank lending you the HELOC loan may also charge some fee associated with loan applications and monthly or annual maintenance of the HELOC account.

With the Dai stablecoin, you are locking up some ethers as the collateral asset in exchange for Dai. It is intended as a stable cryptocurrency whose unit value is pegged to one US dollar. The advantage of such stablecoins is they can leverage all essential capabilities of blockchain technology. At the same time with Dai, it can help to realize the full potential of a cryptocurrency and decentralized network.

Here is how Dai stablecoin works. It has two cryptocurrencies: one is Dai and the other one is Maker (MRK). Maker is a smart contract platform on Ethereum that allows anyone to deposit ethers as a collateral asset; in return, it generates a certain amount of Dai on the Maker platform. You can then use Dai just like any other cryptocurrency. You can then send Dai to anyone, pay for your coffee, or any goods and services, as long as the merchants accept it.

Maker introduces some key components in the Maker platform, including collateralized debt position (CDP), target rate feedback mechanisms (TRFM), and platform governance.

The CDP is a smart contract, which holds collateral assets deposited by a user and actively manages the collateral debt ratios. Here is how it works:

1. The user first needs to send a transaction to Maker to initiate the creation of a CDP.
2. Once a CDP is created, it then sends another transaction to deposit the ethers as the collateral.

3. After that, whenever the user needs some Dais, it can send transactions to get the amount of Dais from the CDP. Behind the scene, the CDP will accrue the debt and manage the debt ratio, and lock out certain collateral until the debt is paid, or additional ethers are deposited.

4. When the user wants to retrieve its ethers, it has to pay down the debt in the CDP, plus any stability fee the platform may charge. Stability fees are paid with Maker.

5. Once it is debt free and the stability fee is paid, the user can end the transaction to get all the collateral back.

Let us say 1 ether is at 100 US dollars, and 1 Dai is 1 US dollar, and the system debt ratio is 75%. If you deposited 10 ethers, which is worth 1,000 US dollars, you are allowed to take 750 US dollars worth of loan, or 750 Dais. You can take a one-time loan of 750 Dais, or take out Dais multiple times, but the total loan amounts to not more than 750 Dais. The 10 ethers will be locked out in the CDP until 750 Dais are paid back. If the ether price increases, you may be able to borrow more Dais. But if the ether price drops, you may have to deposit more ethers, or have to return some Dais, to maintain the debt ratio.

Maker uses the autonomous feedback mechanism to stabilize the Dai, which they call **target rate feedback mechanism** or **TRFM**. It is designed to allow the Dai stablecoin system to adjust the target rate and maintain the stability of the Dai market price around the target price, which is pegged to the US dollar with a ratio of 1:1.

The governance of the Maker platform is established at the system level, which is done through on-chain voting from MKR voters. The Maker platform allows the internal governance variables to be modified through some designated smart contract, also called an active proposal smart contract. Any MKR account holder can come up and deploy smart contracts to propose changes to the governance variable. The MKR voters then vote for the active proposal from all proposals with their MKR tokens. The smart contract with the highest number of votes will be designated as the active proposal smart contract and be granted permission to make the system changes.

 You can check out the Dai stablecoin white paper for more details (https://makerdao.com/whitepaper/DaiDec17WP.pdf).

# Making sense of cryptoeconomics

You may have played or remember Second Life, a massive multiplayer 3D online game in a virtual world, developed by the San Francisco-based firm Linden Lab and launched in June 2003. According to Wikipedia, by 2013, Second Life had approximately one million regular users. Second Life has an internal economy, which is powered by the Linden dollar, or L$. Linden dollar is a virtual token for use only within the Second Life platform. You can buy or rent assets using L$. You can provide services and get paid with L$. The game itself is an autonomous, self-sustainable and self-sufficient virtual world, where, as a virtual being, you can do anything, almost in parallel with the real world we are living in.

Think of the network effect of a blockchain as a second life. The blockchain and cryptocurrencies enable a new autonomous, self-sustainable, and self-sufficient decentralized digital world. In the decentralized world, the blockchain network exhibits all the basic elements of an economic system, which is what people refer to as cryptoeconomics. Like the parable of blind men and an elephant, cryptoeconomics is just like another elephant coming into the crypto world, which has since, caused a lot of confusion. Some may logically think it is a subfield of economics; some think it is not.

Cryptoeconomics refers to the network effect created by blockchain technology; it involves combinations of cryptography, computer networks, and game theory, making the network an autonomous, self-sustainable, and self-sufficient crypto-world. Value creation and transfer are made possible in the digital and crypto-form, and ownership of any value, whether properties or assets, is established and proven with cryptographic technologies.

When Satoshi developed the Bitcoin, the first decentralized digital currency, he implemented a PoW protocol to secure the Bitcoin blockchain network through cryptography and to fuel the system with an incentive system. The actor, the miner in this case, gets rewarded with Bitcoin for computation effort in creating new blocks. Similarly, in a PoS system, where Ethereum is shifting to, the actors or validators stake their crypt-assets to ensure the security of the network.

It is such a fascinating topic. The economic incentives built inside the protocol encourage all network actors to follow good economic practices while maintaining the network's autonomy and sustainability. Smart contracts maintain the government, law and order, and the network protocol defines the monetary policy of the cryptocurrency and crypto-tokens.

 For more information about cryptoeconomics, you can check out the link https://github.com/L4ventures/awesome-cryptoeconomics.

# Working with decentralized data and content storage

Data and content management are two of the main capabilities in many of the real-world business applications, such as information portals, Wikipedia, and ecommerce and social media applications. There is no exception in the decentralized world. During the EVM discussion, we briefly looked at the EVM capability for storing data on Ethereum.

Although it is convenient, it is not generally intended to be used for data storage. It is very expensive too. There are a few options application developers can leverage to manage and access decentralized data and contents for decentralized applications, including Swarm (the Ethereum blockchain solution), IPFS and BigchainDB (a big data platform for blockchain). We will cover them in the rest of this section.

## Swarm

Swarm provides a content distribution service for Ethereum and DApps. Here are some features of Swarm:

- It is a decentralized storage platform, a native base layer service of the Ethereum web 3 stack.
- It intends to be a decentralized store of Ethereum's public record as an alternative to an Ethereum on-chain storage solution.
- It allows DApps to store and distribute code, data, and contents, without jamming all the information on the blockchain.

Imagine you are developing a blockchain-based medical record system, you want to keep track when the medical records are added, where the medical records are recorded, and who has accessed the medical records and for what purpose. All these are the immutable transaction records you want to maintain in the blockchain. But, the medical records themselves, including physician notes, medical diagnosis, and imaging, and so on, may not be suitable to be stored in the Ethereum blockchain. Swarm or IPFS are best suited for such use cases.

A typical Ethereum DApp application architecture for such use cases may look like the diagram here:

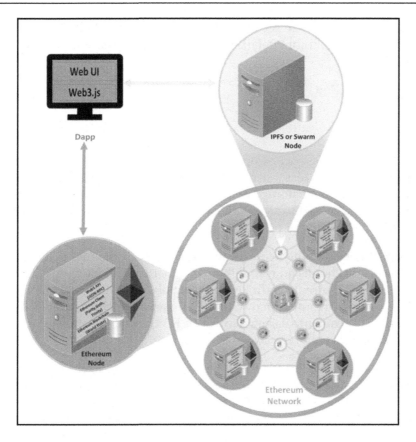

DApps can create, manage, and store data and content directly into a decentralized file system, like IPFS and Swarm, and access and retrieve the data and content using a Swarm hash. When DApps submit all transactions to the Ethereum network, the transactions can reference the Swarm resources with the referenced Swarm hash.

Internally, Swarm maintains a specific type of content addressed distributed hash table (DHT) across the decentralized nodes. File or content uploaded into the Swarm network is treated as the blobs, and chopped into different chunks. A Merkle tree is then created out of all those chunks, and is used to ensure the content integrity. Trunks are further distributed to participating nodes and stored into the DHT. When an access request is made, the content is served by the node(s) closest to the address of a chunk.

Swarm offers several APIs for accessing and managing the contents, including a **CLI (command-line interface)** and JSON-RPC APIs. JavaScript packages are available through the erebos, swarm-js or swarmgw packages, which can be leveraged by most of the UI/JavaScript- based DApps.

If you would like to see more documentation and APIs, check out the Swarm site for more details (`https://swarm-guide.readthedocs.io/en/latest/`).

# IPFS

IPFS is similar to Swarm; it is a peer-to-peer distributed filesystem that was designed to store and share the content across a decentralized network. Both IPFS and Swarm offer the decentralized data and content storage with content addressable hash, generated directly from the content. Both are used to store any kind of content, which can be referenced from the transactions in the Blockchain network.

Behind the scenes, there are quite a few technical differences; mainly, in terms how each chop large datasets into chunks and store them in a distributed network. IPFS may be thought of as a single BitTorrent swarm, exchanging objects within one Git repository. Swarm may be seen as more integrated with the Ethereum blockchain, and has an incentivized system for content sharing. However, Filecoin can be an overlay on top of IPFS for providing a similar incentivized system.

The DApp application architecture in the *Swarm* section applies to IPFS too. In the same way, IPFS offers several APIs for accessing and managing the contents, including a CLI interface, JSON-RPC APIs, and an HTTP interface. JavaScript packages and Go library are available too, which can be leveraged by most of the UI/JavaScript or Go-based DApps.

You can check out the IPFS site for more details (`https://docs.ipfs.io/reference/api/cli/`).

# BigchainDB

BigchainDB is a decentralized database combining both traditional database and data management capabilities and blockchain features. As a blockchain database, BigchainDB is complementary to other decentralized systems, such as decentralized file storage like IPFS or Swarm, and smart contract blockchains like Ethereum or EOS. It is another alternative for storing decentralized data and content. It can be used as the data storage for traditional applications, or can be leveraged as the decentralized data storage for decentralized blockchain platforms, like Ethereum. Although it can be used as a file repository, it is not recommended since it is best suited to structured or unstructured data.

Within the Ethereum community, there is a lot of interest in integrating BigchainDB with Ethereum smart contracts. Some EIPs and **POCs (prototype of concept)** were proposed to explore such integration options. One of the PoCs is to leverage the Oraclize service to retrieve data from BigchainDB within a smart contract. On successful retrieval of data, the smart contract evaluates and executes the logic and performs the requested operation. As the diagram shows, there are two ways a DApp can integrate with BigChainDB. One is to directly interact with BigchainDB as the decentralized data storage through HTTP GET and POST. The second option is to leverage Oraclize service in smart contracts to access external data from BigChainDB:

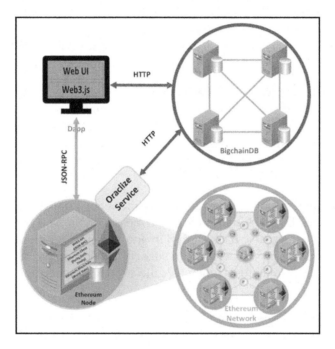

This process uses the following rules:

- BigchainDB offers several interfaces for connecting to BigchainDB servers and storing and retrieving data from the blockchain database, including a CLI interface and HTTP APIs.
- When storing data in the database, you will need to use HTTP POST to send the data to the database server. You use the HTTP GET interface to retrieve data from the database.
- BigchainDB also provides database drivers for developers to connect to the network servers from high-level programming languages, like Java, Python. and JavaScript/Node.js.

If you are interested in more documentation and APIs, check out the BigchainDB site for more details (`https://docs.bigchaindb.com/en/latest/index.html#`).

# Decentralized messaging with Whisper

We are living in an eventful and reactive world. We subscribe to newsletters, and follow people and companies on Twitter, Facebook, or LinkedIn. We buy and sell stocks when the stock prices get to some predefined limits. In a traditional application scenario, an event-driven architecture with a messaging service might be a popular choice for this kind of use case to make the event source and event consumer integrate together asynchronously.

Whisper is a decentralized messaging mechanism designed for asynchronous low-bandwidth, uncertain latency communication and data transmission between decentralized applications. It is almost the same in concept as **JMS (Java Message Service)** in the Java world, or newer ones like Kafka. A message is an atomic unit of work of data passed from the source application to one or more destination applications. It is up to the receiving party to look into the messages and take action.

Messages can be handled in both the request/reply model or publish/subscribe model. In the request/reply model, DApp A needs to send a message to DApp B in one message channel, and expects the response back from B in another message channel. In the publish/subscribe case, a group of DApps can subscribe messages with a certain topic, and will be able to receive such messages whenever the source system publishes a message about the topic.

As the following diagram shows, when DApp A needs to send a message to B, it will send the messages to the decentralized network. Here, the Whisper nodes will relay the messages to all Whisper nodes, and the targeted receiver or the subscriber, DApp B, will be able to pick up the messages from any of the nodes. Let's have a look at the following diagram:

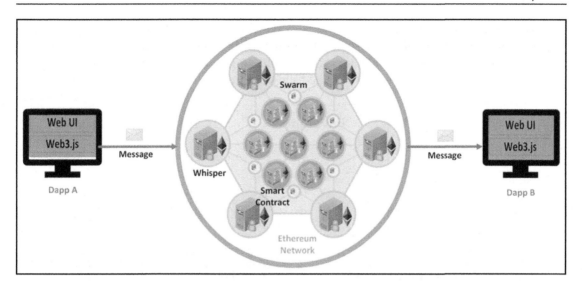

The following list further explains the process:

- Behind the scene, Whisper maintains the messages similar to a **distributed hash table (DHT)**, and uses a datagram messaging protocol, like UDP, for relaying messages between the Whisper nodes.
- A message in Ethereum is a data packet with of to 64KB in size, normally about 256 bytes. It is neither suitable for large data exchanges, nor for real-time communication.
- Typical usages of messages include low-latency signaling messages from one DApp to one or more receiving DApps, or high-latency publication messages.
- Whisper provides low-level APIs for DApps to send or watch the messages. During the transmission of a message, it is packaged within an envelope, which is encoded with the **recursive length prefix (RLP)** encoding schema, something along the lines of:

[expiry: P, ttl: P, [topic0: B_4, topic1: B_4, ...], data: B, nonce: P]

Visually, the envelope structure looks like the one shown in the following diagram, where expiry is the field as the intended expiry date/time for the message, ttl is the time to live given in seconds, which means the message should no longer be transmitted once it is past the *time to live* time. Let's have a look at the following image:

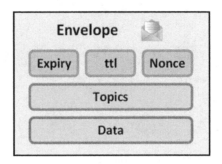

The nonce here is conceptually similar to the nonce in the PoW; it is an arbitrary value intended to demonstrate proof of work in composing the message. Topics are a set of indexes intended to help the message recipients watch and find the expected messages.

Whisper provides low-level APIs in web3.shh for DApps to send or watch the messages.

Messages can be sent as anonymous or public messages, can be signed or not signed, can be encrypted or sent as plain messages. It can be sent to one or more recipients, or published to anyone. When sent as signed messages, the message sender will sign the messages with the SHA-256 hash to show the authenticity of the owner of the messages. When encrypted, it can be encrypted using symmetric key, or public and private key pairs. Whoever owns the symmetric key or private keys can decrypt the messages.

 You can check out the Ethereum wiki site for more details regarding Whisper (https://github.com/ethereum/wiki/wiki/Whisper-pages).

# Summary

In this chapter, we examined various scalability initiatives in Ethereum, discussed how different on-chain and off-chain scalability solutions work, as well as the roadmap to Ethereum 2.0. You learned basic concepts of ICO, STO, IEO, stablecoins, and a variety of token standards, including the ERC-20 and 721 token standards. At the end, we went over decentralized filesystems, like IPFS, Swarm, and BigchainDB, and a decentralized messaging system, like Whisper, to give you the complete toolset you need to develop the full-fledged DApps.

In the next chapter, we will introduce Solidity, the smart contract programming language in Ethereum. We will dive into the details of the programming language structure, and we will discuss the best practices in writing a smart contract in Solidity.

# 2
# Section 2: Blockchain Development Cycle

Solidity is the most popular programming language when it comes to developing smart contracts. In this section, you will learn how to write a smart contract with Solidity and develop your very first cryptocurrency.

This section comprises of the following chapters:

# 4
# Solidity Fundamentals

In this chapter, we will dive into the details of Solidity, the most popular smart contract programming language. We will look at the features of the Solidity programming language and will provide an overview of Solidity's development tools. We will learn about various Solidity language fundamentals, including the structure of a contract, contract patterns, and exception handling. We also cover smart contract security and best practices.

At the end of this chapter, we will show you a complete example of a real-world smart contract that's been developed in Solidity, and demonstrate how you can functionally test your smart contract.

The following topics will be covered in this chapter:

- Introducing Solidity
- Learning the fundamental programming structure in Solidity
- Understanding inheritance, abstract contracts, and interface
- Examining smart contract execution under the hood
- Mastering advanced programming concepts in Solidity
- Putting it all together – rental property

# Technical Requirements

For all the source code of this book, please refer the following GitHub link :

```
https://github.com/PacktPublishing/Learn-Ethereum
```

# Introducing Solidity

Solidity is a JavaScript-like, general-purpose, object-oriented language that's designed to run smart contracts on the Ethereum network. It was developed by Gavin Wood, Christian Reitwiessner, Alex Beregszaszi, and several Ethereum core contributors.

Solidity is a statically typed contract language that contains state variables, functions, and common data types. It allows DApp developers to implement business logic functions in a smart contract. The contract verifies and enforces the constraints at compile-time, as opposed to runtime. Similar to Java, the Solidity code is compiled into bytecode that can be executed on the **Ethereum Virtual Machine (EVM)**. Unlike other compiled languages, the bytecode that's generated across platforms will remain the same, provided that the input parameters to the compiler and the compiler version remain the same. Once compiled, the contracts are uploaded to the Ethereum network. The blockchain will assign an address to the smart contract. Any user with permissions on the blockchain network can call a contract function to execute the smart contract.

Here is a typical flow diagram showing the process from writing contract code to deploying and running it on the Ethereum network:

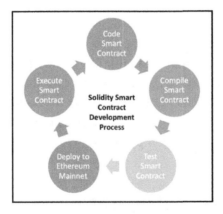

This can be further explained with the following steps:

1. We start by coding smart contracts in Solidity and compiling them into bytecode.
2. Then, we deploy and test our smart contract in the test environment, including a local simulated non-mining environment and the Ethereum testnet.
3. Once the smart contracts have been thoroughly tested, we can deploy a smart contract to the Ethereum mainnet and let the DApps invoke and execute the smart contracts.

# Tools for the Solidity development environment

As we discussed in the *DApp Development Tools* section of `Chapter 2`, *Ethereum Architecture and Ecosystem*, there are quite a few development tools available to make smart contract development easier. Which one to use is truly a personal choice. The following are the tools we are going to use to build, monitor, and deploy smart contracts on the Ethereum platform:

- Browser-based IDEs
- Standalone IDEs with Solidity plugins
- Command-line development management tools

## Browser-based IDEs

There are quite a few browser-based IDEs you can use to develop Solidity smart contracts. The advantage of such tools is that you don't need to download anything on your own desktop or laptop. You simply need to point your favorite browsers to the IDE's site and start coding.

In this section, we will be looking at online browser-based tools such as Remix and EthFiddle. Let's go over them now:

- **Remix**: Remix is a powerful open-source IDE for coding, compiling, testing, and debugging smart contracts in Solidity:
  - It is a browser-based development environment that allows you to program in Solidity within your browser.
  - It allows you to compile Solidity code in all available versions, and supports three runtime environments for testing and debugging, including JavaScript VM, Injected Web3, and the Web3 provider.
  - In addition, it allows you to see all transaction logs, events, inputs, and outputs, as well as gas consumption for the transactions.

You can start Remix by connecting your browser to `https://remix.ethereum.org/`. The following is a screenshot of the UI of Remix:

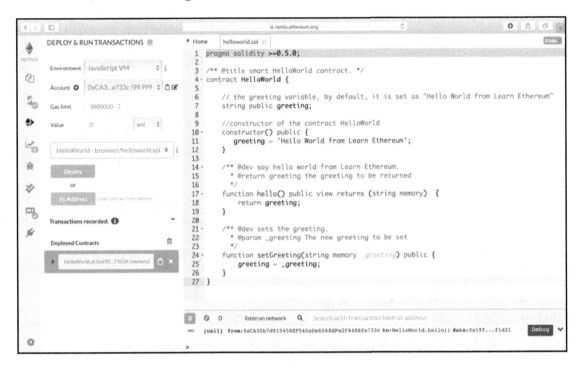

- **EthFiddle**: EthFiddle is another simple Solidity browser-based development tool. You can quickly test and debug smart contract code and share a permalink to it. One feature that makes EthFiddle stand out is its potential to perform security audits. The following screenshot shows the software interface:

You can start coding with EthFiddle by connecting your browser to the EthFiddle site at `https://ethfiddle.com`.

# Standalone IDE with Solidity plugins

Many popular IDEs, including **Visual Studio Code (VSC)**, IntelliJ, and Atom, support smart contract development with a Solidity plugin. Those of you who are interested can follow the link from the ConsenSys site, `https://media.consensys.net/an-definitive-list-of-ethereum-developer-tools-2159ce865974`, to download Solidity plugins for your favorite IDEs.

The following is a screenshot of Solidity development being conducted with VSC:

To get started, you can download Microsoft **VSC** from the website, `https://code.visualstudio.com`. Once you have installed VSC, you can go to the extension tab (the last one on the left-hand side in the preceding screenshot) of VSC to search for Solidity extensions and install the necessary plugins.

# Command-line development management tools

For the folks who are used to command-line development environments and like to develop software through scripting and automation, the following are a few options you can explore:

- Truffle (`https://truffleframework.com/`)
- Embark (`https://github.com/embark-framework/embark`)
- DApp (`https://dapp.tools/dapp/`)
- Builder (`https://buidler.dev`)

Truffle is one of the most popular development environments and testing frameworks and is an asset pipeline for Ethereum. For information on Truffle's major features, you can refer to the following link: `https://www.ifourtechnolab.com/blockchain-technology`.

We will discuss these in more detail in the next chapter, where we will be using Truffle to develop a DApp for an ERC20 token.

# Learning the fundamental programming structure in Solidity

Let's get a taste of Solidity's code and use an example to show you the layout and constructs of a smart contract. We will begin with the most basic smart contract example, HelloWorld.sol, as shown in the following screenshot:

```solidity
1   pragma solidity >=0.5.0;
2
3   /** @title smart HelloWorld contract. */
4 - contract HelloWorld {
5
6       // the greeting variable, by default, it is set as "Hello World from Learn Ethereum"
7       string public greeting;
8
9       //constructor of the contract HelloWorld
10 -     constructor() public {
11          greeting = 'Hello World from Learn Ethereum';
12      }
13
14 -     /** @dev say hello world from Learn Ethereum.
15       * @return greeting the greeting to be returned
16       */
17 -     function hello() public view returns (string memory)  {
18          return greeting;
19      }
20
21 -     /** @dev sets the greeting.
22       * @param _greeting The new greeting to be set
23       */
24 -     function setGreeting(string memory _greeting) public {
25          greeting = _greeting;
26      }
27  }
```

Solidity's file extension is .sol. It is similar to .js for JavaScript files and .java for Java source code. The preceding code defines a smart contract called HelloWorld, which has has a contractor for setting the initial greeting, defines a setGreeting method to reset the greeting, and a hello method for the authorized party to get the greeting. In the rest of this section, we will go over the fundamentals of the Solidity programming language, including the following:

- The layout of a Solidity source file
- Structure of a contract
- State variables
- Functions
- Function modifiers

# The layout of a Solidity source file

A Solidity source file is typically composed of the following constructs:

- `pragma`
- Comments
- `import`
- Contract definition

You can have many of those constructs in one Solidity source file. We will briefly go over the first three constructs in this section, and then discuss the contract construct in detail in the following section.

## Pragma

The `pragma` keyword in line 1 simply says that the source code file will need to compile with a compiler that's version 0.5.0 or later. Anything newer does not break functionality. `<= x.y.z` means the version of x.y.z or a newer one. The `^0.5.2` symbol implies another condition—the source file will not work on compilers lower than version 0.5.2, nor on any version beyond 0.6.0.

## Comments

Just like any other modern language, comments are used to make the source code easier to understand for the readers or developers. They are ignored by the compiler. The comment can be a single lined comment starting with `//` or a multi-lined comment starting with `/*` and ending with `*/`.

Comments can be used to document the inputs and outputs of a function. In the preceding example, there are comments to define the input parameter using `@param` in line 22 and the output parameter via `@return` in line 15.

## Import

The `import` keyword in Solidity is very similar to JavaScript's past version, ES6. It is used to import libraries and other related features into your Solidity source file. It is often used to make the source codes more modularized.

The following are a few ways to import a Solidity source file:

```
import "HelloWorld.sol";
```

The preceding line of code can be used to import all the global symbols from a local Solidity source file:

```
import "openzeppelin-solidity/contracts/token/ERC20/StandardToken.sol";
```

The preceding line of code can be used to import a file from the Zeppelin library from the local library with a defined path:

```
import
"http://github.com/OpenZeppelin/openzeppelin-solidity/contracts/token/ERC20
/ERC20.sol";
```

The preceding line of code imports an `ERC20.sol` file from the public repository.

You can import a file and define a new global symbol as follows:

```
import * as MyContract from "BaseContract.sol";
```

The preceding code imports from `BaseContract` and creates a new global symbol called `MyContract`, containing the global symbol's member from the import file, that is, `BaseContract.sol`.

Another Solidity-specific syntax equivalent to the preceding import is as follows:

```
import "BaseContract.sol" as MyContract;
```

Instead of importing all the global symbols from the imported file, you can import specific symbols and name some of them alias, as shown here:

```
import {symbol1 as alias, symbol2} from " BaseContract.sol";
```

Depending on your import statement, the compiler will use either file path to locate the source file. The path can be a relative path, something like `../orders/OpenOrder.sol`, or an absolute path such as `/home/evergreen/orders/OpenOrder.sol`, or a URL pointing to the public URL, as shown here.

# Structure of a contract

Contracts in Solidity are similar to classes or objects in most object-oriented languages. A contract defines the following constructs:

- Data or state variables
- Functions
- Events and modifiers
- User-defined types in enums or structs
- Collections with mappings

Functions can access and modify the state variables or user-defined types of variables. When calling a function on a different contract, the called function will not have access to the state variables from the caller contract. Smart contracts are deployed to the Ethereum network, and will only react to the call from an external account or contract through IPC, HTTP, or RPC.

# State variables

State variables are values that are permanently stored in contract storage and are used to maintain the contract's state. As shown in the preceding `HelloWorld` contract, greeting is the state variable and is defined as a `string` type with a visibility of X.

The visibility of a state variable can be defined as `public`, `private`, or `internal`, as follows:

- The `public` variable: The compiler automatically generates the getter method.
- The `private` variable: The variable is only visible to the smart contract itself, and not even to the child contracts.
- The `internal` variable: This can be used if you want the state variable to be visible to the smart contract and its child contracts.

# Built-in data types

Solidity is a statically typed language. Developers who are familiar with languages such as JavaScript and Python will find Solidity syntax easy to pick up. Each variable needs to specify the data type. Depending on the data type, a declared variable will have a default value, which is an initial default value whose byte representation is all zeros.

Data types in Solidity can be either of the following:

- **Value types**: This will always be passed by value
- **Reference types**: This means it will be passed by reference

Solidity defines a large number of built-in data types, which allow you to define the complex types using enums, structs, and mapping.

The basic data types in Solidity are as follows:

| Types | Operators | Example | Note |
|-------|-----------|---------|------|
| Boolean (bool) | !, &&, ∥, ==, != | `bool transferable = true;` | The booleans are true or false expressions. By default, it is false. |
| Integer (int8 to int256) | Comparison operators: <=, <, ==, !=, <=, <, Bit operators: &, ∣, ^, +, -, unary -, unary +, *, /, %, **, <<, >> | `int quantity = 10;` | Signed integer, signed of 8 up to 256 bits, in the step of 8. |
| Unsigned Integer (uint8 to uint256) | Comparison operators: <=, <, ==, !=, <=, < Bit operators: &, ∣, ^, +, -, unary -, unary +, *, /, %, **, <<, >> | `uint threshold = 100;` | Unsigned integer, unsigned of 8 up to 256 bits, in the step of 8. |
| Fixed size byte array (bytes1, bytes2, ..., bytes32) | Comparison operators: <=, <, ==, !=, <=, <, Bit operators: &, ∣, ^, ~,<<, <<, get array data : array[index] | `uint8[5] memory odds = [1,3,5,7,9];` | Fixed size byte arrays are defined using the byteN keyword, the N being any number from 1 to 32. It limits the size, is a lot cheaper, and will save you gas. |
| Dynamically-sized array (bytes, strings) | | `/**bytes array **/ bytes32[] empIds /**string array **/ bytes32[] public names` | Solidity supports a dynamically-sized byte array and a dynamically-sized UTF-8- encoded string. |

| Hexadecimal literals | | `hex"1AF34A"` | Hexadecimal literals are prefixed with the keyword hex and are enclosed in single or double-quotes. |
|---|---|---|---|
| Rational or integer literals | | `100, 1.23, 1e23` | The rational or integer literals |
| String literals | | `Hello World` | String literals are normally written with either single or double quotes. |

For example, the following code snippet defines various data types:

```solidity
1  pragma solidity >=0.5.0;
2
3  contract MiscTypes {
4
5      address payable payor; // defining address type payor
6      string hello = 'Hello World'; // defining the string
7      bytes32[] public names;    /**string array **/
8      bytes32[] empIds;    /**bytes array **/
9
10      uint term; // defining unsigned integer lease term
11      bool transferable = true; // defining boolan type
12      int quantity = 10; // define an integer
13      uint threshold = 100; // defining unsigned threshold
14      uint8[5] odds = [1,3,5,7,9]; //defining an array
15
16  }
```

The address is also a built-in data type in Solidity:

- It comes in two flavors: address, which holds a 20-byte value (size of an Ethereum address), and address payable, which adds additional members transfer and send.
- Address payable is an address you can send ether to, while a plain address doesn't allow payment.

- Address literals are the hexadecimal literals that pass the address checksum test, for example, the Ethereum account address `0xcc89c02fb64a6249914a923f3fdd947821f96121` we generated in `Chapter 2`, *Ethereum Architecture and Ecosystem*.

In addition to the hexadecimal value of the address, the address type comes with a balance you can access, as well as the function transfer or sender for you to send the ether to. The key attributes and functions are shown in the following table:

| Member or function | Return Type | Notes |
|---|---|---|
| `<address>.balance` | uint256 | Balance of the address in Wei. |
| `<address payable>.transfer(uint256 amount)` | bool | Send the given amount of Wei to address, reverts on failure, forwards 2,300 gas stipend, not adjustable. |
| `<address payable>.send(uint256 amount)` | bool | Similar to transfer. |
| `<address>.call(bytes memory)` | bool, bytes memory | Issues a low-level CALL with the given payload, returns a success condition and returns data, forwards all available gas, adjustable. |
| `<address>.delegatecall(bytes memory)` | bool, bytes memory | Issues a low-level DELEGATECALL with the given payload, returns a success condition and return data, forwards all available gas, adjustable. |
| `<address>.staticcall(bytes memory)` | bool, bytes memory | Issues a low-level STATICCALL with the given payload, returns a success condition and return data, forwards all available gas, adjustable. |

A contract has a contract address. It also provides functions so that you can issue the contract invocation.

# User-defined data type

In addition to those built-in data types, Solidity allows the user to define user-defined data types too, including the enum, struct, and mapping data types:

- **Enum**: Enum is one way to create a user-defined data type in Solidity. The meaning of the enum type in Solidity is almost the same as the enum in C or C++. It is used to define a set of integer constants represented by identifiers. The values of those integers start from 0 and are subsequently incremented by 1.

The following code snippet defines an enum type of four seasons:

```solidity
1  pragma solidity >=0.5.0 <0.7.0;
2
3  contract FourSeasonContract {
4      enum Season { Spring, Summer, Autumn, Winter}
5      Season season;
6      Season constant defaultSeason = Season.Spring;
7
8      function construct() public {
9          season = defaultSeason;
10     }
11
12     function setSeason(uint _value) public {
13         season = Season(_value);
14     }
15
16     function getSeason() public view returns (uint){
17         return uint(season);
18     }
19 }
```

As we can see, the enum enumerates the value of season (line 4) as `Spring`, `Summer`, `Autumn`, and `Winter` or as 0, 1, 2, and 3. It also defines a `defaultSeason` variable as `Season.Spring` or a value of 0.

- **Struct type**: Similar to C and C++, a struct is a user-defined complex data type built using things of other types. A struct type can be put inside a mapping or array and can have an array or mapping as its named field, but a struct can't have a named field of its own type.

The following code snippet shows a struct definition:

```
struct person {
        uint age;
        string firstName;
        string lastName;
        string emailAddress;
        String cellPhone;
}
```

As we can see, a `person` is a struct of named fields of `age`, `firstName`, `lastName`, `emailAddress`, and `cellPhone`. Given a `person` struct, the attributes can be referred to as `person.age`, `person.firstName`, and so on.

- **Mapping**: Mapping in Solidity is a collection of key-value pairs, similar to a hashtable or hashmap in Java. The key can be any built-in type, bytes, or a string. Value can be any type, including user-defined types such as contract types, enums, mappings, and structs. However, the key data is not stored in a Solidity mapping—only its keccak256 hash is used to look up the value.

The following is a mapping of addresses and orders:

```
1   pragma solidity >=0.5.0;
2
3 - contract Orders {
4
5 -     struct Order {
6           string buyer;
7           string product;
8           uint quantity;
9       }
10
11      mapping (address => Order) orders;
12
13 -     function setOrder(address _address, string memory _buyer, string memory _product, uint _quantity) public {
14          Order storage order = orders[_address];
15          order.buyer = _buyer;
16          order.product = _product;
17          order.quantity = _quantity;
18      }
19
20 -     function getOrder(address _address) view public returns (string memory, string memory, uint) {
21          return (orders[_address].buyer, orders[_address].product, orders[_address].quantity);
22      }
23
24  }
25  |
```

As shown in line 11, it defines a key-value pair mapping structure with an address as the key, and an Order struct as the value. Given an address as the key, you can query an order's mapping structure to get the Order struct for that address, as shown in line 21.

# Functions

Functions are the executable units of code within a contract. The following is a function structure in Solidity:

```
function (<parameter types>) {access modifier} [pure|view|payable] [returns
(<return types>)]
```

As we can see, a function can define the following:

- **Input parameters**: Data that's passed into the function
- **Access modifiers**: Scope of access
- **Output parameters**: The return values

We will go over these in detail in the upcoming sections.

# Input parameters

Input parameters can be passed into functions. They are declared the same way as variables are. In the following Orders example, we define setOrder using the input parameters, that is, _address, _buyer, _product, and _quantity, as shown in the following code snippet:

```
13 ▾    function setOrder(address _address, string memory _buyer, string memory _product, uint _quantity) public {
14           Order storage order = orders[_address];
15           order.buyer = _buyer;
16           order.product = _product;
17           order.quantity = _quantity;
18       }
```

The following list explains some of the code in the function:

- At line 13, we used `string memory` as an input parameter.
- At line 14, we used `Order storage` to create an order struct. This is because a string is a dynamically-sized array.
- Arrays, structs, and mappings in Solidity are reference types.

- All the other data types we discussed are called value types.
- All the data that has value types in the function call are passed by value.
- EVM creates an independent copy of the data.
- All the data with reference types need to explicitly define a data location where the reference type data is stored.

There are three data locations defined in Solidity, as follows:

- **Memory**: Its lifetime is limited to a function call
- **Storage**: The storage where the state variables are stored
- **Calldata**: This is only available for external function call parameters and is used as a special data location that contains the function arguments

Data location may be omitted if you are using an older version of the Solidity compiler, but it is required since version 0.5.0. During a function call, an input parameter with a reference type may be passed by reference, or by copy, depending on the specified data location. The following rules define the assignment and conversion rules between data locations:

|  | Memory | Storage | Calldata |
|---|---|---|---|
| Memory | Reference | Copy | Copy |
| Storage | Copy | Reference when assigning data from storage to local storage, otherwise Copy | Copy |
| Calldata | Copy | Copy | Copy |

Take the example from the *Mapping* list in the *User-defined data type* section:

1. We defined a local storage variable (line 14) and a mapping of orders (line 11).
2. Inside the setOrder function, the order local storage variable is a reference to the orders state variable.
3. At line 21, when the getOrder function is called, the reference from the orders state variable will be returned to the buyer, and the product to the caller.
4. A conversion happens from local storage to string memory, and a separate memory copy of the buyer or product is created as a string.

In this case, quantity is a value type. A copy is always provided as part of the return.

# Output parameters

A function may take only the input parameters and return nothing, as we've seen already in many setter methods. The output parameters can be declared after the `returns` keyword, as shown in the following code snippet:

```
20 ▾   function getOrder(address _address) view public returns (string memory, string memory, uint) {
21         return (orders[_address].buyer, orders[_address].product, orders[_address].quantity);
22     }
```

The same data location applies to the outputs, too. Unlike C, C++, or Java, Solidity may return multiple outputs. In this example, three output values are returned. Two string outputs return the string value of buyer and product, and the one integer value that's returned represents the quantity being ordered.

# Access modifiers

You can define the access modifier for your function. It can be either internal or external.

An internal keyword may be omitted. If the access specifier is not declared, it is considered to be `internal` by default. An internal function can only be called from the current contract or inherited ones, whereas the external functions are specified to be called by an external account or contract. External functions consist of an address and a function signature, and they can be passed via and returned from external function calls.

In addition to internal or external modifiers, a function can have public or private visibility, too. When a function is declared as private, it is only visible to the current contract. When a function is public, it can be treated as internal and external.

# The pure, view, and payable functions

Functions can be declared as **pure**, **view**, or **payable**, depending on whether it can receive ether or if it needs to access the state. Some earlier versions of Solidity had a constant as the alias to view, but it was dropped in v0.5.0:

- **Pure function**: A pure function means it won't read or modify the state.
- **View function**: A view function means it won't modify the state.
- **Payable function**: A payable function means it can receive ether.

The state means anything EVM holds beyond the input parameters, including state variables, events, contracts, ether, and more. The following are considered as modifying the state:

- Writing to or updating the state variables.
- Constructing other contracts using constructors or self-destructing using self-destruct.
- Emitting events or sending ether via calls.
- Making calls to other non-view or non-pure functions, or any low-level call.
- Using an inline assembly that contains certain opcodes for modifying the state.

The following are considered as reading the state:

- Accessing state variables, the balance of any address, or its own balance
- Accessing any of the members of a block, tx, or msg (with the exception of msg.sig and msg.data)
- Calling any function which may read or modify the state
- Using an inline assembly that contains certain opcodes for reading the state

# Constructor and destructor functions

A **constructor** is also a type of function and is declared for creating new contracts. A contract has only one constructor, which means you can't overload a constructor. A constructor is called to initialize the smart contract when the smart contract is deployed.

As you can see from the preceding `HelloWorld` example, a constructor is declared like this:

```
//constructor of the contract HelloWorld
constructor() public {
    greeting = 'Hello World from Learn Ethereum';
}
```

In the case of `FourSeasonContract`, the code looks as follows:

```
Season constant defaultSeason = Season.Spring;

function construct() public {
    season = defaultSeason;
}
```

When `FourSeasonContract` is deployed, the following occurs:

1. The contract will be initialized with the `Spring` season.
2. A contract can be destructed via the `selfdestruct` method or the `suicide` method.

The `suicide` method has been deprecated since Solidity version 0.5.0.

# Fallback function

A contract can have exactly one **fallback** function. A fallback function is an unnamed external function without any input or output parameters. EVM executes the fallback function on a contract if none of the other functions match the intended function calls. For example, the following code snippet defines a fallback function on the `FallbackHelloWorld` contract (lines 9-11):

```
1   pragma solidity >=0.5.0;
2
3   /** @title Fallback HelloWorld contract. */
4 ▾ contract FallbackHelloWorld {
5
6       // the greeting variable
7       string greeting;
8
9 ▾     function() external {
10          greeting = 'Alternate message from Learn Ethereum';
11      }
12  }
```

When the preceding contract is called to receive ether via the send function, the send function will return false since the fallback function is not payable. To receive ether and add it to the total balance of the contract, the fallback function must be marked payable, as shown here:

```
15  // The Rent contract keeps all payments it received;
16 ▾ contract Rent {
17      function() external payable { }
18  }
```

You may wonder when and how the Rent contract balance was updated. In fact, in the case someone calls the transfer or send method on this contract address, EVM will add the transferred amount to the rent contract's balance, prior to the fallback function call.

# Function overloading

Similar to other object-oriented languages such as C++ and Java, Solidity supports function overloading too. Function overloading means that you may define multiple functions with the same name, but with different input parameter types.

The following code snippet shows use of function overloading:

```
1   pragma solidity >=0.5.0;
2
3 - contract OverloadedOrders {
4
5 -     struct Order {
6               string buyer;
7               string product;
8               uint quantity;
9       }
10
11      mapping (address => Order) orders;
12
13 -     function setOrder(address _address, string memory _buyer, string memory _product, uint _quantity) public {
14          Order storage order = orders[_address];
15          order.buyer = _buyer;
16          order.product = _product;
17          order.quantity = _quantity;
18      }
19
20 -     function setOrder(address _address, string memory _buyer, string memory _product) public {
21          Order storage order = orders[_address];
22          order.buyer = _buyer;
23          order.product = _product;
24          order.quantity = 1;
25      }
26
27 -     function getOrder(address _address) view public returns (string memory, string memory, uint) {
28          return (orders[_address].buyer, orders[_address].product, orders[_address].quantity);
29      }
30
31      // The following function will not compile
32 -     //function getOrder(address _address) view public returns (string memory) {
33      //      return orders[_address].buyer;
34      //}
35  }
```

As shown in the preceding code, the OverloadedOrders contract defines two overloaded setOrder methods. One of the overloaded setOrder methods takes three parameters (lines 13-18), while the other one takes four input parameters (lines 20-25).

Return types don't count as part of overloading resolution. As shown in lines 31-34 in the preceding example, a getOrder(address _address) function with the same name and the same set of input parameter types as the other function will cause a compilation error—even the set of return types are different.

# Function modifiers

Those of you who are familiar with **aspect-oriented programming** (**AOP**) in Python or Java may see the similarity here with the function modifier in Solidity. AOP is a programming paradigm that improves functional modularity and increases the reuse of the common function. By separating cross-cutting concerns, this allows different aspects of behavior that are not central to the business logic (such as logging, transaction management, guarding certain rare conditions, and so on) to be added to a function without cluttering the code, which is core to its functionality.

Similar to AOP, modifiers in Solidity can be used to change or augment the behavior of a function. They are inheritable properties of contracts and may be overridden by derived contracts. It is very handy, especially in Solidity and Blockchain, since smart contracts are considered to be immutable once deployed, and new needs or conditions may come up after the initial development is done.

For example, in the previous OverloadedOrders smart contract, you may want to restrict anyone from ordering large quantities of a certain product. One way to do that is to modify the setOrder function itself so that it handles different conditions. The issue with this approach is that smart contracts are immutable. The better approach is to leverage a function modifier to check those conditions prior to the execution of the existing setOrder function.

The following code snippet shows use of a function modifier:

```
1   pragma solidity >=0.5.0;
2
3 ▾ contract Orders {
4
5 ▾     struct Order {
6             string buyer;
7             string product;
8             uint quantity;
9       }
10
11      mapping (address => Order) orders;
12
13      // The same setOrder function will be restricted to not more than 100 quantity;|
14      function setOrder(address _address, string memory _buyer, string memory _product, uint _quantity)
15 ▾    public costs(_quantity) {
16          Order storage order = orders[_address];
17          order.buyer = _buyer;
18          order.product = _product;
19          order.quantity = _quantity;
20      }
21
22      // restrict large quantity orders, limit to up to 100;
23 ▾    modifier costs(uint _quantity) {
24          require(
25              _quantity <= 100,
26              "Large quantity orders are not allowed."
27          );
28          _;
29      }
30
31 ▾    function getOrder(address _address) view public returns (string memory, string memory, uint) {
32          return (orders[_address].buyer, orders[_address].product, orders[_address].quantity);
33      }
34
35  }
```

We can see the following in the preceding example:

1. We define a modifier, cost, (uint _quantity) (lines 22-29) to make sure the quantity that's ordered is no more than 100. It will throw an exception if the caller orders more than 100.
2. At line 15, we added the costs function modifier to the existing setOrder function.
3. The _ at line 28 means to continue with the original logic in the setOrder function.

Once the smart contracts have been deployed, you may not be able to change the original Orders smart contract due to immutability. Therefore, during design time, you might define a generic modifier in the base contract so that it can be extended in the future. The extension can be done by overriding the generic modifier in the child contract or overriding the setOrder function with an additional modifier. These are the kinds of design choices you have to make to ensure the flexibility and extensibility of your smart contract. We will discuss inheritance and overriding later.

# Events

Events in Solidity are used to track the execution of a transaction that's sent to a contract. DApps can subscribe and listen to these events through the web3 JSON-RPC interface.

The following code snippet shows how to use events:

```solidity
1   pragma solidity >=0.5.0;
2
3   contract Rent {
4       // define events notifying rent is paid
5       event RentPaid(
6           address indexed _from,
7           string indexed _tenant,
8           uint _rent
9       );
10
11      function deposit(string memory _tenant) public payable {
12          //emit event notifying rent is paid
13          emit RentPaid(msg.sender, _tenant, msg.value);
14      }
15  }
```

As we can see, when the tenant deposits the monthly rent, in addition to receiving the rent in ether, it also emits an event, RentPaid, for the DApps to subscribe to and receive from:

- Events, along with event data, are recorded as special transaction logs on the blockchain
- They stay in the blockchain as long as they can
- Any indexed event fields, such as the _from and _tenant fields, are stored separately as part of topics
- They can be searched or subscribed to
- The non-indexed fields will be stored as part of the transaction log data portion
- It can be displayed, but may not be used to search or subscribe to events

By current definitions, only up to three fields can be indexed per event. Similar to function modifiers, events are inheritable members of contracts. We will discuss inheritance later.

# Global variables, contextual variables, and functions

Before we wrap up the fundamental elements of a contract, let's briefly discuss some other important constructs in Ethereum and Solidity, including global or contextual variables such as address, block, msg, and tx, as well as the member functions of those constructs. We discussed addresses in detail in the *Built-in data types* section. Some of the variables are declared as constant, which means the value cannot change through reassignment, and it can't be redeclared after compile time. In Solidity, a state variable can be declared as constant. It does not allow reassignment to blockchain data (for example, `this.balance` and `block.blockhash`), or execution data (`tx.gasprice`).

The following table shows the Solidity global variables and their built-in functions:

| Global variables and Functions | Descriptions |
|---|---|
| `blockhash(uint blockNumber) returns (bytes32)` | Returns the hash of the given block. This only works for the 256 most recent, excluding current, blocks. |
| `block.coinbase (address payable):` | Returns the current block miner's address. |
| `block.difficulty (uint):` | Returns the current block's difficulty. |
| `block.gaslimit (uint):` | Returns the current block's gas limit. |
| `block.number (uint):` | Returns the current block's number. |
| `block.timestamp (uint):` | Returns the current block's timestamp in seconds since the `uint` epoch. |
| `gasleft() returns (uint256):` | Returns remaining gas. |
| `msg.data (bytes calldata):` | Returns complete call data. |
| `msg.sender (address payable):` | Returns the sender of the message (current call). |
| `msg.sig (bytes4):` | Returns the first four bytes of the call data (that is, the function identifier). |
| `msg.value (uint):` | Returns the number of Wei that was sent with the message. |
| `now (uint):` | Returns the current block timestamp (alias for block.timestamp). |

| tx.gasprice (uint): | Returns the gas price of the transaction. |
|---|---|
| tx.origin (address payable): | Returns the sender of the transaction (full call chain). |

 There are other utility functions for math, encryption, error handling, and so on. Those of you who are interested should check out the Solidity site (https://solidity.readthedocs.io/en/v0.5.8/) and look at the utility functions for the version you are using.

# Understanding inheritance, abstract contracts, and interfaces

There are four important pillars of **object-oriented programming (OOP)**, as follows:

- Inheritance
- Encapsulation
- Abstraction
- Polymorphism

All of the preceding concepts play a critical role in influencing modern programming language design and software development. Inheritance enables code reuse and extensibility. Encapsulation refers to information hiding and bundling data within methods to avoid unauthorized direct access to the data. Abstraction is the process of exposing only the necessary information and hiding the details from other objects. Polymorphism allows functional extensibility via the overloading and overriding functions.

Like most modern object-oriented language, such as Java or C++, Solidity supports OOP concepts through inheritance, abstract contracts, and interfaces. In fact, it supports a superset of these features from both Java and C++. Let's go over them now:

- **Interface**: This defines all the methods a smart contract needs to implement, but may not have any implementation itself.
- **Abstract contract**: This is a smart contract definition, but not all the functions are fully implemented. It is similar to the abstract class in Java and C++. A method with only the function definition is called an abstract method.
- **Inheritance**: This allows one contract or abstract contract to reuse the attributes and behaviors from other contracts.

Encapsulation and abstraction are directly supported by fundamental constructs in Solidity, namely those we discussed in the *Fundamental programming structure in Solidity* section. Here, we discussed function overloading, which is one example of polymorphism. Another example is function overriding, which will be discussed along with the inheritance.

# Interface

In Solidity, the interface is similar to the one in Java. It defines all the methods for a contract to implement, but the interface itself doesn't implement any methods. You may define complex types inside an interface, but you can't define state variables or constructors for an interface.

All the methods in an interface are external functions and provide an API (application programming interface) with definitions between contracts and its clients. Unlike Java, the interface in Solidity can't extend from another interface.

For example, the following interface defines the get and set methods for all the Order contracts to implement:

```
 3 ▾ interface OrderInterface {
 4
 5 ▾     struct Order {
 6             string buyer;
 7             string product;
 8             uint quantity;
 9         }
10
11         enum OrderType { PhoneOrder, MailOrder, InternetOrder}
12
13         function setOrder(address _address, string calldata _buyer, string calldata _product, uint _quantity) external;
14         function getOrder(address _address) view external returns (string memory, string memory, uint);
15     }
16
```

In addition, it defines one enum type, OrderType, and one struct type, Order. Implementing contracts can refer to them as OrderInterface.OrderType or OrderInterface.Order, respectively.

# Abstract contract

Abstract contracts in Solidity are similar to the abstract class in Java. Like interface, it defines all the methods for a contract to implement, but it may implement some default or common methods and leave some methods for the subcontracts to implement. Its definition is almost the same as the contract definition; the compiler marks a contract as an abstract contractor if there are any methods left to be implemented by other contracts.

You may define state variables or complex type variables in an abstract contract. It may implement an interface, too, as shown here. In that case, it inherits all the methods that were defined in the interface. The `AbstractOrders` contract is marked as abstract due to the fact that one of the methods (`setOrder`) in `OrderInterface` is left for the subcontracts to implement:

```
16
17 - contract AbstractOrders is OrderInterface{
18       mapping (address => OrderInterface.Order) orders;
19
20 -     function setOrder(address _address, string memory _buyer, string memory _product) public {
21           Order storage order = orders[_address];
22           order.buyer = _buyer;
23           order.product = _product;
24           order.quantity = 1;
25       }
26
27 -     function getOrder(address _address) view public returns (string memory, string memory, uint) {
28           return (orders[_address].buyer, orders[_address].product, orders[_address].quantity);
29       }
30   }
31
```

Similar to other object-oriented programming languages, an abstract contract is useful for defining some base template methods and making the entire contract design more modular and extensible.

# Inheritance

A contract can extend from other contracts, abstract contracts, or interfaces. Inheritance is an important capability in most object-oriented languages, including Solidity. As shown in the following examples, the `Orders` contract has been rewritten to extend from the `AbstractOrders` contract. It implements the `setOrder` methods, in addition to reusing the get and set methods from its parent contract, `AbstractOrders`:

```
32 ▾ contract Orders is AbstractOrders {
33
34       // The same setOrder function will be restricted to not more than 100 quantity;
35       function setOrder(address _address, string memory _buyer, string memory _product, uint _quantity)
36 ▾     public costs(_quantity) {
37           Order storage order = orders[_address];
38           order.buyer = _buyer;
39           order.product = _product;
40           order.quantity = _quantity;
41       }
42
43       // restrict large quantity orders, limit to up to 100;
44 ▾     modifier costs(uint _quantity) {
45           require(
46               _quantity <= 100,
47               "Large quantity orders are not allowed."
48           );
49           _;
50       }
51   }
```

Abstract contracts or interfaces are not instantiable. When the `getOrder` or `setOrder` methods are invoked by an external account or contract, only the `Orders` contract will be instantiated.

Unlike Java, but similar to C++, Solidity supports multiple inheritance in the form of copying code, which includes polymorphism. Even if one instantiable contract extends from another instantiable contract, during the invocation, only one contract instance is created.

# Multiple inheritance and the diamond problem

The diamond problem refers to the case where one contract extends from two other contracts, and both extend from a common parent contract, as shown here:

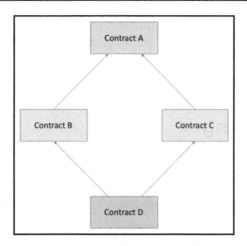

Solidity follows the path Python is taking when it comes to resolving the diamond problem and uses C3 linearization to force a certain kind of order in the base classes.

We can see the following in the following code snippet:

- Both B and C extend A, while D extends B and C in that order, where B is the most likely base for D, but also requests C to override B in the case of conflicts.
- Contract E is allowed since E extends A and B, and B is a subcontract of A.
- F is not allowed since E can't request contract A to override contract B, which is contrary to the fact that B is a subcontract of A:

```
1   pragma solidity >=0.5.0;
2
3 ▾ contract A {
4   }
5
6 ▾ contract B is A {
7   }
8
9 ▾ contract C is A {
10  }
11
12 ▾ contract D is B, C {
13  }
14
15 ▾ contract E is A, B{
16  }
17
18 ▾ //contract F is B, A { This won't compile
19  //}
```

Multiple inheritance is useful, but also quite complicated. The order in the inheritance definition is essential in determining which ways the overriding functions are applied. Comprehensive testing and additional caution need to be exercised in such a case. The best advice is to avoid the diamond problem if you can.

# Function overriding

Function overriding refers to the ability of one method in the subcontract to override the behaviors of the same method on the base contract. For the examples here, contract H extends from G, and also overrides the isGood function. When the isGood function is called on contract H, true is returned from isGood on contract H. On the contrary, contract I extends from G without overriding the isGood function. When the isGood function is called on contract I, the isGood function from base contract G will be applied to I, and return false:

```
21 ▾ contract G {
22 ▾     function isGood() pure public returns (bool) {
23           return false;
24       }
25   }
26
27 ▾ contract H is G {
28 ▾     function isGood() pure public returns (bool) {
29           return true;
30       }
31   }
32
33 ▾ contract I is G {
34   }
35
```

So far, you have learned about the fundamentals of the Solidity programming language, as well as the advanced object-oriented features supported by Solidity. In the next section, we will discuss how smart contract execution works within EVM.

# Examining smart contract execution under the hood

When interacting with smart contracts on the Ethereum blockchain, the Ethereum web3 API or JSON-API interface uses the contract's **application binary interface** (ABI) as the standard way to encode and decode the methods we call, as well as the input and output data. The same applies to calls from outside of the blockchain and calls between contracts. Data is encoded according to its type, as described in the ABI specification.

All the functions and events within the smart contract can be described using JSON descriptors, as shown in the following screenshot. A JSON description of the deposit (_tenant string memory) method is shown in the red box, while the RentPaid event is shown in the purple box:

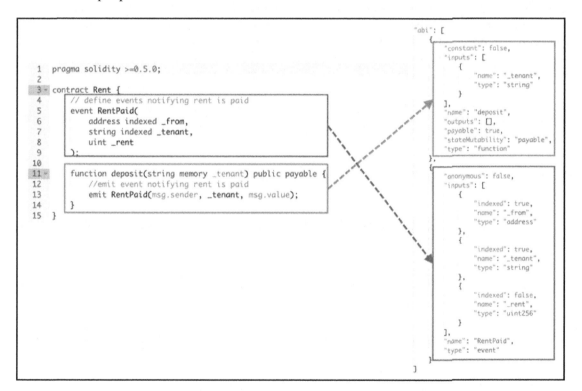

When the deposit method is called, it will generate a function selector, which is calculated as the first 4 bytes of the keccak256 hash of the deposit method signature; something like 0xba8dc1a6 out of (0xba8dc1a692093d8abd34e12aa05a4fe691121bb6) or bytes4(keccak256("deposit(string)")). The function arguments are then ABI encoded into a single byte array and concatenated with the function selector, as shown here, where the red portion is the function selector and the rest is ABI encoded data.

The following image shows an encoded method call of the deposit() method:

```
0xba8dc1a6a26e11860000000000000000000000000000000000000000000000
0000000000000000000020000000000000000000000000000000000000000000
0000000000000000000000054461766964000000000000000000000000000000
0000000000000000000000000000
```

This data is then sent to the contract address on the blockchain, which is able to decode the arguments and execute the smart contract code within the EVM. During execution, when the event is emitted, it will generate some logs and their output, as shown in the following screenshot. In addition, if you use Remix, you can also see the ether (in the value box) that was transferred, as well as the transaction gas and execution gas being paid.

The following is the screenshot from the deposit() method call using Remix:

[vm] **from:**0xca3...a733c **to:**Rent.deposit(string) 0xba8...21bb6 **value:**500000 wei **data:**0xa26...00000 **logs:**1 **hash:**0x714...f1029

| status | 0x1 Transaction mined and execution succeed |
|---|---|
| transaction hash | 0x714f4e0c4945c46f63cbeee0fd585d44c9c60ddd6dc2e913152bf8bc8ccf1029 |
| from | 0xca35b7d915458ef540ade6068dfe2f44e8fa733c |
| to | Rent.deposit(string) 0xba8dc1a692093d8abd34e12aa05a4fe691121bb6 |
| gas | 3000000 gas |
| transaction cost | 24702 gas |
| execution cost | 2598 gas |
| hash | 0x714f4e0c4945c46f63cbeee0fd585d44c9c60ddd6dc2e913152bf8bc8ccf1029 |
| input | 0xa26...00000 |
| decoded input | { <br>     "string _tenant": "David" <br> } |
| decoded output | {} |
| logs | [ <br>   { <br>     "from": "0xba8dc1a692093d8abd34e12aa05a4fe691121bb6", <br>     "topic": "0xed50f965bb41e8192d57bdadc4bc0c5295f8ae70894374beec05ddf4c797f5fc", <br>     "event": "RentPaid", <br>     "args": { <br>       "0": "0xCA35b7d915458EF540aDe6068dFe2F44E8fa733c", <br>       "1": { <br>         "indexed": true, <br>         "hash": "0x8bc4a6a03b3e46d76558234e949e4354d8712c68e011cde3f296a8cb18b78762" <br>       }, <br>       "2": "500000", <br>       "_from": "0xCA35b7d915458EF540aDe6068dFe2F44E8fa733c", <br>       "_tenant": { <br>         "indexed": true, <br>         "hash": "0x8bc4a6a03b3e46d76558234e949e4354d8712c68e011cde3f296a8cb18b78762" <br>       }, <br>       "_rent": "500000", <br>       "length": 3 <br>     } <br>   } <br> ] |
| value | 500000 wei |

 For more details regarding ABI, you can refer to the Ethereum ABI specification at https://solidity.readthedocs.io/en/v0.5.3/abi-spec.html.

Earlier, in the *Layout of a Solidity source file* section, we showed you different ways of importing a library. In the case where the library only supports internal or pure functions, EVM will execute the called function code as a normal method call via a JUMP Opcode. The same is applied when a child contract inherits all the functions from a base contract and the function from the base contract is called.

In the case where the library has external functions, the library needs to be deployed. Similar to a contract deployment, the deployed library has a contract address for the user of the library to call. When an external function from the library is called, EVM will execute the `delegatecall` feature on the calling contract. All such external functions will be executed in the context of the calling contract.

The address of the deployed library has to be linked to the final bytecode of the calling contract. One way to do that is via the command-line compiler linker option. Those of you who are curious should check out Solidity's documentation for more details regarding library linking: `https://solidity.readthedocs.io/en/v0.5.11/contracts.html?highlight=linking#libraries`.

# Mastering advanced programming concepts in Solidity

So far, you have learned about the Solidity programming language's fundamentals, as well as object-oriented concepts in Solidity. To develop real-world smart contract applications, we have to understand the difference between safe and unsafe code practices. Once deployed, a smart contract is considered immutable. Therefore, we have to design smart contracts to be flexible, extensible, and maintainable. There are costs associated with running smart contracts on the Ethereum network, and so we have to develop cost-effective smart contracts.

In this section, we will discuss some advanced topics when it comes to programming Solidity smart contracts, including the following:

- Smart contract security
- Best practices and design patterns
- Writing upgradable smart contracts
- Economic consideration in developing smart contracts

# Smart contract security

Smart contracts are immutable and public records on the blockchain. Once they are deployed onto the Ethereum network, they act as the digital legal contracts between transacting parties. Many of the smart contract functions are account payment-related; therefore, security and testing become absolutely essential for a contract before it's deployed on the main network. The economical sides of execution cost should be considered as well, since all of the smart contract execution steps cost gas.

As a general coding practice, it is always recommended to check math calculations for overflows and underflows to ensure that the appropriate assertions are being made about function inputs, return values, and contract state, and to ensure that the only authorized parties can transact with your contract. When it comes to Solidity, it is always advised to pay special attention to the external contract calls and smart contract execution cost, as well as many reentrancy issues associated with DAO attacks.

In this section, we are going to go over some security practices that will help you design and write flawless Ethereum smart contracts. Most IDEs, such as Remix, have static analysis tools to help us pinpoint some potential security and coding issues, which may give you a quick pointer as to where your smart contracts may be vulnerable.

 Those of you who are interested should check out the ConsenSys site, `https://consensys.github.io/smart-contract-best-practices/`, which maintains a comprehensive list of security best practices for developing secure smart contracts. The paper by the Securify folks, `https://files.sri.inf.ethz.ch/website/papers/ccs18-securify.pdf`, is worth a read. If you want to have your contract checked, upload it to `https://securify.chainsecurity.com`.

# Keep contracts simple and modular

This means writing clean code. Most object-oriented programming practices apply to smart contract development with Solidity too. Have a modular design and try to keep your smart contract small and simple. Move unrelated functionality to other contracts or libraries. Simplify the contract inheritance hierarchy and avoid unnecessary complexity in OO design. Complicated code is difficult to read, understand, and debug, and it is also error prone. It takes much more time to test every kind of scenario.

In addition, pay special attention to the functional difference between built-in global functions, such as `send()`, `transfer`, and `value()` when you're handling fund transfer, which has been exploited to launch DAO attacks. Beware of the semantic limitation of global variables, for example, block.timestamp, which may or may not be able to satisfy your particular business needs for your smart contract.

Solidity itself is still very rudimental and may lack the built-in functionality you enjoyed from other programming languages, such as Java or Python. It is advised that you take advantage of some well-written libraries or tools where possible. The following two are worth exploring:

- **Dappsys**: This is safe, simple, and flexible when it comes to building Ethereum contracts. It has solutions for common problems in Ethereum/Solidity, including Whitelisting, Upgradable ERC20-Token, ERC20-Token-Vault, Authentication (RBAC), and so on. The tools can be found on Dappsy's GitHub site (`https://github.com/dapphub/dappsys`).
- **OpenZeppelin**: This is an open framework of reusable and secure smart contracts in the Solidity language. It is similar to Dappsys, but more integrated into the Truffle framework. OpenZeppelin can be found at `https://github.com/OpenZeppelin/openzeppelin-solidity`.

# Use the checks-effects-interactions pattern

You should always exercise extreme caution when transacting with other external contracts as it may introduce several unexpected risks or errors. External calls should be treated as untrusted as they may execute malicious code. These kinds of calls should be considered as potential security risks and avoided if possible. The following is an example of a DAO reentrancy attack:

```
1   pragma solidity >=0.5.0 <=0.7.0;
2
3   // THIS CONTRACT is INSECURE - DO NOT USE
4 ▾ contract Escrow {
5       mapping(address => uint) escrowBalances;
6
7 ▾     constructor() public payable {
8           escrowBalances[address(this)] = 1000000;
9       }
10
11      function depositToEscrow(uint _amount) public
12 ▾     {
13          escrowBalances[msg.sender] = _amount;
14      }
15
16 ▾     function withdrawFund() public {
17          //external call
18          uint currentBalance = escrowBalances[msg.sender];
19          (bool withdrawn, ) = msg.sender.call.value(currentBalance)("");
20          if (withdrawn) escrowBalances[msg.sender] = 0;
21      }
22  }
23
24 ▾ contract Hacker {
25      Escrow e;
26      uint public reentrancy;
27      event withdrawnEvent(uint c, uint balance);
28
29 ▾     constructor(address vulnerable) public {
30          e = Escrow(vulnerable);
31      }
32
33 ▾     function attack() public {
34          e.depositToEscrow(1000000);
35          e.withdrawFund();
36      }
37
38 ▾     function () external payable {
39          reentrancy++;
40          emit withdrawnEvent(reentrancy, address(e).balance);
41 ▾         if (reentrancy < 10) {
42              e.withdrawFund();
43          }
44      }
45  }
```

In the preceding code snippet, line 19 is an external call that allows Hacker's fallback function at line 38 to repeatedly withdraw the Escrow funds from the Escrow account until all the funds in the Escrow account are drawn. During the recursive calls to the fallback function on line 38, since the sender's Escrow account balance had never had the chance to be updated, this allows money to be repeatedly withdrawn.

As shown in the following event log, Escrow accounts start with 5,000,000 Wei. Hacker deposited 1,000,000 Wei when `withdrawFund` was called on line 35. It repeated the reentrancy calls through the fallback function and ultimately depleted the funds in the Escrow accounts:

```
{
        "from": "0xbd9835ad1196cf677ceb121238dbb3e73aacbd2b",
        "topic": "0x3b61951fc932292485cba1e08064bb726e076b036de1105afabb777abbf8ffb9",
        "event": "withdrawnEvent",
        "args": {
                "0": "1",
                "1": "4000000",
                "c": "1",
                "balance": "4000000",
                "length": 2
        }
},
{
        "from": "0xbd9835ad1196cf677ceb121238dbb3e73aacbd2b",
        "topic": "0x3b61951fc932292485cba1e08064bb726e076b036de1105afabb777abbf8ffb9",
        "event": "withdrawnEvent",
        "args": {
                "0": "2",
                "1": "3000000",
                "c": "2",
                "balance": "3000000",
                "length": 2
        }
},
{
        "from": "0xbd9835ad1196cf677ceb121238dbb3e73aacbd2b",
        "topic": "0x3b61951fc932292485cba1e08064bb726e076b036de1105afabb777abbf8ffb9",
        "event": "withdrawnEvent",
        "args": {
                "0": "3",
                "1": "2000000",
                "c": "3",
                "balance": "2000000",
                "length": 2
        }
},
{
        "from": "0xbd9835ad1196cf677ceb121238dbb3e73aacbd2b",
        "topic": "0x3b61951fc932292485cba1e08064bb726e076b036de1105afabb777abbf8ffb9",
        "event": "withdrawnEvent",
        "args": {
                "0": "4",
                "1": "1000000",
                "c": "4",
                "balance": "1000000",
                "length": 2
        }
},
{
        "from": "0xbd9835ad1196cf677ceb121238dbb3e73aacbd2b",
        "topic": "0x3b61951fc932292485cba1e08064bb726e076b036de1105afabb777abbf8ffb9",
        "event": "withdrawnEvent",
        "args": {
                "0": "5",
                "1": "0",
                "c": "5",
                "balance": "0",
                "length": 2
        }
}
```

The preceding contract vulnerability is called reentrancy. To avoid this, you can use the checks-effects-interactions pattern, as shown in the following example screenshot (lines 63-64). It actually resets the balance before the external calls. The function reads the escrowBalances value and assigns it to a local variable (line 62), before resetting escrowBalances to 0 on line 63. These steps are fulfilled to make sure that the message sender can only transfer to their own account and can't make any changes to state variables. The balance of a user will be reduced before the ether is actually transferred to them. If any error occurs during the transfer, the whole transaction will be reverted, including the reduction transfer amount of balance in the state variable. This approach can be described as optimistic accounting because effects are written down as completed before they actually take place.

The following code snippet shows a safe contract (lines 48-67) and a failed hacker contract (lines 69-90):

```
47   // THIS CONTRACT is considered as safe
48 ▾ contract SafeEscrow {
49       mapping(address => uint) escrowBalances;
50
51 ▾   constructor() public payable {
52           escrowBalances[address(this)] = 1000000;
53       }
54
55       function depositToEscrow(uint _amount) public
56 ▾     {
57           escrowBalances[msg.sender] = _amount;
58       }
59
60 ▾     function withdrawFund() public {
61           //external call
62           uint currentBalance = escrowBalances[msg.sender];
63           escrowBalances[msg.sender] = 0;
64           (bool withdrawn, ) = msg.sender.call.value(currentBalance)("");
65           if (!withdrawn) revert();
66       }
67   }
68
69 ▾ contract FailedHacker {
70       SafeEscrow se;
71       uint public reentrancy;
72       event withdrawnEvent(uint c, uint balance);
73
74 ▾     constructor(address vulnerable) public {
75           se = SafeEscrow(vulnerable);
76       }
77
78 ▾     function attack() public {
79           se.depositToEscrow(1000000);
80           se.withdrawFund();
81       }
82
83 ▾     function () external payable {
84           reentrancy++;
85           emit withdrawnEvent(reentrancy, address(se).balance);
86 ▾         if (reentrancy < 10) {
87               se.withdrawFund();
88           }
89       }
90   }
```

Although the preceding approach prevents repeated withdrawal from the Escrow account, it may not stop reentrancy. As a side effect of reentrance, it continues to burn gas. In the next section, we will discuss techniques that we can use to avoid such issues.

# DoS with block gas limit

The issue with this approach is that the fallback function (on line 83 in the previous section) was repeatedly called 10 times. Even though your funds are safe, this burns additional gas. If it wasn't for line 86, an infinite loop would have occurred and run until all the gas had been burned. This is called a DoS attack with a block gas limit.

The Ethereum blockchain transaction can only process a certain number of steps due to the block gas limit, so be careful when using loops in smart contract logic. When a number of iteration costs go beyond the gas limit, the transaction will fail and the contract can be stalled at a certain point. In this case, attackers may potentially attack the contract and manipulate the gas.

To stop reentrance, it is advised to use the send or transfer method instead of line 19 or line 64, respectively. It is also good practice to check if there are enough funds to be drawn by the `withdrawFund` function on line 60-66. This can be done through an explicit condition check before the `msg.sender.call.value()` call or by using an additional function modifier on `withdrawFund` itself.

# Handle errors in external calls

As we discussed earlier, Solidity has some low-level call methods: `address.call()`, `address.callcode()`, `address.delegatecall()`, and `address.send()`. These methods only return false when the call encounters an exception. Therefore, handling errors in external calls is very important, as shown in the following code snippet. If you use a good IDE, it will remind you about these kinds of warnings. Let's take a look at the following code:

```solidity
1    pragma solidity >=0.5.0;
2
3    /** @title some unsafe examples. */
4    contract SomethingUnsafe {
5
6        function fundTransfer(address payable _payee) public {
7
8            // good
9            if(!_payee.send(100)) {
10               // handle error
11           }
12
13           //don't do this, you will get a warning
14           _payee.send(20);
15
16           // this is doubly dangerous, as it will forward all remaining gas and doesn't check for result
17           _payee.call.value(55)("");
18
19           // if withdraw throws an exception, the raw call() will only return false and
20           //transaction will NOT be reverted
21           _payee.call.value(50)(abi.encode(keccak256("withdraw()")));
22
23       }
24   }
```

As the comments indicate, this is not the best way to handle external calls. The warnings in Remix's static code analysis also provide suggestions when it comes to handling the return value of the external call. The best practice in such cases is to check the return value of those calls and have the appropriate error handling logic at hand when the call fails.

# Best practices in smart contracts

Design patterns are a set of best practices and reusable solutions for certain common problems in software development. Like any other **object-oriented programming (OOP)** language, common OOP design patterns and sound design principles apply to smart contract development in Solidity too. In this section, we will discuss some of the popular ones that are used in the Ethereum community, including the following:

- Access restriction
- State machine

# Access restriction

Access restriction is a Solidity security pattern. It only allows authorized parties to access certain functions. Due to the public nature of the blockchain, all the data on the blockchain is visible to anyone. It is critical to declare your contract function, state, with restricted access control and provide security against unauthorized access to smart contract functionality.

The following code snippet shows the details of functional modifiers:

```
46      // define function modifier restricting to landlord only
47 ▾    modifier onlyLandlord() {
48          if (msg.sender != lease.landlord) revert();
49          _;
50      }
51
52      // define function modifier restricting to tenant only
53 ▾    modifier onlyTenant() {
54          if (msg.sender != lease.tenant) revert();
55          _;
56      }
57
58      // define function modifier restricting actions per state
59 ▾    modifier inState(LeaseState _state) {
60          if (state != _state) revert();
61          _;
62      }
63
64      // define function modifier requiring pay in full
65 ▾    modifier payInFull(uint _rent) {
66          if (_rent < lease.rent) revert();
67          _;
68      }
```

The preceding code is for a rental property leasing application, which we will demonstrate at the end of this chapter. This is what we have here:

- We have defined four different function modifiers to restrict contract execution to the right stage, and by the right party.
- The onlyLandloard and onlyTenant modifiers only allow the landlord and tenants to be able to execute the code.
- The payInFull modifier only accepts the monthly rent if it is paid in full. The inState modifier, on the other hand, only allows certain actions to be performed at different stages of leasing the application.

The following code snippet shows how the functional modifiers can be used to enforce access restriction:

```
76      /* Lease signed by the tenant */
77      function signLease() public
78      inState(LeaseState.Created)
79      onlyLandlord
80 ›    {▦}
87
88      /* tenant move in */
89      function moveIn() public
90      onlyTenant
91      inState(LeaseState.Signed)
92      onlyTenant
93 ›    {▦}
97
98      /* pay the monthly rent, and keep a record */
99      function payRent() public payable
100     onlyTenant
101     inState(LeaseState.Started)
102     payInFull(msg.value)
103 ›   {▦}
108
109     /* terminiate the lease*/
110     function terminateLease() public
111     onlyLandlord
112 ›   {▦}
```

This is what the preceding code shows us:

- The signLease() function can only be invoked by the landlord, and only once the lease has been created.
- The moveIn() function can only be called by the tenant, and only once the lease has been signed off by the landlord.
- Once moved in, the tenant can pay the full rent with the payRent() function call.

The preceding example shows the access restrict pattern via functional modifiers that have been applied to a contract. The function modifier is one of Solidity's most powerful features. If used right, it can greatly improve code readability and remove a lot of duplicate and spaghetti code.

# State machine

State machine is a behavioral design pattern. It allows a contract to alter its behavior when its internal state changes. A smart contract function call typically moves a contract's state from one stage to the next. The basic operation of a state machine has two parts:

- It acts as a workflow of different business processes or steps, with each being represented as independent business functions. The outcomes from each step are a sequence of independent states. Each step knows its preceding states and subsequent states.
- The smart contract traverses through a sequence of such states where the next state is determined by the present state and input conditions. A new state can be added with limited impact being made on other states or the behaviors at other stages.

As the following code snippet shows, LeaseState defines the four stages of leasing an application:

```
24   // Define the state machine for leasing
25   enum LeaseState {Created, Signed, Started, Terminated}
26
```

First, the landlord creates a lease for the tenants to apply for. Once the tenant has applied, the lease contract will be signed by the landlord. The lease will be effective once the tenant moves in. When the lease term is due, the lease contract will be terminated.

The smart contract ensures the right action is taken at any state by using the inState modifier, as shown here:

```
58      // define function modifier restricting actions per state
59 ▾    modifier inState(LeaseState _state) {
60          if (state != _state) revert();
61          _;
62      }
```

The following shows the actual business logic for signing the lease. Once the lease is signed, the lease state is marked as LeaseState.Signed. The function can only be called by the landlord, and after the lease is actually created in a state of LeaseState.Create:

```
76      /* Lease signed by the tenant */
77      function signLease() public
78      inState(LeaseState.Created)
79      onlyLandlord
80 -    {
81          lease.tenant = msg.sender;
82          lease.signedTimestamp = block.timestamp;
83          state = LeaseState.Signed;
84
85          emit leaseSigned(lease.tenant, lease.signedTimestamp);
86      }
```

Through this state transition, all business processes for the rental leasing application can be implemented. If a new state needs to be added, for example, the LeaseState.Applied state for someone who actually applied to lease the rental property, it won't change any other state, except for LeaseState.Signed. This provides great flexibility in making the smart contract code extensible.

# Writing upgradable smart contracts

Earlier, in the *What is Solidity?* section, we briefly discussed the smart contract development process. In reality, once the smart contract has been deployed to the Ethereum mainnet, it doesn't mean the end of the smart contract's life cycle. Bugs may show up. The code may need to be refined, and new requirements may come up. Due to the immutable nature of smart contracts, as well as the gas cost of frequent smart contract deployment or state variable migration, writing upgradable smart contracts becomes critical in the Ethereum blockchain.

Writing upgradable smart contracts means designing and coding for easy upgrades and maintenance. The following are a few practical tactics every smart contract developer should practice:

- Design for flexibility and extensibility. Many of the OO design best practices, including inheritance, polymorphism, encapsulation, and abstraction, apply to smart contract development too. A good design will allow us to add new functionalities without breaking the existing code. It makes the software implementation less brittle.
- Keep smart contracts modular and simple. This simple and modular design makes testing easier and less buggy.
- Separate large contracts into multiple small contracts so that each one can be enhanced and deployed independently.

These tactics may help you avoid unnecessary upgrades, but the software changes are inevitable. In fact, the Ethereum inventor did provide a way to get around immutability with the addressability of smart contracts: the public addresses of smart contracts. In this section, we will introduce the following two design patterns that were developed by the Ethereum community to address the upgradability issues of smart contracts:

- Contract proxy and delegate pattern
- Eternal storage pattern

# Contract proxy and delegate

This is a proxy design pattern and a popular technique that decouples DApps from the actual smart contract implementation and has the proxy as the agent sitting in-between them.

As shown in the following diagram, DApps only need to know the address of the `OrderProxy` smart contract address, and always invoke methods on the proxy. `OrderProxy` maintains a list of addresses regarding the different versions of actual smart contract implementations and knows which one is the latest version. If the smart contract needs to be upgraded, the newer version of the contract implementation will be deployed to the blockchain. The address to the latest version can be dynamically reset with the setter method on the proxy contract. Through the modifier, you can ensure that only the contract owner has permission to repoint the address to the newer version.

The following diagram depicts a contract hierarchy in the contract proxy and delegate design pattern:

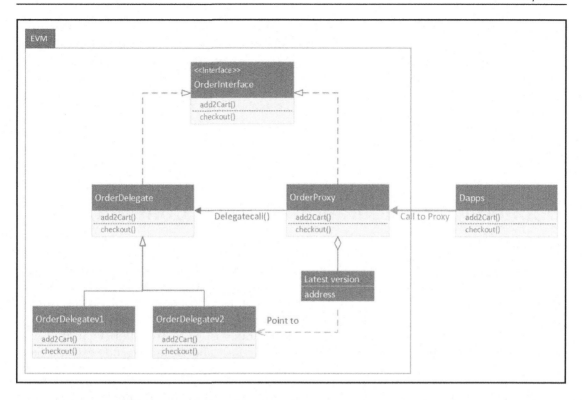

When the invocation comes, the proxy will look up the address of the latest version and delegate the call to the `OrderDelegate` smart contract via `delegatecall()` methods. In Ethereum, `delegatecall` allows the delegate (latest version of the `Order` implementation) to use the caller's context (in this case, the `OrderProxy` contract) to execute the logic, including gas, storage, balances, and so on. Since the `delegatecall()` function only returns true or false, you will need to use inline assembly to make a `delegatecall` if you need to get the return results from the target functions.

# Eternal storage

The proxy approach works well for upgrades when the logic changes. Storage changes are more complicated since they may involve storage data migration. It is always recommended to decouple the logic changes and the storage changes and develop upgrade strategies for software changes or storage changes accordingly. In some cases, unstructured containers, such as mappings, which includes mappings of mappings, may be the best option so that you avoid constant data structure changes. The gas and economic cost of storage data migration are two of the key considerations in determining whether data migration is feasible or not. Plan for storage migration if needed.

Eternal storage is another option we can use to deal with software upgrades with storage data changes. The idea is to create an Eternal storage data contract encapsulating the legacy data and to always leverage an Eternal storage data contract to read and update the storage data. It becomes the custodian of the legacy data.

 Those of you who are interested can check out Zepplino's blog about proxy patterns at `https://blog.zeppelinos.org/proxy-patterns/`.

# Economic consideration of smart contract execution

Developers from the centralized world may not pay too much attention to the execution costs and computing capacity that's needed for running centralized applications. Most of the computing costs are considered to be washouts of the total data center cost. Everything on the blockchain has a cost associated with it, which is measured with gas in the Ethereum network. This includes all the operations under the hood of EVM execution, including ABI encoding and decoding, copying data between storage locations, and Opcode executions.

A good design not only emphasizes a simple, clean, modular, and correct implementation of the business logic, but needs to consider the economic effects in running the smart contracts as well. The economic aspects reflect the following perspectives:

- The coding options in selecting cost-effective language constructs, and avoiding unnecessary and costly operations, make a difference in the total gas cost. Every Opcode has a cost associated with it; some are expensive while others are quite trivial.
- The data locations for calldata, stack, memory, or storage, where the data are temporarily or permanently stored, play a critical role in developing cost conscientious smart contracts.
- Factors related to the cost of deploying smart contracts on the Ethereum blockchain versus the cost of each complex smart contract may have to determine whether we use on-chain data versus off-chain data. On-chain data storage is considered to be very costly. While the off-chain data storage's cost may be low, the cost to oraclize the off-chain data and bring it on-chain for critical execution in smart contracts isn't trivial either.
- Individual function calls, and how often they are invoked, contribute to the total cost of your DApps.

Regarding on-chain data usage, stack variables are normally the cheapest to use and can be used for any value types, that is, anything that is 32 bytes or less. They are packed as 32 bytes at the EVM level. Calldata is the read-only byte array, and every byte of the calldata costs gas, so a function with more arguments or a large calldata size will always cost more gas. It is relatively cheap to load variables directly from calldata, rather than copying them to memory. However, for complex types or dynamic-sized arrays, you may not have many options except resorting to memory data storage.

In EVM, memory is a linearly addressable read-writable byte array. Complex types, including structs, arrays, and strings, must be stored in memory, and the size can be dynamically expanded. When making external smart contract calls, all the arguments have to be copied into a memory location, which incurs costs. Compared to storage data, it is still cheap, but the cost of memory can grow quadratically.

Storage is the most expensive data location and should be used with extra caution. Storage in Ethereum is a persistent and read-writable key-value store that maps keys to values. Both are 256-bit words. Between the read and write operations, the write operation is much more expensive. The storage location is allocated per contract. A smart contract can only read or write to its own storage; it has no access to the storage of external contracts. All the storage locations are initially defined as zero. All the state variables and mappings are stored in the storage location.

In Ethereum, all of these operations are associated with Opcodes. We provided a list of Opcodes in EVM and their associated gas costs in Chapter 2, *Ethereum Architecture and Ecosystem*. There are no hard and fast rules when it comes to developing cost-effective smart contracts. Those of you who are interested should check out the EVM specification and make informed design and coding decisions.

# Putting it all together – rental property leasing

In this section, we will implement and deploy a smart contract for a real-world rental property leasing use case.

The business process for a rental property being leased starts with the landlord creating a rental property listing and allowing the tenants to apply and sign the leasing agreement. Once the tenant moves in, they have to pay monthly rent to the landlord, and once the lease term is due, the lease is terminated. If the tenant misses a rent payment, the landlord has the option to start an eviction, and if the tenant terminates the lease early, they have to pay the early termination penalty.

The following is the high-level diagram of our rental property lease contract:

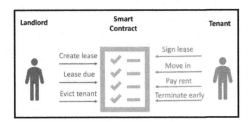

As we explained earlier, the smart contract is developed using a combination of the access control design pattern and the state machine design pattern. Those of you who are interested can check out the complete source in this book's GitHub repository at https://github.com/PacktPublishing/Learn-Ethereum/blob/master/Chapter4/LeaseContract.sol. The following is the smart contract code skeleton for such a use case:

```solidity
  2 ▾ contract LeaseContract {
  3 ▸     struct Lease {▢} // Define the structure for Rental property Lease Agreement
 15       enum LeaseState {Created, Signed, Occupied, Terminated} // Define the state machine for leasing
 16       Lease public lease; // Lease as the state variable
 17 ▸     struct Deposit {▢} // Keep a record of all payments and account balance
 21       Deposit[] public deposits;
 22       uint public balance = 0;
 23       uint public totalReceived = 0;
 24       uint public securityDeposited;   // keep track of security deposit received;
 25       LeaseState public state; //keep track of state transition of leasing application
 26 ▸     constructor(uint _rent, uint _term, uint _securityDeposit, uint _earlyPenalty, string memory _location) public payable {▢}
 36
 37 ▸     modifier inState(LeaseState _state) {▢} // define function modifier restricting actions per state
 41 ▸     modifier onlyLandlord() {▢}   // define function modifier restricting to landlord only
 45 ▸     modifier notLandlord() {▢}      // define function modifier excluding the landlord
 49 ▸     modifier onlyTenant() {▢}      // define function modifier restricting to tenant only
 53 ▸     modifier payInFull(uint _rent) {▢}      // define function modifier requiring pay in full
 57
 58       event securityDepositPaid(address indexed _tenant, uint _amount, uint _timestamp);
 59       event leaseSigned(address indexed _tenant, uint _signedTimestamp);
 60       event rentPaid(address indexed _tenant, uint _timestamp);
 61       event leaseTerminated(address indexed _by, string _reason, uint _timestamp);
 62
 63       /* Lease signed by the tenant */
 64 ▸     function signLease() public payable inState(LeaseState.Created) notLandlord {▢}
 73
 74       /* tenant move in */
 75 ▸     function moveIn() public onlyTenant inState(LeaseState.Signed) onlyTenant {▢}
 79
 80       /* pay the monthly rent, and keep a record */
 81 ▸     function payRent() public payable onlyTenant inState(LeaseState.Occupied) payInFull(msg.value + balance) {▢}
 88
 89       /* terminiate the lease when it is mature*/
 90 ▸     function leaseDue() public inState(LeaseState.Occupied) onlyLandlord      {▢}
 98
 99       /* evict the tenant for missing pay*/
100 ▸     function evict() public inState(LeaseState.Occupied) onlyLandlord {▢}
107
108       /* terminiate the lease early by the tenant*/
109 ▸     function terminateEarly() public payable inState(LeaseState.Occupied) onlyTenant {▢}
116   }
```

Let's use Remix to test our contracts. As shown in the preceding screenshots, we have five ether accounts in the Remix environment. We will use `0xca3...` as the landlord account and `0x147...` as the tenant account. We will select the JavaScript VM option. Let's get started:

1. The landlord deploys `LeaseContract` and creates an instance of the lease contract, where the landlord address, `0xca3...`, is set as the landlord, with rent, term, security deposit, early termination penalty, and property location initialized through the constructor, as shown in the following screenshot:

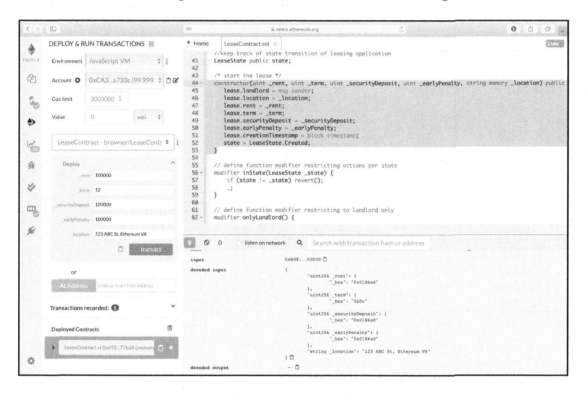

2. Once the lease smart contract has been deployed, the tenant, in this case, switches to the tenant account, `0x147…`, and signs the lease with the initial security deposit. Only the tenant can perform this operation, and only after the lease contract has been created. The following screenshot shows this step:

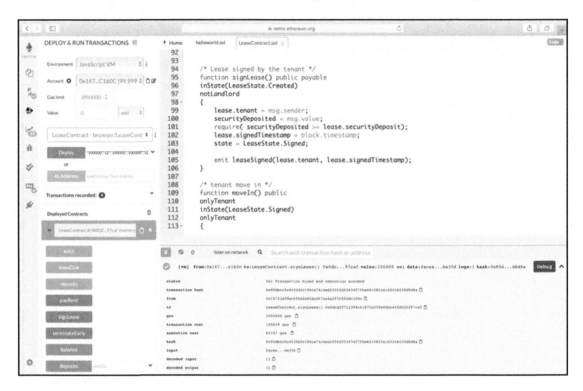

3. In the same way, once the lease has been signed, the tenant can move in with the `moveIn` operation. At this stage, the lease state is changed to 2, that is, the `Occupied` state. The following screenshot shows the Remix editor screen for this step:

4. At this stage, the tenant has to pay the monthly rent. To invoke the `payRent()` function on the lease contract, the tenant will need to deposit enough for rent payment. By enough, we mean that the value the tenant sends in, plus the balance on the account, should be able to cover one month's rent, as indicated by lines 122 and 126. The following screenshot shows the Remix editor screen for this step, where the state was set as 2, that is, `Occupied`:

5. The following screenshot shows the result of 12 monthly rent payments by the tenant. `totalReceived` is updated to 12, which means 12 rent payments have been made:

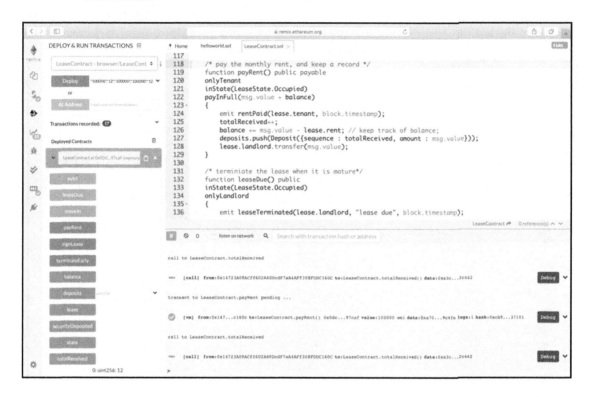

6. Once the lease term is due, you can terminate the lease by invoking the `leaseDue()` method on the lease contract, as shown in the following screenshot. The state will be updated to 3, that is, `terminated`. The security deposit is returned to the tenant, and the remaining balance will be transferred to the landlord:

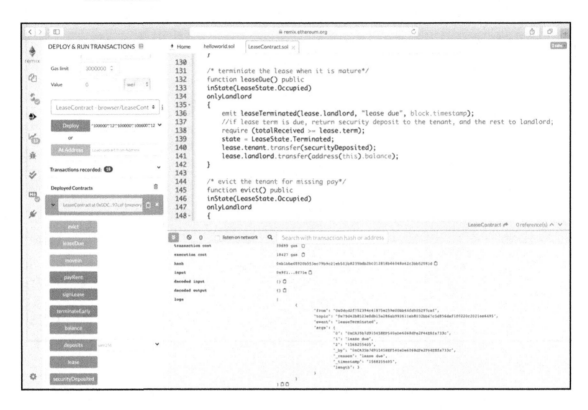

7. Before the lease is due, if the tenant decides to terminate the lease early, by contract, they have to pay the penalty and lose the security deposit. As shown in the following screenshot, the tenant paid 150K for breaking the lease and requesting the early termination. Due to this, the `leaseTeminated` event is logged:

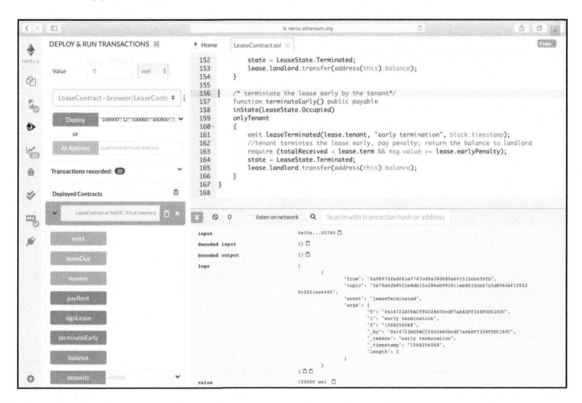

8.  At the same time, if the tenant misses a rent payment, the landlord can terminate the lease and start the eviction process. As shown in the following screenshot, the landlord issued the `evict()` call after the tenant missed the rent payment prior to the lease being due. The balance on the lease contract was not enough to cover the rent:

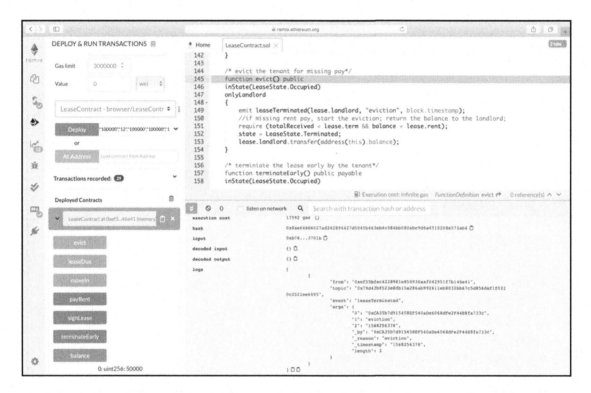

Here, we have shown a working example of a smart contract for a real-world rental property lease application. You should be able to continue to refine and improve the code and make it match the real-world complexity of lease applications even more.

# Summary

In this chapter, we learned how to start smart contract development in Solidity using the most popular Solidity development IDEs. We discussed the Solidity programming fundamentals and basic language constructs. By exploring common patterns and security best practices, we learned how to write better code to avoid contract vulnerabilities. Finally, we showed you a real-world rental property lease smart contract and demonstrated how to use Remix to deploy and test our example.

In the next chapter, we will show you how to develop your very first cryptocurrency and full stack of decentralized applications.

# 5
# Developing Your Own Cryptocurrency

In this chapter, we will provide an overview of smart contract open source libraries and review ERC token standards. Then, we will create a new cryptocurrency called `MyERC20Token` based on the ERC-20 token standard using Solidity. We will also create a non-fungible `DigitalArtERC721Token` token for a decentralized art marketplace based on the ERC-721 standard. After reading through this chapter, you should be able to create your own cryptocurrency.

This chapter is organized around four major topics, as follows:

- Understanding token standards
- Setting up an Ethereum development environment
- Creating an ERC-20 token—`MyERC20Token`
- Creating an ERC-721 token—`DigitalArtERC721Token`

## Technical Requirements

For all the source code of this book, please refer the following GitHub link :

```
https://github.com/PacktPublishing/Learn-Ethereum
```

## Understanding token standards

In `Chapter 3`, *Deep Research on Ethereum*, we learned about the ERC-20 and ERC-721 token standards. ERC-20 is the most popular Ethereum blockchain technical standard for tokens to be issued on Ethereum. The tokens are used as digital currency and are interchangeable.

Before the ERC token standard, the numerous **Initial Coin Offerings (ICOs)**, startups, and decentralized applications (**DApps**) had created their tokens with many different standards. After the release of the ERC-20 standard, things have changed and become much more streamlined.

The benefits of ERC-20 tokens include the following:

- Reducing the risk of contract breaking
- Reducing the complexity of token interactions
- Allowing for lots of different use cases to emerge on top of these standards
- Uniform and quicker transactions
- Confirming transactions more efficiently
- Enhancing token liquidity

However, ERC-20 tokens do not have built-in regulatory limitations by design, so there are no restrictions when it comes to transferring them. This kind of token is known as a **utility token**. When dealing with security regulations, token holders must know that your trading is subject to federal security regulations and that many additional constraints apply to these regulations. Since the ERC-20 token is widely adopted in the industry, currently most of the security token ERC standard proposals are ERC-20-compatible, which means that potentially all wallets and exchanges supporting ERC-20 will support these tokens as well. In ERC-20 standards, when a user trades these tokens, all of the token supply can be treated as the same value; it is interchangeable.

The ERC-20 token is a **Fungible Token (FT)**. An FT is a core characteristic of cryptocurrencies. It can be easily replaced by something identical, and it is interchangeable with ease, such as Bitcoin. On the other hand, a **Non-Fungible Token (NFT)** is a special type of cryptographic token that has unique information or attributes. NFTs are therefore irreplaceable or non-interchangeable. For this purpose, the ERC-721 token was created as a standard.

ERC-721 is for collectibles, which are not interchangeable. These types of tokens are called non-fungible tokens. ERC-721 is an NFT standard, also known as **deeds**. It was created in January 2018 and was proposed by William Entriken, Dieter Shirley, Jacob Evans, and Nastassia Sachs. The most well-known example of ERC-721 is the **CryptoKitties** game. In this game, there are thousands of CryptoKitties. Each cat has unique genes and owns a name, color, shape, price, and other characteristics. The player can collect and breed adorable kittens. Each of CryptoKitties' collectible digital assets can be traded, sold, and bought by a player. Crypto Stamps is another great example that comes from the official national postal service in Austria. It's real post stamps with a digital NFT version for people to collect.

In the following sections, we will kick off the most exciting part—developing our own tokens, including ERC-20 and ERC-721. I am sure that an eager developer like you can unlock the power of blockchain quickly.

# Setting up an Ethereum development environment

To start with smart contract development, you will need to install development tools. Let me introduce you to a popular DApp development tool—Truffle. Follow the instructions in the next section to obtain the Ethereum development tools and start an Ethereum private local blockchain environment (primarily used to run/deploy your smart contract to a local blockchain).

## Working with Truffle

Truffle is an end-to-end Ethereum DApp development tool that provides a development environment for writing, compiling, testing, and deploying smart contracts and DApps. You can use HTML, CSS, and JavaScript for the frontend and Solidity for smart contracts, and you use the web3.js API to interact with the UI and the smart contract. Truffle Boxes provide helpful boilerplate code that contains helpful modules, Solidity contracts and libraries, frontend code, and many other helpful files. Truffle Boxes help developers to quickly get started with their DApp project. The Truffle command line uses the following format:

```
truffle [command] [options]
```

Here are the frequently used options that can be found in the command-line tools:

| Command | Description |
|---|---|
| compile | Compile Solidity contract files |
| console | Command-line interface for interacting with the deployed smart contract |
| create | This command helps to create a new contract, new migration file, and basic test |
| debug | Experiment on a particular transaction in a debugger session |
| deploy/migration | Deploy a contract to the blockchain network |
| develop | Interact with a contract using the command line in a local development environment |
| init | Install a package from the Ethereum package registry |

With the preceding commands, we can do the following:

- Create a Truffle project
- Compile smart contracts
- Deploy smart contracts to a designated blockchain

We just saw a truffle command, so let's install Truffle in our development environment. We will assume that you have npm installed in your environment; if not, please refer to the Node.js installation guide (https://nodejs.org/en/download/package-manager/). Open the command line and run the following command:

```
npm install -g truffle
```

This will install Truffle in your local drive. In this book, we will use Truffle version 5.0.15. Also, make sure that Solidity has been upgraded to version 0.5.2 or above.

Run the following command if you haven't upgraded to the newer version of solc-js, a JavaScript binding for the Solidity compiler:

```
npm install -g solc@latest
```

To run smart contracts, you need to deploy smart contracts to the blockchain. The Truffle site provides a Ganache private blockchain that is very easy to use as your local private blockchain development environment. Let's take a quick look at what Ganache is.

Ganache is a private Ethereum blockchain that helps you to interact with smart contracts in your DApps. Here are some of the features that Ganache provides:

- Displays blockchain log output
- Provides advanced mining control
- Built-in block explorer
- Ethereum blockchain environment

Ganache has a desktop application as well as a command-line tool. This is what the desktop version of Ganache looks like:

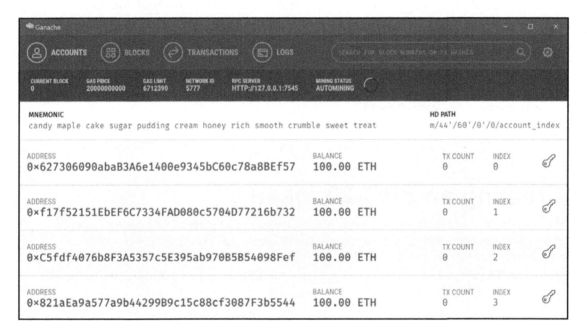

The Ganache command line uses the following format:

```
ganache-cli <options>
```

Here are some frequently used options in the command-line tools:

| Options | Description |
|---|---|
| -a or --accounts | This for the number of accounts to generate at startup. |
| -e or --defaultBalanceEther | Configure the default test account ether amount; the default is 100. |

| | |
|---|---|
| -b or --blockTime | Specify the block time in seconds as a mining interval. If this option is not specified, Ganache will instantly mine a new block when a transaction is invoked. |
| -h or --host or --hostname | Specify hostname to listen on; the default is 127.0.0.1. |
| -p or --port | Specify the port number; the default is 8545. |
| -g or --gasPrice | Specify the gas price in wei (defaults to 20,000,000,000). |
| -l or --gasLimit | The block gas limit (defaults to 0x6691b7). |
| --debug | Display VM opcodes for debugging purposes. |
| -q or --quiet | Run ganache-cli without any logs. |

Now that we are familiar with the commands in Ganache, it is time to install a Ganache private blockchain in our development environment. This is quite straightforward.

Open the command line and install Ganache's command-line interface, as follows:

```
npm install -g ganache-cli
```

This will install Ganache in your local device.

# Creating an ERC-20 token

We have set up our working environment, so we can now start to add code as we walk through the explanation. In this section, we will create our cryptocurrency, called MyERC20Token. For this project, we will be using the Truffle framework and Solidity language. The idea of MyERC20Token is to use the ERC-20 token standard and issue our token.

Here is a list of token features we are going to build:

- The token name is MyERC20Token, with the symbol as MTK.
- The token must follow the ERC-20 standard.
- The token must specify the initial supply during its creation.
- The token owner can assign someone to the admin role.
- The admin can add an account to a whitelist and remove the account from the whitelist.
- The admin can lock or unlock the coins of anyone's account through a whitelist.
- The admin can transfer the administrator role to any other address.

- Anyone who is in the whitelist must be able to buy or sell the
  `MyERC20Token` coin using Ether.
- When calling `transfer` or `transferFrom`, it must check whether or not a
  transfer can be approved so that the coins can be moved to other people's
  accounts. A negative balance should not be allowed.
- The admin must be able to lock or unlock the coins of anyone's account.
- The admin can mint amounts of tokens to the total supply.
- The admin can burn amounts of tokens from the total supply.

We will use the `truffle init` command to download a basic project template for our
initial project, named `MyERC20Tokens`.

Create a `MyERC20Tokens` project directory and navigate to the directory to run the
following command:

```
truffle unbox tutorialtoken
```

The `truffle unbox` command will download Truffle's boilerplate project. It will create a
basic `truffle` tutorial. The token project structure is shown in the following screenshot:

The tutorial token project has a self-contained set of files, which includes the following:

- HTML, JavaScript files for web page display, and interaction between the
  frontend and smart contract
- Smart contract files under the `contracts` folder

- The `migrations` folder for smart contract deployment
- The `test` folder for unit tests

Now that we have the project set up, we will create our `MyERC20Tokens` smart contract.

Many desktop IDEs can be used to develop a smart contract, such as Visual Studio Code, Atom, and Sublime Text. You can also use an online IDE such as Remix. We will explore Remix in more detail in `Chapter 6`, *Smart Contract Development and Test Fundamentals*.

For the `MyERC20Tokens` project, we will use Visual Studio Code. There are many Solidity plugins available, such as Solidity, Solidity language support to support syntax highlight, and auto-completion. You can download extensions from **Visual Studio Marketplace**. Follow these steps to get started:

1. Open the `MyERC20Tokens` project in Visual Studio Code.
2. Create a file called `MyERC20Token.sol` in the `contracts` folder.

This will create an empty Solidity file. With the basic project set up, it is time to implement `MyERC20Tokens` features. We will start with ERC-20's basic features. The project's source code can be found in this book's GitHub repository, at `https://github.com/PacktPublishing/Learn-Ethereum`. In this chapter, we will explain how we can implement token logic. In the next section, we will do the unit test and run the example in the blockchain environment.

# Creating basic token information

Each ERC-20 token should have basic token information, such as name, symbol, and more. In our case, the token name is `MyERC20Token` and the symbol is `MTK`. We will also define the total token supply while we initialize the token.

Let's create a `TokenSummary` struct to hold the basic token information, as shown in the following code snippet:

```
pragma solidity ^0.5.2;
....
TokenSummary public tokenSummary;
mapping(address => uint256) internal balances;
uint256 internal _totalSupply;
struct TokenSummary {
    address initialAccount;
    string name;
    string symbol;
  }
```

```
    constructor(string memory _name, string memory  _symbol,
    address initialAccount, uint initialBalance)
public payable {
        addWhitelist(initialAccount);
        balances[initialAccount] = initialBalance;
        _totalSupply = initialBalance;
        tokenSummary = TokenSummary(initialAccount, _name, _symbol);
    }
```

In the preceding code, we initialized the token name, symbol, initial balance, and total supply through the constructor. We also assigned the token owner as whitelisted at the time of smart contract creation. We will discuss the whitelist function in the upcoming section. The initial balance will be stored in a storage mapping known as `balances`.

# Defining and implementing the ERC-20 interface

Each ERC-20 token must implement the following six mandatory functions. We define the ERC-20 token interface as follows. `MyERC20Token` will implement the ERC-20 interface:

```
interface ERC20 {
    function transfer(address to, uint256 value) external returns (bool);
    function approve(address spender, uint256 value) external returns
(bool);
    function transferFrom(address from, address to, uint256 value) external
returns (bool);
    function totalSupply() external view returns (uint256);
     function balanceOf(address who) external view returns (uint256);
     function allowance(address owner, address spender) external view
returns (uint256);
    event Transfer(address indexed from, address indexed to, uint256
value);
    event Approval(address indexed owner, address indexed spender, uint256
value);
}
contract MyERC20Token is ERC20 {
}
```

In the preceding code, `totalSupply()` returns the total token supply. We provided the total supply while instantiating the contract. For the implementation of `MyERC20Token` `totalSupply()`, it just needs to read the `totalSupply` variable. As shown in the following code, `_totalSupply` is returned, which is initialized with `initialBalance`:

```
    function totalSupply() public view returns (uint256) {
        return _totalSupply;
    }
```

The `balanceOf()` function gets the balance of the account for the given address. Similarly, we can read the balance from balance's mapping storage per input account address, as shown in the following code:

```
function balanceOf(address account) public view returns (uint256) {
    return balances[account];
}
```

In the `transfer()` function, we need to make sure that the target address is valid and that the sender has enough tokens to transfer to the target address. The contract will deposit the requested amount of tokens to the target address. The `emit Transfer` event will log the transaction in the blockchain.

In short, the `transfer()` function allows a certain amount of tokens to be transferred from the owner's account to another account and must fire the transfer event. You can see this implementation in the following code:

```
function transfer (address to, uint256 value) public returns (bool
success) {
        require(to != address(0) && balances[msg.sender]> value);
        balances[msg.sender] = balances[msg.sender] - value;
        balances[to] = balances[to] + value;
        emit Transfer(msg.sender, to, value);
        return true;
    }
```

The `approve()` function allows the spender to withdraw a certain amount from your account. First, the function checks whether the spenders' account is valid, and then approval is sent to the spender to transfer an amount. The approval process will be emitted to the blockchain transaction log. You can see the implementation in the following code:

```
function approve(address spender, uint256 value) public returns (bool) {
        require(spender != address(0));
        allowed[msg.sender][spender] = value;
        emit Approval(msg.sender, spender, value);
        return true;
    }
```

The `allowance()` function returns the allowance amount from the owner. With transfer approval in the `approve()` function, the allowance will be returned, as shown in the following implementation:

```
function allowance(address owner, address spender) public view returns
(uint256) {
    return allowed[owner][spender];
}
```

The `transferFrom()` function sends the specified number of tokens from the `from` address to the `spender` address. This method is used for the withdrawal process, allowing contracts to transfer tokens on your behalf. You can see its implementation in the following code:

```
function transferFrom(address from, address spender,uint256 value) public
(bool) {
        require(spender != address(0) && value <= balances[from] && value
<= allowed[from][msg.sender]);
        balances[from] = balances[from] - value;
        balances[spender] = balances[spender] + value;
        allowed[from][msg.sender] = allowed[from][msg.sender] - value;
        emit Transfer(from, spender, value);
        return true;
    }
```

So far, we have implemented the ERC-20 interface. Now, let's work on token permissions. Some token functions only allow admins to have access privileges. To enable token permission control, we need to create specific roles, for example, the `admin` role.

# Assigning an admin role

The `MyERC20Token` contract owner has permissions to add and remove admins. To only grant permission to the owner to assign an admin, we need to use the access restriction design pattern we discussed in Chapter 4, *Solidity Fundamentals*. Access restriction is a Solidity security pattern. It only allows authorized parties to access certain functions. Due to the public nature of the blockchain, all of the data on the blockchain is visible to anyone. It is critical to declare your contract function, the state with restricted access control, and provide security against unauthorized access to smart contract functionality. As such, we define `onlyOwner` as a modifier to only allow owner access functionality and `onlyAdmin` as a modifier to only allow admin access functionality. Here is the owned contract:

```
contract owned {
    address public owner;
    mapping(address => bool) admins;
...
    modifier onlyOwner { require(msg.sender == owner); _; }
    modifier onlyAdmin() { require(admins[msg.sender] == true);  _; }
    function transferOwnership(address newOwner) onlyOwner public {
owner=newOwner; }
    function isAdmin(address account) onlyOwner public view returns (bool)
{return admins[account]; }
    function addAdmin(address account) onlyOwner public {
        require(account != address(0) && !admins[account]); admins[account]
```

```
= true;
        }
    function removeAdmin(address account) onlyOwner public {
        require(account != address(0) && !admins[account]); admins[account]
= true;
        }
    }
```

So far, we've defined the owner and admin modifier and enabled token role-based access permission. Next, we will build a token whitelist function to allow individual accounts to be added to the whitelist by the admin. Let's do it.

# Working with the whitelist function

A whiteList function is a method where a token owner can control who holds their tokens. The MyERC20Token contract defines the following whitelist-related functions:

- The admin can add an account to the whitelist and remove the account from the whitelist.
- Using the previously defined onlyAdmin function, we can write addWhiteList and store whitelist addresses in mapping storage.
- By reading whitelisted storage, we can check the target address, that is, IsWhiteList. The admin can remove the account from whitelisted storage.

Take a look at the implementation in the following code:

```
contract Whitelist is owned {
    mapping(address => bool) whitelist;
    function addWhitelist(address account) onlyAdmin public{
        require(account != address(0) && !whitelist[account]);
        whitelist[account] = true;
    }
    function isWhitelist(address account) public view returns (bool) {
        return whitelist[account];
    }
    function removeWhitelisted(address account) public onlyAdmin {
        require(account != address(0) && whitelist[account]);
        whitelist[account] = false;
    }
}
```

Anyone who is on the whitelist will be able to buy or sell tokens using the `validateTransferRestricted()` method. It checks whether the target address is in the whitelist address pool. Based on the result, it verifies that all of the required buyer and seller accounts must be in the whitelist. The function also provides built-in messages and a code management solution. Let's take a look at the following code:

```
uint8 public constant SUCCESS_CODE = 0;
string public constant SUCCESS_MESSAGE = "SUCCESS";
uint8 public constant NON_WHITELIST_CODE = 1;
string public constant NON_WHITELIST_ERROR =
"ILLEGAL_TRANSFER_TO_NON_WHITELISTED_ADDRESS"
 modifier verify (address from, address to, uint256 value) {
    uint8 restrictionCode = validateTransferRestricted(to);
    require(restrictionCode == SUCCESS_CODE,
messageHandler(restrictionCode)); _;
 }
  function validateTransferRestricted (address to) public view returns
(uint8 restrictionCode) {
    if (!isWhitelist(to)) { restrictionCode = NON_WHITELIST_CODE;
    } else { restrictionCode = SUCCESS_CODE; }
 }
  function messageHandler (uint8 restrictionCode) public pure returns
(string memory message) {
    if (restrictionCode == SUCCESS_CODE) {message = SUCCESS_MESSAGE;}
    else if(restrictionCode == NON_WHITELIST_CODE){message
=NON_WHITELIST_ERROR;}
  }
    function transfer (address to, uint256 value) public verify(msg.sender,
to, value)  returns (bool success) {}
    function transferFrom(address from, address spender,uint256
value) public verify(from, spender, value) returns (bool) {}
```

We have built the whitelist functions, and we can allow and restrict some accounts to functions based on the whitelist. Next, we will look at the lock and unlock account functions.

# Locking and unlocking an account

The `MyERC20Token` contract requires an admin who has the ability to lock or unlock the coins of anyone's account. The pausable contract defines the `whenNotPaused` and `whenPaused` modifiers. By checking the `paused` flag, the smart contract can toggle between the paused and not paused contract state. The following code shows this implementation:

```
contract Pausable is owned {
    event PausedEvt(address account);
```

```
    event UnpausedEvt(address account);
    bool private paused;
    constructor () internal { paused = false; }
    modifier whenNotPaused() {require(!paused);   _; }
    modifier whenPaused(); {require(paused);   _; }
    function pause() public onlyAdmin whenNotPaused {
        paused = true;   emit PausedEvt(msg.sender);
    }
    function unpause() public onlyAdmin whenPaused {
        paused = false; emit UnpausedEvt(msg.sender);
    }
}
```

We can apply the modifier to `MyERC20Token`:

```
function transfer (address to, uint256 value) public verify(msg.sender, to,
value)
whenNotPaused  returns (bool success) {}
function transferFrom(address from, address spender,uint256 value) public
verify(from, spender, value) whenNotPaused returns (bool) {}
function burn(uint256 value) public whenNotPaused onlyAdmin returns (bool
success) {}
function mint(address account, uint256 value) public whenNotPaused
onlyAdmin returns (bool) { }
```

We can now lock and unlock our smart contract. In some cases, we also need to control our token supply, which will be done through the functions to increase (`mint`) and remove (`burn`) tokens. Let's take a look at how to build the `mint` and `burn` functions.

# The mint and burn tokens

We have implemented most of the `MyERC20Token` features. One more useful feature that's widely used in many stablecoins is the `mint` and `burn` functions. By using the `burn` and `mint` functions, the platform can maintain its 1-to-1 peg to USD. All of the mint and burn transactions are tracked in the blockchain transaction.

The `burn` function reduces the target address' token values and total supply values. The `mint` function increases the target address' token values and total supply values. Here is the implementation:

```
function burn(uint256 value) public whenNotPaused onlyAdmin returns (bool
success) {
    require(balances[msg.sender] >= value);
    balances[msg.sender] -= value;
    _totalSupply -= value;
```

```
      emit Burn(msg.sender, value);
      return true;
  }
   function mint(address account, uint256 value) public onlyAdmin returns
(bool) {
      require(account != address(0));
      _totalSupply = _totalSupply += value;
      balances[account] = balances[account] + value;
      emit Transfer(address(0), account, value);
      return true;
  }
```

By doing this, we have defined and implemented all of our MyERC20Token features. We will need to write a unit test and run truffle test to verify these functions. In the next section, we are going to define and implement another popular ERC token – the ERC 721 token. We will also write a smart contract called DigitalArtERC721Token for that. Let's get started.

# Creating ERC 721 token – the DigitalArt token

For an artist, when they want to sell their product, it is often hard to connect dealers and collectors. If they manage to connect with dealers and collectors, the party on the other side may not be interested in buying the artist's product. Selling their art to the next owner may take a long time due to the many layers of the middleman. The entire process is not transparent and not efficient. Blockchain, however, is a technology that can provide you with opportunities to make the process more transparent.

An art gallery is a great example of an ERC-721 token use case. ERC-721 tokens are non-fungible tokens and essentially have a unique identity that can be used to represent digital ownership. The token itself is genetically traceable. When a digital art owner assigns a unique token ID, along with the original author's information, the art token can be used to track the entire transaction history when product ownership is transferred to its current owner. Other information can also be attached to the token for tracing, such as the artist's information, the painting topic, a description, and the sales agreement.

# Designing the decentralized digital art marketplace

The decentralized digital art platform provides the artist with a place to sell their arts, and thereby a buyer finds a marketplace. It has the following features:

- It allows artists to easily sell their product without a third party, with no hidden fee during the transaction
- All art trading history is available in the blockchain; it is transparent
- The user can browse digital arts in the art gallery
- Each piece of art shows its product information
- The product owner can resell the art with the desired price
- Once a deal has been completed, the ownership of the art will be transferred, and the buyer will pay the seller for the art

In order to develop a smart contract, we need to set up the project.

# Setting up the DigitalArtERC721Token project

We used `truffle suite` to create `MyERC20Token` in the previous section. Let's create a `DigitalArtERC721Token` Truffle project using the same Truffle project setup process we used earlier. The project source code can be found in this book's GitHub repository at `https://github.com/PacktPublishing/Learn-Ethereum`. Under the `contracts` folder, create a Solidity file called `DigitalArtERC721Token.sol`.

Import the project into your IDE and open `DigitalArtERC721Token.sol`. We are now ready to implement our ERC-721 token.

With the basic project set up, it is time to implement the features for `DigitalArtERC721Token`. We will start with ERC-721's basic features.

# Creating the basic token information

Each ERC-721 token should have basic token information, such as name, symbol, and more. In our case, the token name is `DigitalArtToken`, and the symbol is `DT`. We set up a token name and symbol when we initialize the token. Here is the implementation:

```
string private _name;
string private _symbol;
```

```
constructor (string memory name, string memory symbol) public {
    _name = name; _symbol = symbol;
}
function name() external view returns (string memory) {return _name;}
function symbol() external view returns (string memory) {return _symbol;}
}
```

In the preceding code, we provide a token name and symbol when instantiating the contract. The `name()` and `symbol()` methods provide the token name and symbol-related information. When instantiating `DigitalArtToken`, we start by defining and implementing the ERC-721 interface, which is what we will do next.

# Defining and implementing the ERC-721 standard

Each ERC-721 token must implement the following nine mandatory functions. We will define the ERC-721 token interface as shown in the following code, and `DigitalArtERC721Token` will implement the ERC-721 interface. Here is the ERC-721 interface:

```
contract ERC721 {
event Transfer(address indexed from, address indexed to, uint256 indexed
tokenId);
event Approval(address indexed owner, address indexed approved, uint256
indexed tokenId);
event ApprovalForAll(address indexed owner, address indexed operator, bool
approved);
function balanceOf(address owner) public view returns (uint256 balance);
function ownerOf(uint256 tokenId) public view returns (address owner);
function approve(address to, uint256 tokenId) public;
function getApproved(uint256 tokenId) public view returns (address
operator);
function setApprovalForAll(address operator, bool _approved) public;
function isApprovedForAll(address owner, address operator) public view
returns (bool);
function transferFrom(address from, address to, uint256 tokenId) public;
function safeTransferFrom(address from, address to, uint256 tokenId)
public;
}
```

The `balanceOf`, `approve`, and `transferFrom` functions are quite similar to the ones in the ERC-20 token implementation. The `transfer()` function enables the transfer of token ownership from one address to another. In the following `transfer()` function implementation, `_tokenOwner` defines a mapping from the token ID to the owner. `_ownedTokensCount` defines the amount of ERC-721 tokens that are owned by the owner:

```
mapping (address => uint256) private _ownedTokensCount;
mapping (uint256 => address) private _tokenOwner;
function _transfer(address _from, address _to, uint256 _tokenId) private {
    _ownedTokensCount[_to]++;
    _ownedTokensCount[_from]--;
    _tokenOwner[_tokenId] = _to;
    emit Transfer(_from, _to, _tokenId);
}
```

The `balanceOf()` function in the following code gets the total number of tokens for the given address:

```
function balanceOf(address _owner) public view returns (uint256) {
    return _ownedTokensCount[_owner];
}
```

The `ownerOf()` function in the following code returns the unique address of the owner of a token by providing the `tokenId` variable:

```
function ownerOf(uint256 _tokenId) public view returns (address _owner)
{
    _owner = _tokenOwner[_tokenId];
}
```

The `transferFrom()` function in the following code transfers ownership of an NFT. The function that's required from the address is the token owner. The token transfer is approved prior to the call transfer:

```
function isOwnerOf(uint256 tokenId, address account) public view returns
(bool) {
    address owner = _tokenOwner[tokenId];
    require(owner != address(0));
    return owner == account;
}
function isApproved(address _to, uint256 _tokenId) private view returns
(bool) {
    return _tokenApprovals[_tokenId] == _to;
}
function transferFrom(address _from, address _to, uint256 _tokenId) public
{
    require(_to != address(0));
```

```
        require(isOwnerOf(_tokenId, _from));
        require(isApproved(_to, _tokenId));
        _transfer(_from, _to, _tokenId);
}
```

The `approve()` function in the following code approves another entity's permission in order to transfer a token on the owner's behalf. The function requires the message sender to be the owner of `tokenId`. The approved token is stored in the mapping storage of `tokenApprovals`:

```
mapping (uint256 => address) private _tokenApprovals;
function approve(address _to, uint256 _tokenId) public {
        require(isOwnerOf(_tokenId, msg.sender));
        _tokenApprovals[_tokenId] = _to;
        emit Approval(msg.sender, _to, _tokenId);
}
```

The `setApprovalForAll()` function in the following code enables or disables the approval of a third party (`operator`) to manage all of the assets for `msg.sender`:

```
mapping (address => mapping (address => bool)) private _operatorApprovals;
function setApprovalForAll(address operator, bool _approved) public {
        require(operator != msg.sender);
        _operatorApprovals[msg.sender][operator] = _approved;
        emit ApprovalForAll(msg.sender, operator, _approved);
}
```

The `getApproved()` function in the following code gets the approved address for a single NFT. This function verifies and makes sure that the transaction senders are the owners of the token and that the token transfer gets approved:

```
    function _exists(uint256 tokenId) internal view returns (bool) {
        address owner = _tokenOwner[tokenId];
        return owner != address(0);
    }
    function getApproved(uint256 tokenId) public view returns (address
operator) {
        require(_exists(tokenId));
        return _tokenApprovals[tokenId];
    }
```

The isApprovedForAll() function checks whether another address is allowed for an operator:

```
function isApprovedForAll(address owner, address operator) public view
returns (bool) {
  return _operatorApprovals[owner][operator];
}
```

So far, we have implemented the ERC-721 interface. Our token core logic is ready. Now, it'ss time to look at how we can define our art information in the smart contract.

# Defining the art and art transaction struct

When artists sell their art, they need to enter basic art information. When the buy and sell functions of DigitalArtERC721Token are invoked, we are able to trace all of the arts-related transactions. In the following code, we are defining the Art and ArtTxn structs in the smart contract:

```
struct Art {
    uint256 id;
    string title;
    string description;
    uint256 price;
    string date;
    string authorName;
    address payable author;
    address payable owner;
    uint status;
    string image;
}
struct ArtTxn {
    uint256 id;
    uint256 price;
    address seller;
    address buyer;
    uint txnDate;
    uint status;
}
```

Each art has its own token ID, title, description, price, author name, author address, owner address, and URL that's linked to the image.

The art transaction keeps track of these arts transaction records; it has a token ID, price, seller, buyer, transaction date, and status information.

# Creating a non-fungible digital art token

When art authors want to publish and sell their product, they need to fill in all art detail information:

- In our smart contract, we define a `status` field to track the sale's status. A status of `1` means that the token has a sale status. When it changes to `0`, this means it has been sold. Its ownership is transferred and is moved to the off-market gallery.
- Create a token by invoking a `mint` method, then `emit` the transaction event.
- Create an initial index value and assign it as a token ID. The index will keep increasing when creating a token to make sure it's unique. When we create a new art token, we store the art in the `Art[]` array. The token ID is the same as the array index.
- When a token is created for sale, `pendingArtCount` will keep track of the total number of digital pieces of art that have a selling status.

Here is the implementation in detail:

```
Art[] public arts;
uint256 private pendingArtCount;
function createTokenAndSellArt(string memory _title, string memory
_description,
string memory _date, string memory _authorName,  uint256 _price, string
memory _image) public {
      require(bytes(_title).length > 0, 'The title cannot be empty');
      require(bytes(_date).length > 0, 'The Date cannot be empty');
      require(bytes(_description).length > 0, 'The description cannot be
empty');
      require(_price > 0, 'The price cannot be empty');
      require(bytes(_image).length > 0, 'The image cannot be empty');
Art memory _art = Art({
id: index, title: _title, description: _description, price: _price,date:
_date, authorName: _authorName, author: msg.sender, owner: msg.sender,
status: 1, image: _image });
    uint256 tokenId = arts.push(_art) - 1;
    _mint(msg.sender, tokenId);
emit LogArtTokenCreate(tokenId,_title, _date,
_authorName,_price,msg.sender,msg.sender);
      index++;
      pendingArtCount++;
}
```

We were able to create the art token and list the art in the art market. Next, we will implement the buyer functions.

# Implementing the buyArt() function

The users can find art through the art gallery. If they like digital art, they can place an order to buy the art without going through the middleman. Let's implement the function, as shown in the following code:

```
mapping(uint256 => ArtTxn[]) private artTxns;
function buyArt(uint256 _tokenId) payable public {
        (uint256 _id, string memory _title, ,uint256 _price, uint
_status,,string memory _authorName, address _author,address payable
_current_owner, ) =  findArt(_tokenId);
        require(_current_owner != address(0));
        require(msg.sender != address(0));
        require(msg.sender != _current_owner);
        require(msg.value >= _price);
        require(arts[_tokenId].owner != address(0));
        _transfer(_current_owner, msg.sender, _tokenId);
        if(msg.value > _price) msg.sender.transfer(msg.value - _price);
        _current_owner.transfer(_price); arts[_tokenId].owner = msg.sender;
        arts[_tokenId].status = 0;
 ArtTxn memory _artTxn = ArtTxn({id: _id, price: _price, seller:
_current_owner, buyer: msg.sender, txnDate: now, status: _status });
        artTxns[_id].push(_artTxn);
        pendingArtCount--;
emit LogArtSold(_tokenId,_title,  _authorName,_price,
_author,_current_owner,msg.sender);
    }
```

The `buyArt()` function verifies whether the buyer has enough balance to purchase the art. The function also checks whether the seller and buyer both have a valid account address. The token owner's address is not the same as the buyer's address. The seller is the owner of the art. Once all of the conditions have been verified, it will start the payment and art token transfer process. `_transfer` transfers an art token from the seller to the buyer's address. `_current_owner.transfer` will transfer the buyer's payment amount to the art owner's account. If the seller pays extra Ether to buy the art, that ether will be refunded to the buyer's account.

Finally, the `buyArt()` function will update art ownership information in the blockchain. The status will change to `0`, also known as the sold status. The function implementations keep records of the art transaction in the `ArtTxn` array.

# Implementing the resellArt() function

When the art owner wants to resell their art with desired prices, they can republish the art product in the decentralized digital market. The art to be resold will be available to purchase in the art gallery. Here is the implementation in detail:

```
function resellArt(uint256 _tokenId, uint256 _price) payable public {
    require(msg.sender != address(0));
    require(isOwnerOf(_tokenId,msg.sender));
    arts[_tokenId].status = 1;
    arts[_tokenId].price = _price;
    pendingArtCount++;
    emit LogArtResell(_tokenId, 1, _price);
}
```

The resellArt() function verifies whether the sender's address is valid and makes sure that only the current art owner is allowed to resell the art. Then, the resellArt() function updates the art status from 0 to 1 and moves to the sale state. It also updates the art's selling price and increases the count of the current total pending arts. emit LogArtResell() is used to add a log to the blockchain for the art's status and price changes.

# Implementing the findArt() function

The user finds art details through the findArt() function by passing the art token ID. This will return the token ID, title, description, price status, publish date, author name, author address, owner address, and image information. The following code block shows the code implementation for this:

```
function findArt(uint256 _tokenId) public view    returns (
        uint256, string memory, string memory, uint256, uint status,
    string memory, string memory, address, address payable, string memory) {
    Art memory art = arts[_tokenId];
        return (art.id, art.title, art.description, art.price,    art.status,
    art.date, art.authorName, art.author, art.owner,art.image);
    }
```

The preceding function will return art detail based on tokenId. In Chapter 7, *Writing a UI for DApps*, we will learn more about this smart contract as we use DApps in detail there. Next, we will implement findMyArts() to list all of the art pieces under the owner's account.

# Implementing the findMyArts() function

The findMyArts() function returns the current account's user list of owned digital art token IDs. It checks whether the art owner's address is the same as the current account user's address:

```
function findMyArts()  public view returns (uint256[] memory _myArts) {
        require(msg.sender != address(0));
        uint256 numOftokens = balanceOf(msg.sender);
        if (numOftokens == 0) { return new uint256[](0);
        } else {
            uint256[] memory myArts = new uint256[](numOftokens);
            uint256 idx = 0; uint256 arrLength = arts.length;
            for (uint256 i = 0; i < arrLength; i++) {
                if (_tokenOwner[i] == msg.sender) { myArts[idx] = i;
idx++; }
            }
            return myArts;
        }
    }
```

The function makes sure that the sender's address is valid. Then, it loads the number of tokens the owner has.

If there are art tokens that belong to the owner, it will load them from the myArts array by checking whether the token owner's address matches the current account owner's address. Next, we will look at the findAllPendingArt() function so that we can list the art in the market as for sale.

# Implementing the findAllPendingArt() function

This function returns all of the art pieces that have a selling status in an art gallery by comparing the art status with the sale status:

```
function findAllPendingArt() public view  returns (uint256[] memory,
address[] memory, address[] memory,  uint[] memory) {
    if (pendingArtCount == 0) {
      return (new uint256[](0),new address[](0), new address[](0), new
uint[](0));
        } else {
            uint256 arrLength = arts.length;
            uint256[] memory ids = new uint256[](pendingArtCount);
            address[] memory authors = new address[](pendingArtCount);
            address[] memory owners= new address[](pendingArtCount);
            uint[] memory status = new uint[](pendingArtCount);
```

```
            uint256 idx = 0;
            for (uint i = 0; i < arrLength; ++i) {
                Art memory art = arts[i];
                if(art.status==1) {
                    ids[idx] = art.id; authors[idx] = art.author;
                    owners[idx] = art.owner; status[idx] = art.status;
idx++;
                }
            }
            return (ids,authors, owners, status);
        }
    }
```

The findAllPendingArt() function loops through all of the art in the market. It will check whether the art status is pending, which means that these art pieces are still on the market for sale. Once it finds the pending status, it will add it to the display list. Then, we can use the return pending art list to display the art work details in the web UI.

Next, we will discuss how to get all art transactions.

# Getting all art transactions through getArtAllTxn()

When a user makes a deal for an art trade, the transaction records are stored in the artTxns mapping storage. By reading this value, we will get all of the transaction history for the digital art trade. Here is the code implementation:

```
function getArtAllTxn(uint256 _tokenId) public view  returns (uint256[]
memory _id, uint256[] memory _price,address[] memory seller,address[]
memory buyer, uint[] memory _txnDate ){
  ArtTxn[] memory artTxnList = artTxns[_tokenId];
   uint256 arrLength = artTxnList.length;
   uint256[] memory ids = new uint256[](arrLength);
   uint256[] memory prices = new uint256[](arrLength);
   address[] memory sellers = new address[](arrLength);
   address[] memory buyers = new address[](arrLength);
   uint[] memory txnDates = new uint[](arrLength);
   for (uint i = 0; i < artTxnList.length; ++i) {
     ArtTxn memory artTxn = artTxnList[i];
      ids[i] = artTxn.id;prices[i] = artTxn.price;
      sellers[i] =artTxn.seller; buyers[i] =artTxn.buyer; txnDates[i]
=artTxn.txnDate;
   }
   return (ids,prices,sellers,buyers, txnDates);
 }
```

The `getArtAllTxn()` function retrieved the `ArtTxn[]` array storage from `artTxns` by passing in a `tokenId`. If the art token was traded in the past, that information would be stored in the `ArtTxn[]` array in the blockchain. This means that we can look at the transaction history. We can view past transaction details, including who owned the token and when, when the token owner sold the token and for what price, and so on. The entire art transaction is traceable in the blockchain. Information regarding the art deal is transparent.

# Summary

In this chapter, we covered the most popular ERC token standards – ERC-20 and ERC-721. We set up a Truffle project and developed an ERC-20 token called `MYERC20Token`. We also implemented the ERC-20 interface with many additional token functions. Finally, we continued to implement ERC-721 for a digital art non-fungible token, which we used for an art trade.

In the next chapter, we will continue our learning journey and start to learn about Ethereum tools and unit tests.

# 3
# Section 3: Ethereum Implementations

In this section, we will continue with our DigitalArt token DApp development and unit testing. We will also explore various Ethereum tools and frameworks.

This section comprises of the following chapters:

- Chapter 6, *Smart Contract Development and Test Fundamentals*
- Chapter 7, *Writing a UI for our DApps*
- Chapter 8, *Ethereum Tools and Frameworks*

# 6
# Smart Contract Development and Test Fundamentals

In this chapter, we will show you how to use Remix to develop and debug a smart contract. We will explore various options for the Truffle suite tool. We will also cover smart contract unit tests by testing the smart contract we wrote in the previous chapter.

The purpose of this chapter is to help you to understand various development tools, unit tests, and security tests and to help you to brush up on your Ethereum development knowledge and skills. This chapter is organized around three major topics:

- Understanding Remix development fundamentals
- Understanding development using Truffle and unit testing
- Security testing

First, let's take a look at one of the most popular online development tools—Remix!

## Technical Requirements

For all the source code of this book, please refer the following GitHub link :

`https://github.com/PacktPublishing/Learn-Ethereum`

# Understanding Remix development fundamentals

In Chapter 5, *Developing Your Own Cryptocurrency*, we discussed the ERC-20 and ERC-721 smart contracts and wrote smart contract functions. Now, we can do a quick code verification using the Remix online IDE before we use Truffle to write a unit test. We learned about a basic Remix online IDE feature in Chapter 4, *Solidity Fundamentals*. In this section, we will explore more Remix features, namely the following:

- Working with the Solidity compiler
- Analysis
- Testing
- Deploying and running transactions
- Debugging

Remix provides both online and local versions to work with. The online version is available at https://remix.ethereum.org. To install Remix on our local device, run the following npm command:

```
npm install -g remix-ide
remix-ide
```

Once it has been installed successfully, run the remix-ide command and open localhost:8080, as shown in the following screenshot:

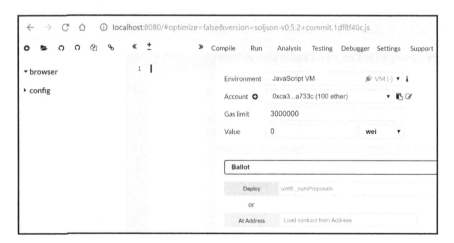

Now, let's write some code and compile it.

# Working with the Solidity compiler

The Solidity version we're using is 0.5.2 and above, so you need to select a Solidity compiler version equal to or higher than 0.5.2. When auto compile is selected, it will detect each change on a smart contract and compile it. Alternatively, you can manually click the **Start to Compile** button; it will trigger the file compile process.

When clicking the **Detail** button, it will display compiled contract information, including the ABI, contract name, metadata, function's hash, and user document. This is shown in the following screenshot:

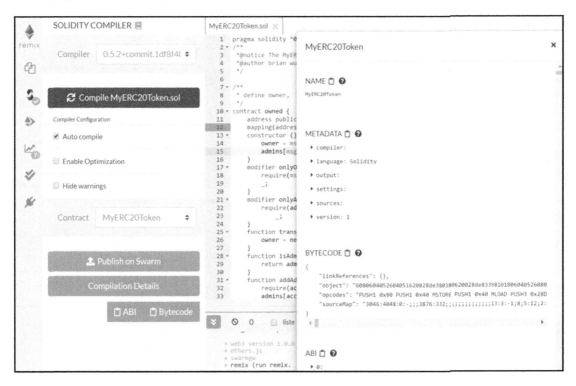

The contract drop-down manual has a drop-down option when there are multiple contracts. The **Publish on Swarm** button provides support for pushing the metadata of the target smart contract to a swarm. This metadata can be used to verify the smart contract source code or to retrieve the web3 JSON interface via a remote swarm. Swarm is a decentralized data storage. Once successfully published, the screen will show the buzz-raw URL location. The smart contract that's published to Swarm, as shown in the following screenshot, can be used to verify the smart contract source code:

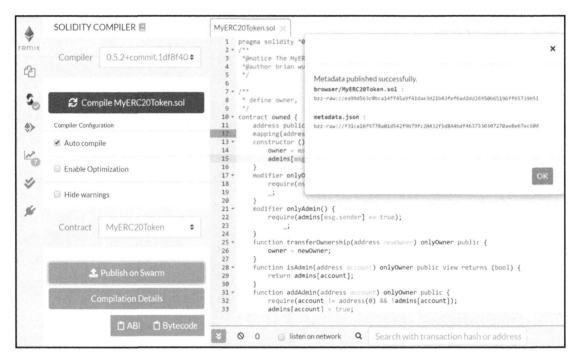

When there is a warning or error, as shown in the following screenshot, it will show the relevant message during the contract session. It is very helpful to address contract issues during development:

```
Static Analysis raised 28 warning(s) that requires your attention.  ✖
Click here to show the warning(s).
```

```
remix_tests.sol:2:1: Warning: Source file does no✖
library Assert {
^ (Relevant source part starts here and spans acr
```

```
browser/ballot_test.sol:2:1: Warning: Source file✖
import "remix_tests.sol"; // this import is autom
^ (Relevant source part starts here and spans acr
```

We just reviewed the Remix compile feature; next, we will take a look at the analysis feature.

# Analysis

This section provides information after each contract compiles. It applies the best practice rules on security, gas, and economy, as well as other miscellaneous areas. This information helps you write good quality code and follow best practices.

Here are a few Remix analyzers:

| Category | Analyzer Item | Reason |
|---|---|---|
| Security | Transaction origin. | When using `tx.origin`, the owner can never be a contract. We should avoid using `tx.origin`. |
| Check effects | Could cause reentrancy issues. | |
| Inline assembly | Inline assembly can access the EVM at a low level; this could bypass Solidity security features. | |

| | | |
|---|---|---|
| Block timestamp | There is no cryptographic way to verify the timestamp itself; semantics may be unclear. | |
| Low-level calls | Semantics may be unclear. | |
| `Block.blockhash` usage | Semantics may be unclear. | |
| Self-destruct | The function can be used to forcibly send ether to any contract unconditionally. This could cause a security issue. | |
| Gas and economy | Gas costs | Gives warning that gas value is too high |
| This on local calls | Invocation of local functions via `this`. | |
| Delete on dynamic Array | When an array is large, it could cause an **Out Of Gas (OOG)** exception. | |
| A `for` loop iterates over the dynamic array | The unbounded or large number iteration is an anti-pattern and could cause OOG exception. | |
| Miscellaneous | Constant functions. | Checks whether the function is constant |
| Similar variable names | A very similar name can cause confusion. | |
| no return | When a function has a return type, but the implementation doesn't return any. | |
| Guard conditions | Use require appropriately. | |
| Result not used | Avoid the case where the result of an operation was not used. | |
| String length | Be aware that byte length is not equal to String length. | |
| Delete from dynamic array | It will leave a gap. | |

Remix also supports unit testing, so let's take a quick look while we're here.

# Testing

Remix unit testing allows you to generate a Solidity contract test file with `suffixed_test`. The test file contains a set of minimum test methods for running unit testing. You can add more unit test functions in the test file. After it runs the tests, it will display a test result, as shown in the following screenshot:

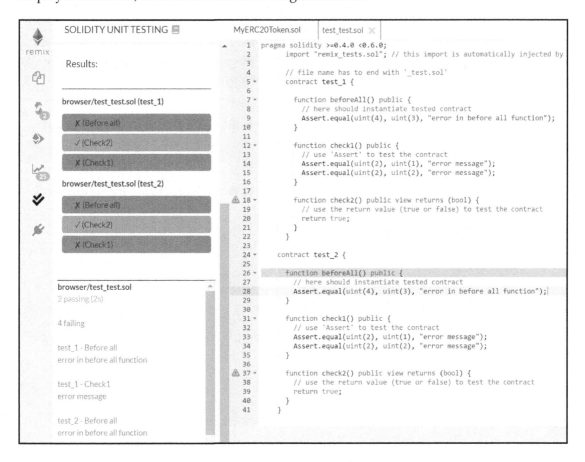

We can see that the Remix unit test generates a unit test report. The failed test cases are shown in red. The success test cases are displayed in green. You can fix failed unit tests based on the test result.

# Deploying and running transactions

The Remix IDE provides three types of environments to execute transactions:

- **JavaScript VM**: The sandbox environment runs emulated blockchain transactions in your browser. It provides 10 test addresses with 100 ether by default. This mode is convenient for quick prototyping and verification of a smart contract.
- **Injected provider**: The provider connects to an external tool such as MetaMask.
- **Web3 provider**: The provider connects to the remote node with geth or other Ethereum clients. It can directly connect to a private network and Ethereum blockchain.

In this section, we will use a JavaScript VM to deploy and run the MYERC20Token smart contract:

1. Select a JavaScript VM.
2. In the **Contract** drop-down menu, select MYERC20Token. Enter the following contract information:

   ```
   name: 'MyERC20Token.'
   symbol:'MTK'
   initialAccount: the first account address
   initialBalance: 100000000000000000000
   ```

   Now, as shown in the following screenshot:

3. Adjust the gas limit if needed. For this example, we will use 6,000,000 as the gas limit.
4. Click on **Deploy**:

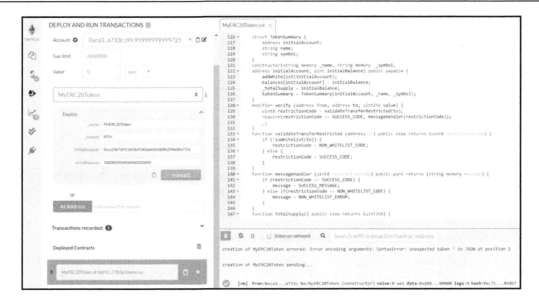

This should deploy `MYERC20Token` to the JavaScript VM emulated blockchain.

5. Verify `balanceOf` by entering the first account address. The `balanceOf` run will be invoked and you will see the balance is `100000000000000000000`, as shown in the following screenshot:

6. Verify that token transfer isn't allowed between non-whitelist accounts. So far, only the first account (contract owner) is assigned as a whitelist; when ether is transferred from the first to a second account, the transaction should be reverted. This is shown in the following screenshot:

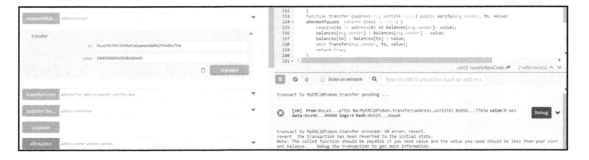

7. Verify that `validateTransferRestricted` passes the second account address, since it is not in the whitelist. We should see that **NON_WHITELIST_CODE 1** is returned, as shown here:

8. Verify `messageHandler` by entering 1 as the restriction code. The message should return **ILLEGAL_TRANSFER_TO_NON_WHITELISTED_ADDRESS**, as shown here:

9. Verify that only the contract owner is allowed to add the account as the admin using the following steps:

   1. Select the first account (owner) and verify that the second account is not an admin by calling `isAdmin()` with the second account address. The function should return `false`, as shown in the following screenshot:

   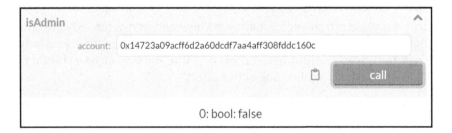

   2. Select the second account and add it as an admin by calling `addAdmin()`. Since the second account is not the owner, we should see the transaction showing an error message in the console, as shown here:

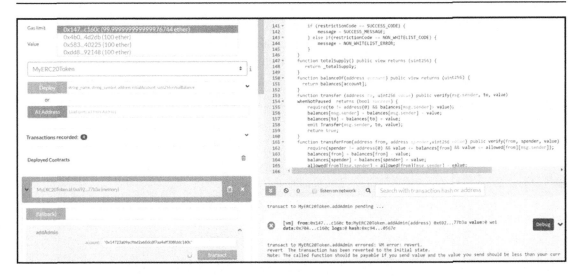

3. Select the first account and add the second account as an admin by calling `addAdmin()`. Since the first account is the owner, the second account should be added as an admin, as shown here:

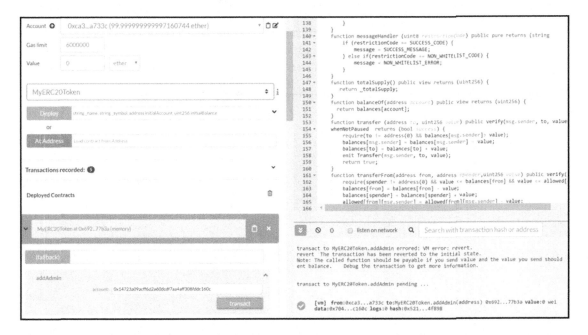

10. Allow the contract admin to whitelist an account. Select the admin account (the first or second) and add the second account to the whitelist by calling `addWhitelist()`. We will see that the second account is in the whitelist, as shown here:

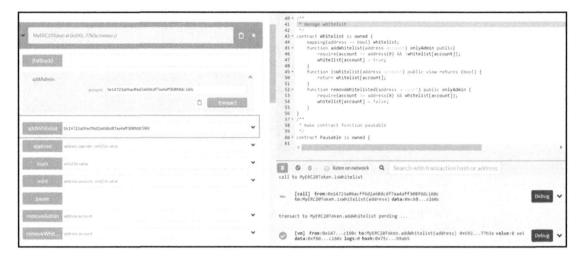

11. Do not allow transfers when a contract is paused. Select the first account (owner) to pause the contract. Transfer a certain amount to the second account. We will see that the transfer failed with an error message being displayed, as shown here:

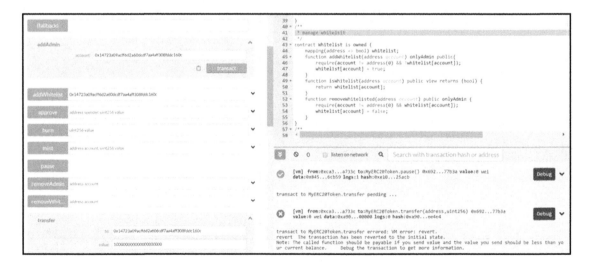

12. Now, we need to allow transfers between whitelisted accounts. Let's transfer 100,000,000,000,000,000 wei (0.1 ether) from the first account to the second. The 0.1 ether should transfer to the second account, as shown in the following screenshot:

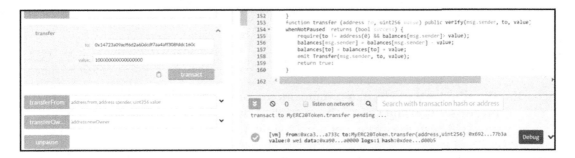

13. Allow the use of `transferFrom` between whitelisted accounts:
    1. Select the second account and call `approve()` by entering the first account as a spender and the value amount as 100,000,000,000,000,000 wei (0.1 ether).
    2. Then, switch to the first account and call `transferFrom()` by entering the second account as **from**, the first account as **spender**, and 100,000,000,000,000,000 wei (0.1 ether) as the **value**. The 0.1 ether will be transferred from the second account to the first account, as shown here:

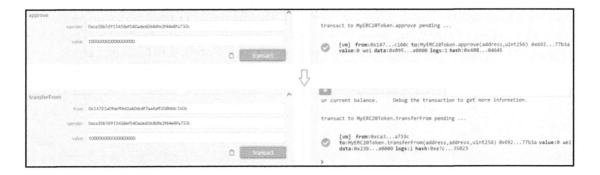

14. The admin should mint a certain amount of tokens—select an admin account (the first or second) and call the mint method by entering a target address and a certain amount of weis. This will mint the token amount to the target account, as shown here:

15. The admin should burn a certain amount of tokens. Select an admin account (the first or second) and call the **burn** method by entering a certain amount of wei. This will burn the token amount, as shown here:

We just reviewed how to invoke transactions in Remix. In the next section, we'll learn how to debug smart contracts in Remix.

# Debugging

The Remix Terminal logs the transaction result for each execution. You can debug it when you want to understand each step in more detail. The debugger button shows up on the right-hand side of the message information in the Terminal. You can also find a debugger icon on the left-hand side of the menu bar and search for a transaction hash or a block number and transaction index, as shown in the following screenshot:

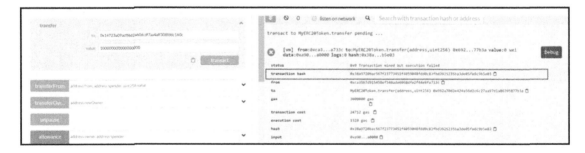

The debugger enables you to step through a Solidity smart contract and check each transaction step's state information to track down the bug. Similar to other popular IDE debuggers, the Remix debugger provides a group of debugger step buttons to let you play each step of the transaction. These include a step over the back breakpoint, step into back breakpoint, step into forward breakpoint, step over forward breakpoint, jump out (jump out of the current call) breakpoint, jump to the previous breakpoint, and jump to the next breakpoint. When the debugger starts from a breakpoint, you can run through each step by clicking one of the aforementioned buttons. One panel highlights the location in the source code where the current execution is happening.

In the following screenshot, the left panel contains the state viewer's contents, which displays basic information about the current step:

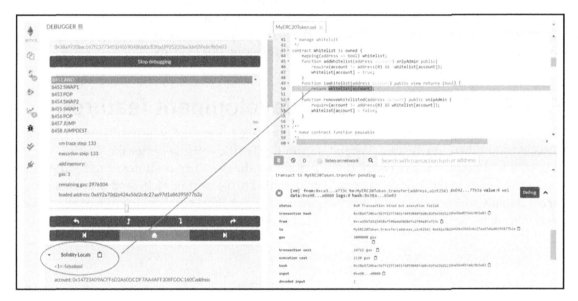

This is further detailed in the following items:

- **VM trace step**: This traces the index for the current VM trace step
- **Execution step**: This traces the index for the current execution step
- **Add memory**: This allocates memory
- **Gas**: This shows the gas expense in the current step
- **Remaining gas**: This shows the details of gas left
- **Loaded address**: This is the currently executing code address

At this stage, you should be familiar with the Remix IDE and with developing smart contracts using Solidity. In the next section, we will explore another very popular DApp development toolkit—Truffle.

# Understanding development using Truffle and unit testing

Truffle is a great tool that helps you to easily develop, compile, test, and deploy your smart contract in your development environment. You can use Truffle to easily set up a project and hook your frontend code with your deployed contract. In Chapter 5, *Developing Your Own Cryptocurrency*, we installed Truffle and briefly introduced the basic Truffle commands. In this section, we will cover Truffle development and unit testing in detail. First, let's take a look at the Truffle console and development features.

## The Truffle console and development features

The Truffle console provides a command-line interface to connect external clients, such as Ganache and Ethereum Testnet. When you run the Truffle console under the Truffle project, it will point to the network definition under the develop section in the Truffle config, as shown in the following code. The default Truffle port is 7545, and our Ganache server default port is 8545. Since we use Ganache as our local blockchain environment, we need to update the Truffle config (truffle.js) port number to 8545:

```
networks: {
    development: {
        host: "127.0.0.1",
        port: 8545,
        network_id: "*" // Match any network id
    }
}
```

Let's connect the local Ganache network through the Truffle console:

1. Start Ganache—open the Terminal and enter the ganache-cli command. This will start a local Ganache server; the default port is 8545. The Terminal will look as follows:

```
C:\Users\xunwu>ganache-cli
Ganache CLI v6.1.0 (ganache-core: 2.1.0)

Available Accounts
==================
(0) 0x0d1a8b4d7b1038b7e2970ce888e71da461c78a21
(1) 0x9dbb119fa9758a7620da8c467cb023b0e3dbd93b
(2) 0x6f49e7540ba480db4a6d58c9bf87ecbe7e25588e
(3) 0x4e725cec024edde16ef93f7d24857820401c4243
(4) 0x73a281052795c25e2a3121867eceaa17eba44d63
(5) 0x7c44663eaea825bac4324f99d4d67882e06d3da9
(6) 0xf89ead4d7be40ecdaf8aa77bdc8e4b9fdf59246f
(7) 0x46ce3fb037978cf1620e5103c4419ad02a00bbce
(8) 0xc1857cf79ebdfe5722d57fdd15945ba205205e64
(9) 0x5593a2dbe91334b5c3550d9e056b2c6c638529b2


Private Keys
==================
(0) e6b968cb2ec803b1cf899660eb70a3f27525206e8920c6370595603ae5fc3d57
(1) a0c4c69890194f2ba94f2a4c6e4982a053881b7d35aadca78ed35c2e06db07bd
(2) c7a544b397f86187398391ed12118a0a64631ed473fa1778a5fb3507dbd7316e
(3) 76e08ffe0b52cfed1e0b55bf672ae6c2135868c093481132e40d228c5a97245c
(4) 15c2723e6eb142e0c36decc39bfa24e5203674897d167a5583f5eebf53ffeae3
(5) dcb914121549681ed5d5f52d425616c2788901320d70a4d325e1f728df5bcd33
(6) 01a270a81149f73ae7443dff95cd7f3d0e0615c44d181087927d8b4e3101c1df
(7) 47ef44851c5d8ad249409e10e217444b29cb6947363c9b67d0b87168231f41aa
(8) d47b1b2809346dc475a0eb24478a4a4416f1d07332e59e31cdc7b94d6fd697c5
(9) 86654d33df370c67a6c36c64ff18654c343657c8cfc55774d484d1b86426805a


HD Wallet
==================
Mnemonic:      seed tired mean knee plug wrap advice skull grain number paddle want
Base HD Path:  m/44'/60'/0'/0/{account_index}

Listening on localhost:8545
```

2. Run the Truffle console under the `MYERC20Token` project, as shown here. It will connect to the Ganache local development network:

```
D:\documents\publish\Learn Ehereum\sourcecode\MyERC20Token>truff console
Warning: Please rename truffle.js to truffle-config.js to ensure Windows compatibility.
truffle(development)>
```

3. Then, you can compile and migrate to deploy a smart contract to the Ganache network. To compile, run the `compile` command, as shown in the following screenshot:

```
truffle(development)> compile
Warning: Please rename truffle.js to truffle-config.js to ensure Windows compatibility.

Compiling your contracts...
===========================
> Compiling .\contracts\MyERC20Token.sol
> Artifacts written to D:\documents\publish\Learn Ehereum\sourcecode\MyERC20Token\build\contracts
> Compiled successfully using:
   - solc: 0.5.8+commit.23d335f2.Emscripten.clang

truffle(development)>
```

4. To migrate, run the `migrate` command, as shown in the following screenshot:

```
truffle(development)> migrate
Warning: Please rename truffle.js to truffle-config.js to ensure Windows compatibility.

Compiling your contracts...
===========================
> Everything is up to date, there is nothing to compile.

Warning: Please rename truffle.js to truffle-config.js to ensure Windows compatibility.
Warning: Please rename truffle.js to truffle-config.js to ensure Windows compatibility.

Starting migrations...
======================
> Network name:    'development'
> Network id:      1558983611160
> Block gas limit: 0x6691b7


1_initial_migration.js
======================

   Deploying 'Migrations'
   ----------------------
   > transaction hash:    0x7e79d8556333cb4e27f50a9a016a58a7eee2fa1e51a468f5f0bb9d09e2bed15c
   > Blocks: 0           Seconds: 0
   > contract address:    0xD4C80e58028d1e37cde78A46bF78Ac7D635615Cb
   > block number:        1
   > block timestamp:     1558983929
   > account:             0x0D1a8b4d7B1038b7e2970ce888e71dA461C78A21
   > balance:             99.99453676
   > gas used:            273162
   > gas price:           20 gwei
   > value sent:          0 ETH
   > total cost:          0.00546324 ETH
```

The pre-generated `migrations.sol` file uses a different Solidity version, so if you run into an error, you may need to change the Solidity version of the `migrations.sol` file.

You can do the same thing through the `truffle develop` command. The `truffle develop` command provides a development blockchain environment for quick development and testing. The development network provides default accounts with ether for development purposes.

If you have deployed the smart contract through the Truffle console, you can close the Truffle console and open a new one. Also, close the Ganache Terminal.

Now, let's launch the Truffle development blockchain using the `truffle develop` command in a new Terminal:

1. Run `truffle develop` under the `MYERC20Token` project. It will connect to the Truffle development network at `localhost:9545`, as shown in the following screenshot. You may need to update the Truffle config port number to `9545`:

```
Warning: Please rename truffle.js to truffle-config.js to ensure Windows compatibility.
Truffle Develop started at http://127.0.0.1:9545/

Accounts:
(0) 0xab9f5070c46ceee39256f932a18163370ebd5cdd
(1) 0xcbf70d83734a61cd7dea8f84a93daed4d3770727
(2) 0xcb193bd308830d99766f9554606133b5c5496be3
(3) 0x7de69fd5072c4d7f1ef0017f39952ab49e01f33a
(4) 0xf2d95866e1df175a44f682ba18609312c6ae1261
(5) 0x962a2250f2fd3219c6e1ca3457c672c0a3a17a0b
(6) 0x5fa5a619980536339550d51bb1c51b3dacc8f7e1
(7) 0x507ed48597b65db0bdc5e746e7a0dad6d8b26fcf
(8) 0x4758efa1863e1a753839b9bc9d49772c1ab8ac3e
(9) 0x9fb39a7f6e199aee24c6fdc7b7d5e837bcd2557e

Private Keys:
(0) a25c3b3d94dab6647ca268262658bc42fecf14d33e54aa5689bf2776f9bd3bff
(1) 78a30e6f56b9acbb25e163d3cbb23c302184dba04cfefe9c38337ff64cd1a666
(2) 502ba8bd241465432ab3a027510c586519fc4f7cb2643498cd5321bed4b1a875
(3) dc1653a201964a9aa5e50e30fa563a5b52fbe353e94b4c9e6a31282047289b25
(4) e291ad9ff8d2d1699c4c2150713956fb3d4903b8ff2e2d5feb42cdf8ee63c21e
(5) 803ac07c9b346939b3e5b1c58a8b1fc500629f5e3841be7764370161278d063c
(6) 37d8ecd64cdfc8bdb128f5ce8834e965e11c5fcf978808bfb533e6999e41e8c3
(7) ca56d1873626e69b1ce326c2f6058a1ccf29eb40c6cc5595dc45d9c741815083
(8) 90c07bd9bb5820b5a01d19177a3990fec104461c10b41db4316236a6ba899743
(9) 715d68e1e295e5360d5cfc61a52ff8bcb80db38113ae50e3c63a8e477a04e6a2

Mnemonic: post put will jeans chaos exile chat fade reflect drama fog inquiry

▩▩  Important ▩▩  : This mnemonic was created for you by Truffle. It is not secure.
Ensure you do not use it on production blockchains, or else you risk losing funds.

truffle(develop)>
```

2. Then, run the `compile` and `migrate` commands to deploy a smart contract to the development network, as shown in the following screenshot:

The Truffle console shows compilation and deployment statuses. Once successfully deployed to a blockchain, we can see the transaction hash and other block information returned and displayed on the screen.

# Running a Truffle migration

The `truffle migrate` command is used to deploy our smart contracts. The migrations contract keeps track of the status of migrations on the current network, such as which contract has been completed and which contract is still pending migration. When running the `migrate` command, it will point to the project's migrations directory. To deploy the contract, the migration starts from the first migration file, `migrations/1_initial_migration.js`, as shown here:

```
var Migrations = artifacts.require("./Migrations.sol");
module.exports = function(deployer) {
    deployer.deploy(Migrations);
};
```

Add more new migrations by increasing the numbered prefixes to deploy other contracts. For example, in `MyERC20Token`, we will add a new migrations file, `migrations/2_deploy_contracts`, as shown here:

```
var MyERC20Token = artifacts.require("./MyERC20Token.sol");
module.exports = (deployer, network, accounts) => {
deployer.then(async () => {
    try {
       const ownerAddress = accounts[0];
       await deployer.deploy(MyERC20Token, "MyERC20Token", "MTK",
ownerAddress, '100000000000000000000');
       } catch (err) {
         console.log(('Failed to Deploy Contracts', err))
       }
    })
}
```

This will deploy our `MyERC20Token` smart contract. The migration files use a deployer to control the deployment tasks; these tasks can perform synchronously with the proper order. You can add more contracts, as shown in the following code block:

```
var Contract1 = artifacts.require("./Contract1.sol");
var Contract2 = artifacts.require("./Contract2.sol");
var Contractn = artifacts.require("./Contractn.sol");
module.exports = (deployer, network, accounts) => {
deployer.then(async () => {
    await deployer.deploy(Contract1)
    await deployer.deploy(Contract2)
    .....
    await deployer.deploy(Contractn)
}
```

Each deploy function on the deployer will queue up using the `promise` function. These tasks will be executed in the correct order. The current deployment tasks depend on the execution of the previous task.

# Truffle unit testing

The Truffle framework has a built-in testing framework to support two-way tests; you can write a test using JavaScript or Solidity.

All test files will be located under the `test` folder. For JavaScript tests, it allows the `.js`, `.ts`, `.es`, `.es6`, and `.jsx` file formats; however, `.sol` is for the Solidity test file. In this section, we will write unit tests for `MyERC20Token` using the JavaScript test file. The JavaScript test is based on the popular Mocha testing framework. Let's get started:

1. Create `MyERC20Token.js` under the `test` folder.
2. Import an initialized test class setup:

   ```
   var MyERC20Token = artifacts.require("./MyERC20Token.sol");
   ....
   before(async () => {
           token = await MyERC20Token.new(name, symbol,
   initialAccount, initialBalance)
           tokenTotalSupply = await token.totalSupply()
           SUCCESS_CODE = await token.SUCCESS_CODE()
           SUCCESS_MESSAGE = await token.SUCCESS_MESSAGE()
           NON_WHITELIST_CODE = await token.NON_WHITELIST_CODE()
           NON_WHITELIST_ERROR = await token.NON_WHITELIST_ERROR()
   })
   beforeEach(async () => {
       senderBalanceBefore = await token.balanceOf(sender)
       recipientBalanceBefore = await token.balanceOf(recipient)
   })
   ```

In the preceding code, we first imported the `MyERC20Token.sol` smart contract. Then, we initialized the contract test data, including test accounts, initial balance, and so on. We also instantiated a new `MyERC20Token` contract by passing a predefined name and symbol and `initialAccount` and `initialBalance`. We use the ES6 async/await function to run an `async` method and get the result.

The contract is a function that will hold the instance of the smart contract.

Before writing the function, we need to prepare test conditions before all the other test cases are run:

1. Test the basic information of the contract, for example, a token summary and initial account balance, as shown in the following snippet:

```
it('should has token name and symbol', async () => {
const tokenSummary = await token.tokenSummary();
    assert(tokenSummary[1]===name)
    assert(tokenSummary[2]===symbol)
})
it('should mint total supply of tokens to initial account', async
() => {
    const initialAccountBalance = await
token.balanceOf(initialAccount)
    assert(initialAccountBalance.eq(tokenTotalSupply))
})
```

`truffle test` uses the Chai framework-enabled BDD test-driven approach, as shown in the following screenshot. You can check out `https://www.chaijs.com/` for more details:

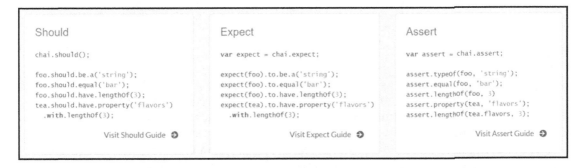

2. In the test contract whitelist-related function, the test will make sure that a transfer is not allowed between non-whitelist accounts, and that only an admin can add a whitelist account. Let's take a look at a few of these steps:

   - Test to make sure that a transfer between non-whitelisted accounts is not allowed. If the `approve` and `transferFrom` functions are called when the account is not whitelisted, then it will throw an exception. The following code handles the exception:

   ```
   it('should revert use of transferFrom between non-
   whitelisted accounts', async () => {
       let revertedTransfer = false
   ```

```
try {
    await token.approve(owner, transferValue, { from:
sender })
    await token.transferFrom(sender, recipient,
transferValue, { from: owner })
} catch (err) {
    revertedTransfer = true
}
assert(revertedTransfer)
})
```

- Test to make sure that a contract admin is allowed to add an account to the whitelist. The isWhitelist function performs a whitelist account check. The addWhitelist function is used to add the account as whiteList, as shown in the following block of code:

```
it('should allow contract admin to whitelist an account',
async () => {
    const operatorIsNotWhitelisted = await
token.isWhitelist(operator)
    assert(!operatorIsNotWhitelisted)
    await token.addWhitelist(operator, { from: operator })
    const operatorIsWhitelisted = await
token.isWhitelist(operator)
    assert(operatorIsWhitelisted)
})
```

3. Test a contract-admin-related function to make sure that the owner account can add and remove admins and check whether the account is an admin. In the following unit test, we will check whether the recipient account is an admin by calling the isAdmin function. Once verified, we can then add it to the admin account via the addAdmin function:

```
it('should allow only contract owner add account as admin', async
() => {
    const isAdmin = await token.isAdmin(recipient, { from: owner })
    assert(!isAdmin)
    let revertedAddAdmin = false
    try {
        await token.addAdmin(operator, { from: thirdAcct })
    } catch (err) {
    revertedAddAdmin = true
}
    assert(revertedAddAdmin)
    await token.addAdmin(operator, { from: owner })
```

```
const operatorIsAdmin = await token.isAdmin(operator)
assert(operatorIsAdmin)
})
```

4. Now, we need to test to make sure a paused account can make any transfers.
   Sometimes, we need to pause an individual account in an emergency case. Once
   the account has been paused, we should not allow the token transfer function.
   We will get an exception while performing this unit test case. Here is the unit test
   code:

```
it('should not allow transfer when contract is paused', async () =>
{
    await token.pause({ from: owner })
    let revertedTransfer = false
    try {
    await token.transfer(recipient, transferValue, { from: sender
})
    } catch (err) {
    revertedTransfer = true
    }
    assert(revertedTransfer)
    await token.unpause({ from: owner })
})
```

5. Then, test to allow a whitelist account to transfer ethers. The following unit test
   shows this case. First, we use the transfer function to transfer ether from the
   sender's account to the recipient's account. Then, we verify that the recipient's
   account's ether gets added to the exact amount sent from the sender. We use
   the **Big Numbers (BN)** function to compare ether values. The implementation is
   shown in the following code:

```
it('should allow transfer between whitelisted accounts', async ()
=> {
    await token.transfer(recipient, transferValue, { from: sender
})
    const senderBalanceAfter = await token.balanceOf(sender)
    const recipientBalanceAfter = await token.balanceOf(recipient)
    assert.equal(
        senderBalanceAfter.valueOf(),
        new BN(senderBalanceBefore).sub(new
BN(transferValue)).toString())
    assert.equal(
    recipientBalanceAfter.valueOf(),
    new BN(recipientBalanceBefore).add(new
BN(transferValue)).toString()
    )
})
```

6. At the end of our unit test, we will test the contract mint and burn functions that were performed by the admin. As an admin, users can burn a certain amount of tokens when needed. The burn function is used for this purpose. After the tokens have been burnt, the total supply of tokens will be reduced. The remaining token amount should be the total supply, minus the burnt token amount. Here is the code:

```
it('should admin burn certain amount tokens', async () => {
    const senderBalanceBefore = await token.balanceOf(sender)
    const tokenTotalSupplyBefore = await token.totalSupply()
    await token.burn(transferValue, { from: owner })
    const senderBalanceAfter = await token.balanceOf(sender)
    const tokenTotalSupplyAfter = await token.totalSupply()
    assert.equal(
        senderBalanceAfter.valueOf(),
        new BN(senderBalanceBefore).sub(new
BN(transferValue)).toString()
    )
    assert.equal(
        tokenTotalSupplyAfter.valueOf(),
        new BN(tokenTotalSupplyBefore).sub(new
BN(transferValue)).toString()
    )
})
```

The mint function will work similarly but will add new tokens to the total supply.

With all of the preceding MyERC20Token test cases defined, you can run truffle test in the Truffle console or test it in truffle develop. The full code can be found in this book's GitHub repository. You should see the passed test result, as follows:

```
truffle(develop)> test
Warning: Please rename truffle.js to truffle-config.js to ensure Windows compatibility.
Using network 'develop'.

Compiling your contracts...
===========================
> Everything is up to date, there is nothing to compile.

Warning: Please rename truffle.js to truffle-config.js to ensure Windows compatibility.

  Contract: MyERC20Token
    √ should has token name and symbol (39ms)
    √ should mint total supply of tokens to initial account
    √ should revert transfers between non-whitelisted accounts (77ms)
    √ should revert use of transferFrom between non-whitelisted accounts (114ms)
    √ should detect restriction for transfer between non-whitelisted accounts
    √ should return non-whitelisted error message for whitelist error code
    √ should allow only contract owner add account as admin (141ms)
    √ should allow contract admin to whitelist an account (84ms)
    √ should not allow transfer when contract is paused (179ms)
    √ should allow transfer between whitelisted accounts (95ms)
    √ should allow use of transferFrom betwen whitelisted accounts (151ms)
code:0
    √ should detect success for valid transfer
    √ should ensure success code is 0
    √ should return success message for success code
    √ should admin burn certain amount tokens (118ms)
    √ should admin mint certain amount tokens (122ms)

  16 passing (2s)
```

We just learned how to write a unit test in the Truffle project. To quickly start developing a new project, Truffle also provides some toolsets to help you achieve this goal. Truffle Box is one of these tools.

# Truffle Box

Truffle Box provides a collection of DApp boilerplates that allow you to quickly set up your DApp project. To create a box, you can run the `truffle unbox` command:

```
truffle unbox {USER_NAME || ORG_NAME}/{REPO_NAME}
```

In this section, we will build a web interface for Cheshire—fast CryptoKitties DApp development—using Truffle Box. CryptoKitties is a popular Ethereum game. Players can purchase, collect, breed, and sell blockchain cats. Cheshire implements the minimum CryptoKitties DApp API, as shown here:

```
/kitties
/kitties/:id
/user/:address
```

The installation process is quite simple:

1.  Install the Cheshire box by running the following command:

    ```
    truffle unbox endless-nameless-inc/cheshire
    ```

    The output will be as follows:

    ```
    D:\documents\publish\Learn Ehereum\cheshire>truffle unbox endless-nameless-inc/cheshire

    √ Preparing to download
    √ Downloading
    √ Cleaning up temporary files
    √ Setting up box

    Unbox successful. Sweet!

    Commands:

    Start Cheshire:          yarn start
    Open Cheshire dashboard: yarn run dashboard
    Run Cheshire script:     yarn run script ./scripts/yourscript.js
    Mine blocks:             yarn run mine <num blocks>
    Help / System status:    yarn run help
    Compile contracts:       truffle compile
    Migrate contracts:       truffle migrate
    Test contracts:          truffle test
    ```

2.  Run `yarnstart` under the project folder, as shown here:

    ```
    async start() {
    await this.startTestnet()
    await this.compileContracts()
    await this.deployContracts()
    await this.startApiServer()
    await this.loadAccounts()
    await this.runSetupScript()
    ..
    }
    ```

The `yarn start` command will do the following:

1.  Start the Ethereum testnet (in our case, it is `ganache-cli`).
2.  Compile the start contract.
3.  Deploy `KittyCore.sol`, `GeneScience.sol`, `SaleClockAuction.sol`, and `SiringClockAuction.sol` to the Ganache testnet.
4.  Start a local CryptoKitties API server.
5.  Load the required accounts.
6.  Run the setup scripts at `/scripts/setup.js`.

7. Open a page at `http://localhost:4000`. You should see the Cheshire dashboard page, as shown here:

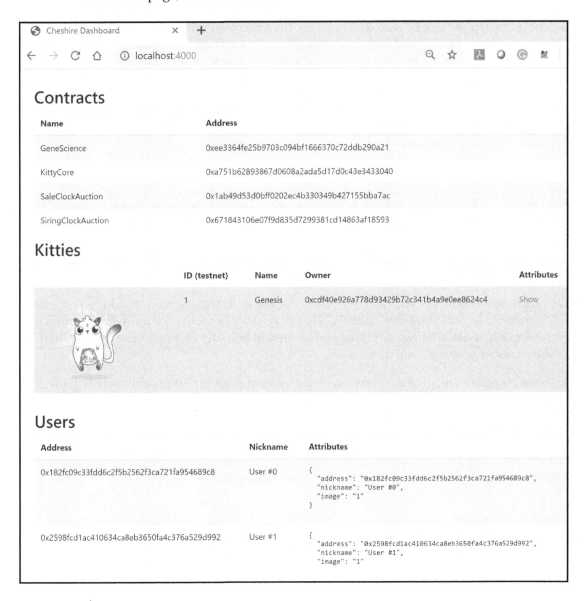

Cheshire automatically imports the Genesis kitty. You can query the Genesis kitty from the browser by entering the kitty's ID by going to `localhost:4000/kitties/1`. The result will be displayed on the page.

# Security testing

Smart contracts are self-executable and self-enforcing programs; once deployed to a decentralized public blockchain, the smart contract becomes immutable and fully transparent. Everyone in the blockchain has access to it. A smart contract can be designed to transfer and manipulate funds in user accounts for payment purposes. For example, a token amount can be transferred from one account to another account in the ERC-20 token standard. Since it is public and decentralized in nature, it becomes much more sensitive from a security perspective. The potential cost of vulnerabilities and the bounty available is an incentive for hackers to spend time and resources to find and exploit security bugs and loopholes in smart contract codes.

The most notable attack is the **Decentralized Autonomous Organization (DAO)** attack. DAO is an organization that acts as a finance venture capital fund for the crypto and blockchain space. On June 17, 2016, a hacker found a security bug in the smart contract. He asked the DAO to give the ether back multiple times before the smart contract balance was updated. Around $50 million worth of ether was stolen by hackers in a few hours. This resulted in the DAO being shut down and Ethereum being hard forked. The Ethereum community split into two parts—Ethereum and Ethereum Classic.

Writing a smart contract is not an easy task; even the most experienced developers cannot be guaranteed to write bug-free code. Following security best practice guidelines, utilizing better security tools, writing unit tests, and so on will help developers prevent accidental mistakes, security scams, and more.

In this section, we will give an overview of the current popular Ethereum security tools. This includes the following test tools:

- Static and dynamic analysis
- Linters

The following is a pictorial representation of both test tools:

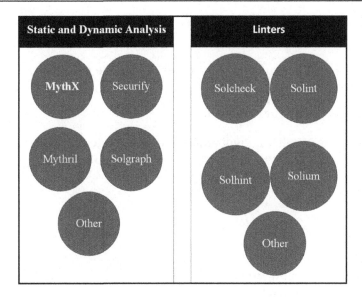

The preceding diagram shows the current popular tools for static and dynamic analysis and lints. Let's look at static and dynamic analysis first.

# Static and dynamic analysis

Static and dynamic analysis is a tool that can quickly analyze and validate Solidity code. It detects serious vulnerabilities or bugs to prevent security breaches on smart contracts. These are many blockchain static and dynamic analysis tools such as MythX, Securify, Mythril, Solgraph, and more. We'll be discussing MythX and Securify in the upcoming sections.

# MythX

MythX is a security analysis tool from ConsenSys. It can be used as a security verification plugin for the Truffle framework. It is an open source Ethereum security analysis tool for smart contracts and helps to detect many common Solidity security and EVM bytecode vulnerabilities. The MythX tool supports many popular IDEs, such as Truffle plugins, the VS Code Solidity extension, Ramuh (for MythX Desktop Notifications), Mythos (the MythX Simple CLI Client), and PythX (a Python MythX CLI).

In this section, we will set up MythX with a Truffle testing environment to test our smart contract:

1. Install the MythX Truffle plugin under the Truffle project using the following command:

   ```
   npm install truffle-security
   ```

Once the plugin is installed, it will automatically update the project's configuration file (`truffle-config.js`) with the `truffle-security` plugin configuration, as shown here:

```
module.exports =
{ plugins: ["truffle-security"],
..
}
```

2. To get a free account, you can go to `https://mythx.io/` and sign in with MetaMask, as shown here:

3. Update your API password, as shown in the following screenshot:

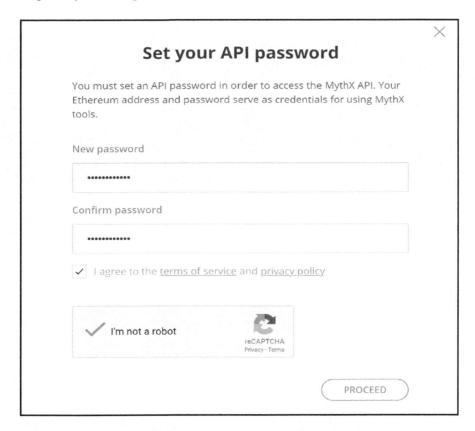

4. Once you have set up a free account, set the following properties:

- Set `MYTHX_ETH_ADDRESS` and `MYTHX_PASSWORD` in your project environment from the command line
- Set `MYTHX_ETH_ADDRESS=0x12345678000000000000000000000000-your-address`
- Set `MYTHX_PASSWORD='Put your password in here!'`

5. Now, you can start a security test for your smart contract by entering the following command:

```
truffle run verify
```

The Terminal will display the security test result, similar to the following screenshot:

```
D:\documents\publish\Learn Ehereum\sourcecode\MyERC20Token>set MYTHX_ETH_ADDRESS=0x22a29f5b8290e7f655a7

D:\documents\publish\Learn Ehereum\sourcecode\MyERC20Token>set MYTHX_PASSWORD=YourPassword

D:\documents\publish\Learn Ehereum\sourcecode\MyERC20Token>truffle run verify
Warning: Please rename truffle.js to truffle-config.js to ensure Windows compatibility.
Welcome to MythX! You are currently running in Free mode.

      ERC20 |****************************************************************| 100% || Elapsed: 60.5s 🔒 completed
MyERC20Token |****************************************************************| 100% || Elapsed: 6.9s 🔒 completed
    Pausable |****************************************************************| 100% || Elapsed: 16.4s 🔒 completed
   Whitelist |****************************************************************| 100% || Elapsed: 15.2s 🔒 completed
       owned |****************************************************************| 100% || Elapsed: 13.6s 🔒 completed

D:/documents/publish/Learn Ehereum/sourcecode/MyERC20Token/contracts/MyERC20Token.sol
    1:0    warning  A floating pragma is set                      SWC-103
   98:23   warning  Local variable shadows a state variable       SWC-119
  104:0    error    The binary addition can overflow              SWC-101
  169:21   warning  Local variable shadows a state variable       SWC-119
```

As we can see, it is quite straightforward to use MythX for your smart contract security tests. There are many other similar security tools available. In the next section, we will discuss an online security analyzer—Securify.

# Securify

Securify is an open platform online security scanner for smart contracts. It is supported by the Ethereum Foundation and ChainSecurity. Securify supports online web-based and offline backend versions. The scanned security report is based on Solidity vulnerability patterns. The following screenshot shows the view of Securify. You can visit the website by going to `https://securify.chainsecurity.com`:

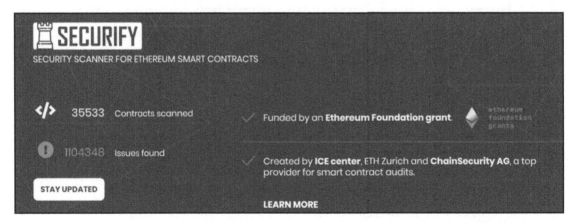

Securify uses security compliance and violation patterns to generate a smart contract security report. Here is a list of some of the properties and patterns:

- Locked ether
- Ether liquidity
- No writes after call
- Restricted writes
- Validated arguments
- Restricted transfer
- Handled exception
- Transaction ordering dependency

Open Securify Web; you can copy paste the smart contract code, as shown in the following screenshot. Moreover, if you click **Scan Now**, the security scan process will start. Once the scan is completed, the test result will be returned.

Here is our `MyERC20Token` test result:

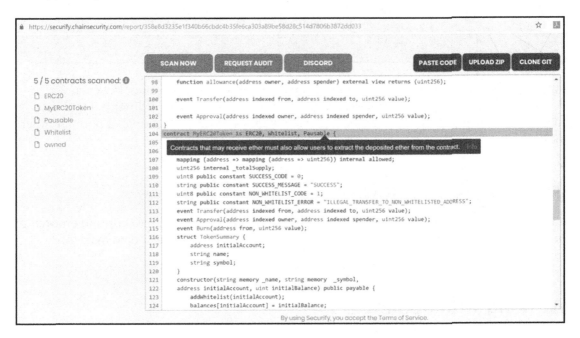

Securify will highlight the potentially vulnerable line of code when you click the **Info** button; detailed instructions and examples are provided to explain the result, as shown in the following screenshot:

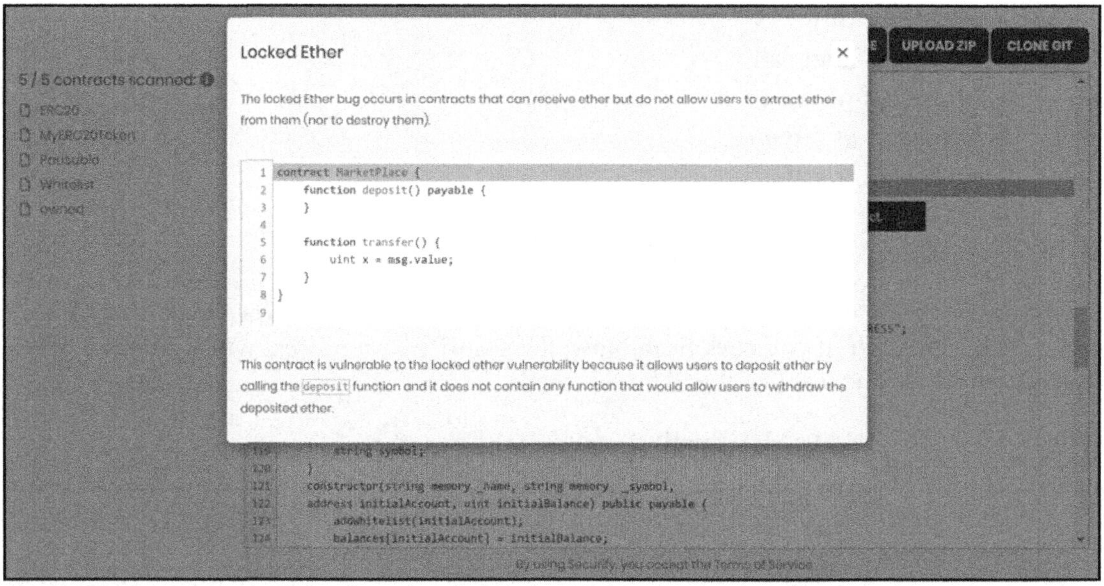

In this section, we reviewed some popular static and dynamic analysis tools. When we develop a smart contract, the code style and quality are also critical. A linter is a tool that can provide such help. In the next section, we will quickly review a couple of popular linter tools.

# Working with a linter

Lint, or a linter, is a tool that improves code quality by analyzing source code and enforcing rules for style and composition. It reports errors, bugs, and stylistic errors to make code easier to read and review.

## Working with solhint

Solhint is an open source linter for smart Solidity contracts. By executing `solhint`, it will generate a lint report to help improve code quality.

Let's set up `solhint` to see how it works:

1. Install `solhint` by running the `npm` command, as shown here:

```
npm install -g solhint
```

2. Navigate to the Truffle project folder. If you haven't generated a `solhint` confirmation file, simply enter the following command:

```
Path to your project/MyERC20Token>solhint init-config
```

If you open the generated configuration file, `.solhint.json`, you will see that it is just a simple JSON content:

```
{
    "extends": "solhint:default"
}
```

It uses the default `solhint` configuration setting.

3. Now, you can run a lint test by entering the following command:

```
solhint contracts/MyERC20Token.sol
```

The generated lint report will be displayed on the console, as shown here. It gives format suggestions to let you clean up Solidity code:

```
D:\documents\publish\Learn Ethereum\sourcecode\MyERC20Token>solhint contracts/MyERC20Token.sol

contracts/MyERC20Token.sol
   23:13   error   Expected indentation of 8 spaces but found 12                        indent
  148:8    error   Expected indentation of 8 spaces but found 7                         indent
  151:7    error   Expected indentation of 8 spaces but found 6                         indent
  161:2    error   Line length must be no more than 120 but current length is 138  max-line-length
  168:3    error   Expected indentation of 4 spaces but found 2                         indent
  169:3    error   Expected indentation of 4 spaces but found 2                         indent
  170:5    error   Expected indentation of 8 spaces but found 4                         indent
  171:3    error   Expected indentation of 4 spaces but found 2                         indent
  172:3    error   Expected indentation of 4 spaces but found 2                         indent
  177:4    error   Expected indentation of 4 spaces but found 3                         indent
  178:3    error   Expected indentation of 4 spaces but found 2                         indent
  179:5    error   Expected indentation of 8 spaces but found 4                         indent
  180:5    error   Expected indentation of 8 spaces but found 4                         indent
  181:5    error   Expected indentation of 8 spaces but found 4                         indent
  182:5    error   Expected indentation of 8 spaces but found 4                         indent
  183:5    error   Expected indentation of 8 spaces but found 4                         indent
  184:2    error   Expected indentation of 4 spaces but found 1                         indent
  185:3    error   Expected indentation of 4 spaces but found 2                         indent
  186:5    error   Expected indentation of 8 spaces but found 4                         indent
  187:5    error   Expected indentation of 8 spaces but found 4                         indent
  188:5    error   Expected indentation of 8 spaces but found 4                         indent
  189:5    error   Expected indentation of 8 spaces but found 4                         indent
  190:5    error   Expected indentation of 8 spaces but found 4                         indent
  191:3    error   Expected indentation of 4 spaces but found 2                         indent
  192:3    error   Expected indentation of 4 spaces but found 2                         indent
  193:8    error   Expected indentation of 8 spaces but found 7                         indent
  194:3    error   Expected indentation of 4 spaces but found 2                         indent

✖ 27 problems (27 errors, 0 warnings)
```

In the preceding test result, it shows 27 indent format errors. We can then fix these smart contract formats based on the report. This will help improve code quality.

# Summary

In this chapter, we covered the Remix IDE, including how to compile, deploy, and debug a smart contract. We also explored the Truffle suite, including commands to build and deploy our MYERC20Token smart contract and how to write a unit test and run it. We then had an overview of security testing tools, including static and dynamic analysis tools, such as MythX and Securify, and we set up a linter tool—solhint.

In the next chapter, we will write frontend code using React.js and use web3.js to interact with backend smart contracts and to build an end-to-end decentralized digital art market DApp.

# 7
# Writing UI for the DApps

Generally, a **decentralized application (DApp)** is a two-tier application, comprising two main components, a frontend UI layer written by HTML, JavaScript, or web3.js and a smart backend contract that runs in the blockchain network.

We learned how to write a smart contract using the Ethereum development tool in the previous chapter, and to run a unit test to verify that all the Solidity functions worked well. To let an end user enable calls to our smart contract, we will need to build a UI to interact with the smart contracts.

In this chapter, we will learn how to write a UI to build a decentralized digital art market DApp, using the popular JavaScript framework React and web3.js. The chapter comprises five major topics, as follows:

- Knowing about DApps
- Working with a Web3 JavaScript API
- Setting up a DApp development environment
- Building frontend UI components
- Running a decentralized digital art market DApp

# Technical requirements

For all the source code of this book, please refer to the following GitHub link: `https://github.com/PacktPublishing/Learn-Ethereum`.

# Knowing about DApps

A DApp is an application that uses smart contracts to run. Smart contracts are deployed on an **Ethereum Virtual Machine** (**EVM**). It is similar to a client-server two-tier architecture, where there is no need for any middlemen to operate. A DApp can have a frontend (web) that makes calls to its backend (smart contract) through the web3.js API.

To interact with a blockchain smart contract, web3.js typically connects with a wallet—one of the most popular browser wallets is MetaMask. The wallet will connect with a backend blockchain node instance and send a request to the blockchain.

The following diagram shows a typical DApp architecture and the flow interactions between the frontend and backend:

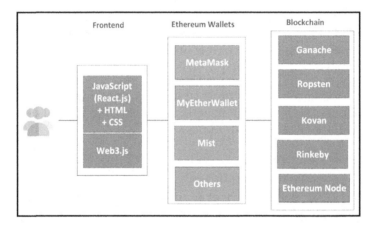

In this chapter, we are going to follow the preceding diagram to build our decentralized digital art market DApp. A frontend tier on the client side will use React and the **Material Design for Bootstrap** (**MDB**) framework. The backend will be an Ethereum network, which has a smart contract deployed. We will use the most popular Ethereum browser wallet to connect to the backend blockchain. In the development stage, we will use Ganache as our local Ethereum network.

MetaMask is a browser-based Ethereum wallet; it provides a friendly user interface to manage user Ethereum accounts and interact with DApps through the Ethereum web3 API. The client can call, send, and receive blockchain transactions in a secure way. Alternatively, currently, MetaMask supports add-ons in Chrome, Firefox, Opera, and the new Brave browser. When open in the browser, MetaMask will inject the web3 library and will be accessible to all JavaScript websites. In our DApp development, we will use a Chrome plugin.

# Working with Web3 JavaScript API

Basically, web3.js is an Ethereum JavaScript API, which provides a collection of libraries for interacting with local or remote Ethereum networks. The connection between web3js and Ethereum is made by using the HTTP, WebSocket, or IPC protocol. In the following table, we will quickly review several important web3.js API concepts:

| API reference | Description | Example |
|---|---|---|
| web3-eth | This package provides an API to interact with the Ethereum blockchain and smart contracts. | `getBalance, sendTransaction, coinbase, getBlockNumber, getAccounts` |
| web3-shh | This package provides an API to interact with the Whisper protocol for broadcasting. | `web3.shh.post({` `symKeyID: identities[0],` `topic: '0xffaadd11',` `payload: '0xffffffdddddd1122'` `}).then(h => console.log(`Message` `with hash ${h} was successfuly sent`))` |
| web3-bzz | This package provides an API to interact with the Ethereum swarm, the decentralized file storage platform. | `web3.bzz.currentProvider` `web3.bzz.download(bzzHash [,` `localpath])` |
| web3-utils | This package provides a collection of utility functions for Ethereum DApps and other web3.js packages. | `web3.utils.toWei(number [, unit])` `web3.utils.isAddress(address)` |

To get the web3.js library, you need to install `web3` in your project. You can run one of the following commands based on your project settings:

- **npm**: `npm install web3`
- **yarn**: `yarn add web3`
- **bower**: `bower install web3`
- Alternatively, directly use the **CDN (Content Delivery Networks)** link

With web3.js installed, to instantiate `web3`, here is a typical JS code. The following code shows how to handle chains when you have MetaMask installed in your browser, or it can use your local Ganache instance. For simplicity, we haven't dealt with all of the other cases, such as when as user has already granted the site permissions to access MetaMask and MetaMask is locked:

```js
export const getWeb3 = () =>
    new Promise((resolve, reject) => {
    window.addEventListener("load", async () => {
    // load modern dapp browsers or newer version of metamask...
    if (window.ethereum) {
        const web3 = new Web3(window.ethereum);
        try {
        await window.ethereum.enable();
        resolve(web3);
        } catch (error) {
        reject(error);
        }
    } else if (window.web3) {
        // load older metamask provider
        const web3 = window.web3;
        console.log("Injected web3 detected.");
        resolve(web3);
    } else {
        //connect to local ganache instance
        const provider = new Web3.providers.HttpProvider("http://127.0.0.1:7545");
        const web3 = new Web3(provider);
        console.log("No web3 instance injected, using Local web3.");
        resolve(web3);
    }
    });
});
```

You first check if we use a modern DApp browser or a newer version of the MetaMask wallet. With `window.ethereum.enable()`, we request access to wallet accounts.

If an Ethereum provider is not detected, we will load an injected older version of a wallet provider, like MetaMask. The default will point to a local Ganache instance; in the preceding example, we connect to the `7545` port instances.

This will load our `web3` instance, which connects to the blockchain instance.

# Setting up a DApp development environment

In Chapter 5, *Developing Your Own Cryptocurrency*, and Chapter 6, *Smart Contract Development and Test Fundamentals*, we created the `DigitalArtERC721Token` Truffle project and learned how to use a Truffle tool to compile and deploy the smart contract to our local Ganache instance. We start a Ganache server using the CLI tool. In this chapter, we will use Ganache desktop as our local development blockchain instance and continue to complete our frontend DApp code. Let's first install Ganache.

## Installing Ganache desktop

To install the desktop version of Ganache, please follow the given steps:

1. Go to the Truffle suite website, download and install Ganache desktop: `https://truffleframework.com/ganache`.

2. Once installed, open it. This is what the desktop version of Ganache looks like:

In the preceding screenshot, we notice that:

- The desktop displays many blockchain properties, such as **Current Block**, **Gas Price**, **Gas Limit**, **Network ID**, **RPC Server**, **Mining Status**, and so on.
- A developer can check **ACCOUNTS** information; Ganache creates 10 default accounts; each of them has 100 ether as default. Each address has an associated unique private key and index.
- The **BLOCKS** tab provides an entire history of blocks mined.
- The **TRANSACTIONS** tab provides the entire transaction history.
- The **LOGS** tab provides log information.

3. Once we have installed Ganache, we then need to set up our project workspace.

# Creating a development workspace

When we open Ganache desktop, it has the option to create a new workspace. As shown in the following screenshot, **QUICKSTART** is an option to quickly and easily install your workspace with just one click. The **NEW WORKSPACE** option provides more configuration options for workspace creation:

1. Click **NEW WORKSPACE**; it will navigate to the workspace configuration page.
2. Define your workspace name and point to our `DigitalArtERC721Token` **Truffle** configuration file—`truffle-config.js` and save it. This will create a Truffle development workspace for our project.

 The project source code can be cloned from the Packt GitHub site: `https:/ /github.com/PacktPublishing/Learn-Ethereum`.

The following is how the workspace configuration looks:

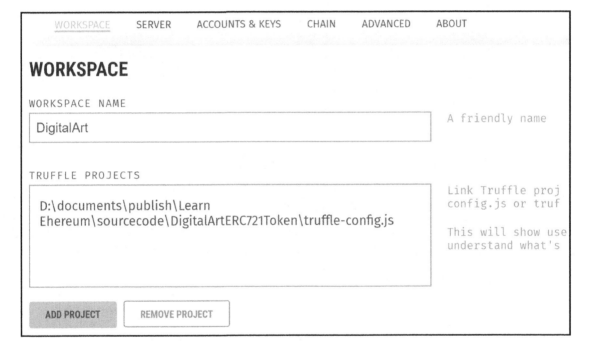

3. Click the **CONTRACTS** tab in Ganache as shown in the following screenshot. We can see that the `DigitalArt` smart contract hasn't deployed yet:

Next, let's set up our DApp client-side project using React.

# Setting up the project for our DApp

We assume that you have installed the `Navigate project` root folder for `DigitalArtERC721Token`. Before we start to create the React project, we need to do the following:

1. Install the `create-react-app` node command-line interface as shown here:

```
npm install -g create-react-app
```

2. Now, we can run the `create react-app` command to create a React project. Under the project root folder, run the following command to create a React project:

```
npm create-react-app dapp
```

3. Once we create the DApp react project, navigate to `dapp`.
4. Run `npm start` or `yarn start` to bring up the web server as shown here:

```
npm start
```

5. Now, we can run the React application through the browser
at `http://localhost:3000/`. The project structure will look like the following:

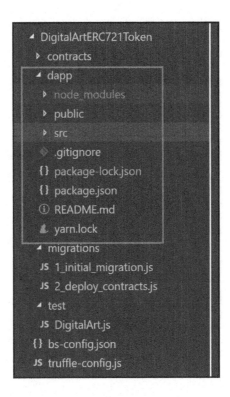

Since `create-react-app` doesn't allow you to read a file from outside the `src/` directory, the Truffle compiler will generate compiled files in the `build` folder under the root project. This will cause the DApp to not read the smart contract ABI information. To solve this, fortunately, Truffle provides an elegant solution. You just need to add a `contracts_build_directory` entry in the `truffle.js` project or the `truffle-config.js` (in Windows) file; here is what we will change:

```
const path = require("path");

module.exports = {
  contracts_build_directory: path.join(__dirname, "./dapp/src/abi"),

  networks: {
```

Now, we run the `truffle compile` command:

```
truffle compile
```

The compiled smart contract will move to `./dapp/src/abi`.

Here is the compiled smart contract in the `src/abi` folder:

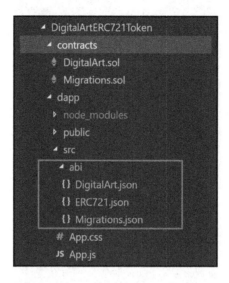

At the next step, let's deploy our smart contract.

# Deploying a smart contract

With all the required components and configuration set up, now we can deploy our contract to a Ganache network. Open the terminal under the project root folder, and run the `deploy` command as follows:

```
truffle deploy
```

Once the deployment is successful, we should see that the contract status will be changed to **Deployed**. This is how the desktop deployment status under the **CONTRACTS** tab will look:

We can also verify deployment and check the transaction hash under the **TRANSACTION** tab. The Truffle migration transaction is displayed. The contract owner address is our first account from Ganache:

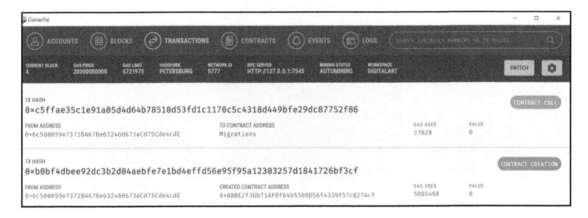

Our project is ready to run, but we need a wallet to connect to our Ganache blockchain. We will use the popular MetaMask wallet to do this.

# Installing MetaMask and connecting to Ganache

In `DigitalArtERC721Token`, we use MetaMask as the browser wallet to connect to the blockchain. Installing MetaMask will follow the standard chrome extension installation process. You can refer to the MetaMask website `https://metamask.io` for more details.

Once you have MetaMask, perform the following steps:

1. Once MetaMask is installed in your browser, you need to connect to the Ganache desktop. The Ganache desktop runs on `http://localhost:7545` by default.

2. Open MetaMask and click on **Custom RPC** to connect our Ganache desktop instance. The screenshot shows the following output:

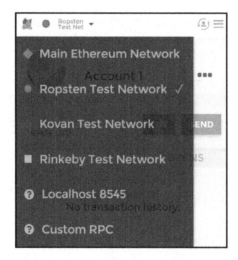

3. Give the network a name and a new RPC URL, which is `http://localhost:7545`. As shown in the following screenshot, leave the remaining fields as default, then click Save. This will connect MetaMask with the Ganache desktop:

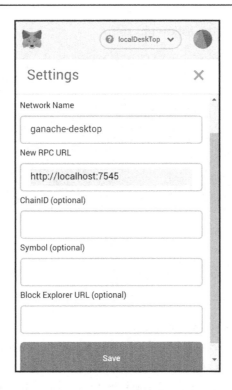

# Setting MetaMask Ganache accounts

You may have noticed that MetaMask only has one default account after we connect with the Ganache server. This account has zero ether balance, which is created by MetaMask by default. To import the Ganache wallet address to MetaMask, we can use a private key or JSON file.

In Ganache desktop, perform the following steps:

1. Click the key icon under the **ACCOUNTS** tab, the pop-up screen will display the private key information for the preferred address selected as shown here:

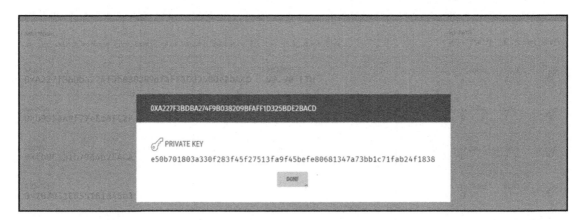

2. Copy the private key information.
3. Then click on the **Account** button in the MetaMask upper-right corner.
4. Click **Import Account**. The new account screen will display.
5. Paste the private key string in the input box, then click **Import**.

This will import the selected Ganache account address and balance. The import screen is shown here:

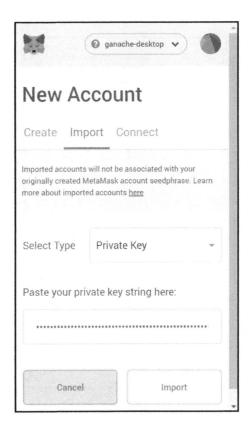

Once connected to the Ganache desktop blockchain, the private key associated with the account will display in MetaMask. In our case, this account has around 99 ethers as shown here:

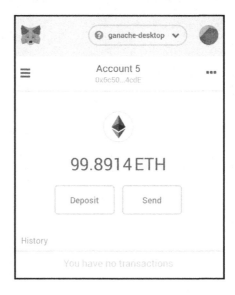

Do the same thing for two more accounts—let's import a total of three accounts for our project for testing purposes. You can see the details of the three accounts in the following screenshot:

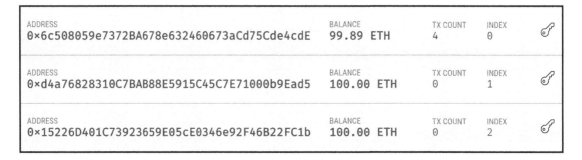

At this stage, we have set up our DApp development environment. Now it is time to build our frontend DApp logic.

# Building frontend UI components

In this section, we will build our decentralized digital art market DApp frontend components. Before we start to write the code, we will install all the dependencies needed in the project.

# Setting up project dependencies

In our DApp frontend, we will use the MDB framework as a UI CSS framework, react-route as a URL router navigation library, and Truffle contract as a utility to read the compiled contract ABI file. Web3 is used to communicate with the backend blockchain network. The following is the list of the npm dependencies defined in `package.json`:

```json
{
    "name": "dapp",
    "version": "0.1.0",
    "private": true,
    "dependencies": {
        "@babel/runtime": "^7.4.4",
        "mdbootstrap": "^4.8.1",
        "react": "^16.8.6",
        "react-dom": "^16.8.6".
        "react-router-dom": "^5.0.0",
        "react-scripts": "3.0.1",
        "truffle-contract": "^4.0.15",
        "web3": "^1.0.0-beta.35"
    },
}
```

Install all these dependencies by running the `install` command as shown here:

```
npm install
```

After installing all the necessary dependencies, we will instantiate our smart contract instance.

# Getting the instance of a deployed contract

In the web3 section, we learned how to instantiate a web3 instance. To call a deployed contract instance from the blockchain network, web3 provides an API—`web3.eth.Contract(JSON Interface, address, options)`—for this purpose. The next screenshot shows how we can get the `DigitalArtContract` instance:

```
import DigitalArtContract from './abi/DigitalArt.json '

export const getInstance = async (web3) => {
    const networkId = await web3.eth.net.getId();
    window.user = (await web3.eth.getAccounts())[0];
    const deployedNetwork = DigitalArtContract.networks[networkId];
    window.instance = new web3.eth.Contract(
        DigitalArtContract.abi,
        deployedNetwork && deployedNetwork.address,
        {
            from: window.user
        }
    );
    return window.instance;
}
```

We first load the compiled `DigitalArt.json` ABI file. By reading `networkId` through the web3 API—`web3.eth.net.getId()`, we can find the network address from the ABI file—`network[networkId]`.

We then call the web API (`web3.eth.Contract`) to get the contract instance. To build the frontend components, we will start building a navigation bar. Then we can navigate different pages.

# Building a navigation bar

Once we get a smart contract instance, it will be quite easy to get the token name and symbol information and display it on our navigation bar. Here is the code to get symbol:

```
const symbol = await contractInstance.methods.symbol().call()
```

Note that `contractInstance.methods.myMethod([param1[, param2[, ...]]]).call(transactionObject, blockNumber, callback])` in web3 is used to return a result from a read-only method. This `call()` function does not send any transaction in EVM.

The `params` call transaction object can be an optional input, as shown here:

- `from`: Caller address
- `gasPrice`: The call transaction gas price in wei
- `gas`: The maximum number of gas limits

> While using `call()`, the function doesn't change any state. There is another `send()` method; it can alter the smart contract state. The `myContract.methods.myMethod([param1[, param2[, ...]]]).send(options[, callback])`
> send method will send a transaction to the smart contract and execute its method.

We also need to add a few `nav` buttons to switch between different views:

- **ART GALLERY**: Displays digital art and sells products. The user can buy the products.
- **PUBLISH YOUR ARTS**: The page for digital art producers. Owners initially sell their products creating an ERC721 token.
- **MY WALLET INFO**: Displays wallet information, including address, balance, and owned digital art products. It also provides a personal collector's gallery, allowing the owner to resell their products when the price changes.

The navigation bar looks like the following:

The UI code for the navigation bar is as follows:

```
componentDidMount = async () => {
  const web3 = await getWeb3();
  const contractInstance = await getInstance(web3);
  window.user = (await web3.eth.getAccounts())[0];
  const symbol = await contractInstance.methods.symbol().call()
  this.setState({ symbol: symbol });
        const name = await contractInstance.methods.name().call();
  this.setState({ name: name });
}

render() {
  return (
    <nav className="navbar navbar-expand-lg navbar-dark stylish-color">
      <div className="navbar-brand">
        <a className="navbar-item text-white" href="/">
          <strong>
            <i className="fa fa-coins"></i>Decentralized Art Market ( {this.state.name} | {this.state.symbol})
          </strong>
        </a>
      </div>
      <form className="form-inline  my-2 my-lg-0 ml-auto">
        <a  className="btn btn-outline-white btn-md my-2 my-sm-0 ml-3" href="/">Art Gallery</a>
        <a className="btn btn-outline-white btn-md my-2 my-sm-0 ml-3" href="/publishArt">Publish Your Art</a>
        <a className="btn btn-outline-white btn-md my-2 my-sm-0 ml-3" href="/myWallet">My Wallet Info</a>
      </form>
    </nav>
```

We display the token name and symbol on the navigation bar. We also defined the navigation link. When **Publish Your Art** is clicked, the page will navigate to the **Art Publish** page. **My Wallet Info** will link to **MyWallet** page. Next, we will build the art gallery page.

The DApp source code is available at GitHub: `https://github.com/Packt-Publishing/Learn-Ethereum`.

# The ART GALLERY page

The **ART GALLERY** page has two functions:

- Display selling digital art products

- Buy the product

**Display selling digital art products**: The `DigitalArt` smart contract defines the `findAllPendingArt` method and returns all the digital arts currently on sale in the digital art market. Here is the code to load the products for sale:

```
const result = await
this.state.contractInstance.methods.findAllPendingArt().call();
```

Notice that we get `contractInstance` from the reacting state, instead of the query blockchain every time. This is because we cached `contractInstance` after we get `Instance` for the first time. It will help the page performance. The following is how we do it:

```
componentDidMount = async () => {
        const web3 = await getWeb3();
        const contractInstance = await getInstance(web3);
...
        this.setState({ contractInstance: contractInstance });
    }
```

With the `return` function, we loop through each pending artwork to get the art's detailed information, including the title, description, price, published date, author, and image, and then display it in a web page. We store the image URL in the blockchain; in the actual real-world DApp, you can point to decentralized storage like IPFS, Swarm, and so on.

Here is the code logic:

```
ids = result[0];
let _total = ids.length;
if(ids && _total>0) {
  let row;
  if(_total<=3) {
    row = 1;
  } else {
    row = Math.ceil(_total/3);
  }
  let columns = 3;
  this.setState({ rows: [], columns: [] });
  let rowArr = Array.apply(null, {length: row}).map(Number.call, Number);
  let colArr = Array.apply(null, {length: columns}).map(Number.call, Number);
  this.setState({ rows: rowArr, columns: colArr });
  let _tokenIds= [], _title =[], _desc= [], _price= [], _publishDate= [], _image =[], _author=[];
  let idx =0;
  this.resetPendingArts();
  for(let i = 0; i<row; i++) {
    for(let j = 0; j < columns; j++) {
      if(idx<_total) {
        let tokenId= ids[idx];
        const art = await this.state.contractInstance.methods.findArt(tokenId).call();
        const priceInEther = web3.utils.fromWei(art[3], 'ether');
        _tokenIds.push(art[0]);
        _title.push(art[1]);
        _desc.push(art[2]);
        _price.push(priceInEther);
        _publishDate.push(art[5]);
        _image.push(art[9]);
        _author.push(art[6]);
      }
      idx++;
    }
  }
```

We build the art gallery page. As a buyer, the DApp should provide a function to let a buyer purchase digital art products. Let's write the code.

**Buy the product**: The DigitalArt smart contract defines the `buyArt` method for the user who wants to purchase digital art. Here is the code to buy products:

```
async buyArt(tokenId, priceInEther) {
  try {
    const priceInWei = window.web3.utils.toWei(priceInEther, 'ether');
    await this.state.contractInstance.methods.buyArt(tokenId).send({
      from: this.state.user, gas: 6000000, value: priceInWei
    })
    window.location.reload();
  } catch (e) {console.log('Error', e)}
};
```

In this method, we use the web3 API for sending a transaction; as we mentioned before, `send()` will modify the smart contract state:

```
contractInstance.methods.myMethod([param1[, param2[, ...]]]).send(options[,
callback])
```

Similar to the `call()` method, the `options` parameter input can pass from `gasPrice` and `gas`.

It can also pass additional parameter values when the send method of a transaction requires a balance transfer. The value unit for the transfer transaction is wei.

Here we use `web3.util.toWei` to convert ether units to wei and pass a value to the `send` method as a transaction value parameter. It will update when we switch to a different account in the MetaMask wallet.

We have completed the art buyer side,so now we also need an art owner side, which allows the buyer to publish and sell their arts.

## The PUBLISH YOUR ARTS page

As we discussed earlier,the **PUBLISH YOUR ARTS** page is the place for the art owner to do the following:

Initially,they publish their product on the digital art market by creating an ERC721 token.

Here is the code for how to publish products:

```
await this.state.contractInstance.methods.
  createTokenAndSellArt(title,description, date, authorName, price,
imageValue)
  .send({from: this.state.user })
```

The web3 calls the smart contract `createTokenAndSellArt` function with the `send()` transaction. It will create an ERC721 token and then publish the art in the decentralized digital art market.

## The MY WALLET INFO page

The **MY WALLET INFO** page has three functions:

- Displaying wallet information
- Displaying owned digital art products
- Reselling owned digital products

**Display wallet information:** To display wallet information, we can utilize the web3 API. We have discussed similar APIs before; here is the code:

```
const web3 = await getWeb3();
window.web3 = web3;
const contractInstance = await getInstance(web3);
window.user = (await web3.eth.getAccounts())[0];
const balanceInWei = await web3.eth.getBalance(window.user);
var balance = web3.utils.fromWei(balanceInWei, 'ether');
const networkId = await web3.eth.net.getId();
const networkType = await web3.eth.net.getNetworkType();
```

Note that `web3.eth.getBalance()` is to get user ether balance.

**Display owned digital products:** the DigitalArt smart contract defines the `findMyArt()` method and returns the list of current `tokenIds` for the wallet owner. With `tokenId`, we can perform a query on the `findArt()` method to get the details of each digital art product, including the title, description, publish date, author, and status. Let's have a look at the following code:

```
const result = await
this.state.contractInstance.methods.findMyArts().call();
..
const art = await
this.state.contractInstance.methods.findArt(tokenId).call();
```

The following code shows how we can get owned `tokenIds` and look through to get information on each art product:

```
async loadMyDigitalArts(web3) {
    try {
        let ids;
        const result = await this.state.contractInstance.methods.findMyArts().call();
        let _total = result.length;
        if(_total>0) {
            let row;
            if(_total<=3) {
                row = 1;
            } else {
                row = Math.ceil(_total/3);
            }
            let columns = 3;
            let rowArr = Array.apply(null, {length: row}).map(Number.call, Number);
            let colArr = Array.apply(null, {length: columns}).map(Number.call, Number);
            this.setState({ rows: rowArr, columns: colArr });
            let _tokenIds= [], _title =[], _desc= [], _price= [], _publishDate= [], _image =[], _author=[], _status=[];
            let idx =0;
            this.resetPendingArts();
            for(let i = 0; i<row; i++) {
                for(let j = 0; j < columns; j++) {
                    if(idx<_total) {
                        let tokenId= result[idx];
                        const art = await this.state.contractInstance.methods.findArt(tokenId).call();
                        const priceInEther = web3.utils.fromWei(art[3], 'ether');
                        _tokenIds.push(art[0]);
                        _title.push(art[1]);
                        _desc.push(art[2]);
                        if(art[4]==1) {
                            _status.push("In selling");
                        } else {
                            _status.push("Publish");
                        }

                        _price.push(priceInEther);
                        _publishDate.push(art[5]);
                        _image.push(art[9]);
                        _author.push(art[6]);
```

After the buyer purchases and owns the digital art products, he will be able to resell these products with a specific price in the market. Therefore, we need to write a related function to resell the arts.

**Resell owned digital products:** for owned digital arts, if the art products are still in sell status, the page won't provide a sell button, because it is still in sell status. However, for those not in sell status, the owner can resell the products at the desired price.

Here is how we do that:

```
async submitArtSell() {
  try {
    const priceInWei = window.web3.utils.toWei(this.state.sellPrice, 'ether');
    await this.state.contractInstance.methods.resellArt(this.state.sellTokenId, priceInWei).send({
      from: this.state.user, gas: 6000000
    })
    window.location.reload();
  } catch (e) {console.log('Error', e)}
};
```

We invoke `resellArt` by bypassing `TokenId`, the price of the digital art. The parameters in send method pass the buyer address and gas fee.

This ends our frontend code development. Since this book is primarily about blockchains, we will skip most of the HTML React code in this section; you can check the detailed code from this book's GitHub repository.

Next step is to run our DApp!

# Running the decentralized digital art market DApp

Once you are ready, you can start your web server by running `yarn start` in the root project folder. During project initializing, you will see the web page and MetaMask connect request popup, as in the following screenshot:

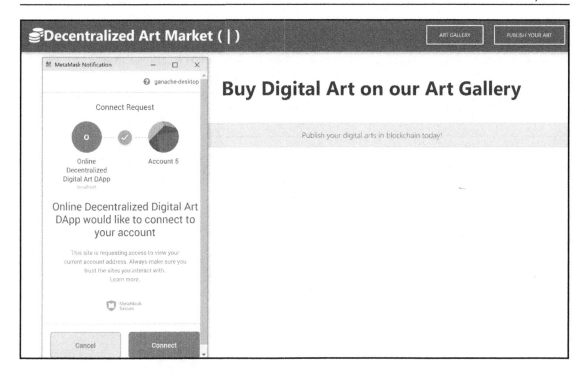

Accept connection by clicking the **Connect** button. The home page will display empty when selling the product at the beginning.

# Publishing your art (the first account)

Fill in all the necessary digital art information, then click **SUBMIT**. The submit request—the `createTokenAndSellArt()` method—was detected by MetaMask. The pop-up screen will automatically show up as you confirm the transaction request with the gas fee. Here is a screenshot:

Accept the pop-up request and confirm. MetaMask will forward the transaction to the connected blockchain and invoke the related transaction. In our case, it is a `createTokenAndSellArt` method for the `DigitalArt` smart contract.

Once the transaction is successfully processed in the blockchain, our home page will display our first digital art for sale from the author:

Great. Next, let's look at my wallet info.

# My wallet info (the first account)

As we discussed before, **MY WALLET INFO** page has three functions:

- Displaying wallet information
- Displaying owned digital art products
- Reselling owned digital products

**Display wallet information**: click the **MY WALLET INFO** tab, at the top of the page; we will see the current user's account information, including `address`, `networkId`, `networkType`, and `balance`:

My Address: 0x6c508059e7372BA678e632460673aCd75Cde4cdE            NetworkId: 5777

Balance: 99.88484612 (ether)            NetworkType: private

**Owned digital art products**: it displays the author and the product after he/she published his/her product:

1. Notice that the first account balance is 99.88 ether at this moment.
2. Repeat the same process, submit the author's second product—`A silent moment`.
3. Let's switch to the second account in the MetaMask wallet and refresh the page.
4. Do a similar process as for the first account. We should see two digital art products are published in the market, as shown in the following image:

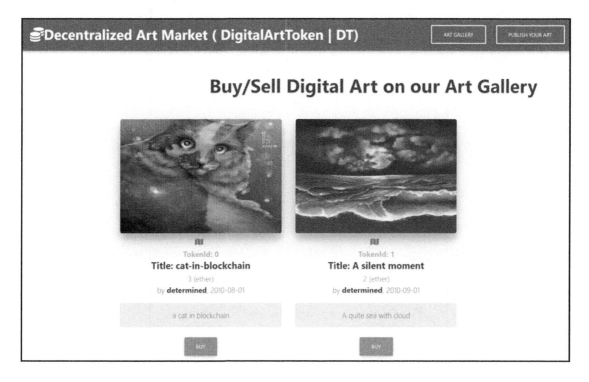

The confirmed transaction history also stored in the MetaMask wallet under the associated account.

We can see that there are two transactions:

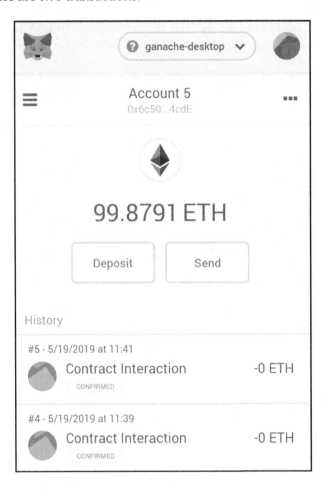

The transaction information is also displayed in the Ganache desktop under
the **TRANSACTION** tab. Open the Ganache desktop, and you will see similar information:

Click the **Contract Call** link; we can see the `createTokenAndSellArt` function invoked in the blockchain. The Contract Call link shows the details like how much gas is used in this transaction call, and what the gas limit is:

Under the **BLOCK** tab, we can see **BLOCK 6** was successfully mined. It also shows the block hash and transaction hash information. We also know when the block was mined. In an actual Ethereum public network, that information is public and transparent:

We have now deployed our smart contract and learned the basic Ganache desktop features. It is time to interact with our digital art market DApp.

# Publishing your art (the second account)

Similar to the first account, the DApp can support, publish, and submit art from the second account. The second account submits a digital artwork called `gril`:

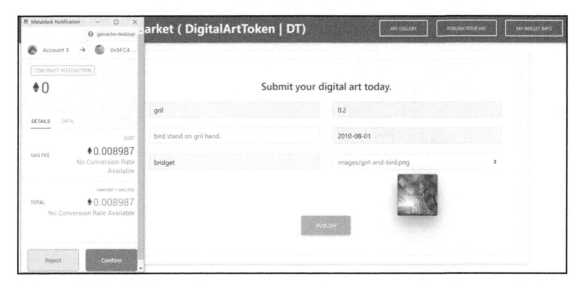

Enter the price of the art, its name, and owner information, then click **PUBLISH**. The example is shown in the preceding screenshot. It will submit a digital art product for the second account.

# My wallet info (the second account)

In the second account's **MY WALLET INFO** page, the page will show related wallet information and a digital artwork titled `gril` as an owned and published product. Here is the wallet info page:

Next, we will buy digital art from the second account.

# Buying art (the second account)

As the second account user, let's assume you want to buy digital art. Click the `cat-in-blockchain` digital art **BUY** button and confirm the MetaMask transaction popup as shown in the following image:

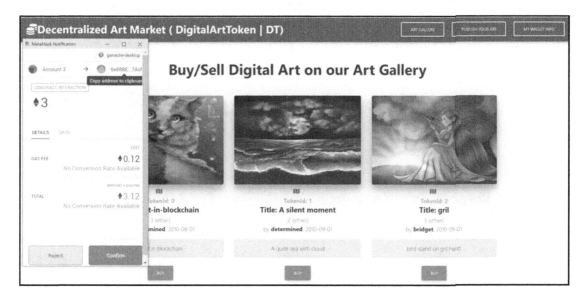

After a successful transaction, the second account user should now own the `cat-in-blockchain` product. You may notice the **PUBLISH** button is available for `cat-in-blockchain` since it is not in selling status. In the following image, the `gril` digital doesn't have the **PUBLISH** button; this art is still in the market for sale. This account user can resell the product:

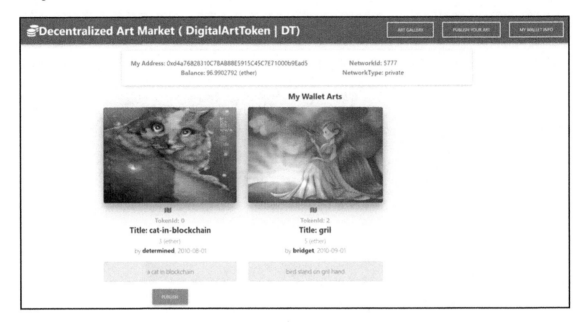

Let's navigate to the home page. As shown in the following screenshot, we can see **A silent moment**, and **gril** are up for sale, whereas `cat-in-blockchain` is off the market. This worked as expected:

**Verify ownership transferred:** Switch to the first account, which originally owned `cat-in-blockchain`. Now, ownership has been transferred to the second account. There is only **A silent moment** remaining as shown in the following screenshot:

**Verify ether balance transfer:** We verify most of our smart contract functions. We also need to check that the original owner also gets paid by the second owner.

We have noted that the first account initial balance is 99.88 ether after publishing the art. The **cat-in-blockchain** price is 3 ether. After selling the digital art, the first account balance should be 102.88 ether.

Open the first **MY WALLET INFO** account; we can see the account balance is 102.88 ether, as shown here:

Awesome! We have verified ownership transfer and balance payment. Before we end this section, there is still one more function that we need to verify—reselling art.

# Reselling art

Now it is time to verify the last function: resellArt().

1. Switch to the second account.
2. Select cat-in-blockchain and click the **PUBLISH** button.
3. A pop-up screen opens for asking the selling price.

4. Enter the desired selling price (ether units), as shown in the following screenshot.

5. Click **SUBMIT**:

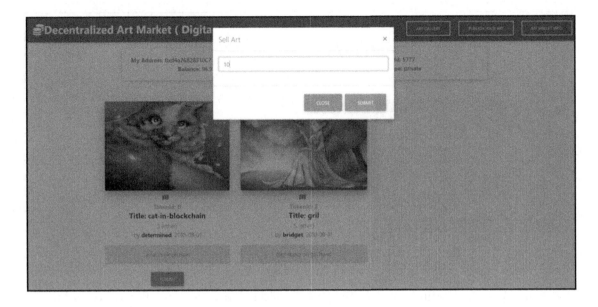

6. Accept and confirm the transaction popup from MetaMask, as shown in the following screenshot:

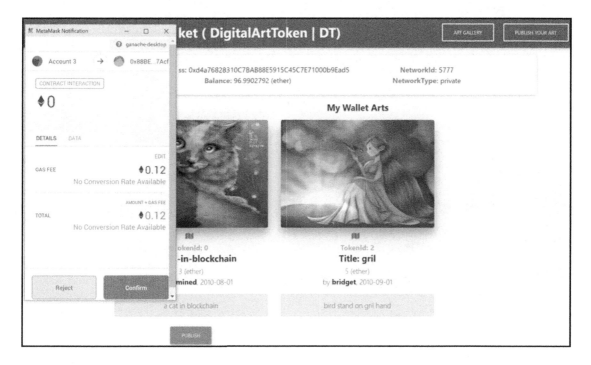

With successful submission, `cat-in-blockchain` in the second user wallet is now in sell status. The prices are updated to 10 ether, as shown in the following screenshot:

My Address: 0xd4a76828310C7BAB88E5915C45C7E71000b9Ead5

Balance: 96.98917462 (ether)

NetworkId: 5777

NetworkType: private

## My Wallet Arts

TokenId: 0

**Title: cat-in-blockchain**

10 (ether)

by **determined**, 2010-08-01

a cat in blockchain

TokenId: 2

**Title: gril**

5 (ether)

by **bridget**, 2010-09-01

bird stand on gril hand

On the following **Art Gallery** page, `cat-in-blockchain` is shown on the **Decentralized Art Market** for sale:

If you have followed the whole example and were able to run to this step, congratulations! You will be able to develop an end-to-end DApp.

# Summary

In this chapter, we covered the popular DApp concept, and learnt about the web3 JavaScript API. After setting up the development environment, we built our digital art market DApp. Finally, we ran through the application and verified all of the functions we have built so far. We have learned in detail how to build the end-to-end DApp with a smart contract and tools.

In the next chapter, we will continue our learning journey and explore how to monitor smart contracts.

# 8
# Ethereum Tools and Frameworks

In this chapter, we will explore the popular tools and frameworks that you come across frequently while starting to learn Ethereum. This will help you get a grasp on the big picture of the Ethereum ecosystem and apply this knowledge to Ethereum project development. The topics that we will cover in this chapter are as follows:

- Understanding the Ethereum development tools and framework
- The Ethereum client API
- Ethereum storage
- Ethereum messaging – Whisper
- Popular smart contract libraries

## Technical requirements

To find the source code for this book, please refer to the following GitHub link:

`https://github.com/PacktPublishing/Learn-Ethereum.`

# Understanding the Ethereum development tools and frameworks

For the DApp software development life cycle, efficient use of the popular tools, frameworks, and libraries can help reduce the time from prototype to production and reduce the risk of the smart contract. Since more people are using and testing these tools, they tend to be more stable.

There are many different Ethereum development tools and frameworks the market today, all of which represent different standards. Here are some of the most popular tools and frameworks:

- Truffle
- Embark
- Infura
- DApp
- Waffle

In Chapter 6, *Smart Contract Development and Test Fundamentals*, we discussed the Truffle tool. In this section, we will review one of the popular tools listed here—Infura. For other tools, please visit their official websites to learn more.

# Working with Infura

Infura provides a collection of full node interfaces that allow the client application to access the Ethereum network in a scalable, secure, and reliable way. ConsenSys provides Infura service to maintain these Ethereum and **InterPlanetary File System (IPFS)** nodes. Developers don't need to worry about the complexity of running these Ethereum and IPFS nodes. MetaMask uses Infura as the Ethereum provider to connect to the Ethereum blockchain. The following diagram shows the technical architecture of how a web client connects with IPFS and the Ethereum node through Infura:

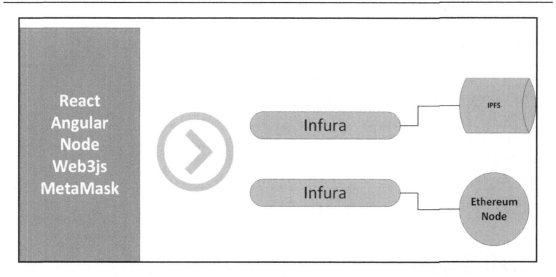

To start working with the Infura service, you need to sign up for an account from the Infura website: `https://infura.io/register`. At the time of writing, the latest available version is Infura V3.

Once you've signed up, you can create a project to start your DApp development. The website will provide you with an access token to connect to the relevant Ethereum network. After creating a project, you should see the following page:

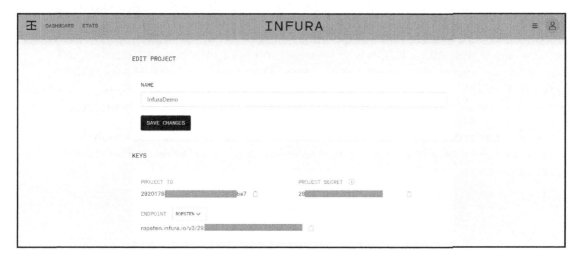

Infura provides links for various environments, including the main Ethereum network and other popular test networks. These environments are listed in the following table:

| Env | Link |
| --- | --- |
| Main Ethereum Network | `https://mainnet.infura.io/v3/YOUR-PROJECT-ID` |
| Rinkeby Test Ethereum Network | `https://rinkeby.infura.io/v3/YOUR-PROJECT-ID` |
| Ropsten Test Ethereum Network | `https://ropsten.infura.io/v3/YOUR-PROJECT-ID` |
| Görli Test Ethereum Network | `https://goerli.infura.io/v3/YOUR-PROJECT-ID` |
| IPFS Gateway | `https://ipfs.infura.io/ipfs/` |

Next, let's explore Infura's Ethereum API.

# Working with the Infura Ethereum API

You can build and invoke Ethereum nodes through the Infura load-balanced nodes by calling the Ethereum API. Just write a regular JSON RPC over both HTTPS and WebSockets code; you can use popular Ethereum client libraries and frameworks to access node information.

 When an API needs to support the Pub/Sub feature, a WebSockets endpoint is the better choice; it also provides JSON-RPC filter support, for example, `eth_newFilter`, which creates a filter in the node to notify us when a new block arrives, and more.

Let's create a simple Infura DApp to get account and node information from the Görli testnet; we will use web3.js for this. In our Infura DApp, we will use the newer Görli test network. Ropsten is not immune to spam attacks, causing the gas prices to inflate due to its 51% attack rate. Görli is based on the clique consensus and is supported by multiple clients.

Before we start exploring the Ethereum API for Infura, let's get some ether in the Görli testnet. As shown in the following screenshot, you can get ether and send ether requests from `https://goerli-faucet.slock.it/`:

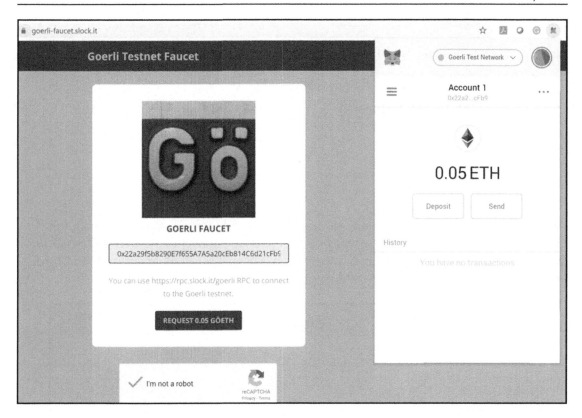

 **TIP**

To find other testnet faucets, for example, the Ropsten test network, you can use the following link: `https://faucet.metamask.io/`.

Now that we have ethers in our wallet account, it is time to write some simple Infura Ethereum APIs to experience how to interact with the blockchain. Let's write a simple HTML script, as follows:

```html
<html>
<header>
    <title>Infura</title>
    <script
src="https://cdn.jsdelivr.net/gh/ethereum/web3.js@1.0.0-beta.36/dist/web3.m
in.js" integrity="sha256-nWBTbvxhJgjslRyuAKJHK+XcZPlCnmIAAMixz6EefVk="
crossorigin="anonymous"></script>
    <script src="https://code.jquery.com/jquery-3.4.1.min.js"
integrity="sha256-CSXorXvZcTkaix6Yvo6HppcZGetbYMGWSFlBw8HfCJo="
crossorigin="anonymous"></script>
```

```
    <script>
    if (typeof web3 !== 'undefined') {
        web3 = new Web3(web3.currentProvider);
    } else {
        // Set the provider you want from
        Web3.providers
        web3 = new Web3(new
Web3.providers.HttpProvider("https://goerli.infura.io/v3/<your infura
projectID>"));
    }
    </script>
</header>
</html>
```

First, we load the `web3.min.js` and `jquery` libraries and then set up providers. In this case, we have MetaMask as our current provider and we connect to the Görli testnet. The project provides Görli Infura address information. You can select other environment Infura links as well. This is shown in the following screenshot:

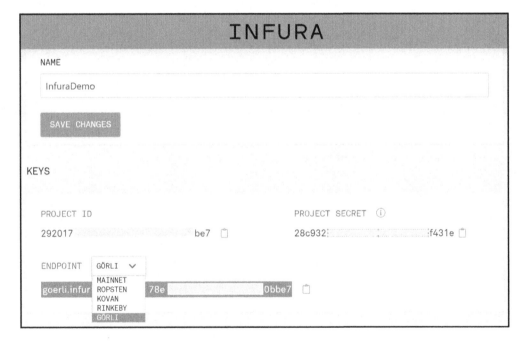

Let's write a query to get the latest block information from Infura:

```html
<body>
<div>
    <h2>Latest Block</h2><span id="lastblock"></span>
</div>
<script>
    web3.eth.getBlockNumber(function (err, res) {
        if (err) console.log(err)
        $( "#lastblock" ).text(res)
    })
</script>
</body>
```

The preceding code will connect to Infura through web3.js and return the most recent block number from the blockchain. We use the `web3.getBlockNumber` API to achieve this. In the web page, the block number will be displayed on the screen, as shown here:

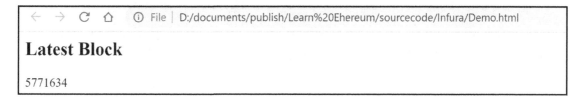

Similarly, we can use the web3 API to get the balance and query other nodes' information. Here is the code for this:

```javascript
web3.eth.getBalance("your metamask account address", function (err, res) {
    if (err) console.log(err)
    $( "#balance" ).text(res)
})
web3.eth.getNodeInfo(function (err, res) {
    if (err) console.log(err)
    $( "#nodeInfo" ).text(res)
})
```

The `getBalance()` function returns the current account balance, while `getNodeInfo()` returns node information. The UI information is shown here:

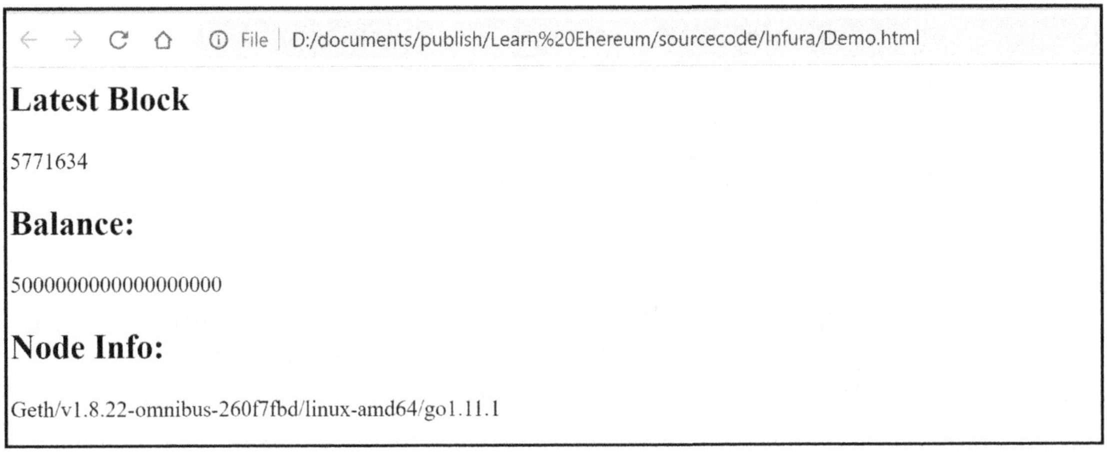

```
←  →  C  ⌂    ⓘ File | D:/documents/publish/Learn%20Ehereum/sourcecode/Infura/Demo.html
```

**Latest Block**

5771634

**Balance:**

5000000000000000000

**Node Info:**

Geth/v1.8.22-omnibus-260f7fbd/linux-amd64/go1.11.1

We just saw how easy it is to use the web3 API, to connecting with the Infura blockchain environment. Remix also provides very easy integration with Infura. Let's have a look.

# Using Remix with Infura

We can deploy the ERC20 token smart contract shown in Chapter 5, *Developing Your Own Cryptocurrency*, from Remix to the Infura Ropsten testnet easily. Just use an injected Web3 instance by using MetaMask, which is already connected to Ropsten testnet through Infura. If you need ethers for test, you can get them from `https://faucet.metamask.io`:

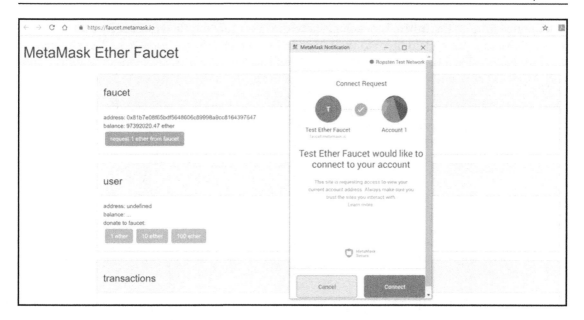

Follow the regular deployment process; the smart contract will be deployed to the Ropsten testnet in a few clicks, as shown here:

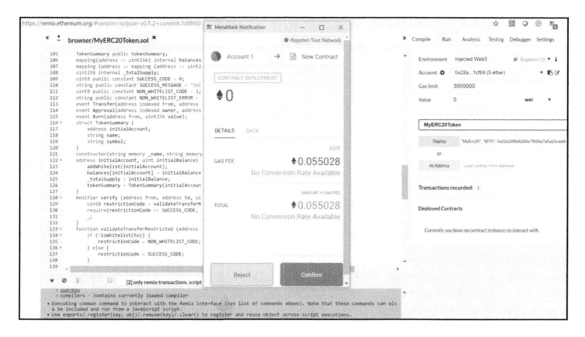

After connecting to the Infura blockchain network, you can call the smart contract function; as usual, MetaMask will connect to the testnet and execute transactions. You don't even need to install a local blockchain instance. Due to this, smart contract development becomes very easy and convenient. You just need to connect to the network provided by Infura.

You can also easily transfer amounts from one account to another by using the send ETH method from the MetaMask wallet. The following example shows that we sent 2 ethers from one account to another:

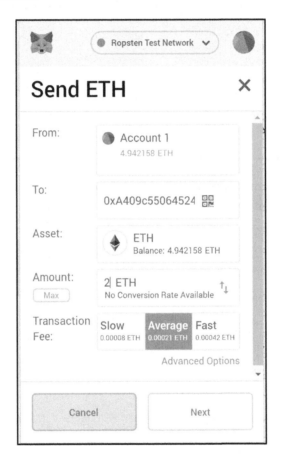

Click **Next** and confirm the transaction. Once the transfer has completed, we can verify that the ether was sent in Etherscan. Etherscan is the block explorer and analytics platform for the Ethereum blockchain. You can easily search, confirm, and validate smart contract transactions that have been deployed on the Ethereum blockchain using this platform. In Chapter 10, *Deployment of your Smart Contract*, in the *Monitoring smart contracts* section, we will discuss more the Etherscan tool in more detail.

The following screenshot shows our transactions in **Etherscan**:

As we can see, Infura has undoubtedly provided an easy solution to help developers build DApps on the Ethereum network. A developer can focus on their application development and utilize infrastructure supported by Infura.

We have quickly reviewed Ethereum's popular tools and framework. I hope you have enjoyed what you have learned so far. Next, we will review the Ethereum client API.

# The Ethereum client API

The Ethereum client API allows you to connect to the Ethereum node and send a transaction to the blockchain. Through the Ethereum client, you can create and run a smart contract. There are many client libraries that have been written by different programming languages. Here is a list of some of them:

| Ethereum client API | Programming language |
|---|---|
| web3.js | JavaScript Web3 |
| ethers.js | Similar to JavaScript Web3 |
| EthereumJS | Provide collections of utility functions |
| Web3.py | Python web3 API |
| web3j | Java web3 API |
| web3.php | PHP web3 API |
| Nethereum | .net Web3 API |
| ethereum.rb | Ruby Web3 API |
| Web3.hs | Haskell Web3 API |
| KEthereum | Kotlin Web3 API |
| Ethereumex | Elixir JSON-RPC client for the Ethereum blockchain |

Java, as one of the most popular and influential programming languages, has a large number of developers and programmers. The Ethereum Web3j library allows Java developers to interact with the blockchain. In the next section, we will discuss the Web3j API. If you are not familiar with Java, you can skip the next section.

# Working with Web3j

Web3j is a Java client library that can connect to an Ethereum node. Similar to Web3 JavaScript, it can be used to interact with a smart contract on the Ethereum node. It can generate a Java smart contract from Solidity contract files.

First, let's set up the Web3j environment, as shown in the following steps:

1. Install the Solidity compiler, `solc`, and run the following command to install it:

```
npm install -g solc
```

2. Install `web3j` using the `run brew` command (at the time of writing, we used `web3j-4.2.0`):

```
brew tap web3j/web3j

brew install web3j
```

Once `solc` and `web3j` have been installed, you will see the following screen:

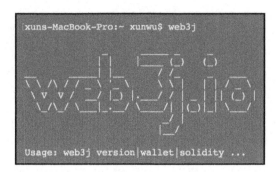

 We use macOS to set up the `web3j` environment; for other OS environments, please check the Web3j official website: `https://docs.web3j.io/getting_started/`.

3. Compile and translate the smart contract into a Java class. We will use the `helloWord` smart contract as an example. Here is the smart contract:

```
pragma solidity >=0.4.22 <0.6.0;
contract helloWorld {
    function getMessage() public pure returns (string memory) {
        return "Hello World!";
    }
}
```

4. Run the `solc` command, as shown here, to generate the `bin` and `abi` files:

**solcjs helloworld.sol --bin --abi --optimize -o compile/**

Once the command runs successfully, you will see that the following two files are generated:

- `helloworld_sol_helloWorld.abi`
- `helloworld_sol_helloWorld.bin`

5. Generate a Java class from the smart contract by running the following command:

```
web3j solidity generate --javaTypes -b
helloworld_sol_helloWorld.bin -a helloworld_sol_helloWorld.abi -o .
-p com.packt.learnethereum
```

The result of the preceding command will look as follows:

Copy the generated Java class into a Java project. In the next step, we will build out the Java Maven project.

6. Set up a Web3j Maven project. Use your favorite Java IDE (Eclipse or IntelliJ) to create a Maven project and add the following dependency to the Maven project. We used version 4.2.0 in this example:

```xml
<!-- https://mvnrepository.com/artifact/org.web3j/core -->
  <dependency>
        <groupId>org.web3j</groupId>
        <artifactId>core</artifactId>
        <version>4.2.0</version>
  </dependency>
```

This will load the Web3j library into your project.

7. Deploy a smart contract. In our example, we will deploy the `helloWorld` smart contract to Infura through MetaMask.

8. In MetaMask, select **Inject web3** as **Environment** and connect MetaMask to the Infura Ropsten test network. Then click **Deploy**. The deployed contract address can be found for the deployed contract by clicking the copy icon, as shown here:

When clicking on **Deploy**, MetaMask confirms this in a popup. Check and click the **Confirm** button. This will deploy the contract to the remote Ropsten network. Here is a screenshot of confirming transactions:

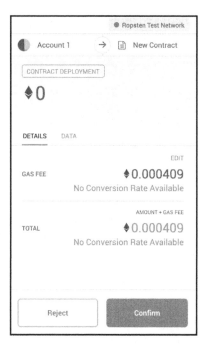

Let's get some basic blockchain information through the Web3j API:

- Get `web3ClientVersion` through the Web3j API, as shown here:

```
Web3j web3j = Web3j.build(new
HttpService("https://ropsten.infura.io/v3/your key"));
Web3ClientVersion web3ClientVersion =
web3j.web3ClientVersion().send();
```

  This will return the web3 client version. `Web3j.build` instantiates the Web3j instance. Then, you can use `web3j.web3ClientVersion().send()` to get the client version. The Web3j Infura API provides the specific Infura-Ethereum-Preferred-Client header. This allows the client to connect to the blockchain network through Infura.

  You can get account-, balance-, and transaction-related information through the Web3j API as follows:

- Get the block number with `ethBlockNumber()`, as shown here:

```
web3j.ethBlockNumber().sendAsync().get()
```

- Get the account balance with `ethGetBalance()`, as shown here:

```
web3j.ethGetBalance(address,
    DefaultBlockParameter.valueOf("latest")).sendAsync().get()
```

- Send 1 ether to another account with `sendFunds()`, as shown here:

```
Credentials credentials = Credentials.create("<<your acct proviate
key>>");
Transfer.sendFunds(web3j, credentials, "<<target acct address>>",
BigDecimal.valueOf(1.0),
Convert.Unit.ETHER).send()
```

- Call a smart contract with `load()`:

  We can use the previous Web3j API to generate a Java class load method by passing the deployed contract address, Web3j instance, credential, and default gas provider. This will connect and invoke a remote contract and call-related contract method, as shown here:

  ```
  Helloworld_sol_helloWorld contract =
  Helloworld_sol_helloWorld.load("<<contract address>>", web3j,
  credentials, new DefaultGasProvider());
  String message = contract.getMessage().send();
  ```

Once all of the preceding Web3j functions have been executed, you will see the following output:

```
tWeb3ClientVersion: Geth/v1.8.22-omnibus-260f7fbd/linux-amd64/go1.11.1
Current Block Number: 5793493
firstAcctBalanceBefore: 2999548719000000000
secondAcctBalanceBefore: 7000000000000000000
transactionHash: 0xe056983967f1825ff9b9b89afd98e29134027a735af994c3031792dc529d6122
firstAcctBalanceAfter: 1999527719000000000
secondAcctBalanceAfter: 8000000000000000000
Helloworld message: Hello World!
```

We just reviewed the Web3j Ethereum API. As a Java developer, I hope you now feel comfortable writing some smart contract client APIs to interact with Ethereum.

Next, we will move on to another important topic—Ethereum decentralized storage.

# Ethereum storage

In `Chapter 3`, *Deep Research on Ethereum*, we provided a high-level overview of different decentralized data and storage solutions in Ethereum, including IPFS, Swarm, and BigchainDB. In this section, we will delve into more details and steps to get started with some of the popular decentralized solutions.

In current cloud-based data storage, all data is stored in centralized cloud vendor's servers; data access is through location-based addressing. The vendor handles and controls many background process jobs. Via vendor services, you can upload your data to a cloud server and set up a data recovery strategy to handle availability.

With a security access policy, data encryption, and other approaches, you can secure your data in cloud storage. The centralized storage solution makes data easier to manage, scale, and secure. However, because of this centralized nature, you do not fully control the data. You may face a data breach, data outage, lack of ownership, and other risks.

On the other hand, decentralized data storage stores data in multiple machines on the decentralized network. You can download your file similar to BitTorrent and other **peer-to-peer (P2P)** clients using a distributed P2P file sharing system. The entire file is distributed as smart chunks or data fragments and shared across all the client machines that have participants in the file download process. You can start sharing your client node as soon as you start downloading a small piece of the file. One of the main issues with the BitTorrent protocol is the lack of incentive for the user to run the client without rewards. Many of the download feeds come from a few hosts. The decentralized data storage migrates a similar issue by way of monetary rewards.

There is already enormous decentralized cloud storage offerings for blockchain applications on the market. We will review two of the most popular Ethereum storage solutions:

- **Interplanetary File System (IPFS)**
- Swarm

IPFS uses Filecoin as the incentive layer. For SWARM, the Ethereum Geth client is built in the incentive components.

# Knowing the IPFS protocol

IPFS is a protocol and decentralized network that stores and delivers information by content instead of by location. Each IPFS file, including the blocks it contains, has a unique cryptographic hash. When you search IPFS files, the network will look up the nodes storing the contents by unique cryptographic hash. An IPFS support file can be accessed in a variety of ways, including FUSE and HTTP. Since each IPFS file has its own unique hash, which will remove file duplications in the network when content is changed, the address will also change and a new hash key will be generated. **Inter-Planetary Name System (IPNS)** is a decentralized naming system that can create and update human-readable and mutable links for IPFS content.

The IPNS address will use the `/ipns/` prefix, followed by the hash of a public key. It is associated with content information that's signed by the paired private key. When publishing new content, the content can be encrypted and signed with a private key.

Here is an example of an IPNS address link:

```
/ipns/QmOuTrFhUKA3ZodhzPWHbCFgcPMFWF4QsxXbkWfEpkitDa
```

You can publish an `ipns` address as follows:

```
const addr = '/ipfs/QmOuTrFhUKA3ZodhzPWHbCFgcPMFWF4QsxXbkWfEpkitDa'
ipfs.name.publish(addr, function (err, res) {
..
});
```

Similar to BitTorrent, IPFS will allow users to both receive and host content. We have introduced the basics of IPFS. Now, let's run a hands-on IPFS example.

# Installing IPFS

To start using IPFS, we need to install it. We will use a Unix environment for our IPFS example. The tools will allow us to upload and view the content on the IPFS network:

1. First, we will install `go`. Afterward, we get the latest security updates. Then, we will extract the files after downloading them. Finally, we will move the package to the `/usr/local` directory:

```
apt-get update
apt-get install build-essential
wget https://dl.google.com/go/go1.12.6.linux-amd64.tar.gz
sudo tar -xvf go1.12.6.linux-amd64.tar.gz
sudo mv go /usr/local
```

2. For IPFS to work properly, we need to set up the Go software environment variables. Create a file called `/etc/profile.d/go.sh`. Add the following Go software environment variables to the file:

```
#/bin/bash
export GOROOT=/usr/local/go
export GOPATH=$GOROOT/work
export PATH=$PATH:$GOROOT/bin:$GOPATH/bin
```

3. Reboot Ubuntu using the following command and verify whether `go` has installed successfully:

```
reboot
go version
```

You should see the `go version` output in the console.

4. To install `ipfs`, you may need to log in as an admin user by running `sudo -i`. Then, run the following command to install IPFS:

```
go get -u -d github.com/ipfs/go-ipfs
cd $GOPATH/src/github.com/ipfs/go-ipfs
make install
```

Here is a screenshot that shows the output of the preceding command:

```
ubuntu@ip-172-31-41-161:~$ sudo -i
root@ip-172-31-41-161:~# go get -u -d github.com/ipfs/go-ipfs
root@ip-172-31-41-161:~# cd $GOPATH/src/github.com/ipfs/go-ipfs
root@ip-172-31-41-161:/usr/local/go/work/src/github.com/ipfs/go-ipfs# make install
go version go1.12.6 linux/amd64
bin/check_go_version 1.12
go install  -asmflags=all=-trimpath="/usr/local/go/work" -gcflags=all=-trimpath="/usr/local/go/work"
pfs
go: finding github.com/ipfs/go-ipfs-blockstore v0.0.1
```

Once IPFS has been successfully installed, the output will show the version of `go-ipfs-blockstore`. In our installation, this is `v0.0.1`.

# Starting an IPFS node

Once installed successfully, enter the `ipfs init` command to start your IPFS node. You will see your IPFS node ID:

```
ubuntu@ip-172-31-41-161:~$ ipfs init
initializing IPFS node at /home/ubuntu/.ipfs
generating 2048-bit RSA keypair...done
peer identity: QmasretZGnmUBZQ4Za5S2m62qWU5nju2uaveRp5QvEzmFU
to get started, enter:

        ipfs cat /ipfs/QmS4ustL54uo8FzR9455qaxZwuMiUhyvMcX9Ba8nUH4uVv/readme
```

Run the following command and the welcome page will be displayed:

```
ipfs cat /ipfs/<nodeID>, the IPFS
```

This is what the welcome page will look like:

```
ubuntu@ip-172-31-41-161:~$ ipfs cat /ipfs/QmS4ustL54uo8FzR9455qaxZwuMiUhyvMcX9Ba8nUH4uVv/readme
Hello and Welcome to IPFS!

IPFS

If you're seeing this, you have successfully installed
IPFS and are now interfacing with the ipfs merkledag!

-------------------------------------------------------
| Warning:                                            |
|   This is alpha software. Use at your own discretion! |
|   Much is missing or lacking polish. There are bugs. |
|   Not yet secure. Read the security notes for more.  |
-------------------------------------------------------

Check out some of the other files in this directory:

  ./about
  ./help
  ./quick-start     <-- usage examples
  ./readme          <-- this file
  ./security-notes
```

We now have the initial IPFS node. To start the IPFS service, run the following command:

```
ipfs daemon
```

Here is the result of the preceding command:

```
[ubuntu@ip-172-31-41-161:~$ ipfs daemon
Initializing daemon...
go-ipfs version: 0.4.22-dev-810cb60
Repo version: 7
System version: amd64/linux
Golang version: go1.12.6
Swarm listening on /ip4/127.0.0.1/tcp/4001
Swarm listening on /ip4/172.31.41.161/tcp/4001
Swarm listening on /ip6/::1/tcp/4001
Swarm listening on /p2p-circuit
Swarm announcing /ip4/127.0.0.1/tcp/4001
Swarm announcing /ip4/172.31.41.161/tcp/4001
Swarm announcing /ip6/::1/tcp/4001
API server listening on /ip4/127.0.0.1/tcp/5001
WebUI: http://127.0.0.1:5001/webui
Gateway (readonly) server listening on /ip4/127.0.0.1/tcp/8080
Daemon is ready
```

Run the following command in a new Terminal to view the nodes in the network that we're directly connected to:

```
ipfs swarm peers
```

Here is the resulting screen:

```
ubuntu@ip-172-31-41-161:~$ ipfs swarm peers
/ip4/104.131.131.82/tcp/4001/ipfs/QmaCpDMGvV2BGHeYERUEnRQAwe3N8SzbUtfsmvsqQLuvuJ
/ip4/104.236.179.241/tcp/4001/ipfs/QmSoLPppuBtQSGwKDZT2M73ULpjvfd3aZ6ha4oFGL1KrGM
/ip4/128.199.219.111/tcp/4001/ipfs/QmSoLSafTMBsPKadTEgaXctDQVcqN88CNLHXMkTNwMKPnu
/ip4/138.197.186.92/tcp/4001/ipfs/QmQ6pkvmp45Gd1LbnuCV3jF1Ta24AGHvd5qLrJgtTnvWJ3
/ip4/139.178.69.3/tcp/4001/ipfs/QmdGQoGuK3pao6bRDqGSDvux5SFHa4kC2XNFfHFcvcbydY
/ip4/218.16.123.42/tcp/14003/ipfs/QmRUipdchtUzVuistKMxUxe7ZDFuscWkwn8HnySwzQQZi2
```

We have installed IPFS in our machine. Next, we will run a simple example so that you can see how we can use IPFS.

# Running an IPFS example

First, we will take a look at how to publish a simple page to IPFS and how to view the published content in IPFS.

## Publishing a simple page in the command line

We will first create an HTML file—learn-ethereum-ipfs.html—and add some content to it, as shown in the following code block:

```
<html>
<body>
<h1>Learn Ethereum</h1>
<h2>Hello IPFS</h2>
</body>
</html>
```

Then, we will add it to IPFS by running the following command:

```
ipfs add -w learn-ethereum-ipfs.html
```

The result is shown here. We can see the **74 B** size of the file at 100% load in IPFS:

```
ubuntu@ip-172-31-41-161:~$ ipfs add -w learn-ethereum-ipfs.html
added QmUnLXNyWTqh2qbmZoyfqzR8qXRBtSeFe4RCKmRf2tGj2v learn-ethereum-ipfs.html
added QmNdDqo9xkNDCjNhVeNgkUXcYpQ3K5G5ZT4BUUUqJxrx8u
74 B / 74 B [===============================================================] 100.00%
ubuntu@ip-172-31-41-161:~$
```

QmUnLXNyWTqh2qbmZoyfqzR8qXRBtSmFm4RCKmRf2tGj2v is the address ID that was assigned by IPFS; you can view the upload file content from the IPFS gateway: https://gateway.ipfs.io/ipfs/QmUnLXNyWTqh2qbmZoyfqzR8qXRBtSmFm4RCKmRf2tGj2v.

Here is a screenshot of the resulting screen:

We just published content to IPFS through the command line. We can also do this by writing a program that publishes content to IPFS.

## Publishing and querying IPFS via Infura

In this example, we will write a simple JavaScript to publish and query data to IPFS via Infura:

1. To start the project, just create a project folder. Navigate to the project folder and run the following command to initialize a node IPFS project:

```
npm init -yes
ipfs-mini
```

2. Create the publish side node file, PublishData.js, as shown in the following code block. First, we use the ipfs-mini library and connect to https://infura via ipfs.infura.io:5001. Then, we call ipfs.add to add data to IPFS:

```
const IPFS = require('ipfs-mini');
const ipfs = new IPFS({host: 'ipfs.infura.io', port: 5001,
protocol: 'https'});
const myData = "Hello IPFS Infura";
ipfs.add(myData, (err, data) => {
   console.log("IPFS HASH:", data);
});
```

We will see that the hash value is returned after the `ipfs.add` function, like so:

```
ubuntu@ip-172-31-41-161:~/ipfs$ node PublishData.js
IPFS HASH: QmRF2XAkJbQYNQYYscr7ctUkhEUdyFWQfwBdXQiZaWgMyF
```

We will use the return hash to search for the data on the query side.

3. Write `QueryData.js` on the query side to get the published data from IPFS:

```
const IPFS = require('ipfs-mini');
const ipfs = new IPFS({host: 'ipfs.infura.io', port: 5001,
protocol: 'https'});
const ipfsHash = "QmRF2XAkJbQYNQYYscr7ctUkhEUdyFWQfwBdXQiZaWgMyF";
ipfs.cat(ipfsHash, (err, data) => {
 console.log("Received:", data);
});
```

Similar to `PublishData.js`, we set up the initial IPFS connection by using the `ipfs-mini` library. We call the `ipfs.cat` function to retrieve the published IPFS data. The result is as follows:

```
ubuntu@ip-172-31-41-161:~/ipfs$ node QueryData.js
Received: Hello IPFS Infura
```

Congratulations! You just learned how to publish your own data to decentralized storage—IPFS. In the next section, we will quickly review another similar decentralized storage—Swarm.

# Working with Swarm

We discussed Swarm in Chapter 3, *Deep Research on Ethereum*, in the *Decentralized data and content storage* section. We learned that Swarm is a distributed storage platform and content distribution service, and the native base layer service of the Ethereum Web3 stack. We showed the use case for Swarm and the typical Ethereum DApp application architecture diagram for it. In this section, we will show you how to install Swarm and get started using Swarm for decentralized content storage.

Swarm is very similar to IPFS; it is made up of Ethereum as the storage layer based on the Ethereum web3 stack and supports the Ethereum Geth client. It connects to Ethereum blockchain and requires an Ethereum account. Nodes in the Swarm network use the `bzz` wire protocol, which is based on devp2p/rlpx as a transport protocol for communication among Ethereum nodes. devp2p/rlpx is a TCP-based transport protocol that's used for P2P communication among Ethereum nodes. RLPx carries encrypted messages belonging to one or more capabilities to send and receive packets. One of the primary objectives of Swarm is to allow DApps to efficiently store and share their data with the end user. Swarm is still under development and not fully operational.

The following diagram shows the Swarm distributed storage architecture:

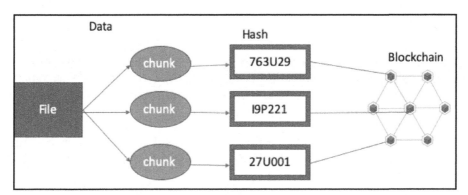

Swarm has a distributed chunk store, which has the basic unit of storage with a fixed maximum size (currently,this is 4 KB). The chunk store is deterministically derived from its addressed content. When any kind of readable source, such as images, texts, or video records, is uploaded to Swarm, the Swarm API layer will chop this data into fixed-sized chunks. A unique cryptographic hash is generated for each chunk. The hashes of these chunks will be used to generate another unique hash of a new chunk. Currently, 128 hashes make up a new chunk. The content gets mapped to a chunk tree. This builds up a Merkle tree, and the root hash of the tree is the address that you use to retrieve the uploaded file. This hierarchical Swarm hash construct allows chunk data within a unique hash, providing data integrity and allowing protected random access. When the chunk is damaged or has been tampered with, the tree can tell by just hashing it.

On top of the chunk Merkle trees, Swarm provides a crucial third layer: manifest files. The manifest defines a document collection for organizing content and defines a mapping between arbitrary paths and files. The metadata in the Swarm manifests are associated with the collection, files, and media mime type. Here is an example:

```
{
   "entries": [{
      "hash": "4b3a73e43......048d",
      "contentType": "text/html; charset=utf-8",
      "path": "index.html"
   },{
      "hash": "69b0a42a9382.....98Ta",
      "contentType": "application/pdf",
      "path": "a.pdf"
   }]}
```

The preceding manifest file specifies a document collection; each document defines its path, unique cryptographic hash, and content type. You can think of a manifest as a dictionary that provides a service for the user and tells them what the content is and where to find it. Swarm exposes the manifest API via the `bzz` URL scheme.

The Swarm node directly connects to the Ethereum network and has the cryptographic hash associated with their bzz-account address. The nodes pool provides a distributed storage and content distribution service.

The actual storage layer of Swarm supports both localstore and netstore, and they have the following properties:

- Localstore has both a memory store and dbstore:
  - In-memory fast cache
  - Persistent disk storage
- Netstore does the following:
  - Implements the distributed preimage archive
  - Extends localstore to a Swarm distributed storage

In the concept of a distributed preimage archive adopted in Swarm, nodes that close to a chunk's address actually host the data, alongside providing information about its content. The access frequency of the chunks determines what the nodes are storing. When nodes reach a certain storage limit, the oldest unaccessed chunks will be purged.

# Installing Swarm

To start a Swarm instance, we need to install both Geth and Swarm on our machine. We will use Ubuntu as our installation environment. The Geth tool is the Go Ethereum standalone client written in the Go language. Geth is an Ethereum client node, and it can verify the block broadcast onto the network. Geth is also responsible for maintaining your local copy of Ethereum's network state.

The simplest way to install Swarm is via the built-in launchpad PPAs (Personal Package Archives):

1. Enable our launchpad repository and run the following command:

```
sudo apt-get install software-properties-common
sudo add-apt-repository -y ppa:ethereum/ethereum
```

2. The following command will help you install a stable version of Swarm:

```
sudo apt-get update
sudo apt-get install ethereum-swarm
```

3. Once installed successfully, verify the Swarm version. It will look like this:

```
ubuntu@ip-172-31-41-161:~$ swarm version
Swarm
Version: 0.4.1-stable
Git Commit: 0b9a3ea4074d1de13521cc902e26ecae08a028ab
Go Version: go1.11.5
OS: linux
```

Next, we will install Geth. Similar to the Swarm installation, we will install Geth on Ubuntu via PPAs.

# Installing Geth

Perform the following steps to install Geth:

1. Enable our launchpad repository and run the following command:

```
sudo add-apt-repository -y ppa:ethereum/ethereum
```

2. Install the stable version of Geth with the following command:

```
sudo apt-get update
sudo apt-get install Ethereum
```

3.  Once installed successfully, verify the Geth version. It will look like this:

```
[ubuntu@ip-172-31-41-161:~$ geth version
WARN [06-24|14:59:59.721] Sanitizing cache to Go's GC limits        provided=1024 updated=666
Geth
Version: 1.8.27-stable
Git Commit: 4bcc0a37ab70cb79b16893556cffdaad6974e7d8
Architecture: amd64
Protocol Versions: [63 62]
Network Id: 1
Go Version: go1.10.4
Operating System: linux
GOPATH=/usr/local/go/work
GOROOT=/usr/local/go
```

Now that Geth and Swarm have been installed, we can run a Swarm example. Let's do it!

# Running an example of Swarm

We just installed Swarm and Geth. To start Swarm, we need an Ethereum account. Use the Geth command-line tool to create a new account, as shown in the following code:

```
geth account new
```

The Terminal will prompt for a password, so enter a password. After that, the console will display this new Ethereum account address. Here is the result:

```
ubuntu@ip-172-31-41-161:~$ geth account new
WARN [06-24|15:01:19.658] Sanitizing cache to Go's GC limits        provided=1024 updated=666
INFO [06-24|15:01:19.659] Maximum peer count                        ETH=25 LES=0 total=25
Your new account is locked with a password. Please give a password. Do not forget this password.
Passphrase:
Repeat passphrase:
Address: {54b0c384e8a15e0346dbf501990968f1d634e84c}
```

We will use this Ethereum account to connect with the Swarm node. To connect to Swarm, use the newly generated Ethereum account and run the following command:

```
$ swarm -bzzaccount
6e7782893d4957f4eb2a4fcd9350b68f1fbf81f558ca84debcd0c8bed7ea122b
```

Replace the hash with your account address key when you run the example. Here is the result:

```
[ubuntu@ip-172-31-41-161:~$ swarm --bzzaccount 54b0c384e8a15e0346dbf501990968f1d634e84c
INFO [06-24|15:05:41.627] Maximum peer count                        ETH=50 LES=0 total=50
Unlocking swarm account 0x54B0c384e8A15e0346dBF501990968f1D634E84c [1/3]
[Passphrase:
INFO [06-24|15:05:50.417] Starting peer-to-peer node                instance=swarm/v0.4.1-0b9a3ea4/linux-amd64/go1.11.5
INFO [06-24|15:05:50.461] New local node record                     seq=1 id=aeb42dabee780e5d ip=127.0.0.1 udp=30399 tcp=30399
INFO [06-24|15:05:50.462] Updated bzz local addr                    oaddr=21b7a0e349b4f9fca1043d8edd5028f48706afea0a2aa721308a6c4e4cff5fee
b62681ebf6f38f7e2072a66d93d44858fd520fd54f7ef80127.0.0.1:30399
INFO [06-24|15:05:50.462] Starting bzz service
INFO [06-24|15:05:50.462] Starting hive                             baseaddr=21b7a0e3
INFO [06-24|15:05:50.462] Detected an existing store, trying to load peers
INFO [06-24|15:05:50.462] hive 21b7a0e3: no persisted peers found
INFO [06-24|15:05:50.462] Swarm network started                     bzzaddr=21b7a0e349b4f9fca1043d8edd5028f48706afea0a2aa721308a6c4e4cff5fee
INFO [06-24|15:05:50.462] Started Pss
INFO [06-24|15:05:50.462] Loaded EC keys                            pubkey=0x048675188971dfe6445afff0a47d0a6fd9addb018e91cc99f82eb46b2ab9bf8
45afff0a47d0a6fd9addb018e91cc99f82eb46b2ab9bf822e
INFO [06-24|15:05:50.462] Streamer started
INFO [06-24|15:05:50.464] IPC endpoint opened                       url=/home/ubuntu/.ethereum/bzzd.ipc
INFO [06-24|15:05:50.467] Started P2P networking                    self=enode://b5da55be6337331786358a3df9611083331d6216f155eaa068f34781ffd
INFO [06-24|15:05:56.440] New local node record                     seq=2 id=aeb42dabee780e5d ip=54.196.105.231 udp=30399 tcp=30399
```

Swarm is fully integrated with the Geth console. To bring up the Swarm Geth console, open another new Terminal and run the Geth command in the console, as follows:

```
geth attach $HOME/.ethereum/bzzd.ipc
```

You will get a result that's similar to the following:

```
[ubuntu@ip-172-31-41-161:~$ geth attach $HOME/.ethereum/bzzd.ipc
WARN [06-25|02:42:26.059] Sanitizing cache to Go's GC limits        provided=1024 updated=666
Welcome to the Geth JavaScript console!

instance: swarm/v0.4.1-0b9a3ea4/linux-amd64/go1.11.5
 modules: accounting:1.0 admin:1.0 bzz:1.0 chequebook:1.0 debug:1.0 hive:1.0 pss:1.0 rpc:1.0 stream:1.0 swarmfs:1.0 web3:1.0

>
```

Once Swarm is running, we can start uploading files to the network. Here, we will use a simple text file that contains Hello Swarm and upload it to Swarm:

```
ubuntu@ip-172-31-41-161:~$ swarm up learn-ethereum.txt
        6e7782893d4957f4eb2a4fcd9350b68f1fbf81f558ca84debcd0c8bed7ea122b
```

As shown in the preceding code block, the console returns the hash key of the uploaded file. The hash is the access-controlled manifest.

You can access the uploaded files through the local HTTP gateway on port 8500, as shown here, at http://localhost:8500/bzz:/<file_hash>:

```
ubuntu@ip-172-31-41-161:~$ swarm up learn-ethereum.txt
6e7782893d4957f4eb2a4fcd9350b68f1fbf81f558ca84debcd0c8bed7ea122b
ubuntu@ip-172-31-41-161:~$ curl http://localhost:8500/bzz:/6e7782893d4957f4eb2a4fcd9350b68f1fbf81f558ca84debcd0c8bed7ea122b/
Hello swarm
```

Alternatively, you can access the file through Swarm's public gateway at `http://swarm-gateways.net/bzz:/<file_hash>`.

Here is a screenshot showing Swarm being accessed using the HTTPS Swarm public gateway:

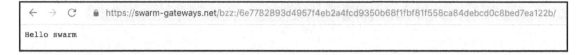

Now we've explored the two most popular decentralized storages—IPFS and Swarm. I am sure you feel comfortable with the concept of decentralized storage now. In the next section, we will discuss an exciting topic: decentralized messages with Whisper.

# Ethereum messages – Whisper

An application typically needs three kinds of resources for application services:

- Compute
- Storage
- Messaging

Ethereum EVM and smart contracts provide compute, while Swarm/IPFS handles large data storage and is the decentralized storage layer. Whisper handles Ethereum messages.

Here is a high-level architecture diagram showing these three in action:

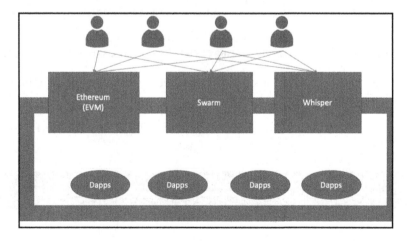

Whisper is an Ethereum P2P communication protocol that allows messaging between DApps. It provides a simple API that we can use to send an encrypted message through the Ethereum blockchain and receive and decrypted messages with the hash key. Whisper is currently at the POC 2 stage and supports the Geth and Parity clients. It can be used for DApps publish-subscribe coordination signaling and building secure, untraceable decentralized communication.

# Whisper protocol

Whisper currently uses the `ssh` protocol string of devp2p. When sending an encrypted message, the message content can be encrypted by default either asymmetrically or symmetrically.

Asymmetric cryptography, also known as public key cryptography, uses public and private keys to encrypt and decrypt data. One key is public and it is shared with everyone. The other is a private key; only the owner can see or access private key information. When encrypting the Whisper message, it uses the standard Elliptic Curve Integrated Encryption Scheme with the SECP-256k1 public key to encrypt a message; the other key is used for decryption. Symmetric cryptography (also known as the **secret key**), on the other hand, uses the hash key with the AES GCM algorithm with a random 96-bit nonce for both encryption and decryption. It typically facilitates one-to-many messages. The sender and receiver use the same symmetric key to encrypt and decrypt the message.

# Whisper envelopes

Whisper envelopes contain the encrypted payload and some metadata in plain format. It is sent and received by Whisper nodes.

Here is the structure of the envelope. It contains topic-related information, as shown in the following diagram:

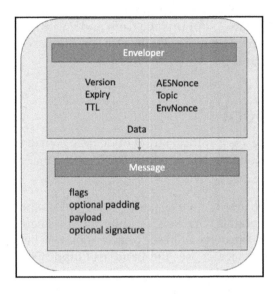

Each field in the Whisper envelope contains important information for the message:

- **Version**: This can be up to 4 bytes (currently one byte containing zero) and indicates the encryption method. If the **Version** is higher than the current one, the envelope cannot be decrypted, and therefore can only be forwarded to the peers.
- **Expiry**: This is the message expiry time (Unix time in seconds).
- **TTL**: This defines the message's time-to-live in seconds.
- **Topic**: This is 4 bytes of arbitrary data.
- **AESNonce**: This is used in symmetric encryption and represents 12 bytes of random data.
- **Data**: This is encrypted byte array data.
- **EnvNonce**: This is 8 bytes of arbitrary integer data that's used for **Proof-of-Work (PoW)** calculations.

# Whisper message

Envelope's payload has encrypted byte array data; it is the Whisper message in plain format.

Here is the message's structure:

```
[ flags, optional padding, payload, optional signature]
```

Let's explain the structure in more detail:

- **Flags**: There's a single byte for the flag to specify the message has a signature.
- **Padding**: This is used to align the message size, and it can contain random data.
- **Signature**: This is the signature that's used for sending the message. It is the ECDSA signature of the Keccak-256 hash of the unencrypted data.
- **Payload**: This is the payload of the message.

Whisper messages are sent to all Whisper nodes with TTL and PoW consensus to prevent **Direct Denial-of-Service (DDoS)** attacks. The nodes pass envelopes around, and only the receiver who has the private key can read the message.

Now, we understand the basic Whisper message structure. It is time to look at an example.

# Whisper example

To run Whisper, you need to install geth and then connect to a geth node with the Whisper option, as shown here:

```
geth --rpc --shh -ws
```

In the preceding command, we can see the following:

- The --rpc option is used to enable message communication via RPC.
- The --ssh option is used to enable the Whisper protocol.
- The --ws option is used to enable the WebSocket protocol for real-time message communication.

Here is the result after running the preceding command:

```
ubuntu@ip-172-31-41-161:~$ geth --rpc --shh --ws
WARN [06-25|13:38:45.397] Sanitizing cache to Go's GC limits      provided=1024 updated=666
INFO [06-25|13:38:45.399] Maximum peer count                      ETH=25 LES=0 total=25
INFO [06-25|13:38:45.401] Starting peer-to-peer node              instance=Geth/v1.8.27-stable-4bcc0a37/linux-amd64/go1.10.4
INFO [06-25|13:38:45.401] Allocated cache and file handles        database=/home/ubuntu/.ethereum/geth/chaindata cache=333 handles=524288
INFO [06-25|13:38:45.441] Writing default main-net genesis block
INFO [06-25|13:38:45.838] Persisted trie from memory database     nodes=12356 size=1.88mB time=83.849487ms gcnodes=0 gcsize=0.00B gctime=0s
INFO [06-25|13:38:45.840] Initialised chain configuration         config="{ChainID: 1 Homestead: 1150000 DAO: 1920000 DAOSupport: true EIP1
4370000 Constantinople: 7280000  ConstantinopleFix: 7280000 Engine: ethash}"
INFO [06-25|13:38:45.841] Disk storage enabled for ethash caches  dir=/home/ubuntu/.ethereum/geth/ethash count=3
INFO [06-25|13:38:45.841] Disk storage enabled for ethash DAGs    dir=/home/ubuntu/.ethash             count=2
INFO [06-25|13:38:45.841] Initialising Ethereum protocol          versions="[63 62]" network=1
INFO [06-25|13:38:45.867] Loaded most recent local header         number=0 hash=d4e567…cb8fa3 td=17179869184 age=50y2mo1w
INFO [06-25|13:38:45.867] Loaded most recent local full block     number=0 hash=d4e567…cb8fa3 td=17179869184 age=50y2mo1w
INFO [06-25|13:38:45.867] Loaded most recent local fast block     number=0 hash=d4e567…cb8fa3 td=17179869184 age=50y2mo1w
INFO [06-25|13:38:45.868] Regenerated local transaction journal   transactions=0 accounts=0
INFO [06-25|13:38:45.887] New local node record                   seq=1 id=3ebbfdf612d5bd4b ip=127.0.0.1 udp=30303 tcp=30303
```

**Posting a message**: To post a Whisper message, we need a public key to encrypt a message:

1. First, we will initialize the Whisper client by using the `go-ethereum` Whisper client API and connect to a local Geth node over WebSocket at the default port number `8546`.

2. Then, we will generate public and private keys through the `NewKeyPair` function.

The go-ethereum `whisperv6` package provides a `NewMessage` API to broadcast the message to the network. Here is a code sample for the publish message:

```go
import (
...
    "github.com/ethereum/go-ethereum/common/hexutil"
    "github.com/ethereum/go-ethereum/Whisper/shhclient"
    "github.com/ethereum/go-ethereum/Whisper/whisperv6"
)
    client, err := shhclient.Dial("ws://127.0.0.1:8546")
    keyID, err := client.NewKeyPair(context.Background())
    publicKey, err := client.PublicKey(context.Background(), keyID)
    message := whisperv6.NewMessage{
        Payload:   []byte("Hello Whisper"),
        PublicKey: publicKey,
        TTL:       120,
        PowTime:   3,
        PowTarget: 2,
    }
    messageHash, err := client.Post(context.Background(), message)
```

**Receiving a message:** To receive a Whisper message, we need a private key to decrypt the message:

1. First, we initialize the Whisper client by using the `go-ethereum` Whisper client API and connect to a local Geth node over WebSocket at the default port number `8546`.

2. Then, we call `NewKeyPair` to get the private key with `keyID`.

After that, we get the message using the private key. Here is a subscribe message code sample:

```
client, err := shhclient.Dial("ws://127.0.0.1:8546")
keyID, err := client.NewKeyPair(context.Background())
messages := make(chan *whisperv6.Message)
criteria := whisperv6.Criteria{
    PrivateKeyID: keyID,
}
sub, err := client.SubscribeMessages(context.Background(), criteria,
messages
go func() {
    for {
        select {
            ..
            case message := <-messages:
                fmt.Printf(string(message.Payload)) // "Hello Whisper"
                os.Exit(0)
        }
    }
}()
...
```

Whisper nodes use the devp2p Wire protocol for P2P communication. It is currently in the alpha stage. If you want to learn more, the API documentation can be found on the Whisper GitHub page (`https://github.com/ethereum/wiki/wiki/Whisper`). Now, we will have a look at popular smart contract libraries.

# Popular smart contract libraries

As we have learned so far, developing a secure, reusable, and efficient smart contract is not an easy task. It takes a lot of effort, experience, and testing. Once a smart contract has been deployed to a blockchain, anyone in the blockchain can access it. So, developing a top, secure, and quality smart contract becomes a crucial task for any smart contract developer. Well-tested, reusable, and secured libraries become very important. There are many popular open source Ethereum libraries available, as follows:

- **Modular Libraries**: A library that's used for utilizing EVMs
- **Aragon**: A DAO protocol, including the aragonOS smart contract framework for upgradeability and governance
- **DateTime Library**: A Solidity date and time library

OpenZeppelin is one of the most popular libraries, and we'll discuss it in the next section. It provides many handy tokens and utility libraries.

# Working with OpenZeppelin

OpenZeppelin is an open source framework for Solidity smart contracts. It is one of the most widely used Solidity libraries that provide reusable, secure, and modular smart contract code. All of this smart contract code is fully tested to follow the best practice security patterns. The framework is maintained by the Zeppelin company.

OpenZeppelin libraries provide many useful smart contracts, including access, crowdsale, cryptography, introspection, life cycle, math, ownership, payment, token, and utils. The following table shows all of the library project structures:

| OpenZeppelin libraries | Description |
|---|---|
| access | Provides role-based access control. |
| crowdsale | Provides token-based crowdsale contract libraries. |
| Cryptography | Provides different cryptographic primitives libraries. |
| Introspection | Provides a set of local and global interfaces. |
| Draft | The contract is currently in testing status by OpenZeppelin. |
| Lifecycle | Provides life cycle management for the contract, and supports pausing and unpausing smart contracts via the pauserRole user. |
| math | Provides math-related utilities. |
| ownership | Provides simple authorization and access control mechanisms. |
| payment | Provides payment-related utilities. |

| token | Provides the most popular ERC token utilities. |
|-------|------------------------------------------------|
| utils | Provides miscellaneous smart contract utility functions. |

Let's explore some OpenZeppelin libraries to understand how we can use these utilities.

# Setting up a dev environment

To understand more about OpenZeppelin, let's set up a Truffle project and run a simple example to get started:

1. Set up a Truffle project, create a project folder, and navigate to the project root folder. Then, issue the following Truffle command:

```
npm install truffle
npx truffle init
```

2. Install the OpenZeppelin library and, under the project root folder, run the following npm command:

```
npm install openzeppelin-solidity
```

This should install the OpenZeppelin library under the node_modules directory. A Truffle project can read all of these Solidity classes by using an import-related class.

# Access control

In Solidity smart contracts, role-based access control is used to restrict unauthorized users from accessing certain functions. With defined access control policies, the smart contract can build the security rule around roles and privileges.

To use the OpenZeppelin Roles function, you need to import Roles.sol from the OpenZeppelin access folder. Then, you have to define the roles you want to use. In our example, we define an admin and minter role. Here is an example of how we can create an admin role and a minter role:

```
pragma solidity >=0.4.22 <0.6.0;
import "openzeppelin-solidity/contracts/access/Roles.sol";
contract AclRole {
  using Roles for Roles.Role;
  Roles.Role private admins;
  Roles.Role private minters;
  function onlyAdminRole() view public {
    //only admin can use this function
```

```
      require(admins.has(msg.sender), "You must be admin");
    }
    function onlyMintersRole() view public {
      //only minters can use this function
      require(minters.has(msg.sender), "You must be minter");
    }
    function anyone() public {
      //anyone can use this function
    }
}
```

In the preceding example, we created two role functions:

- `OnlyAdminRole()`: Allows the admin role to access and perform functions
- `OnlyMinterRole()`: Only allows the minter role to access and perform functions

Next, let's take a look at math functions.

# Math

OpenZeppelin libraries provide that `SafeMath` contract, which has the `add`, `sub`, `mul`, `div`, and `mod` methods so that developers can perform safe math operations. Here is the list of functions:

- `add(uint256 a, uint256 b)`
- `sub(uint256 a, uint256 b)`
- `mul(uint256 a, uint256 b)`
- `div(uint256 a, uint256 b)`
- `mod(uint256 a, uint256 b)`

The `add` function is equivalent to Solidity's + operator. For example, we can add certain balance values:

```
balances[msg.sender] = balances[msg.sender].add(_value);
```

The `sub` function is equivalent to Solidity's – operator. For example, we can subtract certain balance values:

```
balances[msg.sender] = balances[msg.sender].sub(_value);
```

The `mul` function is equivalent to Solidity's `*` operator. For example, we can multiply a balance value by two:

```
balances[msg.sender] = balances[msg.sender].mul(2);
```

The `div` function is equivalent to Solidity's `/` operator. For example, we can divide a balance value by 10:

```
balances[msg.sender] = balances[msg.sender].div(10);
```

The `mod` function is equivalent to Solidity's `%` operator. For example, if we only charge a multiple of one ether (such as 1eth, 2eth, and so on), we can use the `weiUnit` mod. After the mod operation, we can find out how much of the remaining ether needs to be returned to the sender:

```
uint weiUnit = 1 * 10 ** 16;
uint returnAmt = msg.value.mod(weiUnit);
uint payAmount = msg.value.sub(returnAmt);
```

# Token

OpenZeppelin libraries provide a set of comprehensive token implementations for ERC20, ERC721, and ERC777. The following screenshot shows the ERC20 implemented by OpenZeppelin libraries. It makes token development much easier and safer:

Let's review ERC20 token libraries.

An ERC20 token keeps track of user address and balance information. The IERC20 interface defines functions and events that all ERC20 tokens must implement:

- **ERC20**: This provides basic implementation for IERC20.
- **ERC20Burable**: This allows the token holder to burn a certain number of tokens.
- **ERC20Mintable**: This allows MonterRole to mint (create) a certain amount of new tokens when needed.
- **ERC20Capped**: This adds caps for the token supply.
- **ERC20Detailed**: This adds name, symbol, and decimal to the ERC20 token's implementation.
- **ERC20Pausable**: Users with `pauseRole` can pause and resume or freeze and resume the token transfer.
- **SafeERC20**: This provides a wrapper around ERC20 token functions such as `safeTransfer`, `safeTransferFrom`, and `safeApprove` via the `callOptionalReturn` (IERC20 token and bytes memory data) function.
- **TokenTimeLock**: This allows the token beneficiary to extract a certain amount of tokens after a specific release time.

Let's utilize OpenZeppelin-developed token smart contract to implement our ERC20 token. We will use ERC20 for basic ERC20 implementation. `ERC20Detailed` is for token detail information such as symbol, name, and decimal.

Here is our `SampleToken` implementation. You can see how easy it is when we use the `openzeppelin` token libraries. Let's take a look at the code implementation here:

```
import "openzeppelin-solidity/contracts/ownership/Ownable.sol";
import "openzeppelin-solidity/contracts/token/ERC20/ERC20.sol";
import "openzeppelin-solidity/contracts/token/ERC20/ERC20Detailed.sol";
contract SampleToken is ERC20, ERC20Detailed, Ownable {
    uint256 public initialSupply  = 100000000000;
    constructor () public ERC20Detailed("SampleToken", "ST", 18) {
        _mint(msg.sender, initialSupply);
    }
}
```

We can see that we just need to extend our smart contract from the `openzeppelin` ERC20 token implementation; you can immediately create your own token by doing this. It makes writing token smart contracts much more straightforward.

## Utils

The OpenZeppelin util libraries provide address, arrays, and the `ReentrancyGuard` utility. Address has a function, `isContract(address account)`, which will return `true` if the account is the contract. Arrays have a function, `findUpperBound(uint256[] array, uint256 element)`, which is a sorted search array and returns the `upperBound` element (first index) that returns a value larger or equal to the element value. `ReentrancyGuard` prevents a reentrance call to a function.

# Summary

In this chapter, we learned about various Ethereum tools and APIs. First, we reviewed Ethereum's development tools and frameworks and explored the Infura framework. Then, we studied the Web3j Ethereum client API. By running examples of IPFS and Swarm, we understood the basics of the Ethereum storage concept. We also went through Ethereum messaging with Whisper. At the end of this chapter, we discussed the most popular smart contract library: OpenZeppelin.

In the next chapter, we will continue with our journey of creating an Ethereum private chain.

# Section 4: Production and Deployment

With Ethereum becoming more well-known, the accelerated development of private and permissioned blockchain technology is increasing in popularity. This intense interest across industries is playing a major role as a stimulant for enterprises to roll out blockchain networks into production. In this context, understanding different types of Ethereum blockchain and being able to create a private network locally will be useful to coders.

This section comprises of the following chapters:

- Chapter 9, *Creating an Ethereum Private Chain*
- Chapter 10, *Deployment of Your Smart Contract*
- Chapter 11, *Building Ethereum Wallets*

# Creating an Ethereum Private Chain

# 9

In this chapter, we will move our focus to Ethereum private chains. For developers, private blockchains are set up for testing purposes. Private chains have advantages over public blockchains in testing. For example, there is no need for nodes syncing or obtaining test ether, as you are the only user, and there are no other smart contracts. But the disadvantage is that the testing won't be as good as real scenarios in a public blockchain, in the absence of other nodes, users, and contracts.

As blockchain technology has matured, enterprises have started to adopt the technology for their own use cases. It's important for you to understand not only the public blockchains but also the private and permissioned ones. Developers should know how to set up their own blockchains.

We will have a look at the difference between public and private blockchains, and take you through the steps for setting up a private blockchain using Ethereum. We will also look at the options flags that we can use with new chains. At the end of this chapter, we will provide a brief overview of popular private blockchains, including R3 Corda, Hyperledger, and Quorum, and their usages in the industry. The chapter will also explain private blockchains in production usages.

We will cover the following topics in the chapter:

- Understanding private and permissioned blockchains
- Setting up a local private blockchain
- Using optional flags with new chains
- Introducing the popular private blockchains in the industry
- Private blockchains in production usages

# Technical requirements

To set up a local blockchain network, you will need one or more local computers connected through the local network. The steps demonstrated in this chapter have been implemented with a Mac machine. It will work almost the same on the Ubuntu server. You will also need to decide which Ethereum client to use. We will use Go-ethereum, the popular Ethereum client from the Ethereum foundation. If you choose a different Ethereum client implementation, follow the detailed instructions on its website, even if it appears to be very similar to Go-ethereum.

There are multiple options available for you to install Go-ethereum or Geth. The simplest way is to complete the following three steps:

1. Download Geth directly from the Geth site: `https://geth.ethereum.org/downloads`.
2. Extract the `tar` file and store the executable file in your local directory.
3. Add the directory to your system path.

Geth can be installed as part of Mist, which we discussed in Chapter 7, *Writing UI for the DApps*. If you intend to build Go-ethereum from source, the following applications will be required. For detailed instructions, you should check the geth site: `https://geth.ethereum.org/install-and-build/Installing-Geth#build-it-from-source-code`:

- Git
- Xcode
- Homebrew

If you plan to create any miner nodes, make sure you have enough RAM set aside for mining. Now that we understand the concept of private and permissioned blockchains, we will introduce how to create a local private blockchain without mining and then with mining.

# Understanding a private and permissioned blockchain

So far, we have extensively discussed Bitcoin and Ethereum as public blockchains. With a public blockchain, anyone can become a node of the network and access all the activities inside it. The key challenges for enterprise adoption are privacy and confidentiality. Enterprises need both of them for legitimate reasons:

- One is that privacy will be enforced by laws and regulations. In Europe, the **General Data Protection Regulation (GDPR)** is the core of digital privacy legislation. In the US, HIPAA in healthcare and KYC/AML in finance require the business to protect consumer privacy. More importantly, privacy and security in general are competitive advantages for enterprises to gain the trust of and retain their customers.
- The second reason is that all businesses and large enterprises deal with crucial product and services information, which make them competitive on the global market. For this reason, enterprises are more likely to join the private and consortium blockchains to avoid exposing sensitive data and transactions to the public.

A private blockchain is sometimes called a **permissioned blockchain**, similar to the way that a public blockchain is sometimes categorized as a permissionless blockchain. It can have all the key features we discussed in the public blockchain, including a decentralized peer-to-peer network, distributed ledger, and security through cryptography. The difference between the public and private blockchain lies in who can join the network, and what rights you can get. You can think of a public blockchain as a public park. Anyone can get into the public park. And once in, you can do all kinds of activities, such as jogging or playing, as long as the policies or rules allow them. Joining a private blockchain is like going to someone's birthday party: you can only join if you've been invited.

In a public blockchain, anyone can join the network and access all transactions. Anyone can be the validator to verify the transactions and create the blocks, and the system relies on the economic perspectives (incentives in the **proof-of-work (PoW)** consensus mechanism, and the disincentives in the **proof-of-stake (PoS)** mechanism) to secure the network. On the contrary, in the private blockchain, only selected nodes can participate in the peer-to-peer network and process the transactions. The system relies on the identity of the entities, whether it is a user or a node, to secure the network.

The difference between permissionless and permissioned blockchain lies in the trust of validators. Permissionless blockchains allow everyone to validate transactions, but only selected users can do so in a permissioned blockchain. In other words, a permissioned blockchain doesn't put its trust in validators.

To help you get a clear picture of the different categories of blockchains, we can summarize the features of blockchains in the following table:

| blockchain | Public permissionless | Public permissioned | Private permissionless | Private permissioned |
|---|---|---|---|---|
| Read/create transactions | Anyone | Anyone | Restricted | Restricted |
| Validate/write transactions | Anyone | Restricted | Anyone | Restricted |
| Validator identity | Highly Anonymous | Moderate Anonymous | Identified | Identified |
| Trust in validators | Yes | No | Yes | No |
| Consensus | PoW | PoS PoA (Goerli Testnet) | Federated Byzantine agreement | Practical Byzantine Fault Tolerance Algorithm /Multisignature |
| Require Token | Yes | Yes | No | No |
| Speed | Slower | Faster | Faster | Faster |
| Energy consumption | Higher | Lower | Lower | Lower |
| Projects | Bitcoin Ethereum Waves | Ethereum after Casper Ripple | LTO Network MONET | Hyperledger Fabric R3 Corda Quorum |

Also, as mainstream blockchain categories, blockchain networks are either permissioned or permissionless. The concept of it being private or public is application specific, and not at the network level. It is based on someone's ability to access the network and also what identification requirements there are. Within those networks, transactions and interactions may be private or public. Whether or not you need privacy or confidentiality is depending on use case. For example, Quorum has tessera nodes for private transactions, Hyperledger has channels for private interactions, and E&Y has nightfall for public Ethereum.

Although Ethereum is launched as a public permissionless blockchain, you can build a local private blockchain with Ethereum too.

In the next section, we will walk you through how to set up a private Ethereum blockchain network.

# Setting up a local private Ethereum blockchain

In addition to the enterprise needs of a private blockchain, there are other reasons for setting up a local private Ethereum blockchain.

As we discussed in `Chapter 4`, *Solidity Fundamentals*, smart contracts are immutable and can be very costly once deployed to the Ethereum mainnet. It is always recommended to follow the best practices in coding, security, and economics, and have the code thoroughly tested before it is deployed on the Ethereum network. With a local private blockchain, it makes it easy and convenient for the developers to test smart contracts and simulate the contract's behaviors. You can even deploy smart contracts to the single instance of a local Ethereum blockchain without running a full node.

In this section, we will show you how to create multiple local nodes and configure and establish the private blockchain, as well as set up mining on the private chain.

In the context of trust model for permissioned blockchain, everyone in a permissioned network is properly identified and not pseudonymous. Therefore, proof of work mining, which will limit 51% takeover, is not required. Unless and until permissioned blockchain gets large enough and it looks like a permissionless network, mining will be necessary again.

# Private blockchains without mining

By creating the genesis block, we will create our private blockchain. The following steps are all you will need to run a non-mining private Ethereum blockchain:

1. Set up the environment.
2. Configure the custom genesis file.
3. Run Geth.

# Setting up the environment

We are going to run the Ethereum client Geth to create a private blockchain with only one user: ourselves. Let's get started:

1. First, open up a Terminal window and navigate to any directory that you want. From there, we are going to create the `hello_world` directory to host the data of the two blocks, as follows:

   `$ mkdir hello_world`

2. We will also create a subdirectory under `hello_world` to host all the logs. First, navigate to the directory we just created, that is, `hello_world`. Next, a directory named `logs` , as follows:

   `$ cd hello_world`
   `$ mkdir logs`

With the directories created, we have set up the environment to configure the genesis file. Let's move on to the next step.

# Configuring the custom genesis file

A genesis block is the starting point of every blockchain. We can configure a genesis block through customizing a `genesis.json` file. There are a few components to be configured within the file, including a `config` struct for initializing the blockchain, and `alloc` to allocate the initial funds. In addition to that, there are a few other configuration parameters for mining and gas limits.

The following is the `config` structure definition in Geth:

```
179  // ChainConfig is the core config which determines the blockchain settings.
180  //
181  // ChainConfig is stored in the database on a per block basis. This means
182  // that any network, identified by its genesis block, can have its own
183  // set of configuration options.
184  type ChainConfig struct {
185      ChainID *big.Int  json:"chainId"  // chainId identifies the current chain and is used for replay protection
186
187      HomesteadBlock *big.Int  json:"homesteadBlock,omitempty"  // Homestead switch block (nil = no fork, 0 = already homestead)
188
189      DAOForkBlock    *big.Int  json:"daoForkBlock,omitempty"    // TheDAO hard-fork switch block (nil = no fork)
190      DAOForkSupport bool       json:"daoForkSupport,omitempty"  // Whether the nodes supports or opposes the DAO hard-fork
191
192      // EIP150 implements the Gas price changes (https://github.com/ethereum/EIPs/issues/150)
193      EIP150Block *big.Int    json:"eip150Block,omitempty"  // EIP150 HF block (nil = no fork)
194      EIP150Hash  common.Hash json:"eip150Hash,omitempty"   // EIP150 HF hash (needed for header only clients as only gas pricing changed)
195
196      EIP155Block *big.Int  json:"eip155Block,omitempty"  // EIP155 HF block
197      EIP158Block *big.Int  json:"eip158Block,omitempty"  // EIP158 HF block
198
199      ByzantiumBlock      *big.Int  json:"byzantiumBlock,omitempty"       // Byzantium switch block (nil = no fork, 0 = already on byzantium)
200      ConstantinopleBlock *big.Int  json:"constantinopleBlock,omitempty"  // Constantinople switch block (nil = no fork, 0 = already activated)
201      PetersburgBlock     *big.Int  json:"petersburgBlock,omitempty"      // Petersburg switch block (nil = same as Constantinople)
202      EWASMBlock          *big.Int  json:"ewasmBlock,omitempty"           // EWASM switch block (nil = no fork, 0 = already activated)
203
204      // Various consensus engines
205      Ethash *EthashConfig json:"ethash,omitempty"
206      Clique *CliqueConfig json:"clique,omitempty"
207  }
```

The `genesis.json` file of a private blockchain can be configured as follows:

```json
{
"config":{
"chainId":0205718128,
"homesteadBlock":0,
"eip155Block":0,
"eip158Block":0
},
"alloc":{}
}
```

Let's take a look at the preceding code:

- `config`: This section holds the main blockchain configuration information. It has properties such as `chainID`, `homesteadBlock`, `eip155Block`, and `eip158Block`. With the exception of `config`, particular protocol upgrades will be available immediately.
- `alloc`: This section is for prefunding the accounts on the blockchain.

In order to keep our blockchain private, we need to customize the genesis block in the genesis.json configuration file:

1. For the private blockchain, set homesteadblock as 0.
2. It's also very important to supply a network ID that's different from the default value of 1 for the main Ethereum network.
3. If you don't plan to prefund the blockchain, the alloc struct can be kept blank.

In the hello_world directory, let's save the genesis.json sample to a file named the same as genesis.json. You can create the file and write it using the editor of your choice. If you happen to use vim, the command is as follows:

```
$ vi genesis.json
```

Right now, we have saved the starting point of a private chain to the environment that we set up. We will use this genesis block to create a database in the next section.

# Running Geth

Once the genegsis.json file has been created, you are ready to start the private Ethereum blockchain. We will start the node in one terminal/process where we can see the logs being written to stdout. In the second terminal, we will use the geth console to get the console. There are advantages of using two terminals:

- Logs from the first terminal are written to stdout instead of being redirected. We know that everything is functional.
- Closing the console in the second terminal doesn't terminate the geth syncing process.

Now, let's see how we can run geth:

1. In dir hello_world, we will start the first node by running the following command:

```
$ geth --datadir block_0 --identity node_0 --verbosity 6 --
ipcdisable --port 30398 --rpcport 8171
```

The following is a list of a few command-line options:

- `--datadir`: It specifies the directory for the database and Keystore to be stored. In our case, it is set as `block_0`, which means the database with the first genesis block on our private blockchain was created under the `block_0` directory. Everything geth persists now will write to `block_0`. The default `datadir` value is listed in the following table:

| Operating system | Datadir |
|---|---|
| Mac | ~/Library/Ethereum |
| Windows | %APPDATA%\Ethereum |
| Linux | ~/.ethereum |

- `--identity` specifies a custom node name.
- `--verbosity` defines the log level.
- `--ipcdisable` disables the IPC-RPC server during the startup.
- `--port` is the network listening port number for the node; the default value is 30303.
- `--rpcport` specifies the `http-rpc` server listening port number; the default is 8545.

2. We will use the geth console to start a session of an interactive JavaScript environment, where we will interact with the first node that we just created. It will show us something like the following:

```
$ geth console
Welcome to the Geth JavaScript console!
instance: Geth/node_0/v1.8.22-stable/darwin-amd64/go1.11.5
modules: admin:1.0 debug:1.0 eth:1.0 ethash:1.0 miner:1.0 net:1.0
personal:1.0 rpc:1.0 txpool:1.0 web3:1.0
```

3. In the console, we can obtain all the node information with the `admin.nodeInfo` command. We will need `enode` later when we want to implement it in the second node as it is a peer to the second node. To check the `enode` of the first node, we can type in the following command:

```
> admin.nodeInfo.enode
"enode://4202d9ac5c1c7c8eea8ae56dbc881fb61230c7447d81b964345bba3841
684f8449e6dce625552c3c881622a6f3dabeee596f3ff61dd212ad14cfb6f687793
ef1@100.100.100.100:30398"
```

Note that we assume that the 30398 port is open for listening. This might not work for users who have their firewall enabled. I used a fake IP address 100.100.100.100, and it will be used several times in this section. To find your own IP address, you can use the following command in your terminal:

```
$ ifconfig|grep netmask|awk '{print $2}'
```

4. Leave the terminal open or save the enode information for the first node somewhere. So far, we have a single node in the network. If we check on peers now, it will be an empty list, as follows:

```
> admin.peers
[]
```

To run multiple nodes of a local blockchain, we will need to make sure they are running on a different port. We will use a different port for the second node by putting down a different value in --port and --rpcport.

5. Let's run the second node with a slightly different command, as follows:

```
$ geth --datadir block_1 --identity node_1  --verbosity 6 --
ipcdisable --port 30399 --rpcport 8173 console 2>>
logs/second_node.log
```

We have two nodes running, but they are unaware of each other's existence. In order to create a peer-to-peer network with these two nodes, we can use the addPeer command.

6. In the current console for the second node, we will add the first node as a peer to the second node, as follows:

```
>admin.addPeer("enode://4202d9ac5c1c7c8eea8ae56dbc881fb61230c7447d8
1b964345bba3841684f8449e6dce625552c3c881622a6f3dabeee596f3ff61dd212
ad14cfb6f687793ef1@100.100.100.100:30398")

true
```

Using `admin.addPeer` to add static nodes at runtime is just adding nodes ephemerally, instead of permanently. If you have restarted the process, you will notice the peer you've added is gone in a new session. `Admin.addPeer` is usually used for debugging purposes. If you would like to add a peer permanently, the peer needs to be manually configured in the `geth` config file called `static-nodes.json`, under the `<datadir>/geth/` path, as shown in the following example:

```
[
"enode://4202d9ac5c1c7c8eea8ae56dbc881fb61230c7447d81b964345bba3841
684f8449e6dce625552c3c881622a6f3dabeee596f3ff61dd212ad14cfb6f687793
ef1@100.100.100.100:30398"
]
```

If you have more static nodes to add, you can keep appending some `enode` URLs to the `static-nodes.json` file, as shown in the following example:

```
[
"enode://4202d9ac5c1c7c8eea8ae56dbc881fb61230c7447d81b964345bba3841
684f8449e6dce625552c3c881622a6f3dabeee596f3ff61dd212ad14cfb6f687793
ef1@100.100.100.100:30398",
"enode://pubkey@ip:port",
...
]
```

7. The console returns `true` when it is successfully executed. We will use the following command to test the connection:

```
> admin.peers
...
```

Furthermore, `admin.peers` will list out the detailed information of the first node; we won't list them all here.

As you can see in the following code snippet, `net.peerCount` will show only 1 peer in your local blockchain network now:

```
> net.peerCount
1
```

Check if the network is listening, with the help of the following command:

```
> net.listening
true
```

That is all you need to start a private blockchain. As we discussed in Chapter 7, *Writing UI for the DApps*, you can configure your development tools to connect to the local blockchain for testing and debugging before you deploy your smart contracts to testnet or mainnet.

# Private blockchains with mining

We have shown you the steps to start a simple private blockchain. With some additional steps, you can set up private blockchains with mining enabled too. We will discuss the steps you need to take to get a mining blockchain up and running in the local environment here:

## Setting up an environment

Let's create another directory for a blockchain with mining. It's very similar to how we set up an environment in the *Private blockchain without mining* section. In the following code, we create two more subdirectories, data and src, under hello_world_mining:

```
$ cd hello_world_mining
$ mkdir data
$ mkdir src
```

When data and src are created, you list the information of the directories under hello_world_mining to verify the names and locations.

## Configuring the custom genesis file

When we created the blockchain without mining, we left the alloc section blank. We will prefund the accounts this time. You may want to tune the difficulty to a lower value in your first attempt. It is better to choose some random value for a nonce, in case it connects to any unknown nodes. Let's have a look at the following configuration:

```
{
"config": {
        "chainId": 135,
        "homesteadBlock": 0,
        "eip155Block": 0,
        "eip158Block": 0
    },

    "alloc" : {
    "0x0000000000000000000000000000000000000001": {"balance": "111111111"},
    "0x0000000000000000000000000000000000000002": {"balance": "222222222"}
```

```
    },

    "coinbase" : "0x0000000000000000000000000000000000000000",
    "difficulty" : "0x00001",
    "extraData" : "",
    "gasLimit" : "0x2fefd8",
    "nonce" : "0x0000000000000107",
    "mixhash" :
"0x0000000000000000000000000000000000000000000000000000000000000000",
    "parentHash" :
"0x0000000000000000000000000000000000000000000000000000000000000000",
    "timestamp" : "0x00"
}
```

The configuration here is the pre-funding
address 0x0000000000000000000000000000000000000001 and the balance
of 111111111 and 222222222 to the
0x0000000000000000000000000000000000000002 address.

Let's take the opportunity to look at the other parameters here:

- coinbase: A 160-bit address that gets the ether rewards from successful mining.
- difficulty: The difficulty level of how hard it is to mine a block when a nonce discovers the block. The higher the value or the difficulty is, the more calculations that need is needed to be done to mine the block. The difficulty of the current block normally calculated using the timestamp and the difficulty of the previous block. Difficulty plays an important role in controlling the frequency of block generation. Difficulty is set to keep the waiting time of generating a block in the target range. When we read difficulty, we can interpret it using its reciprocal. For example, difficulty is set to 0 x 0400 in hexadecimal, which is 1,024 in decimal. The reciprocal of decimal 1,024 is 1/1024. Basically, 1/1024 indicates there will be 1 successful mining out of 1,024 hash operations on average. The faster your machine can finish 1,024 hash operations, the faster your will get a valid block.

- `mixhash` and `nonce`: `mixhash` is a 256-bit hash and nonce is a 64-bit hash. Both of them are used together to verify if the block is cryptographically mined and is a valid block. The verification requirement for them combined is defined in the yellow paper. The reason why both of them are needed rather than just a nonce is that a nonce can be falsified in an attack. It will cost a large amount of computational power of the network to discover the nonce was false. An intermediate calculation, which `mixhash` provides, can help to find out a nonce. And this calculation is not as expensive. So, when a suspicious `mixhash` is found when the block is being validated, the block can be discarded without us having to do any additional calculation to check the nonce.
- `parenthash`: The Keccak 256-bit hash of an entire block header of the parent. It includes both `mixhash` and the nonce.
- `gaslimit`: This is the upper limit of computations that any block can support. We will talk about this in detail in later chapters.
- `timestamp`: This provides the Unix `time()` output at the block's inception. The timestamp helps to verify the order of the blocks on the chain.
- `extraData`: This is an optional space with a maximum of 32 bytes.

By now, you should understand the structure and content of a genesis file. Be my guest and customize a genesis file on your own. Doing so will deepen your understanding.

# Running Geth

With the genesis.json file, let's build the first node in the private blockchain for mining.

1. Let's navigate to the root directory and initialize the blockchain using the `genesis.json` file, as follows:

```
$ cd hello_world_mining/data
$ geth --datadir hello_world_mining/data init
hello_world_mining/genesis.json
```

To make this a bit more interesting, we will set up our own bootnode. A bootnode is a node that can be used to allow any node to join the private network for the first time and find other nodes in the network.

For example, `MainnetBootnodes` is the bootnode of the main Ethereum network. It is defined as follows in `params/bootnodes.go`:

```
var MainnetBootnodes = []string{
 // Ethereum Foundation Go Bootnodes
 "enode://a979fb575495b8d6db44f750317d0f4622bf4c2aa3365d6af7c2843399
 68eef29b69ad0dce72a4d8db5ebb4968de0e3bec910127f134779fbcb0cb6d33311
 63c@52.16.188.185:30303", // IE
 "enode://3f1d12044546b76342d59d4a05532c14b85aa669704bfe1f864fe07941
 5aa2c02d743e03218e57a33fb94523adb54032871a6c51b2cc5514cb7c7e35b3ed0
 a99@13.93.211.84:30303", // US-WEST
 ...
}
```

Other than `MainnetBootnodes`, there are also other predefined bootnodes for test networks:

- **Ropsten test network**: `TestnetBootnodes`
- **Rinkeby test network**: `RinkebyBootnodes`
- **Goerli test network**: `GoerliBootnodes`
- **Experimental RLPx v5 topic-discovery network**: `DiscoveryV5Bootnodes`

As we can see, there are the existing test networks: the Ropsten test network, the Rinkeby test network, the Goerli test network, and the experimental RLPx v5 topic-discovery network. We will talk about them in detail in `Chapter 10`, *Deployment of your Smart Contract*, in the *Deploying smart contract with testnet* section.

Geth supports bootnode creation for private networks too. You will start bootnode at the specified enode address. The following steps are for creating an enode URL and starting the bootnode.

2. If you type the bootnode command, you will get the following warning:

```
$ bootnode
Fatal: Use -nodekey or -nodekeyhex to specify a private key.
```

It complains about a missing private key, which can be generated by a command; . Let's call this key `PrivateBootnode.key`:

```
$ bootnode -genkey PrivateBootnode.key
```

3. As shown in the following code block, we can check if the key was generated:

```
$ cat PrivateBootnode.key
15bdd11dbff8327552ac8ac7fb2c3bca4373e98657dd30d83491cea635dca903
```

4. We can get the enode address of the bootnode by using the −nodekey option:

```
$ bootnode −nodekey PrivateBootnode.key
```

Alternatively, we can use the key from the previous step to generate the enode address:

```
$ bootnode −nodekeyhex
15bdd11dbff8327552ac8ac7fb2c3bca4373e98657dd30d83491cea635dca903 −
writeaddress
c25172a39c2c118290912c181b73376e4e58b8cc3b5178e4aa2f0a929e1739216c9
baa6db990513963bcf6a3cf1652c23d5655cc637f5d611297349f887543d0
```

5. Now, start a new terminal session. We will use the −bootnodes flag to tell geth to use the bootnode we just created. Remember to put enode://before the enode address:

```
$ cd hello_world_mining/
$ geth −−datadir data −−
bootnodes=enode://c25172a39c2c118290912c181b73376e4e58b8cc3b5178e4a
a2f0a929e1739216c9baa6db990513963bcf6a3cf1652c23d5655cc637f5d611297
349f887543d0@100.100.100.100:3031
```

Geth will create a file under hello_world_mining/data/geth.ipc. We will use this file to create a new account.

## Creating a new account

To start mining, we will need to create an ether account on the private blockchain. Let's get started:

1. Let's start a new terminal session with an open and running network connection. The attach sub-command will start a JSRE REPL console for interactive use. The REPL console can also be started by a sub-command console. The difference between the two is that attach starts the console without starting the geth nodes:

```
$ geth attach hello_world_mining/data/geth.ipc
Welcome to the Geth JavaScript console!
instance: Geth/v1.8.22-stable/darwin-amd64/go1.11.5
```

```
modules: admin:1.0 debug:1.0 eth:1.0 ethash:1.0 miner:1.0 net:1.0
personal:1.0 rpc:1.0 txpool:1.0 web3:1.0
```

If you check your account now, it will be an empty list:

```
> eth.accounts
[]
```

2. Now, let's get started and create our very first account in the interactive console. When you create a new account, geth asks for a passphrase:

```
> personal.newAccount()
Passphrase:
```

Make sure you type in a very strong password, and write it down somewhere and keep a few copies. You know the drill. After repeating the passphrase, you will see your new account:

```
Repeat passphrase:
"0xde2d56b4abc0bf860d25781ca4a87772dec8f8a8"
```

3. You can check your account now; it will include the one we just created, as follows:

```
> eth.accounts
["0xde2d56b4abc0bf860d25781ca4a87772dec8f8a8"]
```

4. Let's check the balance of our new account; a 0 balance is expected for now:

```
> web3.fromWei(eth.getBalance(eth.accounts[0]), "ether")
0
```

New accounts can also be created non-interactively without opening the geth console. The --password flag can be used in this case if you have created a password file in plaintext format, as follows:

```
$ geth account new
$ geth account new --password <password file>
```

We have provided two ways of creating a new account:

- Creating the new account interactively with the console
- Using the geth account new command directly

At this point, we have a new account handy. We are going to mine on our local private network in the next section.

# Mining on a local private network

Mining on the local private blockchain can be started with the following command; we will be using `--etherbase` to credit all rewards to the account we just created:

```
$ geth --datadir data --mine --miner.threads=1 --miner.etherbase
=0xde2d56b4abc0bf860d25781ca4a87772dec8f8a8
```

Once started, it will keep running and writing out the logs, as follows:

```
INFO Successfully sealed new block number=1520 sealhash=7c9374...e035e4
hash=25a8c4...d0ae06 elapsed=5.228s
INFO  block reached canonical chain number=1513 hash=7ca5de...5cab58
INFO  mined potential block number=1520 hash=25a8c4...d0ae06
INFO Commit new mining work number=1521 sealhash=8ce312...0bec54 uncles=0
txs=0 gas=0 fees=0 elapsed=173.13µs
```

It will earn you ethers when new blocks are added to the blockchain. It's very realistic to become a billionaire if you keep mining:

```
> web3.fromWei(eth.getBalance(eth.accounts[0]), "ether")
40
> web3.fromWei(eth.getBalance(eth.accounts[0]), "ether")
7175
> web3.fromWei(eth.getBalance(eth.accounts[0]), "ether")
8360
> web3.fromWei(eth.getBalance(eth.accounts[0]), "ether")
9010
```

It must feel good to see the number keep increasing. But to stop the miner, you can use the console `miner.stop()` command.

# Using optional flags with new chains

While we were building a local private blockchain, we used a few command-line options such as `--datadir`, `--identity`, `--verbosity`, and so on. These options are also known as optional flags. They are Ethereum options and are useful for setting up a local blockchain and accessing testnets. Developer chain options support switching to developer mode. Other options are available for Ethash, transaction pools, performance tuning, account, API and consoles, networking, miner, gas price oracles, virtual machines, logging and debugging, metrics, stats, and options, and so on. Let's have a look at the following command:

```
$ geth help or $ geth h
```

The preceding command will give you a full host of Ethash options. Let's have a look at the format of the following command:

```
$ geth [options] command [command options] [arguments]
```

You can implement all the options in the commands using the preceding format.

# Commands

Geth comes with a list of commands and command-line options. Earlier, you saw a few in action, including console, account, attach, and so on. The following is a list of commands that are supported by Geth:

- account
- attach
- bug
- console
- copydb
- dump
- dumpconfig
- export
- export-preimages
- import
- import-preimages
- init
- js
- license
- makecache
- makedag
- monitor
- removedb
- version
- wallet
- help,h

We used `geth account new` to create new accounts in the previous section. Furthermore, `geth account` helps you manage accounts:

```
$ geth account list - gives you a summary of existing accounts
$ geth account update - updates the existing accounts
$ geth account import - imports private keys for new accounts
```

Some additional `geth` commands are as follows:

- `geth import`: This imports the files of a blockchain
- `geth export`: This exports a blockchain to the appropriate files
- `geth copydb`: This creates a local blockchain from a source chain data directory path
- `geth removdb`: This discards a local blockchain and its databases
- `geth init`: This initializes a genesis block from the target genesis JSON file
- `geth js`: This executes the target JavaScript files
- `geth attach`: This connects to nodes in the network
- `geth console`: This opens an interactive JavaScript environment session
- `geth wallet`: This manages presale Ethereum wallets
- `geth bug`: This automatically brings up the page on GitHub, where you can report the bug

For example, a presale Ethereum wallet can be imported with the following import command:

```
$ geth wallet import <path to wallet>presale.wallet
```

There are other commands that are useful for monitoring your local chain and testing, including `dump`, `dumpconfig`, `export-preimages`, `import-preimages`, `license`, `makecache`, `makedag`, `monitor`, and `version`.

# Ethereum options

Ethereum options are widely used in development and testing, especially in setting up a private blockchain. We have encountered quite a few in the previous sections of this chapter:

- `--datadir` and `--identity` are the Ethereum options we used when setting up our local blockchain.

- `--networkid` specifies the network ID:
    - 1 is the default value, referring to the Frontier network.
    - 2 stands for a disused Morden network.
    - 3 is the Ropsten network.
    - 4 is the Rinkeby network.

Separately, Geth provides the following alternate options too:

- `--testnet`: This option will let you connect to the PoW Ropsten network.
- `--rinkeby`: This option supports the proof-of-authority Rinkeby network.
- `--syncmode`: This defines the fast, full, and light sync modes.
- `--whitelist`: This takes block number-to-hash mappings. It requires a comma-separated `<number>=<hash>` format. The whitelist allows you to specify the block hash mappings the chain must have. Peers not on the whitelist will be rejected.

Developers use the whitelist to run the `"fast"` sync mode to avoid landing on the incorrect chain when the Ropsten testnet has a Constantinople chain split. What happens in the` "fast"` sync mode is that `geth` starts downloading every block header. Fast sync starts from the chain with the highest total difficulty. Developers will land on the incorrect chain if the highest total difficulty chain has an unwanted block within it.

The following Ethereum options are also available:

- `--config`
- `--keystore`
- `--nousb`
- `--gcmode`
- `--ethstats`
- `--lightserv`
- `--lightpeers`
- `--lightkdf`

Please use `geth help/h` to look them up, and get yourself familiar with them.

# Developer chain options

Developer chain options are the ones facing developers. There are two useful developer chain options:

- `--dev`
- `--dev.period`

By running `--dev`, a proof-of-authority network will be established. Notice that a prefunded account will be created and mining will be enabled automatically. The default block period will be 0, meaning mining is only enabled when the transaction is in a pending status. Sometimes, developers will save the trouble of creating their own local private chain from scratch by using the one developer mode provides. You can challenge yourself by setting up a private blockchain using the `--dev` flag. It will deepen your understanding of all the kinds of options supported by `geth`.

Let's quickly check the fund in the predefined account using the following steps:

1. You must be very familiar with the console by now. We will bring up the console with the following command:

   **$ geth -dev console**

2. Then, we will double-check if this is the account we are interested in with the help of the following command:

   **> eth.accounts**
   **["0xcbb8c6537505837c43cc54f1440bcf988111ad91"]**

3. If we query interactively using the following command, we will find out the amount of ether the `0xcbb8c6537505837c43cc54f1440bcf988111ad91` account is holding:

   **> web3.fromWei(eth.getBalance(eth.coinbase), "ether")**
   **1.15792089237316195423570985008687907853269984665640564039457584007**
   **913129639927e+59**

   From the result, we know that the account has been funded with `1.15792089237316195423570985008687907853269984665640564039457584007913129639927e+59` ether.

# API and console options

If you have gone through the *Setting up a local private Ethereum blockchain*, you've already encountered a few API and console options:

- `--ipcdisable` and `--rpcport`: The `--ipcdisable` flag disables the IPC-RPC server.
- `--rpcport` decides which listening port to use for the HTTP-RPC server.
- `--rpc` starts the HTTP JSON-RPC server. Alternatively, you can use `admin.startRPC(addr, port)` to start the HTTP JSON-RPC server.
- In order to access RPC via a browser without request failures (due to same-origin policy), `--rpccorsdomain` needs to be supplied with the comma-separated set of domains. Like the following command, we start with `geth` and append the `--rpc`, and `--rpccorsdomain` options with a local host, as follows:

```
$ geth --rpc --rpccorsdomain http://localhost:3000
```

- To enable management APIs, use the flags in the format of `--{interface}api`. For example, `--rpcapi` is for the HTTP endpoint, while `--wsapi` is for the WebSocket. The default `--ipcapi` setting will enable all the APIs for the `ipc` interface, and `db`, `eth`, `net`, and `web3` for the HTTP and WS interfaces. Please enable APIs for different interfaces with caution. All the management APIs are listed in the following table:

| Management API namespaces | Support | Methods |
| --- | --- | --- |
| admin | Nodes management | `datadir, nodeInfo, peers, setSolc, startRPC, startWS, stopRPC, stopWS` |
| debug | Nodes debugging | `backtraceAt, blockProfile, cpuProfile, dumpBlock, gcStats, getBlockRlp, goTrace, memStats, seedHashsign, setBlockProfileRate, setHead, stacks, startCPUProfile, startGoTrace, stopCPUProfile, stopGoTrace, traceBlock, traceBlockByNumber, traceBlockByHash, traceBlockFromFile, traceTransaction, verbosity, vmodule, writeBlockProfile, writeMemProfile` |
| miner | Miner and Ethash DAG management | `setExtra, setGasPrice, start, stop, getHashrate, setEtherbase` |

| personal | Accounts management | ecRecover, importRawKey, listAccounts, lockAccount, newAccount, unlockAccount, sendTransaction, sign |
|---|---|---|
| txpool | Pool and transactions management | content, inspect, status |

Apart from the DApp namespaces such as eth, shh, and web3, geth allows the extra management API namespaces we mentioned previously:

- **Admin** allows access to a few RPC methods, giving better control over the Geth instance
- **Debug** helps developers debug during runtime
- **Miner** provides extra mining settings, and helps developers gain remote control over a mining operation
- Through a personal API, private keys in the key store can be managed
- The txpool API allows developers to access the transaction pool, as well as pending and queued transactions.

# Networking options

Networking options provide us with the flexibility to define the network's details, such as the listening port, the maximum number of peers, the maximum number of attempts for pending a connection, the discovery mechanism in the network, and so on. The following list specifies the various options that are available:

- --bootnodes, --port, --nodekey, and --nodekeyhex are the networking option flags we have come across. Generally, --bootnodesv4 is set for light server and full nodes. --bootnodesv5 is set for light servers and light nodes.
- If you have already connected a few nodes, for example, with 2 nodes, and you don't want any other nodes to be added to the local private network accidentally, set --maxpeers to 2. The default value for maxpeers is 25.
- --nodiscover is used for adding peers manually without the discovery protocol. This flag is used for testing a single node or network with a limited number of nodes.

- Other members of the networking options family are `--maxpendpeers`, `--nat`, `--v5disc`, and `--netrestrict`. In a local private blockchain, `--maxpeers` and `--nodiscover` are frequently used.
- Starting from geth v1.5.4, `--netrestrict` is added to the toolbox. The flag takes an IP address, and geth will only communicate with the peers from this address.

In the following command, we specify `maxpeers` to be 2, disabling the peering discovery mechanism and restricting the network communication to `127.0.0.1`:

```
$ geth --datadir < local data dir> --networkid <network id> --maxpeers 2 --
nodiscover --netrestrict 127.0.0.1
```

We have introduced every member of the networking options family. Feel free to use them and get familiar with them.

# Transaction pool options

Like mining, transaction is a key concept in Ethereum. We discussed how transactions are processed in blockchain in `Chapter 1`, *blockchain and Cryptocurrency*, and how Ethereum processes transactions in `Chapter 2`, *Ethereum Architecture and Ecosystem*. At a high level, once submitted, transactions are broadcasted to the blockchain network and queued in the transaction pool at each node. The miners process transactions and add the blocks to the blockchain. In Ethereum, transactions are processed in an **Ethereum Virtual Machine (EVM)**, and each computation step has a cost in gas associated with it. The sender who's creating a transaction sets both a gas limit and price per gas unit, which together becomes the price in ether that is paid. The winning miner gets rewarded with ethers and collects the transaction fee.

Within the transaction pool at the miner node, transactions are sorted based on gas price. A transaction with a higher price will naturally be completed sooner. But a transaction with a low gas price won't stay in a pool forever in a pending state. Different Ethereum client implementations may behave slightly differently. In geth, the network operators can define how the transaction pool works via transaction pool command-line options when starting up the client. The following is a list of the parameters it can set up:

- `txpool.nolocals` disables price exemptions for locally submitted transactions.
- `txpool.journal` defines a disk journal for a local transaction to survive node restarts. The default is `transactions.rlp`.

- `txpool.rejournal` defines the time interval to regenerate the local transaction journal, by default; it is set to 1 hour.
- `txpool.pricelimit` defines the minimal gas price limit to enforce for acceptance into the pool; by default, it is set to 1.
- `txpool.pricebump` defines the price bump percentage to replace an already existing transaction; by default, it is set to 10.
- `txpool.accountslots` specifies the minimum number of executable transaction slots guaranteed per account; by default, it is set to 16.
- `txpool.globalslots` specifies maximum number of executable transaction slots for all accounts; by default, it is 4,096.
- `txpool.accountqueue` specifies the maximum number of non-executable transaction slots permitted per account; by default, it is 64.
- `txpool.globalqueue` specifies the maximum number of non-executable transaction slots for all accounts; by default, it is set as 1,024.
- `txpool.lifetime` specifies the maximum amount of time non-executable transactions are queued; by default, it is 3 hours.

For example, a node might set a price limit so that it doesn't accept the transactions with the `--txpool.pricelimit` flag. The default value is 1, meaning the miner node will only accept the transaction to the pool if it meets the price of 1. Don't confuse this price limit with `--miner.gasprice` (`--gasprice` is the depreciated version). Furthermore, `--miner.gasprice` is used in mining. If `--txpool.pricelimit` is set in the first place, and mining is enabled later, `--txpool.pricelimit` will be overwritten. The pool will only accept a transaction that is minable.

Every node can use the `--txpool.lifetime` and `--txpool.globalqueue` flags to drop the transactions. Furthermore, `--txpool.lifetime 24h0m0s` will queue non-executable transactions up to 24 hours; the default value is `3h0m0s`. In addition to this, `--txpool.globalqueue 1000` will open 1,000 slots for non-executable transactions, and start to drop the 1001st transaction that is pending. The default value is 1,024. If you have decided to pay more for gas for transactions that have already been sent, you can still bump up the price using `--txpool.pricebump`. Use the same nonce when the transaction is resubmitted. By the time this new transaction is received, it will overwrite the old one.

# Introducing the popular private blockchains in the industry

Earlier, we discussed the enterprise needs of a private or consortium blockchain. In this section, we will provide a brief introduction to the popular ones, including Hyperledger, Corda, and Quorum. There are Ethereum and non-Ethereum variant. Quorum is an Ethereum variant. While Fabric, Sawtooth, and Corda are non-Ethereum variants.

# Hyperledger

Each enterprise or industry has its own set of requirements and unique business cases. Most of the use cases and business capabilities go beyond value transfer and payment settlement, which are sweet spots for cryptocurrency-native permissionless blockchains such as Bitcoin and Ethereum. To gain mainstream enterprise adoption, Hyperledger embraces and builds blockchain technology with the following added design principles:

- **Modular**: A plug in architecture for an enterprise to tailor the blockchains to the needs of the enterprise.
- **Highly secure**: Security and privacy, along with audit and compliance, are business-critical components of any business.
- **Interoperable**: Large enterprises do not exist in isolation, but will have to deal with different blockchains within the enterprise or across its ecosystems to complete large complex business processes. Interoperability between blockchains gives a business a competitive edge.
- **Cryptocurrency-agnostic**: Allows different cryptographic algorithms to be implemented, based on the needs of the business.
- **Complete with APIs**: Enables easy API integration with the rest of the enterprise applications.

With that in mind, the Hyperledger architecture provides abstraction layers for key blockchain components, including consensus algorithms, smart contracts, P2P communication, blockchain state data storage, and cryptocurrencies. It allows the enterprise to swap and plug in different implementations of the abstraction layers that are best suited to the business use cases. In addition to this, it provides identity and policy services to enable identity management, access control, and policy establishment at all layers. On top of all these, it provides API layers to allow the enterprise systems to integrate with the smart contracts on the blockchain.

To support different business and industry needs, Hyperledger comes up with five Hyperledger business blockchain frameworks—Fabric, Sawtooth, Iroha, Burrow, and Indy:

- Hyperledger Fabric and Sawtooth are the most active ones and have seen real-world applications.
- Hyperledger Burrow provides a permissionable smart contract execution environment, similar to a built-in part, using Ethereum EVM specifications.
- Indy is built as the special purpose distributed ledger for digital identity management.
- Iroha is a business blockchain framework that's used for managing digital assets, identities, and data.

# Hyperledger Fabric

Hyperledger Fabric is an early implementation of distributed ledger technology in the Hyperledger umbrella. It is a general-purpose permissioned blockchain, designed with a modular architecture. At a high level, Fabric allows you to configure the blockchain system in any possible way that fits your business scenarios, including the following:

- **State database for the ledger**: This can be configurable to any DBMS. By default, it uses levelDB and CouchDB.
- **Ordering service**: Establishes consensus on the order of transactions and then broadcasts blocks to peers. In its initial implementation of Fabric 1.0, a Kafka implementation of ordering services is provided.
- **Chaincode**: These are smart contracts running in a docker container, and can be developed using any programming language.
- **Membership service**: This can be integrated with an identity management system in the enterprise and enforce the permissions in the private chain.

Channel is another novel concept in Fabric and allows the enterprise or trading partners to establish a separate ledger of transactions. It can be very useful when dealing with sensitive transactions or data where only the participants can share and access the ledger in the channel.

# Hyperledger Sawtooth

Hyperledger Sawtooth is another general-purpose blockchain framework under Hyperledger Umbrella for building both distributed ledgers:

- Compared to Fabric, Sawtooth is more similar to a public blockchain such as Ethereum, but still maintains some design principles.
- Hyperledger enforces modularization, configurability, and flexibility in plugging in different implementations.
- It maintains a cryptographically linked chain of transaction blocks, has a peer-to-peer validator network for relaying transactions between nodes, and relies on the gossip protocol to propagate all transactions to all nodes in the validator network.

While Fabric is a permissioned blockchain, Sawtooth supports both permissioned and permissionless blockchains. Permissions are set at both the network level and the local validator configuration level:

- At the network level, its task is to configure who has permission to join the validator network.
- At the local validator configuration level, it controls whether the validator has permission to access and process the transactions and messages.

Unlike other private blockchains such as Fabric, Corda, or Quorum, where a sensitive or private transaction may not be accessible to all nodes, all transactions in Sawtooth are stored in validators in the network; it relies on the local permissions to enforce transaction privacy.

The consensus in Sawtooth, by design, is pluggable too. Consensus algorithms can be configured at the network level during the initial validator network's setup. They can be switched during the transaction process too. By default, it supports the **Proof of Elapsed Time (PoEt)** consensus protocol, although a voting-based consensus in RAFT is under development. PoET is a Nakamoto-style lottery-based consensus algorithm that relies on Intel's **Software Guard Extensions (SGX)** to select a validator to create blocks based on random waiting times, without using the PoW algorithm.

Similar to Fabric, Sawtooth supports smart contract development in many different programming languages, such as Java, JavaScript, Go, and on. In addition, it supports Solidity and Rust too, which are quite successful in the Ethereum community. One notable difference with transaction processing in Sawtooth is the ability to batch the transactions and ensure all or nothing when processing all the transactions in a batch. This could be quite useful for an enterprise that's dealing with some business scenarios with large, complex transactions.

# Corda

Corda is considered a private permissioned blockchain. It is a specific-purpose distributed ledger technology, built from the ground up, to support the financial and insurance industries. It focuses on transaction privacy using a shared immutable ledger that's agreed upon by all parties through smart contracts.

To maintain the shared immutable ledger, Corda was built according to the following core concepts:

- **State objects**: These are point-in-time facts about the data in the enterprise, like a stock or bond, or customers. It represents the current state of the facts and is updated through transaction processing.
- **Transactions**: These represent the state transition of state objects through a life cycle. Corda employs a UTXO data model to reflect the state transition in the ledger. Both state objects and transactions are persisted in the enclave of a node, which can be any kind of database. A transaction must be validated by the contracts, which is a legal agreement in smart contracts between transacting parties.
- **Flows**: These allow transacting parties to coordinate actions and complete transactions without a central controller.

In Corda, consensus is achieved in two ways:

- One is transaction validity, which is the agreement in smart contract code between transacting parties, and includes all the signatures that are needed to authorize the transactions.
- Another is transaction uniqueness to prevent double spending. Corda introduces the Notary concept to prove the transaction's uniqueness.

Like Hyperledger, consensus in Corda is pluggable, which allows notary clusters to choose a consensus algorithm, fitting the needs of the business transactions. In Corda, a "notary" is an abstraction of an ordering service. A "notary cluster" is a collection of notary nodes using a consensus algorithm among them. This consensus algorithm may or may not be byzantine fault tolerance. Newer high-performance notary services, like crash fault tolerance (CFT) notary services were prototyped, which are based on Atomix, a light-weight Raft-based fault-tolerant distributed coordination framework.

A smart contract can be developed using Java, which is a good selling point for many enterprise developers since Java is a relatively dominant programming language. In fact, it can be written in any JVM language, for example, Kotlin or Scala, and has access to the full capabilities of the language.

Corda is supported by a network of Coda nodes, and only authorized nodes can join the network with permissions. The transaction is only accessible by the transacting parties, which ensures the transaction's privacy.

# Quorum

Quorum is a distributed ledger technology implementation that was customized and extended from Ethereum code base, and provided alternate transaction management and contract privacy fitting the needs of financial industry. More specifically, it forked out of an early version of Geth client implementation.

To address transaction and contract privacy issues with the public version of Ethereum blockchain, Quorum introduced the public and private state, where the public state would be shared and accessed by all nodes, and private state only accessed by nodes with permissions. In a similar way, it puts the read-only restriction on the private contract when it accesses the public state, to prevent the private data been propagated to the public state. You can think Quorum manages to have both public blockchain and private blockchain on the same blockchain. In doing so, it has to customize Geth to manage the global state root and state Pritrica tire, to accommodate the separated public and private state, as well as the transaction/block generation logic impacts because of dual states.

A node can differentiate public transactions (unencrypted payloads) vs private transactions (encrypted payloads). It will ask a transaction manager to decrypt the private transactions, which in turn determines if the node has the permissions to decrypt the message. If it has the permissions then transaction manager will decrypt the transaction payload, and allow the node to process the transaction.

As shown in the picture below, encryption and decryption of transaction payload is delegated to the crypto enclave, which also holds all private keys for all involving parties.

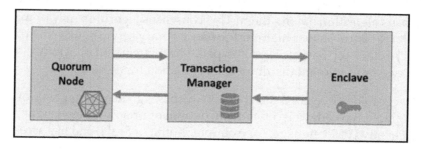

Another key area for customization is to implement Istanbul BFT consensus algorithms instead of using Ethereum Estash based PoW algorithm, where nodes with permissions are invited to a simple voting mechanism through a smart contract. Together with the design of offloading cryptographic computations to the off-chain enclave, it greatly improved transaction performance and increased scalability.

Quorum is widely adopted across the industries. We list out some of the usages of Quorum in the following table:

| Industry | Quorum usages |
|---|---|
| Supply Chain | Starbucks<br>LVMH (luxury goods company) |
| Financial Services | IIN |
| Oil and Gas | VAKT |
| Trade Finance | Komgo |
| Digital | Accenture |

  We won't be able to cover all the use cases here. Readers can refer to the Fortune blockchain 50 articles as further readings on the topic.

# Private blockchains use cases

Assuming that you have been diligently trying out the commands in this chapter, your own private blockchain has started to sail on the local platform. A private blockchain is put into production use in so many aspects of our life: to make payments faster and more secure in the financial world, to lower medical costs in the healthcare industry, and to make the process more transparent in the food supply chain. Our generation is leading the most comfortable and convenient life in history. But there is still room for the game-changing blockchain technology to solve the issues we are facing and improve the current protocols.

# Financial services

blockchain started as the peer-to-peer electronic payment solutions, and quickly found success in broad financial service, banking, and payment industries.

# Payments

There are great opportunities in the payment market considering its size. According to the Global Payments Study by McKinsey in 2018, the revenues of global payments raised 11% in 2017, up to 1.9 trillion dollars. It's the revenue of payment industry, as well as cost for transactions. Blockchain-enabled model further supports banks for frictionless real-time payments with lower costs.

Ripple came into to the picture with blockchain technology. In 2012 Ripple Labs Inc. released a real-time gross settlement system, including currency exchange and remittance network. RippleNet provides service to send money globally by connecting the banks, payment providers and digital asset exchanges. This payment network involves 27 countries. Ripple's solution could be an option to support banks to make transactions directly and bring real-time certainty to settlement. Assuming there are 100 million transactions per year, and annual transactions value as 5 trillion dollars. If you apply the same cost model as Ripple does, which saves up to 38.18 dollars per payment, the annual saving will be 3.82 billion dollars. Lowering the cost of transactions is not the only benefit private blockchain provides to banks, it opens door to opportunities for new use cases, clients, revenue and market. The errors, failures and reconciliation issues that might be happening during transactions can also be lower accordingly.

Ripple is not the only blockchain-based payment service. Mastercard and blockchain company R3 announced partnership for cross-border payment solution 2019 September. Facebook Libra is registering its payment system in Switzerland. And Swiss Financial Market Supervisory Authority (FINMA) published 'stable coin' guidelines on September, 2019.

We may expect objectives like financial inclusion, consumer protection and regulatory compliance to work together towards the same goal. The goal of offering a global currency and robust, secure infrastructure and empowering lives of people all over the world.

## Audit and assurance

During an audit, an organization's financial statements will be evaluated to determine their accuracy and fairness. If all the transactions are recorded in an immutable blockchain as indelible marks, audits will become futile. There is still a chance that blockchain transactions will be logged in the wrong sections of financial statements. Or, the transaction itself may be illegal if, say, it's sent and received between parties, and then it might not comply with regulations. In some cases, it can even be sent as an off-chain agreement.

Internationally, the audit market is dominated by big players such as **PricewaterhouseCoopers (PwC)**, KPMG, **Ernst & Young (EY)**, and Deloitte. All of them are bringing in blockchain innovations.

PwC announced a blockchain auditing service in March 2018. PwC France and Francophone Africa brought together experts specialized in cybersecurity and big data, auditors, and so on in its blockchain lab, located in Paris. The lab collaborated with Request Network, which is a project that's building a decentralized payment system for the Ethereum network.

KPMG, partnered with Microsoft, expanded its blockchain strategy to audit. Microsoft Azure's hybrid cloud capabilities, security at an enterprise level, and extensive compliance certification portfolio were combined by KPMG to break down complex business workflows. The first joint blockchain nodes opened in Frankfurt and Singapore in February 2017.

By April 2018, EY had announced its blockchain analyzer to make the life of the audit team easier in sourcing all transaction data across the organization from multiple ledgers on the blockchain. Auditors will be able to do the following:

- Interrogate the data
- Analyze the transactions

- Identify suspicious transactions by looking at the outliers
- Reconcile transactions

In 2017, Deloitte released 90,000 certificates on the private blockchain, with an international accredited registrar DNV GL. How does this work? As soon as a new certificate is issued, it will be digitized and stored in a private blockchain. In the private network, each certificate is tagged uniquely and can be traced. Simply scanning a QR code made it possible for anyone to verify that a company is certified.

# Healthcare

Healthcare is another industry that has strived to find ways to maintain health quality and lower the overall cost. blockchain has the potential to disrupt the entire industry.

# Medical records

blockchain in healthcare can help improve medical record access. MedRec, a system built on a small-scale private blockchain, prioritizes patient agency, providing a transparent and accessible view of medical history. Similar projects, such as phrOS, were released by the Taipei Medical University Hospital and Digital Treasury Corporation. This sounds exciting, right? Finally, someone is going to do something for electronic health records scattered across different providers!

# Medical costs

Cutting medical costs can be done by using blockchains. ConnectingCare, a project of SimplyVital Health, uses algorithms to forecast medical cost in near-real time. This leads to the next project, Health Nexus, which stores patient data for all the providers to view. And it may also make it possible for patients to sell their medical records to researchers to reduce their medical costs.

# Drugs

Drugs are supposed to heal people or at least cause no harm. But according to the World Health Organization, tens of thousands die from the fake drugs trade, which was worth 30 billion dollars in 2017. FarmaTrust is a project that's designed to put an end to this. It can track and trace the inventory of drugs and provide transparency into the life cycle of the drugs.

Production use cases are not limited to the topics I have listed here. Private blockchains are making it easier to track clinical. It is also helping to secure better healthcare transactions and improve the way patients interact with doctors.

# Food supply chain

Applications a private blockchains are not only impacting us in the financial world and healthcare industry– they are impacting us everywhere.

A news article entitled *one in every five fish sold is mislabeled* drew my attention. I looked into the facts and found that, according to a study from UCLA and Loyola Marymount University, nearly half of the sushi served in Los Angeles may be mislabeled. To tell what's on your plate without carrying around a DNA toolkit, blockchains, with their accountability, can come to the rescue.

Having inherited the immutability of the blockchain, a private blockchain brings unprecedented transparency and efficiency to tracking food sources. Tuna is traced by Bumble Bee Foods using blockchain technology. Walmart deployed Hyperledger Fabric (an implementation of the blockchain framework) in the food supply chain. Tracing the source of contaminated foods used to take seven days, but now it can be as fast as 2.2 seconds. Implementing private blockchains in the airline industry makes ticketing more transparent and secure at a lower cost. In 2018, China's largest retailer, JD.com, launched a blockchain platform, for better enterprise operation management. A private blockchain is marching into the real estate and rental industry, as well as in recruitment for large companies.

# Summary

In this chapter, you learned how to deploy a private Ethereum blockchain, as well as other types of private blockchains. We also provided some real-world use cases of private blockchains in different industries. blockchain is still at the very early stages of its technological revolution. As the technology becomes more mature, we expect it will be very successful and have a profound impact on many industries.

As blockchain technology is being recognized by broader and broader audiences, the development of smart contracts is increasing rapidly. In the time it has taken to write this book, 73,699,065 accounts (externally owned accounts and contract accounts) have been added to the Ethereum main network, holding 107,440,864.655 ether. The number of accounts is 10 times higher than it was two years ago. A total number of 96,108,208 contract internal transactions have been made on Ethereum. Developing and deploying smart contracts is one of the main activities on Ethereum.

In the next chapter, we will go through the deployment of smart contracts in detail.

# 10 Deployment of Your Smart Contract

By now, you should be able to develop and test smart contracts. As the next step in the development cycle, we will need to test the smart contracts in the environment close to the Ethereum main network. Testnets provide such places where a developer can test scenarios very close to the main network. In this chapter, we will get to know how to deploy smart contracts with testnets and how to monitor them after deployment.

By following the deployment steps in this chapter, you should be able to navigate through Ethereum wallets such as MyCrypto and MyEtherWallet to get test ether on testnets and to deploy smart contracts via different wallets. We will go into the details of how to use Etherscan to monitor deployed smart contracts. At the end of this chapter, we will introduce Ethereum block explorers such as Etherscan.

In this chapter, we will go over the following topics:

- Deploying smart contracts with testnet
- Monitoring smart contracts

## Technical requirements

For all of the source code of this book, please refer to the following GitHub link:

https://github.com/PacktPublishing/Learn-Ethereum

# Deploying smart contracts with testnet

We dived into details about smart contract execution under the hood in Chapter 4, *Solidity Fundamentals*, and learned how to develop our own cryptocurrency using smart contracts in Chapter 5, *Developing Your Own Cryptocurrency*. In Chapter 6, *Smart Contract Development and Test Fundamentals*, we showed you how to use Remix to develop and debug a smart contract. We will add a few different aspects of smart contracts here: contract accounts on Ethereum and a little background on smart contracts.

As we discussed in Chapter 9, *Creating an Ethereum Private Chain*, a recipient of a transaction can be an EOA or a contract account. The transaction data is considered an argument to the function. EOA is usually managed by the users through a wallet, while a contract account is handled by a smart contract—basically, a piece of code. We can get a clear picture of two types of accounts by looking at the following table. What EOA and the contract account have in common is they are both identified by an address. The contract account needs code and data storage, and it doesn't have private keys. On the other hand, EOA doesn't need code or data storage, and it has private keys. Let's have a look at the following table:

| Account type | Managed by | Needs code | Data storage | Has private keys | Identified by |
|---|---|---|---|---|---|
| EOA | Users/wallet | No | No | Yes | address |
| contract account | A smart contract | Yes | Yes | No | address |

A smart contract is not a new concept in Ethereum. It was first mooted by Nick Szabo in 1994. At that time, it was defined as a set of promises. Later on, in 2009, when Bitcoin was invented, smart contracts evolved again. By 2014, the name **smart contract** was used to refer to computer programs that ran on the Ethereum virtual machine. The history of smart contracts is summarized in the following screenshot:

| Year 1994 | Year 2009 | Year 2014 |
|---|---|---|
| •First proposed by Nick Szabo<br>•Defination: a set of promises, specified in digital form, including protocols within which the parties perform on the other promises | •Bitcoin was invented and software became open sourced.<br>•The turing-incomplete script language of blockchain technology supports the development of custom smart contract. | •Ethereum was announced<br>•A Turing-complete language is implemented<br>•Smart contract are immutable programs compiled to EVM bytecode.<br>• Written in language: Mutan, LLL, Serpent, and Solidity, Viper, Bamboo, Lisk, Chain. |

Now that we've caught up on the history of smart contracts, let's take a look at testnets and their usages. Testnet is the abbreviation of "test network". Testnets are alternative Ethereum networks, that is, copies of the Ethereum blockchain. Testnets are used for simulating the main Ethereum network's behavior and are for testing purposes. In order to execute smart contracts in the main Ethereum network, virtual fuel must be paid. Virtual fuel is also known as gas. Ether is needed to cover the gas cost. In a testnet, there's usually a service, called a faucet, that will dispense funds as free test ether. With free or unlimited gas, developers can test their smart contracts without using any real ether to cover the cost of gas.

In general, we have two types of testnets:

- Public testnets
- Private testnets

In `Chapter 9`, *Creating Ethereum Private Chains*, we encountered a few public testnets: Ropsten, Kovan, Rinkeby, Goerli, and Morden (decommissioned). Ropsten is a proof-of-work testnet for Ethereum. The rest of them are proof-of-authority testnets. There are different ways to get ether from them. Note that the private blockchain that we set up in `Chapter 9`, *Creating an Ethereum Private Chain*, can be considered a private testnet.

Public testnets are widely used in smart contract and DApps development. We have listed the similarities and differences between popular public testnets in the following table:

| Testnet | Consensus | Block Explorer | Acquire ETH |
|---------|-----------|----------------|-------------|
| Ropsten | Proof-of-work | `https://ropsten.etherscan.io` | Mining |
| Rinkeby | Proof-of-authority | `https://rinkeby.etherscan.io` | Request from a faucet: `https://faucet.rinkeby.io` |
| Goerli | Cross-client proof-of-authority | `https://goerli.etherscan.io` | Request from a faucet: `https://faucet.goerli.mudit.blog` |

Here we've compared four public testnets based on the consensus, the block explorer, and acquiring ETH. Kovan and Rinkeby use proof-of-authority as a consensus. Ropsten uses proof-of-work, while Goerli uses cross-client proof-of-authority. You will have to mine your own test ether on Ropsten, while you can request the ether from a faucet for the other three. Now, let's deploy a smart contract.

# Deploying a smart contract to the Goerli testnet with MyCrypto

In this section, we will look at using MyCrypto for deploying a smart contract to the Goerli testnet. MyCrypto is a web tool where you can create a wallet, manage tokens, and deploy smart contracts as well.

We will break down the deployment process into the following steps:

1. Navigate to MyCrypto using the link here: `https://mycrypto.com/account`. You will see the following screen.
2. On the top-right corner, you will see the **ETHEREUM (AUTO)** option by default, which means you are on the mainnet. Switch to the **GOERLI** testnet by selecting it from the dropdown menu.
3. On the same screen, under the **TOOLS** dropdown menu, select **Interact with Contracts**:

4. The page now will look like what's shown in the screenshot here. Double-check the top-right corner to make sure you have chosen the **GOERLI** testnet.

5. We will be connecting to MetaMask through the **Web3** option, as highlighted by the red rectangle in the following screenshot:

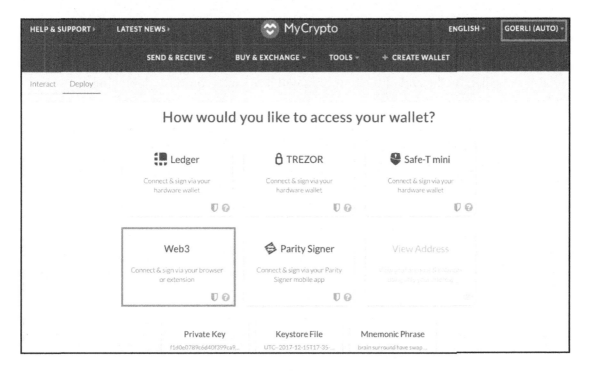

6. After clicking on the Web3 option, the page will update and ask you to unlock your version of Web3. Proceed to connect if you have it installed already. The options are shown in the following screenshot:

We will go over these steps in the next section. For those of you who already have accounts, you can skip the next section, *Opening a MetaMask account*. For those of you who have test ether in their accounts, you can skip the *Getting test ether* section altogether and go directly to *Deploying the smart contract*.

## Creating a MetaMask account

If you don't have a MetaMask account, then this section will take you on a tour of the MetaMask wallet. By the end of the tour, you will have an account for deploying our smart contract:

1. In a Google Chrome browser, as shown here, navigate to `https://metamask.io`. The easiest way to do this would be to get the Chrome extension. Notice the actual MetaMask extension is offered by `https://metamask.io` and has more than 1 million users:

2. Before clicking on the get started option, please verify the MetaMask version you've added is the real one. The URL should be `https://chrome.google.com/webstore/detail/metamask/nkbihfbeogaeaoehlefnkodbefgpgknn`.

3. Follow the instructions on the MetaMask Chrome extension to create an account. As shown in the following screenshot, after setting up a password, you will be shown a backup phrase so that you can back up and restore your account:

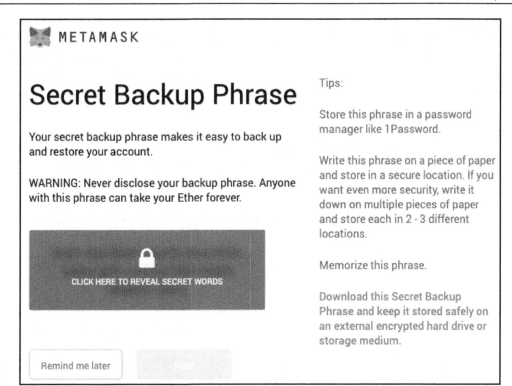

You must note this phrase down somewhere. You will be asked to reselect the words in your backup phrase.

Here are the tips for storing your backup phrase safely: write the phrase on a piece of paper and store it in a secure place. To be more secure, you can write it down separately on a few pieces of paper, and store the copies in different locations.

4. After clicking on **All Done**, you will be able to see your MetaMask account.

If this is your first time creating a MetaMask account, take some time to get familiar with MetaMask as it will be very useful for you to know the features it offers.

# Getting test ether

Now, we have an account with MetaMask. The next step will be to get some test ether. If you already have test ether in your account, feel free to skip this section and go directly to the next section, *Deploying the smart contract*.

Follow these steps to get test ether in your wallet:

1. Log in to your MetaMask account.
2. On the top-right corner of the account home, as shown in the following screenshot, click on the **Main Ethereum Network** dropdown menu. We will be selecting **Goerli Test Network**.
3. Click on the **Deposit** option under the **Goerli Test Network** on the right-hand side of the screen:

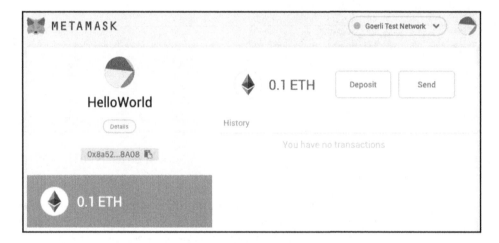

4. Click on **Get ether** in the **Test Faucet** section, as shown here. Then, a new tab for the Goerli testnet faucet will open:

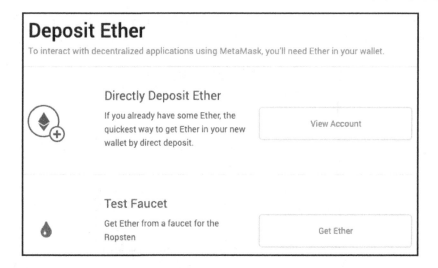

5. Request **0.05** Goerli from the faucet each time by pasting your MetaMask account address, as shown here:

6. After waiting for a little while, you will see a successful deposit message, as shown here:

7. Now, go back to MetaMask. You will see that 0.05 Goerli has been credited to your account. Connect to MetaMask after confirming its **Goerli Test Network**, as shown here:

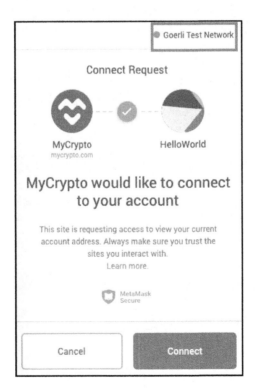

When connecting to MetaMask, check the network in the upper-right corner. If you were using another network previously, it will directly connect to that one.

Once connected, we have everything we need to deploy the smart contract.

# Deploying the smart contract

With the MetaMask account created and test ether deposited to the account, we can start deploying the smart contract. The process involves the following steps:

1. After unlocking Web3 on MyCrypto and connecting to MetaMask, the deployment page is shown. MyCrypto takes the **Byte Code** of our smart contract:

2. We will use the subcurrency example from the following Solidity v0.5.7 document as shown here: `https://solidity.readthedocs.io/en/v0.5.7/introduction-to-smart-contracts.html#subcurrency-example`. Let's take a look at what we have in this piece of code.

The first line shows that the code supports Solidity version 0.5.0 up to, but not including, 0.7.0:

```
pragma solidity >=0.5.0 <0.7.0;
```

In the next few lines of the code, we can see the following:

- The contract is defined as `Coin`.
- An address type variable named `minter` is declared here.
- The address type, 160-bit, suits the need for storing addresses that belong to either contracts or key pairs of the external address.
- The `public` keyword makes it accessible publicly so that people have access to the value of this variable from outside the network:

```
contract Coin {
    // The keyword "public" makes those variables
    // easily readable from outside.
    address public minter;
```

The following line of code serves the purpose of creating a public state variable as well. However, it does the mapping from address type to unsigned integers:

```
mapping (address => uint) public balances;
```

In the next line, an event is declared and will be emitted in the `sent()` function. Once the event is emitted, the listener will be able to access the address `from`, and `to`, as well as unit `amount`. Listening to events that are emitted on the network is not expensive. By receiving arguments like these, transactions can be monitored with ease:

```
// Events allow light clients to react to
// changes efficiently.
event Sent(address from, address to, uint amount);
```

A constructor is a type of special function. Constructors are usually run when contracts are being created and aren't available after that. In the following line of code, the value of `msg.sender` has to be the address that made the external function call:

```
// This is the constructor whose code is
// run only when the contract is created.
constructor() public {
```

```
        minter = msg.sender;
    }
```

In the lines of code that follow, we can see the following:

- The `mint()` and `send()` functions are the ones that are called by contracts or users.
- Notice there are two lines of `require` here.
- The first one says `msg.sender` needs to be the same one that created the contract.
- The second line prevents the amount of coin from exceeding `1e60`. Too many coins may cause the problem of overflow:

```
function mint(address receiver, uint amount) public {
    require(msg.sender == minter);
    require(amount < 1e60);
    balances[receiver] += amount;
}
```

In the following code, we can see the following:

- The `send()` function doesn't have the requirement of who's the sender. Therefore, it can be used by anyone who has enough coin to send.
- When it comes to the case that the amount going to be sent out is bigger than the coins owned, the error message `"Insufficient balance."` will be displayed:

```
function send(address receiver, uint amount) public {
    require(amount <= balances[msg.sender], "Insufficient balance.");
    balances[msg.sender] -= amount;
    balances[receiver] += amount;
    emit Sent(msg.sender, receiver, amount);
    }
}
```

Now, we know the purpose of each line of code in the subcurrency example. The next step is compiling the smart contract. There are quite a few IDEs out there: Remix, SuperBlocks, and EthFiddle are just a few examples. Check out the entire list here: `https://github.com/ConsenSys/ethereum-developer-tools-list#ides`.

Let's look at an example through Remix. Feel free to try the other IDEs:

1. Open Remix via `https://remix.ethereum.org` and create a new file named `subcurrency.sol`:

```
FILE EXPLORERS                subcurrency.sol  ×
 ▾ browser   ⊕  ⊡ ⬚ ⬚        1   pragma solidity >=0.5.0 <0.7.0;
    subcurrency.sol           2
                             3 ▾ contract Coin {
                             4       // The keyword "public" makes those variables
                             5       // easily readable from outside.
                             6       address public minter;
                             7       mapping (address => uint) public balances;
                             8
                             9       // Events allow light clients to react to
                            10       // changes efficiently.
                            11       event Sent(address from, address to, uint amount);
                            12
                            13       // This is the constructor whose code is
                            14       // run only when the contract is created.
                            15 ▾     constructor() public {
                            16           minter = msg.sender;
                            17       }
                            18
                            19 ▾     function mint(address receiver, uint amount) public {
                            20           require(msg.sender == minter);
                            21           require(amount < 1e60);
                            22           balances[receiver] += amount;
                            23       }
                            24
                            25 ▾     function send(address receiver, uint amount) public {
                            26           require(amount <= balances[msg.sender], "Insufficient balance.");
                            27           balances[msg.sender] -= amount;
                            28           balances[receiver] += amount;
                            29           emit Sent(msg.sender, receiver, amount);
                            30       }
                            31 }
```

2. Once the file has been created, move down to the compile tab on the left and choose a compiler. Note that the subcurrency example we chose earlier supports Solidity version 0.5.0 and newer versions. I used 0.5.7 here.

3. As shown here, click on the gray bar, **Compile subcurrency.sol**, to initiate the work:

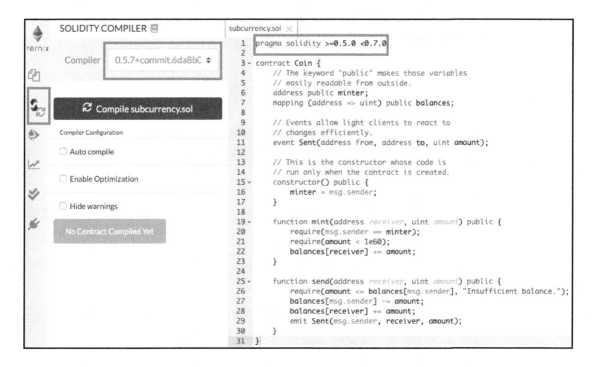

4. When the compilation is done, retrieve the Bytecode by clicking on the button in the bottom-right corner, as shown in the following screenshot. The Bytecode will be copied to the clipboard:

5. Copy the following context to **TextEdit** (on a Mac) or any other text editor of your preference. Then, paste the bytecode under `object`:

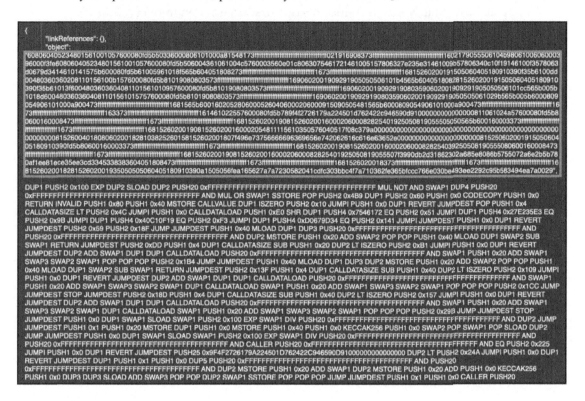

6. Go back to the previous MyCrypto page that we were at, paste the Bytecode there, and hit **Deploy Contract**. The gas price and gas limit will be filled out for you. Note that **Nonce** is 0 since it's our first transaction in the account:

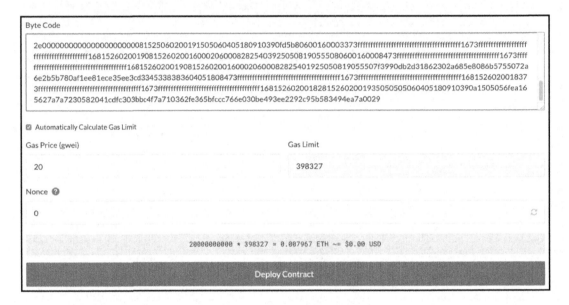

7. The transaction fee will be shown in ether. As we can see, it's about 0.007967 ETH. Click on **Deploy Contract**. MetaMask will let you confirm the transaction, as shown here:

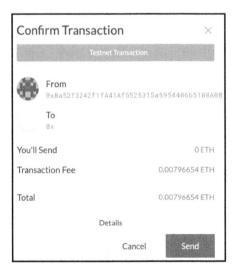

8. Click on **Send**, as shown in the preceding screenshot, and then you will be able to confirm the payment, as follows:

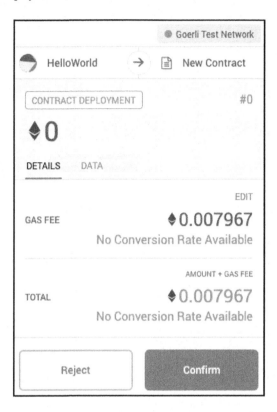

9. In the transaction history of MetaMask, you can view more details about the transaction. If you click on **View on Etherscan** in the following screenshot, a new tab in your browser will open. The URL of the transaction page will be in the following format:

```
https://goerli.etherscan.io/tx/<transaction id>
```

In our case, it is the link shown here, `https://goerli.etherscan.io/tx/`
`0xcb0259addb0f9ec199e1658a7a13af817ab1d0e0d87882f7f39306f1e04b4914`:

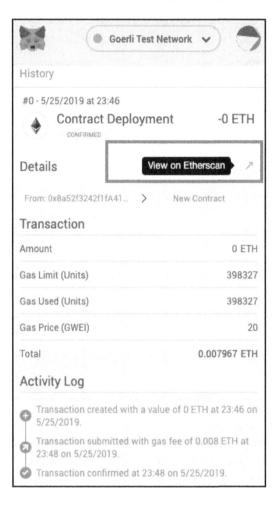

Congratulations! A smart contract has been deployed to the Goerli testnet. You should be able to get the message of deployment on MyCryto as well:

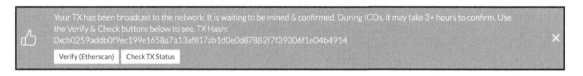

Now, we will take this further and view the smart contract that we just deployed on Etherscan. Etherscan is a powerful tool that allows everyone to develop smart contracts or DApps. We will get to know Etherscan in detail in the other half of `Chapter 6`, *Smart Contract Development and Test Fundamentals*.

# Viewing deployed smart contracts on Etherscan

The page on Etherscan for our deployed smart contract will look something like the following screenshot. As shown in the following screenshot, the **Overview** tab provides information about the transaction hash, block, where it is sent from, and where it was sent to:

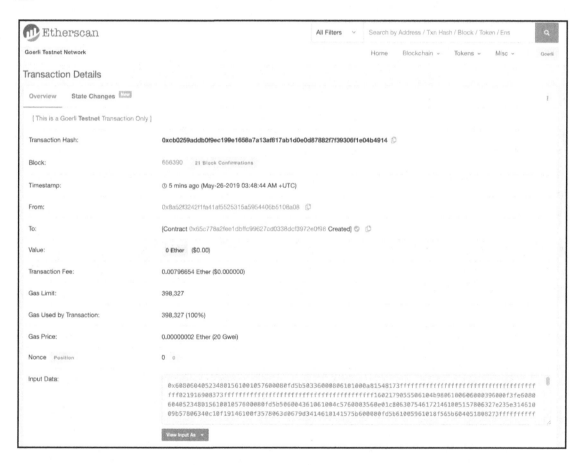

In the **State Changes** tab, you will be able to see the state of the miner, as well as your own account. Let's look at the following screenshot:

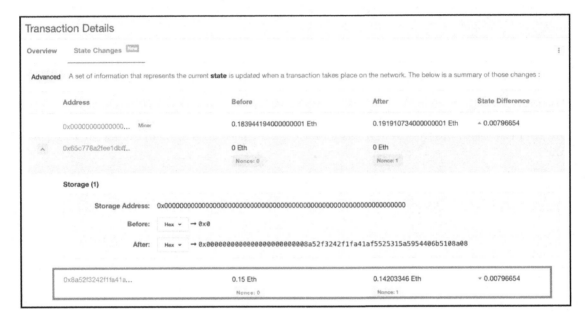

This account had 0.15 Eth when nonce was 0 and moved to ~0.14 Eth after we paid the transaction fee.

# Interacting with the deployed smart contract

After deployment, MyCrypto lets you interact with the smart contract under the **Interact** tab next to the **Deploy** tab.

Let's see this in action:

1. Take the contract address from Etherscan and put it under **Contract Address** in MyCrypto:

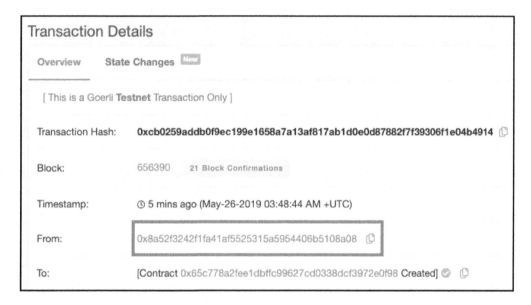

2. Retrieve the ABI. This can be done through Remix by clicking on the **ABI** button on the bottom. I won't show the entire ABI here because of its length:

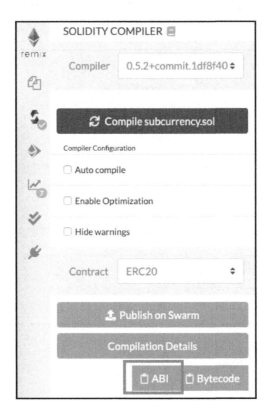

3. Fill in the contract address and ABI information that we just retrieved in *steps 1 and 2* on MyCrypto. You will be able to access the subcurrency smart contract by clicking on the **Access** button on the bottom-left corner, as shown in the following screenshot:

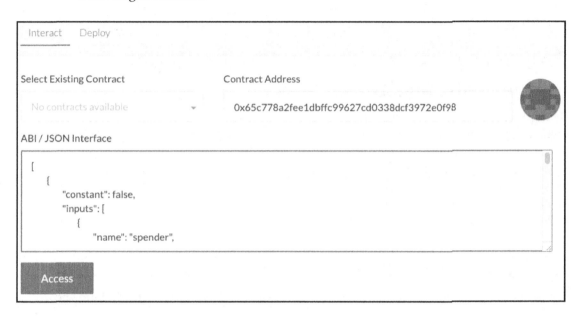

4. We can interact with the smart contract in various ways. An example is shown in the following screenshot:

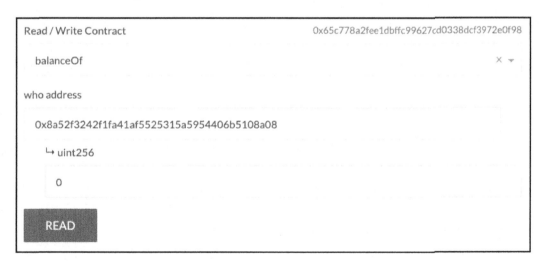

If we check the balance of our account now, it will show 0.

At this point, you should be able to deploy the smart contract with MyCrypto. You have been doing a good job following along. You may repeat this process a few times on your own to get the hang of it if you so wish..

# Deploying a smart contract to the Ropsten testnet with MyEtherWallet

By deploying a smart contract to the Goerli testnet, you have achieved the goal of deploying your smart contract. In this section, we are going to deploy the `MyERC20Token` smart contract (from the *Creating an ERC-20 token—MyERC20Token section in* `Chapter 5`, *Developing Your Own Cryptocurrency*) to a different testnet, that is, the Ropsten testnet, and with a different wallet, that is, MyEtherWallet. By taking different approaches, we will be able to see the little differences between testnets, wallets, and smart contracts. Let's dive right in.

## Accessing or creating a new wallet on MyEtherWallet

For accessing of creating a new wallet on MyEtherWallet, follow the steps that are shown here:

1.  To get started on MyEtherWallet, navigate to `https://www.myetherwallet.com/` and choose **Access My Wallet**, as shown here:

Instead of choosing **Access My Wallet,** feel free to click on **Create A New Wallet**; you will be given three options to create a new wallet:

- **MEWconnect**
- **By Keystore File**
- **By Mnemonic Phrase**

We created our MetaMask wallet by mnemonic phrase, so let's try something different here with the MEWconnect app.

2. As shown in the following screenshot, you can download MEWconnect through the App Store or Google Play:

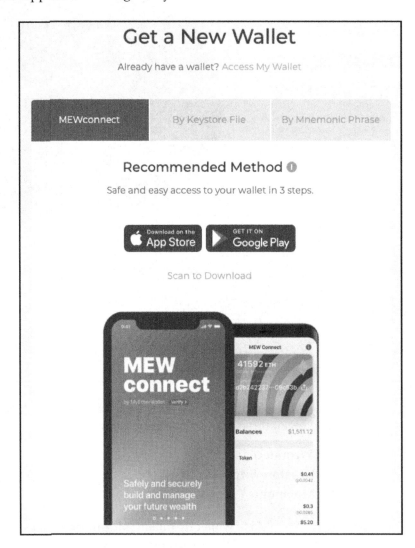

3. With MEWconnect installed on your phone, you can proceed with **Access My Wallet**, as shown in the following screenshot:

## Access My Wallet

Do not have a wallet? Create A New Wallet

| MEWconnect | Hardware | MetaMask | Software |
|---|---|---|---|
| Use MEWconnect to access my wallet | Ledger wallet, FINNEY, Trezor, Digital bitbox, Secalot, KeepKey | Use the MetaMask extension to access my wallet | Keystore file, Private key, Mnemonic phrase  Not recommended |

4. Once you hit **MEWconnect**, MyEtherWallet will let you to scan the QR code on your phone, indicating the wallet is ready to use:

Before you scan the QR code, make sure you switched to the Ropsten testnet on MEWconnect on your phone (like the screenshot shown previously). Otherwise, it will connect to the main Ethereum network by default.

5. Going back to try a few more options, I will connect to the MetaMask wallet here:

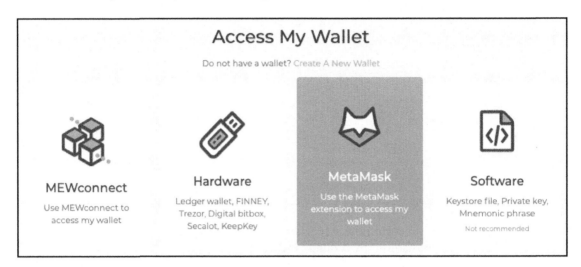

By navigating through MEW, you may find out that, like MyCrypto, MEW supports various activities, mainly the following:

- Making transactions
- Deploying and interacting with smart contracts and DApps

Both MEW and MyCrypto, with their different layouts and features, are good wallets to use.

# Getting test ether

Like we did in the previous section, *Deploying a smart contract to the Goerli testnet*, if you don't have any test ether in your account, make sure you get some. You can do this in two ways, as follows:

- Through the Ropsten Ethereum Faucet: `https://faucet.ropsten.be/`
- Through MetaMask

Now, the account should be loaded with test ether. With this, we are ready to deploy the smart contract.

# Deploying the smart contract

Follow these steps to deploy the smart contract:

1. Log in to the MEW home page.
2. Using the left sidebar, as shown in the following screenshot, select **Contract** | **Deploy Contract**:

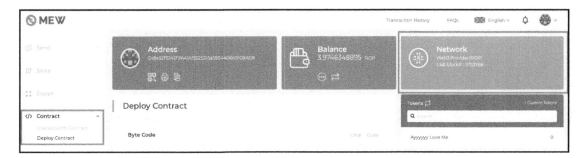

Please make sure that you are connecting to the Ropsten testnet on the MEW web page. If you are not seeing your test ETH balance or `infura.io` (ROP) under the network box, then use the change button to switch.

When we use MyCrypto, only the ABI/JSON interface is needed. With MEW, we also need Bytecode.

3. Compile the MyERC20Token smart contract with Remix, Truffle, or whatever way you prefer and paste in the Bytecode, which is the ABI/JSON interface in MEW. When the ABI/JSON interface is provided, constructor inputs will show up if needed. We will use the following inputs, like we did in `Chapter 6`, *Smart Contract Development and Test Fundamentals*:

```
_name (string): MyERC20Token
_symbol (string): MTK
InitialAccount (address): 0x8a52f3242f1fA41Af5525315a5954406b5108A08
InitialBalance (uint256): 100000000000000000000000
Value in ETH: 0
Contract Name: MyERC20Token
```

4.  You must check for typing errors or whether the type that you entered does not meet the expectations of the smart contract:

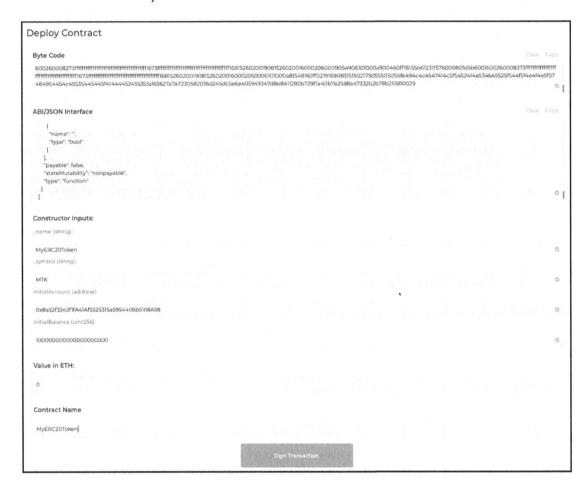

As shown in the preceding screenshot, if each field has a green checkmark on the right, we will be able to sign the transaction. If a green check mark is missing in one of the fields, you won't be able to proceed.

5. Click on **Sign Transaction**:

- If you are using MEW to connect, a confirmation page will be brought up on your phone.
- If you are connecting to the MetaMask wallet, you will need to confirm on MetaMask.

The following screenshot is the screen that you will see for MEW confirmation. It lets you verify the transaction, as shown here:

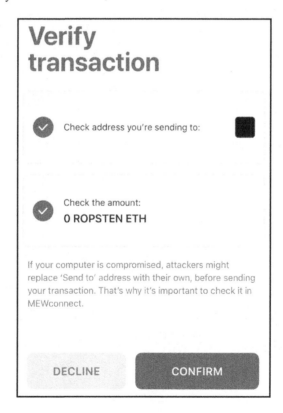

6. On the following confirmation screen, you will have to click on **Confirm and Send**:

The MetaMask confirmation is like the following screenshot. The **DETAILS** tab shows you the gas fee and total cost:

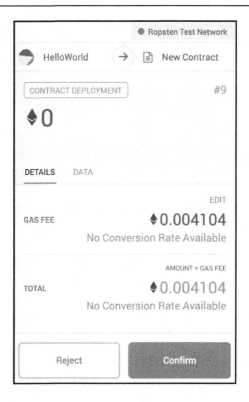

Once confirmed, you will be able to see details about the transaction on the left of the screen and the **Activity Log** on the right:

7. With the MyERC20Token successfully deployed, we can also check the deployment status of our smart contract on Etherscan:

At this point, we have successfully deployed out smart contract, MyERC20Token, to the Ropsten testnet with MyEtherWallet. In this section, we have learned how to deploy smart contracts to different testnets and have a brief idea of how to track them on Etherscan.

# Monitoring smart contracts

Etherscan is one of the popular block explorers. What is an Ethereum blockchain explorer? They are services that let you browse the Ethererum blockchain (mainnet) and testnets. Information on the address, transaction hash, block, contracts, token, and other on-chain activities can be found on block explorers.

There are a few mainstream block explorers, such as the following:

- Etherscan: `https://etherscan.io`
- Etherchain:`https://www.etherchain.org`
- Blockscout: `https://blockscout.com/poa/core/`
- Smart contract watch: `https://github.com/Neufund/smart-contract-watch`

Etherscan is the original block explorer. It provides almost anything you could possibly need. Let's take a tour of Etherscan:

1. First of all, you have to choose the network that you will be using. The default page is the mainnet.
2. Click on the Ethereum symbol on the right-hand corner to switch between the Ethereum mainnet, testnets, and the Tobalaba Energy Web Foundation (EWF). The home page of Etherscan will look as follows:

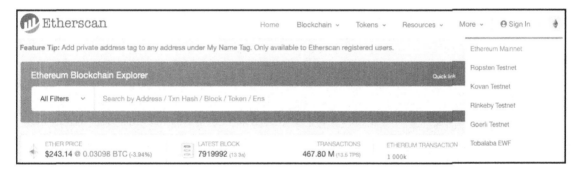

 EWF stands for Energy Web Foundation. It's a blockchain specialized for the energy sector that meets the market and regulators' needs.

3. On the home page, a variety of information is provided. At the top is a search bar for the address, transaction hash, block, token, and Ens. We can also search for the MyERC20Token smart contract we just deployed in the previous section, but make sure you switch to the Ropsten testnet. It will return the same page that we saw at the end of the previous section:

On the top-right corner of the search bar, as shown here, there are quick links to ERC-20 tokens and ERC-721 tokens.

4. The page of the ERC-20 token provides detailed information regarding Ethereum token market capitalization. Token contracts are ranked by prices in descending order. You can rank it by change rate, volume in the last 24 hours, circulating supply market cap (number of outstanding tokens at the current market price), and the number of holders, as shown in the following screenshot:

5. Back to the home page, the ether price, market cap, latest block number, the total transaction counters, transactions per second, difficulty, and average hash rate are listed under the search bar, as shown here. The 14-day-history chart of transaction history is on the right-hand side:

In each section, you can drill down to a page with more information on the topic. If you hold a lot of ether, you can check the page for Ethereum prices frequently. In the following screenshot, the current Ethereum price in USD is listed at the top, and historical prices are in the trend chart here:

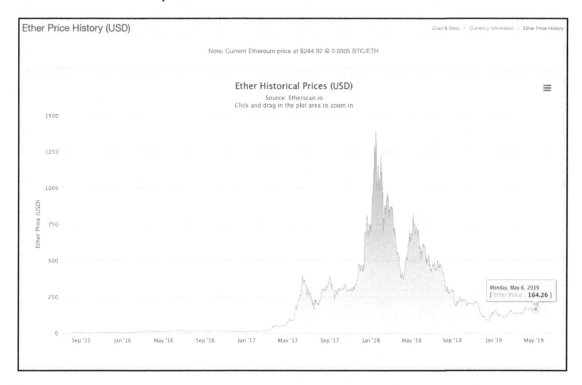

6. Click and drag the plot; it will zoom into the period you are interested in (like the one shown here). Feel free to explore each page in detail, and we will meet each other back on the home page once you are done:

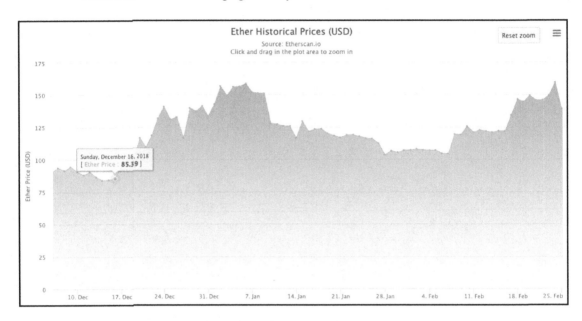

At the top of the site, there are dropdown lists for **Blockchain**, **Tokens**, **Resources**, and **More**. Each one provides topic-specific functionalities:

7. Click on the Blockchain section; it supports view transactions, blocks, uncles, top accounts, and verified contracts. Transactions include completed transactions, pending transactions, and the ones internal to the contracts. Blocks are visible to everyone, including forked blocks, which are the result of chain reorganization. When chain reorganization happens, transactions residing on the blocks of the old chain will cease to exist:

8. Click on the **View Txns** option. It will give us the completed transactions, as shown here:

9. Click on **View Pending Txns** to see the pending transactions, as shown here:

A contract's internal transactions are also captured. Here is an example of those internal transactions on block 8101772:

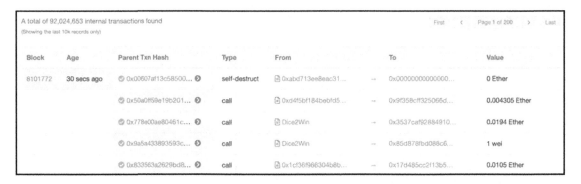

10. Etherscan lets you view uncles under the Blockchain dropdown menu as well. Click on **View Uncles**, and you will be directed to a detailed page of uncle nodes. Newborn uncle nodes are listed on the top. Block height, uncle number, age, miner, and rewards are provided on the page, as shown here:

You can dive into details for one uncle by choosing one of the uncle numbers. Information regarding uncle height, uncle position, block height, hash, parent hash, sha3uncles, miner, difficulty, gas limit, gas used, timestamp, and uncle reward are given, as shown in the following screenshot. It's an uncle node of the height 8100974. Miner was rewarded with 1.75 ether for validating this uncle block. We have provided further reading on uncles at the end of this section:

Uncle #0x6262d04427ddb263f0b5e88701e2818d83924262cf7b6c009b4de860ea8dcee6

Overview

| | |
|---|---|
| Uncle Height: | **8100974** |
| Uncle Position: | 0 |
| Block Height: | 8100975 |
| Hash: | 0x6262d04427ddb263f0b5e88701e2818d83924262cf7b6c009b4de860ea8dcee6 |
| Parent Hash: | 0x7352f26c6afd2684ce5f71f2084892ab34efd6b122a38791455329659ead5d5c |
| Sha3Uncles: | 0x1dcc4de8dec75d7aab85b567b6ccd41ad312451b948a7413f0a142fd40d49347 |
| Mined by: | 0xea674fdde714fd979de3edf0f56aa9716b898ec8 (Ethermine) in 0 secs |
| Difficulty: | 2,127,844,048,990,297 |
| Gas Limit: | 8,000,000 Wei |
| Gas Used: | 4,560,029 Wei |
| Timestamp: | ⏱ 16 mins ago (7/7/2019 12:40:11 AM +UTC) |
| Uncle Reward: | 1.75 Ether |

Let's get back to where we were on Etherscan. Top accounts are listed by ether balance in descending order. Etherscan allows us to see what the richest accounts are in the Ethereum world. As you can see from the following screenshot, the richest account at the time of writing is the one with the name tag **Binance 6**:

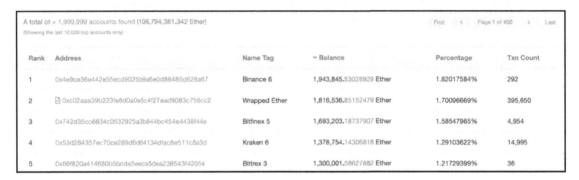

Verified contract pages are only listing contracts with verified source code. On the top-left corner of the following screenshot, the view can be filtered by compiler type—Solidity or Vyper. On the last column, **dApp** (right-hand side of the following screenshot), we can view the **dApp** page and interact with the DApp:

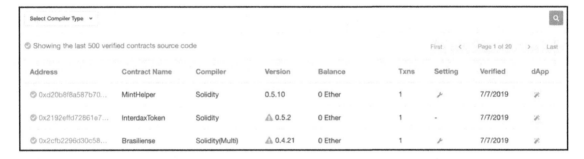

Take the Dapp BSOV on the mainnet as an example. This page allows us to read and write contracts, as shown in the following screenshot:

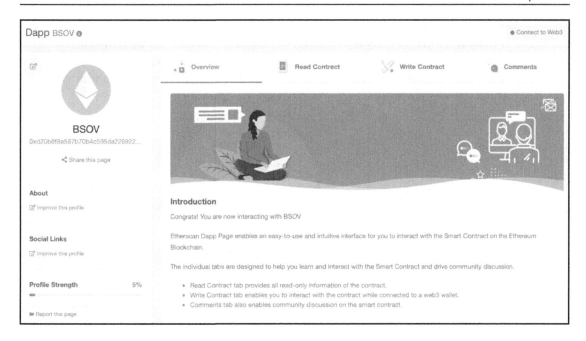

When we read the contract, we are free to query the smart contract's information, as shown in the following screenshot:

While the web3 wallet is not a must for reading contracts, it's required for writing contracts. Once connected to a web3 wallet, you can interact with the smart contract and directly do transactions for writing content such as approving spending and value, where the funds are getting transferred from, and increasing or decreasing allowance:

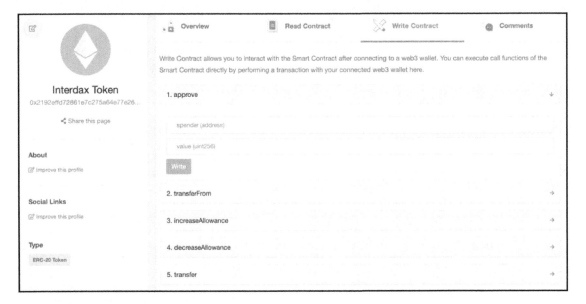

10. Back to the home page again. As shown in the following screenshot, click on the dropdown menu of the tokens. It provides the following view options:

The token tracker lists tokens by market capitalization in descending order. From the rank we in the following screenshot, the top three tokens holding the largest market capitalization are BNB, LEO, and LINK:

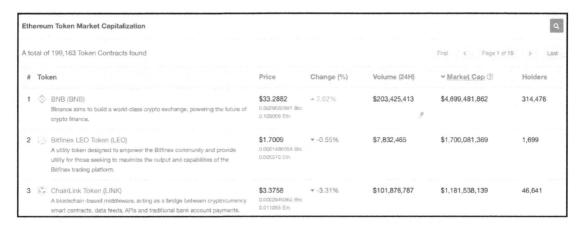

Token transfers between accounts can also be viewed, as shown in the following screenshot. The OCK token with a value of 10 was transferred just 18 seconds before this screenshot was taken:

11. Click on the Ethereum directory on the home page, as shown in the following screenshot. The resources provide the Ethereum directory and charts and stats:

12. There's also a search bar at the top, as shown in the following screenshot. For instance, you can search for any Ethereum wallet. Exchanges for ICOs and others can be located by searching as well. Under the search bar, the most frequently used tools are configured:

These tools are exchanges, wallets, ICOs, news and forums, events, learning resources, smart contracts, mining, and some extra resources. Each section will list the related resources and their websites:

The **Charts and Statistics** page has 26 charts for general information, information on currency, network, blockchain, Ethereum chain data size growth, Ethereum name service, and mining.

A node tracker is available as part of the network's information. You will be able to see the top 10 countries found on most nodes and node stats, as shown in the following screenshot. The heat map on the world map is helpful to locate the countries that are found on most of the nodes in the page. The United States is the top country now, so it has the deepest blue color on the world map. Explore the page and you may find some charts that are very useful to your analysis:

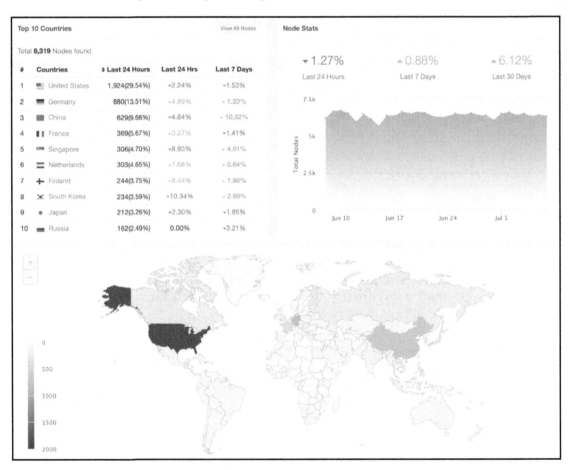

13. The last dropdown menu of Etherscan has four sections: **Developers**, **Swarm & ENS**, **Service Tracker**, and **Misc**:

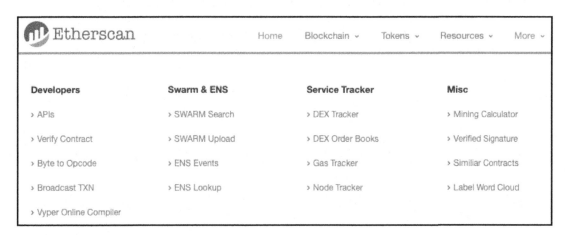

To find out more about this powerful tool, we will introduce using developer APIs in the next section. The following sections provide some further reading regarding the topic of uncle nodes.

# Ethereum developer APIs

Ethereum developer APIs support accessing blockchain data, building DApps, verifying contracts, and so on. GET/POST requests are supported. The upper limit of requests per second is five.

We will show you how to use an Ethereum developer API in the following steps:

1. Before being able to use the API service, a free **API-Key Token** is needed. To get an **API-Key Token**, you will need an Etherscan account. Choose the **API-KEYs** tab and you will be able to create one by naming the app, as shown in the following screenshot:

2. To get the ether balance for a single address, we can use the following link. You should try this with your own address and API key token:
   ```
   https://api.etherscan.io/api?module=account&action=balance&address=<Address>&tag=latest&apikey=<YourApiKeyToken>.
   ```

   Now, we can get the balance of the top account holding the maximum ether. From the top accounts page, we can see it has **1,943,845.53028929** ether. The address of this account is **0x4e9ce36e442e55ecd9025b9a6e0d88485d628a67**:

3. Call the URL with the account address and your API-Key Token. We encourage you to replace the address and API key for the URL with the following format: `https://api.etherscan.io/api?module=accountaction=balance address=<address>tag=latestapikey=<apikey>`.

   For example, we have the following: `https://api.etherscan.io/api?module=accountaction=balanceaddress=0x4e9ce36e442e55ecd9025b9a6e0d88485d628a67tag=latestapikey=2ENS37APDAVA4GY8DUB79X9XKW54Y1W86G`.

4. Check the balance is returned in the message. It matches the one that we have at the top account tracker:

   `{"status":"1","message":"OK","result":"19438455302892962094433357"}`

5. APIs support not only getting the ether balance for a single address, but also multiple addresses (up to 20 accounts) in a single call via `https://api.etherscan.io/api?module=account&action=balancemulti&address=<address 1>,<address 2>...&tag=latest&apikey=<YourApiKeyToken>`.

Other than account APIs, there are APIs for contracts, transactions, blocks, event logs, GETH/Parity Proxy, tokens, stats, and misc tools and utilities. Using contract APIs, we can retrieve a contract ABI or source code. The functionalities of each API are shown in the following table:

| APIs | Functions |
|------|-----------|
| **Accounts** | Get the following by address:<br>• Ether balance<br>• Transactions<br>• ERC-20 token transfer events<br>• Blocks |
| **Contracts** | Get the following information about a verified contract by address:<br>• Contract ABI<br>• Contract source code |
| **Transactions** | Get the following status:<br>• Contract execution status<br>• Transaction receipt status |
| **Blocks** | Get ether rewards of block or uncle by block number |
| **Event Logs** | It supports the following filter parameters:<br>• `fromBlock`, `toBlock`, and address<br>• `topic0`, `topic1`, `topic2`, and `topic3`<br>• `topic0_1_opr`, `topic1_2_opr`, `topic2_3_`, `topic0_2_opr`, `topic0_3_opr`, and `topic1_3_opr` |

| GETH/Parity Proxy | A complete list is available at `https://github.com/ethereum/wiki/wiki/JSON-RPC` |
|---|---|
| Tokens | Get ERC20-Token information:<br>• Total supply by contract address<br>• Account balance by token contract address |
| Stats | Get Ethereum information:<br>• Total supply of ether<br>• Last price of ether<br>• Node size |
| Misc Tools and Utilities | Third-party tools:<br>• `https://github.com/corpetty/py-etherscan-api`<br>• `https:/github.com/sebs/etherscan-api` |

We won't go into detail about each API in the preceding table. Exploring these APIs will be left as homework for you. Now, let's go over some further reading regarding the uncle nodes we mentioned earlier.

# Further reading on uncle nodes

Uncles are also referred to as ommer to be more gender neutral. The concept of uncles is closely related to orphans in blockchain. What are orphans? When a block is mined, this information regarding the new block will be shared across the entire network. But the news about the new block doesn't reach every block at the same time. There is a scenario where a block is solved by two or more miners at the same block height.

Let's explain this with the following diagram. When the miner solved block B, miner C didn't know it had been solved. C continues to solve block B. Block B ends up being solved more than once. The red block, B, becomes an orphan block, and even though it is a valid block, it won't be part of the blockchain:

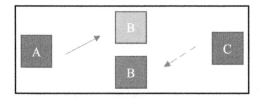

Here is a real-world example on blockchain, as shown in the following table:

- Both blocks share the same height, 578141.
- The orphaned block was created 4 seconds later than the block on the main chain.
- The parties who relayed the block are different.

- There are no next blocks after the orphaned block, but there are blocks after the one on the main chain.
- Because the orphan block is no longer part of the main chain, the block reward in it is not spendable either. Therefore, there is no actual reward for solving the orphan block. When the same block is being produced, a fork happens.

What happens next is the longest blockchain is found and every block migrates to it:

| Height | 578141 (Orphaned) | 578141 (Main chain) |
|---|---|---|
| Hash | 00000000000000000001253a5f37d3763dbe928d21f7d72a708f05268c044179c | 0000000000000000000022ea15acccabee11b79e57db44afeeefc094beb1131b02 |
| Previous Block | 00000000000000000005819c1a3342dde3774952849d1bda1e5ee6cd5839f27c | 00000000000000000005819c1a3342dde3774952849d1bda1e5ee6cd5839f27c |
| Next Block | // | 000000000000000000028e2f65a4f8d0ae92f99c9f3147ca9233cd5f228e6b6ba |
| Time | 2019-05-28 05:54:17 | 2019-05-28 05:54:13 |
| Received Time | 2019-05-28 05:54:17 | 2019-05-28 05:54:13 |
| Relayed By | ViaBTC | AntPool |
| Difficulty | 6.70463E+12 | 6.70463E+12 |
| Bits | 388627269 | 388627269 |
| Number of Transactions | 2326 | 2382 |
| Output Total | 4,255.54726431 BTC | 4,142.21396413 BTC |
| Estimated Transaction Volume | 318.49426642 BTC | 327.23405757 BTC |
| Size | 1097.595 KB | 1099.549 KB |
| Version | 0x20400000 | 0x20000000 |
| Merkle Root | b6323487c4c443954b906af47a9bdfa7011ca9b46739602d1dd1268656bd689b | 4f5b257de8b807959701f33cc9d9f5b8bec62d5d8e887dad06133d9307fc6c82 |
| Nonce | 1615532724 | 1746025253 |
| Block Reward | 12.5 BTC | 12.5 BTC |
| Transaction Fees | 0.86579811 BTC | 0.86019294 BTC |

Ethereum uses a modified version of GHOST to make sure its block time is not 10 minutes (is it is in the Bitcoin blockchain) but without raising the orphan rate. The **Greedy Heaviest Observed Subtree (GHOST)** protocol was introduced in 2013 by Bitcoin researchers. Instead of getting rid of orphans such as Bitcoin, Ethereum includes them as *uncles*. If miners solve uncles, they will still get rewards for it.

# Summary

In this chapter, we started working with different approaches to deploying smart contracts to testnets via Ethereum wallets. We went through deploying smart contracts with the Goerli testnet and Ropsten testnet. Then, we took a close look at how to monitor smart contracts on Etherscan. Finally, we looked at and used some of the useful tools that are provided by Etherscan.

In the next chapter, we will get a better understanding of Ethereum wallet technology, create a hierarchical deterministic wallet, and compare wallets.

# 11
# Building Ethereum Wallets

We briefly introduced bitcoin and Ethereum wallets in Chapter 1, *Blockchain and Cryptocurrency* and Chapter 2, *Ethereum Architecture and Ecosystem*. In this chapter, we will get an overview of Ethereum wallets and learn how to create an Ethereum wallet. We will also look at how to create a non-deterministic wallet. When we have a sound understanding of Ethereum wallets, we will create a **Hierarchical Deterministic (HD)** wallet. We will also discuss the popular third-party Ethereum wallets.

This chapter will cover the following topics:

- Understanding the wallet technology
- Creating an Ethereum wallet
- Working with third-party Ethereum wallets

## Technical requirements

Please refer to the following GitHub link to find the source code for this book:

https://github.com/PacktPublishing/Learn-Ethereum

## Understanding the wallet technology

When we refer to something as a wallet, we assume that it's something that holds money. In fact, an Ethereum wallet does not store any ether or tokens. Wallets keep the private keys that are needed for signing the transactions. An Ethereum wallet, just like a cryptocurrency wallet, can be classified as a non-deterministic or deterministic wallet.

# Understanding non-deterministic and deterministic wallets

What's the difference between these two types of wallets? They are different in how the private keys are backed up. A non-deterministic wallet generates private keys that are random and independent of each other (such as in the left-hand side of the following diagram). There is no particular pattern as to how the keys are derived and hence we need to create a backup of the keys each time there is a new one. In a deterministic wallet, on the contrary, the private keys are related because they originate from the same key called seed, as shown here on the right-hand side of the diagram. Just backing up the seed once will be enough to regenerate all the keys:

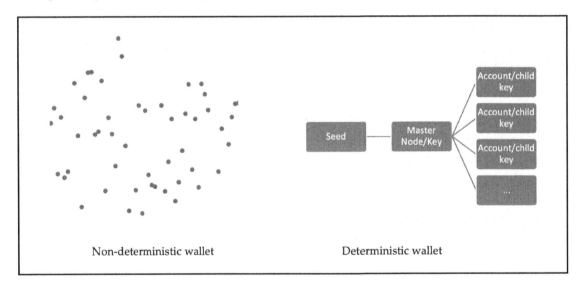

Non-deterministic wallet                    Deterministic wallet

There are three types of wallets:

- Deterministic wallet
- HD wallet
- Armory deterministic wallet

The first wallet, which is used in Ethereum presale, is a non-deterministic wallet. It's considered a rather old style compared to a deterministic wallet. Modern deterministic wallets have advantages over non-deterministic wallets in many aspects, such as backups, security, data storage, accounting, auditing, and access controls. The following list showcases some of these advantages:

- One-time backup for deterministic wallets is so much easier than the cumbersome way a non-deterministic wallet has to be backed up. If you don't create a backup each time, you will risk losing the data, which is referring to ether and smart contracts. For a deterministic wallet, only copying the master seed will be enough. It's less work during the import and export of wallets. For a non-deterministic wallet, the entire list of keys needs to be copied during the migration process.
- In the concept of deterministic wallets, deriving the keys from the seed makes it possible to store the private keys offline. Disabling web server access to private keys offers more privacy and security. Securing the seed takes less effort compared to keeping all the keys safe, which is what non-deterministic wallets need to do.

The HD wallet is the most well-known kind of deterministic wallet. It's also a preferred option among the deterministic wallets if you want to create one since it is well developed. When it comes to the following cases, the HD wallet shows more advantages than other types of deterministic wallet:

- Use cases for creating public keys without accessing corresponding private keys
- Use cases for keys to match the hierarchical structure in an organization context

The first use case shows the security advantage of the HD wallet. Normally, a deterministic wallet holds a single chain of keypairs, which doesn't support selective keypair sharing, while the HD wallet allows such selective sharing on multiple keypair chains that are generated from a single root. In some cases, being able to create public keys without exposing private keys makes the HD wallet available in environments that would normally be a higher security risk. The second use case listed here takes advantage of the hierarchical structure of the design and puts it into the use of real-world cases.

HD wallet has security advantages just mentioned previously, we will bring up another aspect of secure consideration—private key management. It does not only refer to key generation offline (away from the network, such as cold storage. Key sharding and splitting or division of signatures are other alternatives. **Key sharding**, also known as **Shamir's secret sharing**, is basically splitting a key into several pieces, or shards. This makes each shard useless, and the original key would be reconstructed unless enough pieces are assembled to reconstruct. A similar but very different concept to this is **multi-signature wallet**. Readers who are interested in the topic are encouraged to do further reading about this.

With cryptocurrency wallets becoming more and more developed, the protocols and standards need to be shared across the industry. The Ethereum community has been establishing standards over the years. Some of them are known as **Ethereum Improvement Proposals (EIPs)**. Some are on application-level standards, for example, the standard format for smart contracts, known as **Ethereum Requests for Comment (ERC)**. Standards are also followed for wallet creation. There are a few standards that are widely adopted, as follows:

- HD wallets (BIP-32)
- Multipurpose HD wallets (BIP-43)
- Multi-currency and multi-account wallets (BIP-44)
- Mnemonic code words (BIP-39)

**BIP** stands for **Bitcoin Improvement Proposal**. Although there are so many differences between Bitcoin and Ethereum networks today, they still have a lot in common and share standards and protocols.

The mnemonic code words is 128-bit to 256-bit entropy. This entropy will be plugged into a **Password-Based Key Derivation Function 2 (PBKDF2)** function and stretched to a 512-bit seed. The seed will be used in building a deterministic wallet. We will take a look at those standards in detail next.

# Mnemonic code words (BIP-39)

The purpose of BIP-39 is to implement mnemonic code for generating deterministic keys. The standard defines two processes:

- Generating the mnemonic words
- Converting the words into binary seeds

The guideline of BIP-39 is basically transforming randomness generated in computer language to human language. The transformation starts with entropy and ends with a mapped mnemonic sentence, with a middle product checksum. The transformation can be simplified to the following:

*Entropy >>> Checksum >>> Entropy + Checksum >>> Mnemonic sentence*

The initial entropy size is defined as 128 to 256 bits. As entropy becomes more secure, the end product sentence gets longer. If we take a 128-bit entropy, we will get 12 phrases. We summarize the size of value of each step in bits, as shown in the following table:

| Entropy | Checksum | Entropy + Checksum | Mnemonic sentence |
|---------|----------|--------------------|--------------------|
| 128 | 4 | 132 | 12 |
| 160 | 5 | 165 | 15 |
| 192 | 6 | 198 | 18 |
| 224 | 7 | 231 | 21 |
| 256 | 8 | 264 | 24 |

The generation process of mnemonic words can be broken down into the following steps:

1. Generate an initial entropy, that is, a cryptographically random sequence.

   For example, we have entropy in hexadecimal, like so:

   ```
   7f7f7f7f7f7f7f7f7f7f7f7f7f7f7f7f
   ```

2. Generate a checksum of entropy by taking the first *n* bits of entropy's SHA256 hash:

$$n = \frac{length\ of\ entropy}{32}$$

   We won't go into the details of the SHA-256 algorithm here. You can directly take the SHA-256 hash of entropy from any online tool such as `https://emn178.github.io/online-tools/sha256.html`. The hash we get is similar to the following in hexadecimal:

   ```
   8ecee7af753ae153af3163ac2a5d7a73381bfb1dff5f45a06f4e2d673b4ee41c
   ```

Convert the hash from hexadecimal to binary, as follows:

```
10001110110 01110111001 11101011110 11101010011 10101110000
10101001110 10111100110 00101100011 10101100001 01010010111
01011110100 11100110011 10000001101 11111101100 01110111111
11101011111 01000101101 00000011011 11010011100 01011010110
01110011101 10100111011 10010000011 100
```

The next step is to get *n*, which we do by applying the equation we mentioned previously to the 128-bit entropy we had:

$$n = \frac{128}{32} = 4$$

Therefore, *n* is *4*; we are taking the first 4 bits of the hash. It will be 1,000 in our case.

3.  Append the checksum to the end of the entropy. The raw binary of the original entropy will be like the following:

```
01111111011 11111011111 11011111110 11111110111 11110111111
10111111101 11111101111 11101111111 01111111011 11111011111
11011111110 1111111
```

Append 1000 to the end of 128-bit binary. We will get a total of 132 bits (128 + 4 bits):

```
01111111011 11111011111 11011111110 11111110111 11110111111
10111111101 11111101111 11101111111 01111111011 11111011111
11011111110 11111111000
```

4.  Convert the 132-bit binary into decimal, like so:

```
01111111011 11111011111 11011111110 11111110111 11110111111
1019        2015        1790        2039        1983
10111111101 11111101111 11101111111 01111111011 11111011111
1533        2031        1919        1019        2015
11011111110 11111111000
1790        2040
```

5.  Match the word indexes with a word list. We will get the following 12 phrases:

```
1019, 2015, 1790, 2039, 1983, 1533, 2031, 1919, 1019, 2015, 1790,
2040
```

Our resulting 12 phrases are as follows:

- If we use the English list (`https://github.com/bitcoin/bips/blob/master/bip-0039/english.txt`):

    legal winner thank year wave sausage worth useful legal winner thank yellow

- If we use the Japanese list (`https://github.com/bip32JP/bip32JP.github.io/blob/master/test_JP_BIP39.json`):

---

そつう　れきだい　ほんやく　わかす　りくつ　ばいか　ろせん　やちん　そつう　れきだい　ほんやく　わかめ

---

Please try this transformation process on your own and get used to it.

# Stretching mnemonic code words to the seed of the deterministic wallet

Now that we've learned step by step how mnemonic code words are generated, we will go into more detail about how the mnemonic code words are transformed into a seed, which will be used in deterministic wallet creation. The process can be broken down into a few steps:

1. Take the mnemonic code words as a parameter for the PBKDF2 function. We will use the Japanese words from the previous section:

---

そつう　れきだい　ほんやく　わかす　りくつ　ばいか　ろせん　やちん　そつう　れきだい　ほんやく　わかめ

---

2. Take salt as another parameter for the PBKDF2 function. The salt, known as cryptographic salt, is a string. It has two components—a constant mnemonic string and a passphrase provided by the user. The passphrase is generally optional. The purpose of introducing the salt is to make the end product seem more secure.

For example, we use the following Japanese phrase as a passphrase:

$$\boxed{\text{㌔ガバヴァぱばぐゞちぢ十人十色}}$$

3. Use the PBKDF2 function to get a 512-bit mnemonic seed, with parameters from the previous two steps as inputs. What a PBKDF2 function does is basically apply a pseudorandom function—in this case, a **Hash-based Message Authentication Code (HMAC)**, to the inputs.

    The PBKDF2 key derivation function can be described with the following formula:

    $$\text{Seed} = \text{PBKDF2}(\text{PRF}, \text{Password}, \text{Salt}, c, \text{dkLen})$$

    - *RPF*: The pseudorandom function HMAC-SHA512
    - *c*: The number of iterations, which in this case is 2048
    - *dkLen*: The desired bit-length of seed, which is 512

    With the transformation complete, we got our seed:

    ```
    aee025cbe6ca256862f889e48110a6a382365142f7d16f2b9545285b3af64e54214
    3a577e9c144e101a6bdca18f8d97ec3366ebf5b088b1c1af9bc31346e60d9
    ```

The following are a few implementations in different languages for reference:

| Language | Library Path |
|---|---|
| C | https://github.com/ElementsProject/libwally-core |
| C++ | https://github.com/libbitcoin/libbitcoin-system |
| Go | https://github.com/tyler-smith/go-bip39go-bip39 |
| JavaScript | https://github.com/bitcoinjs/bip39 |
| Python | https://github.com/trezor/python-mnemonic |
| Ruby | https://github.com/sreekanthgs/bip_mnemonic |
| Rust | https://github.com/infincia/bip39-rs |
| Swift | https://github.com/CikeQiu/CKMnemonic <br> https://github.com/yuzushioh/HDWalletKit |

More information can be found on the wiki page here:

https://github.com/bitcoin/bips/blob/master/bip-0039.mediawiki. You are welcome to read through for more details.

# HD wallets (BIP-32)

HD wallets follow the BIP-32 standard, which was created on February 11, 2012. The standard was set for mainly two aspects:

- How to use a single seed to derive the tree of keypairs
- How to derive wallet structure from the tree of keypairs

## Deriving a tree of keypairs

Before going in to any details regarding key derivation, we need to understand the concept of extended keys properly. The concept of **extended keys** came into the picture to prevent the derived child keys from entirely depending on the parent key itself. The process for deriving the child keys is as follows:

1. Take the private and public parent key.
2. Extend the key with an extra 256-bit entropy, called **chain code:**

    - If the parent key is a private key, the extended private key will have the prefix `xprv`.
    - If the parent key is a public key, the extended public key will have the prefix `xpub`.

3. The extended keys will be used to produce the child key instead of the original private and public parent keys.

For key derivation, **Child Key Derivation (CDK)** functions are defined. They are functions that are used to derive child keys from a parent key. There will be a different CDK for each computation of the following:

- Compute the private child key from the private parent key.
- Compute the public child key from the public parent key.
- Compute the public child key from the private parent key.

The parent key doesn't need to be the root of the tree, and it can be any node on the tree.

To summarize, there are two ways to generate a child public key:

- Directly from the parent public key
- From the child private key

Notice it won't be possible to compute a private child key from a public parent key.

However, the feature of generating child public keys from parent public keys only is a key feature of the HD wallet. This brought us back to the second point of advantage deterministic wallets have over non-deterministic ones (which we went over in the *Understanding non-deterministic and deterministic wallets* section). With an extended public key on a web server, we can generate as many public keys and addresses as we need. If it wasn't an HD wallet, we would have to store all those pubic keys and addresses on a server, which is more work for maintenance and security. On the other hand, extended private keys can be secured on a separate server or offline cold wallet. Even if the server holding the pubic keys is compromised, the private keys won't be impacted.

Like a coin with two faces, the convenience of generating all the public child keys from the extended public key also comes with risks. Recall the process of generating extended keys. In the second step, we extend the public key with a chain code. If the attacker gets the chain code from the extended public key, it will compromise the non-hardened child key. With the child private key plus the chain code, the attacker will be able to derive the parent private key. Other than extended keys, we will introduce another concept, that is, hardened and normal (unhardened or non-hardened) keys. Here, we simplify the computation of those keys as follows:

- Hardened child key: Hash (parent private key + index)
- Normal child key: Hash (parent public key + index)

For the hardened child key, the linkage between the parent pubic key and private child key is broken. Therefore, the risk of exposing the child and parent private keys is countered.

In the formula for hardened and normal child keys, we are using an index. To generate more than one child key from a certain parent key, an index is very useful to keep things in order. The index is defined as a 32-bit integer. Just like how we distinguish private and public extended keys using prefixes `xprv` and `xpub`, we use different ranges of indexes for hardened and normal child keys:

- Index of hardened child key is in the range $[0, 2^{31})$ or $[0, 2^{31} - 1]$
- Index of normal child key is bigger than $2^{31} - 1$

With all the concepts of keys in mind, let's move on to the key derivation process. Instead of solely using one key, both private and public keys are used in extension with an extra 256 bits of entropy. With all CDKs in place, the key tree can be built. Building the key tree takes on the following process:

1. First, we start with one master extended key.
2. Then, we use the child key derivation function to get level-one derived nodes.

3. Next, we apply child key derivation functions to each of these level-one nodes to derive next-level nodes.
4. Finally, we repeat the same process to build the entire tree.

The keys are in the format of 256 bits, while there are $2^{512}$ possible extended keypairs in total. Because of security considerations, master keys won't be generated, but are generated from seed values instead.

# Deriving wallet structure

Having a tree of key pairs, the structure of a wallet can be imposed on the tree. The default wallet layout is defined like so:

- Each account contains one external and one internal keypair chain.
- Derive public addresses from external keychain.
- The internal keychain is responsible for all the activities that won't be shared with the outside environment.

HD wallets support a lot of use cases, for example:

- Full wallet sharing
- Support for auditing
- Central control from headquarter to branches
- Recurrent transactions among businesses
- Separating incoming and outgoing transactions to prevent fraud

When it's for accounting and auditing purposes, accountants or auditors need to read the history of transactions. For accessing the transactions, wallet owners can generate the public keys at the hierarchical level needed. In terms of access control, the owner of the HD wallet will have the flexibility to determine how much ether others can spend by designing the hierarchy of the wallet.

For implementations, there are quite a few packages in different languages. We are only listing a few here for reference:

| Language | Library name |
|----------|--------------|
| C ++ | mSIGNA: `https://github.com/ciphrex/mSIGNA` |
| Go | btcutil: `https://github.com/btcsuite/btcutil`<br>go-hdwallet: `https://github.com/wemeetagain/go-hdwallet` |

| Java | supernode: https://github.com/bitsofproof/supernode<br>bushido-java-core: https://github.com/bushidowallet/bushido-java-core |
|------|------------------------------------------------------------------------------------------------------------------------------|
| Python | pycoin: https://github.com/richardkiss/pycoin<br>bip32utils 0.3.post4: https://pypi.org/project/bip32utils/ |
| Ruby | money-tree: https://github.com/GemHQ/money-tree |

You can extend your reading to the wiki page of this standard:

https://github.com/bitcoin/bips/blob/master/bip-0032.mediawiki. More math and details are shared on this page.

# HD wallet path

If you have been doing extra reading upon BIP 32, you will have noticed a picture of key derivation, which can be found here: https://github.com/bitcoin/bips/blob/master/bip-0032/derivation.png. In this picture, the master node at depth 0 has a notation of **m**. At depth 1, wallets have notations such as **m/0**, **m/1**, and so on. And for depth 2, wallets have notations such as **m/0/0**, **m/0/1**, ..., **m/i/0**, and **m/i/1**.

This is another convention for keys in HD wallets. All keys are formatted like a path. It's defined as follows:

1. The master private key is **m**.
2. The first normal child of the master private key is **m/o**.
3. The first hardened child of the master private key is **m/o'**.
4. The first normal child of **m/0'** is **m/0'/0** and so on.

The last number of the path describes which is the child of the parent, and the rest of path is the parent. You may see keys such as **M/1/0**. That means it's a public key. Public keys starts with an uppercase **M** while private keys start with a lowercase **m**.

We know one parent extended key can have more than one child key and that the upper limit of numbers of child keys is about 4 billion—2 billion of each hardened and normal child keys. Therefore, the entire tree of HD wallets that are described in BIP-32 can end up being very deep and wide. To reduce the degrees of freedom that BIP-32 offers, BIP-43 and BIP-44 were introduced to further standardize the structure of the tree of HD wallets.

# Multipurpose HD wallets (BIP-43)

BIP-43 uses the first level of the BIP-32 tree structure as `purpose`:

```
m / purpose' /*
```

From the `purpose'` value, we can tell, it's the hardened child key that has been proposed.

HD wallets that follow BIP-43 are only using branch **m/ i' /...** for certain purposes. Index **i** is used to identify the purpose.

# Multi-currency and multi-account wallets (BIP-44)

BIP-44 is actually a particular application of BIP-43. BIP-44 has the title **multi-account hierarchy for deterministic wallets**. It supports the following features:

- Multiple accounts
- Multiple coins
- External chains per account
- Internal chains per account
- Millions of addresses per chain

In BIP-44, five levels in the BIP-32 path are defined like so. Notice that the fourth and fifth level are not hardened derivations like the previous three levels:

```
m / purpose' / coin_type' / account' / change / address_index
```

We will explain each level in detail:

1. The purpose is set to a constant 44'. Notice that a hardened child key is used.
2. The coin type varies, depending on the type of cryptocurrency. We've listed a few that interest us:

| Coin type index | Coin |
|:---:|:---:|
| 0' | Bitcoin |
| 60' | Ether |
| 61' | Ether Classic |
| 1' | Testnet for all coins |

Please take some time to check the whole list: `https://github.com/satoshilabs/slips/blob/master/slip-0044.md`.

3. The account allows independent user identities. Also, different types of coins don't mix together in different accounts.

4. Change is used to identify external and internal chains:
   - The external chain is set as constant 0.
   - The internal chain is set as constant 1.

   In the scope of Ethereum, only the external chain is used to receive the funds. The normal derivation, instead of the hardened derivation that's used here, is used to support exporting the extended public keys to an environment that may not be secured.

5. The address index is a public derivation, the same as change.

Looking into the details of the standards of HD wallets, you should be able to understand any user-facing blockchain application better now.

# Generating a private key in Ethereum

With a sound understanding of wallets, we will go into the details of private key generation in this section. The private key is a key concept in Ethereum. The address of externally owned accounts is determined by a private key. Each address and private key is used to derive that the address is unique. The private key is stored locally only, and won't be shared in transactions. The address of the account and digital signature are shared instead. The creation of a digital signature needs the participation of a private key. The digital signature is then used in authentication that's needed by transactions.

The journey from private key to address is as follows:

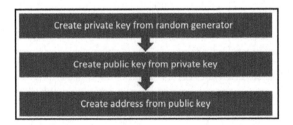

1. The private key in Ethereum is defined as a random number with the format of 256 bits, 32 bytes, a 64-hexadecimal-digits HEX string, and any number between 1 and $2^{256}$.

2. The generation of the private key is an offline activity. It's important to use a true random number generator to generate the private key.

3. `web3.utils` provides a utility function to generate pseudo-random HEX strings given the byte size. The `randomHex` library is using `crypto.randomBytes()` in Node.js, as shown in the following code:

```
$ npm install web3
web3.utils.randomHex(32)

$ npm install randomhex
var randomHex = require('randomhex');
randomHex(32, console.log);
```

Once the private key is generated. The public key can be derived by a private key using the following formula for elliptic curve:

$$Public\ key = Private\ Key * G$$

In the previous formula, the following applies:

- G refers to the *Generator point*.
- The elliptic curve allows the multiplication operation, but it cannot perform the reverse operation: division.

In other words, the public key can be derived easily but it is not possible to use the public key to calculate another private key. The one-way nature of elliptic curve suits our needs for security. This type of cryptography is known as asymmetric cryptography. There is more than one elliptic curve out there. Both Ethereum and Bitcoin use the elliptic curve known as secp256k1. There are a few libraries available for the secp256k1 elliptic curve:

- `secp256k1`: A library wraps the bitcoin `secp256k1` C library.
- `libsecp256k1` **wrapper for OCaml**: A library wraps the `secp256k1` EC(DSA) library into an OCaml library.

The following code will convert a private key into a public key:

```
npm install elliptic-curve
var secp256k1 = require('elliptic-curve').secp256k1
var privateKey =
'278a5de700e29faae8e40e366ec5012b5ec63d36ec77e8a2417154cc1d25383f'
secp256k1.getPublicKey(privateKey)
'03fdd57adec3d438ea237fe46b33ee1e016eda6b585c3e27ea66686c2ea5358479'
```

The previously installed package is a plain JavaScript implementation of elliptic-curve. Compared to RSA cryptography, the elliptic curve is slower, and the JavaScript implementation is even slower. The library is intended to be a fast implementation.

By using the format established by the Standard for Efficient Cryptography Group, the public key is using 65 bytes and 130-hexadecimal characters. Ethereum uses an uncompressed point on the elliptic curve with the prefix `0x04`. The public key that's derived from the private key is a pair $(x, y)$. The final public key we saw from the library is the result of serialization by concatenating $04$, $x$, and $y$, as shown in the following formula:

$$Public\ Key = 04 + x\ in\ 64\ hex + y\ in\ 64$$

An Ethereum address is described as follows in the yellow paper—for a given private key, pr, the Ethereum address A(pr) (a 160-bit value) to which it corresponds is defined as the rightmost 160 bits of the Keccak hash of the corresponding ECDSA public key.

In other words, from a public key to an address, Ethereum implements Keccak-256 to calculate the hash of this public key and rightmost 20 bytes is the Ethereum address. When the public key is used in the calculation, the leading '04' is left out.

# Creating an Ethereum wallet

In this section, we will go through the details of creating an Ethereum wallet. There are a lot of wallet software packages available on the market. For illustration purposes, we will use MyCrypto, the free, open-source wallet for interfacing with the Ethereum network. The desktop version of MyCrypto allows you to create new wallets. You can download MyCrypto Desktop via `https://download.mycrypto.com`. The following are the steps to create a wallet:

1. Open **MyCrypto**.
2. Click on **Create New Wallet** in the left-hand side bar.
3. Navigate to **Create New Wallet** on the next page, as shown in the following screenshot:

4. Click on **Generate a Wallet**.

It will bring you to the next page with two options:

- **Keystore File**
- **Mnemonic Phrase**

Now, we going to create a non-deterministic and HD wallet.

# Creating a non-deterministic wallet

We will start by generating a Keystore file. A Keystore file is an encrypted JSON file. It has a private key, which is the address that will be used for transactions. As we discussed in the previous section, this private key is randomly generated. For security purposes, usually the file is encrypted with a password or passphrase. The password or passphrase is not the seed we mentioned in a deterministic wallet. At the time of logging in to the wallet, you will need both a passphrase or password and the Keystore file. The Keystore file that's generated by MyCrypto can work with Geth and Parity. It's created in such a way that it won't be easily transferred to a mobile device. It's recommended to keep the backup of the file in a USB drive.

# Viewing the Keystore file generated by the geth command

Geth generates a Keystore file. Now, we will take a look at the steps for viewing the file.

In Chapter 9, *Creating an Ethereum Private Chain,* under the *Private blockchain with mining* section, we already created the wallet using Geth. We have provided two ways of creating an account. You must be very familiar with how to create an account with Geth by now:

1. Bring up the geth console and create an account interactively with the following line:

   ```
   > personal.newAccount()
   ```

2. Alternatively, use the geth command directly, as shown in the following code, with or without a password file:

   ```
   $ geth account new
   ```

   The following code is used for creating a file with password:

   ```
   $ geth account new --password <password file>
   ```

    The Keystore file that's generated by geth is usually stored in the Ethereum/Keystore directory on Mac or Windows, and ~/.ethereum/Keystore on Linux. To protect your private key from hackers, private keys cannot be stored as plain text. It is encrypted as a Keystore file by passphrase.

3. Get the location of the Keystore file that was generated by geth, as shown in the following code block. We use the geth account list command to do this:

   ```
   $ geth account list
   Account #0: {054202582efd0cc0034f426d9ac67b5b5c28846f}
   keystore:///Users/SDY/Library/Ethereum/keystore/UTC-
   -2019-05-23T03-57-12.106595000Z-
   -054202582efd0cc0034f426d9ac67b5b5c28846f
   ```

4. Let's take a closer look at this Keystore file. It has address, crypto, id, and version variables. Most of the content is under crypto. Under crypto, there's the cipher, ciphertext, cipherparams, kdf, kdfparams, and mac variables. We can go to the location where the Keystore file is stored and use the cat command on the file to look at the contents of the file.

I have listed the content of our Keystore file here. Let's have a look at it together:

```
$ cat /Users/SDY/Library/Ethereum/keystore/UTC-
-2019-05-23T03-57-12.106595000Z--054202582efd0cc0034f426d9ac67b5b5c28846f
{"address":"054202582efd0cc0034f426d9ac67b5b5c28846f",
 "crypto":{
            "cipher":"aes-128-ctr",
"ciphertext":"a2dca9a02c26003c3158aeb7416bc6e655d8d2257d0f4d945c8982afb3549
b36",
            "cipherparams":{"iv":"b67b26c300bd025cf517b5efb365fbbc"},
            "kdf":"scrypt",
            "kdfparams":{
                          "dklen":32,
                          "n":262144,
                          "p":1,
                          "r":8,
"salt":"d064c6e970cab1078a89a00d2e9b8c37b4736816f9073c08382fdba77c8c58f2"
                        },
"mac":"b26597bcd6826f9d35a9ad0f09b3796f47658f1e14ea25eb868f40616ee08a60"
          },
"id":"346017ef-9e43-475b-a775-0b998a8a98de",
"version":3
}
```

In the preceding file, we encountered the `cipher`, `cipherparams`, `ciphertext`, `kdf`, and `kdfparams` parameters in person. Let's go over what they do:

- `cipher` is the type of symmetric AES algorithm.
- `cipherparams` are the arguments that are needed for the AES algorithm.
- `ciphertext` is the encrypted private key from using the algorithm under `cipher`.
- `kdf` is for the key derivation function, and is mainly used for encryption of the Keystore file.
- `kdfparams` are the arguments that are fed to `kdf`.

Now, we are able to view the Keystore file that's generated by geth and also have a good understanding of each section of the file.

# Creating a non-deterministic wallet with MyCrypto

With a bit of background information on Keystore file, let's create a non-deterministic wallet with MyCrypto. We will skip the Keystore file generation by geth. When we are creating the wallet with MyCrypto, a Keystore file will be generated automatically:

1. Proceed to MyCrypto with a Keystore file. Choose **Generate a Keystore File** on the following page:

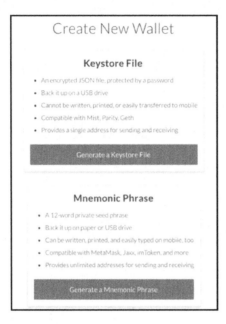

2. On the next screen, you will be asked for a password of at least 12 characters:

3. Now, we need to download the Keystore file, as shown in the following screenshot. Make sure that you have a backup of it because you cannot download it again if you lose it. Please pay attention to the warnings on each page:

4. After securing the Keystore file, you may proceed with the red **Continue** button. The next page will ask you to save your private key. A `.png` file with your address, private key, and QR code is available for download as well. We can print it out as a paper wallet. That content can't be recovered either. Always make sure you back them up and don't share it. At the bottom of the page, there is a link to **Wallet Info**.

5. Now, to unlock the wallet, follow these steps:

   1. Go to **View and Send**.
   2. Select your wallet type as **Keystore file**.
   3. Using the file and password, you will be able to access the new wallet you just created! The following screenshot illustrates this process:

When the wallet is unlocked, it would be good to double-check the wallet is the one you generated and that the address matches the one you saved. Your address and private key can be viewed under the **Wallet Info** tab.

6. If everything checks out fine, you can start sending and requesting ethers and tokens, as shown in the following screenshot.

Always start by sending (or requesting) a small amount of ethers to test the wallet out.

You can go to Etherscan to check the address that's shown on the right-hand side of the wallet, as shown here:

We learned how to use Etherscan in `Chapter 10`, *Deployment of Your Smart Contract*. Now, let's pay a visit to `https://etherscan.io`. We can view the information of our account by searching for its address. You should be able to see the following screen. Copy and paste the address into the search bar of Etherscan:

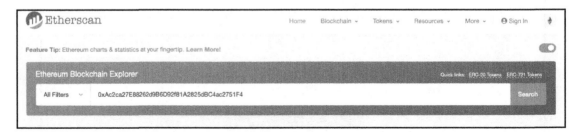

The following screenshot shows my current wallet. As we can see, in the search result here, I have a balance of 0 ether. In the future, transaction history can also be tracked here:

# Creating a non-deterministic wallet with MyEtherWallet

**MyEtherWallet** (known as **MEW**), is another popular Ethereum wallet. Different from working with wallet MyCrypto, we will use geth to create the Keystore file and import it into MyEtherWallet. Here are the detailed steps for creating the wallet:

1. Generate a wallet. We still use the geth account new command, as shown here. You will be typing in the passphrase twice. Write it down somewhere—we will need it later. Here is what geth will respond with when you type in the command:

   ```
   $ geth account new
   INFO [07-24|00:00:39.966] Maximum peer count ETH=25 LES=0 total=25
   Your new account is locked with a password. Please give a password.
   Do not forget this password.
   Passphrase:
   Repeat passphrase:
   Address: {7fd1ba6ff06e9a2a690999d104554a6012ad2856}
   ```

2. Get the keystore file using `geth account list`, as shown in the following code block. Notice that we have two accounts; Account #1 is the one we just created:

   ```
   $ geth account list
   INFO [07-24|00:20:58.332] Maximum peer count ETH=25 LES=0 total=25
   Account #0: {054202582efd0cc0034f426d9ac67b5b5c28846f}
   ```

```
keystore:///Users/SDY/Library/Ethereum/keystore/UTC-
-2019-05-23T03-57-12.106595000Z-
-054202582efd0cc0034f426d9ac67b5b5c28846f
Account #1: {7fd1ba6ff06e9a2a690999d104554a6012ad2856}
keystore:///Users/SDY/Library/Ethereum/keystore/UTC-
-2019-07-24T04-00-52.909854000Z-
-7fd1ba6ff06e9a2a690999d104554a6012ad2856
```

3. Navigate to `https://www.myetherwallet.com` and choose the **Access My Wallet** option. On the next page, select **Software**:

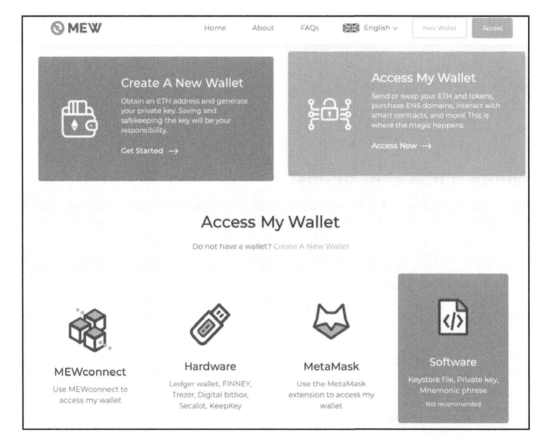

4. Next, we will choose **Keystore File**. After selecting the Keystore file under the location you wrote down, you will be asked for the passphrase of the account. When the passphrase checks out fine, you will be able to access your wallet through MEW:

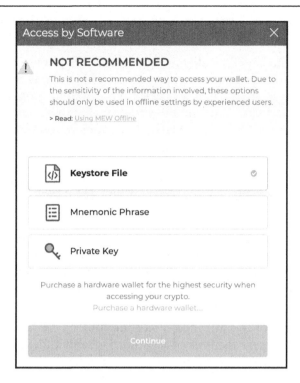

5. On the home page of MEW, you will be able to see the address matches what we had when we created the account with geth—7fd1ba6ff06e9a2a690999d104554a6012ad2856. This is shown in the following screenshot:

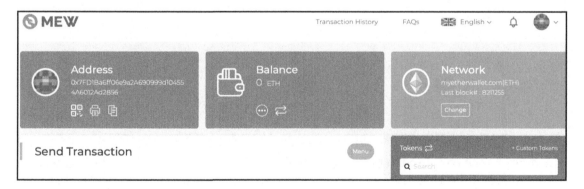

Congratulations, you have successfully created a non-deterministic wallet! Next, we'll create a HD wallet.

# Creating an HD wallet

Now, let's explore creating an HD wallet using a mnemonic phrase. Like a deterministic wallet, an HD wallet also requires you to back up the phrase using a USB drive or using a paper. But unlike the Keystore file that was used in creating the non-deterministic wallet, this one holds a single address. A mnemonic phrase wallet will give you unlimited addresses. When you created your MetaMask in previous chapters, a 12-word phrase was asked for as well. The HD wallet is supported by MetaMask, as well as imToken, Jaxx, and many more.

Let's break down the process of creating an HD wallet using MyCrypto into the following steps:

1. On the first screen of creating the wallet on MyCrypto, you will be given 12 phrases in a numbered order. You will be instructed to write them down instead of copying them to the clipboard. It's recommended to save them offline.

2. After writing them down, confirm all the phrases. You will be able to select the phrases in the same order.

3. As shown here, once confirmed, you could unlock the new wallet in a similar way with a Keystore file type of account. The only thing that's different here is selecting a mnemonic phrase and then typing it in:

The previous screen is used to unlock your wallet. As you can see, you'll be able to access your wallet by following the four specified steps. In the next section, we will look at working with third-party Ethereum wallets.

# Working with third-party Ethereum wallets

Other than the non-deterministic and deterministic ways of categorizing an Ethereum wallet, we can also divide the pie into hardware wallets, desktop wallets, web wallets, mobile wallets, smart contract wallets, and multigeniture wallets. There are custodial wallets abd non-custodial wallets, which depends on whether your private keys are stored by a third party or not. Custodial wallets don't grant you access to private keys, while non-custodial wallets allow full control over your funds. Custodial wallets are trending towards hardware security modules-based solutions, for example Trustology and Anchorage. Another way to classify wallets is as hot and cold wallets. We will show you wallets that are on different platforms and list the features of them. Then, we will go through the steps of how to create two smart contract wallets. At the end of this section, we will talk about hot and cold wallets, and also show you how to create cold wallets.

# Wallets on different platforms

Depending on the form they exist in or the platform they are available on, we call wallets hardware wallets, desktop wallets, web wallets, or mobile wallets. Some wallets don't exist just in one platform, and they can be used on desktop, web, and mobile devices. Smart contract wallets are special; we will talk about this type of wallet in detail in the next section.

Hardware wallets are the safest kind of wallet to manage and trade with ether. As we mentioned earlier, the deterministic wallet provides enhanced security by allowing the owner of the wallet to store the private keys offline. It is the same concept here. Hardware wallets don't grant web server access to private keys naturally when the transactions are being signed and funds are being accessed. The downside is that there is a cost to getting the hardware. There are three popular hardware wallets on the market right now:

- Trezor
- Ledger
- KeepKey

All of them support an extensive list of cryptocurrencies such as Bitcoin, Ethereum, of course, Litecoin, and so on. Ledger and KeepKey also support a bunch of ERC-20 tokens.

Desktop wallets are app wallets that can be downloaded and operated on macOS, Windows, and Linux. Existing desktop wallets are MyCrypto, Exodus, Fetch, Tokenary, HUT34, and Jaxx. MyCrypto, Tokenary, and Jaxx also support mobile wallets.

Web wallets are highly accessible. Without downloading and installation, features such as deploying smart contracts are available. MyCrypto has a web version. The security level of mobile wallets depends on the mobile device.

Let's look at a summary of the third-party wallets. In the following tables, we divided the wallets into groups by the platform they support:

- Hardware and desktop-only wallets:

| Type | Wallet Name | Transaction fees | DApp support | Feature | Access |
|---|---|---|---|---|---|
| Hardware | Trezor | Not applicable | No | | `https://trezor.io` |
| | Ledger | Not applicable | No | | `https://www.ledger.com` |
| | KeepKey | Not applicable | No | | `https://shapeshift.io/keepkey/` |
| Desktop only | HUT34 | Applicable | No | | `https://wallet.hub34.io` |

- Web-only wallets:

| Type | Wallet Name | Transaction fees | DApp support | Feature | Access |
|---|---|---|---|---|---|
| Web only | MetaMask | Applicable | No | Chrome extension | `https://metamask.io` |
| | Portis | Applicable | Yes | User doesn't need to install anything to start using it | `https://www.portis.io` |
| | MyEtherWallet | Not applicable | Yes | Open-source, allows users to interact directly with the Ethereum blockchain. Not necessary to join a centralized exchange. | `https://kb.myetherwallet.com` |
| | SpankCard | Applicable | No | In-browser micropayments wallet | `https://github.com/SpankChain/SpankCard` |
| | Mneumonic generator | Not applicable | No | Online and offline tool for converting BIP39 mnemonic phrases to public and private keys. | `https://github.com/iancoleman/bip39` |
| | Zerion | Applicable | Yes | A trustless banking interface for DeFi, supports loans, investing and trading. Connect to wallets such as MetaMask, Tokenary, and Fortmatic. | `https://zerion.io/en` |
| | Fortmatic | Applicable | Yes | Easy user-onboarding to DApp using phone numbers | `https://fortmatic.com` |

- Mobile-only wallets:

| Type | Wallet Name | Transaction fees | DApp support | Feature | Access |
|------|-------------|------------------|--------------|---------|--------|
| Mobile only | Argent | Not applicable | No | | `https://www.argent.xyz` |
| | Ambo | Not applicable | No | USD deposit | `https://ambo.io` |
| | AlphaWallet | Applicable | Yes | | `https://alphawallet.com` |
| | Balance | Applicable | No | Track token, loans and investments | `https://balance.io` |
| | Coinomi | Applicable | No | | `https://www.coinomi.com/en` |
| | Coinbase | Applicable | No | Pay friends, not addresses | `https://wallet.coinbase.com` |
| | Cypher | Applicable | Yes | | `https://www.cipherbrowser.com` |
| | imToken | Applicable | Yes | | `https://token.im` |
| | Status | Applicable | No | Open source | `https://github.com/status-im/status-react` |
| | Trust | Applicable | Yes | | `https://github.com/TrustWallet/trust-wallet-ios` |
| | WALLETH | Applicable | No | Native Ethereum Android wallet | `https://walleth.org` |

Some wallets support various platforms, as shown in the following table. We list popular wallets and compare some major wallet features, including the following:

- Transactions fees
- DApp support
- Desktop wallet support
- Web wallet support
- Mobile wallet support
- Feather and Access

The following table shows a comparison between the features of the wallets:

| Wallet Name | Transaction fees | DApp support | Desktop Wallet | Web Wallet | Mobile Wallet | Features | Access |
|-------------|------------------|--------------|----------------|------------|---------------|----------|--------|
| **Jaxx** | No | No | Yes | No | Yes | No login required, blockchain news updates | `https://jaxx.io` |

| | | | | | | | |
|---|---|---|---|---|---|---|---|
| **Exodus** | Yes | No | Yes | No | Yes | | `https://exodus.io` |
| **MyCrypto** | Yes | Yes | Yes | Yes | No | Generating Ethereum wallets | `https://mycrypto.com` |
| **Eth lightwallet** | Yes | No | No | Yes | Yes | Lightweight, pure JS Ethereum wallet | `https://github.com/NoahZinsmeister/eth-wallet-light` |
| **Tokenary** | Yes | Yes | Yes | Yes | Yes | Safari extension, swap tokens with nearby friends | `https://tokenary.io` |
| **Fetch** | Yes | No | Yes | Yes | Yes | Chrome extension | `https://hellofetch.co/download` |

There is an open protocol to connect the wallets and Dapps called WalletConnect. The protocol allows the following features on the WalletConnect v1.0.0-beta version:

- Establishes a remote connection between two devices or apps
- Relays payloads by using a Bridge server
- Symmetrically encrypts the payloads using a shared key
- Initiates the connection by one of the two:
    - The QR code displaying by one party
    - Deep link with a standard WalletConnect URI
- Establishes the connection upon the approval of the request by counter-party
- Provides an optional push server which allows the Native applications to notify users when there are incoming payloads for establishing connections

Here are the demo (`https://walletconnect.org/demo`) and GitHub (`https://github.com/walletconnect/`) for WalletConnect. Finding out more about this cool protocol is recommended.

As the number of users grows, more wallets are created. We encourage you to check out the aforementioned wallets and to research any new ones that become available.

# Multi-signature wallets

We will start with analogies. A multi-signature wallet is like a video-game lobby, where the game will only start when each player is ready to go; or like a vault with high security where passwords are needed from more than one manager; or a joint bank account, where signatures are needed from more than one account holder. Now, you have an idea of what a multi-signature wallet is. It's basically a type of wallet that needs more than two signatures to access the funds on a multi-signature address. Let's have a look at the following visual representation:

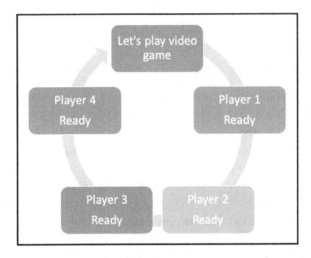

Multi-signature is not a new technology just for Ethereum. It existed in the world of cryptocurrencies even before the time of Bitcoin. The concept of multi-signature can be applied in many use cases, mostly for security purposes. In 2012, it was first implemented for Bitcoin addresses. In the following year, multi-signature wallets were created.

Different from the standard address, which holds only one single key, a multi-signature address is configured from a combination of multiple keys. The most common multi-signature wallet is 2-of-3, meaning a 3-signature address needs two signatures to access funds. Other options exist, for example 2-of-2, 3-of-3, and so on.

A multi-signature wallet has the advantage in terms of security. Imagine managing a single-key address like opening a door with only one lock and one set of keys. Anyone can open the door when they get that key. It's probably a more efficient way to go. But when it comes down to enterprise and business use cases, one key being handled by one individual or sharing one key among multiple key holders is not a good idea from a security perspective. Multi-signature wallets, on the other hand, will still be able to secure the funds when one of the keys is lost. Like setting up multiple locks to your door, even when one set of keys is missing or stolen, the door can't be opened when one key is compromised. Other keys are still needed. For malicious attacks, it will be much more difficult to get all the keys than just getting one key. From the owner's perspective, losing one key doesn't mean losing the funds at the same time. If it's a 2-of-3 type of wallet, with the other two keys, the account holder will still be able to access the funds.

Multi-signature wallets can be a good fit for use cases like the following:

- **Voting for decisions**: A 4-of-6 multi-signature wallet can let a board vote for decisions. Only when the majority of the board members pass the decision will the funds be allocated.
- **Escrowing transactions**: A 2-of-3 wallet can be used among the seller, buyer, and a trusted arbiter. If goods are as expected, both the seller and buyer can sign the transaction for payment. If there is a dispute, the trusted arbiter will step in and provide the signature to either party based on the judgement.
- **Two-factor authentication**: The smart contract wallet is the implementation in this type of use case. We will get into the details about this in next section.

Other than the use cases we mentioned previously, you can do your own research on this topic. There are a few implementations of multi-signature wallets. The project names and links are as follows:

- ConsenSys MultiSig Wallet (`https://github.com/ConsenSys/MultiSigWallet`)

- Gnosis MultiSigWallet (`https://github.com/gnosis/MultiSigWallet/blob/master/contracts/MultiSigWallet.sol`)

- BitGo MultiSig Wallet (`https://github.com/BitGo/eth-multisig-v2`)
- Dapp MultiSig Wallet on Etherscan (`https://rinkeby.etherscan.io/address/0x91e832b89ad21cb15520de239311d5025bb44401#code`)
- Parity MultiSig Wallet (`https://www.parity.io/technologies/`)

The Parity MultiSig wallet got hacked by the MultisigExploit-Hacker in 2017, and more than 30 million worth of ether was stolen. For details of how the hack worked, we encourage you to look at the following article: `http://hackingdistributed.com/2017/07/22/deep-dive-parity-bug/`. It's important to know the vulnerability in the implementation of the MultiSig wallet as a developer.

We can see setting up multi-signature wallets requires deep technical knowledge. This can be a disadvantage of this type of wallet too. Besides, sharing multi-signature wallets with other owners can cause some ownership issues from a legal perspective.

# Smart contract wallets

Smart contract wallets are unique from other types of wallets due to their smart contract functionality. Additional security and recovery features are available for users. Their uniqueness lies in a few aspects. Smart contract wallets use two-factor authentication and allow wallet recovery through your social network, friends, and family. It provides fraud alerts and lockdown in case of an emergency. You have the freedom to set your own blacklists and whitelists. Like an ATM on the street, you can do rate-limited withdraws.

The following are two smart contract wallets in real life:

- Gnosis Safe
- Argent

The Gnosis Safe allows users to manage their funds and interact with decentralized applications. Let's go over how to create a wallet with Gnosis Safe:

1. To create a wallet with Gnosis Safe, go to `https://safe.gnosis.io/#personal` and download the app on your phone, as shown here. You just need to follow the steps shown there and set a password:

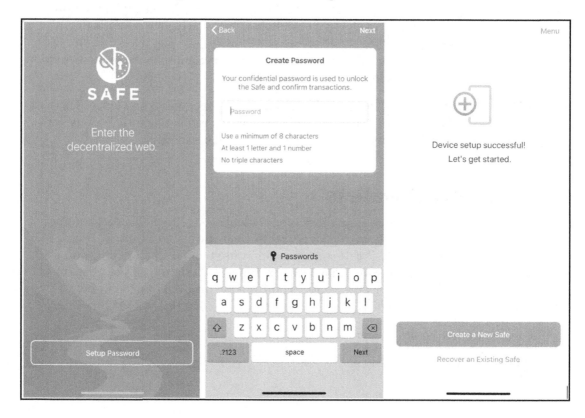

2. Then, when you see the instructions for accessing the browser extension, download and install the Google extension from: `https://chrome.google.com/webstore/detail/gnosis-safe-smart-wallet/iecodoenhaghdlpodmhooppdhjhmibde`:

3. Once it has been installed, log in using the same passcode you set up on your mobile. When the extension is set up successfully, request a QR code. What we will do next is go back to the mobile app and scan the QR code:

4. Then, 12 recovery phrases will be provided when you start to create the safe. You will need to write them down; you will need two of them in the following step. The safe is not free. When you pay your debt of 0.00686 ETH, a new safe will be created for you, as shown here:

Argent is the smart contract wallet that allows you to choose your address for free. But the capacity of the service seems limited at this point. You may need to plan ahead if you need to open an account. The wallet is available for mobile devices. Follow these concise steps to get things up and running quickly:

1. Download it from the Apple Store or Google Play.
2. Reserve a username.
3. Verify your phone and email.
4. Get on the waitlist.
5. Refer your friends to escalate account creation.

I have 5,145 people ahead of me. Good luck with your Argent account:

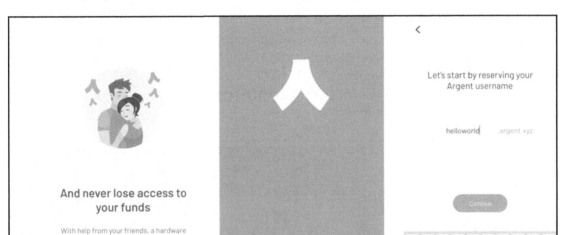

Smart contract wallets are a relatively new type of wallet on the market. We would like you to do your own research regarding any new types of wallet that were made available after this book was written.

# Hot and cold wallets

All wallets can also be either hot or cold. Hot wallets are wallets that store keys online. They are not as secure as a cold wallet. Cold wallets store private keys offline. Let's see a cold wallet in action.

If you were paying attention to the options for creating a wallet on MyCrypto, you would have noticed that there is another option to create a wallet: Parity Signer. It helps in turning a smartphone into a hardware wallet. It's a free app on a mobile device that you can use to create and store your private key. Like mnemonic phrase's way of creating wallets, it allows you to keep more than one address. From the name, you will be able to tell it's compatible with the Parity wallet. It is secure since it never connects to the internet, which is different from a lot of mobile wallets.

Follow these steps to create a wallet with Parity Signer:

1. Download the app to the smartphone.
2. As usual, get it from the Apple Store or Google Play.
3. After installation, open the app and choose `Create New Account` on the **Getting Started** screen.
4. As shown here, on the **CREATE ACCOUNT** page, choose the network, an identicon, and account name:

5. A list of recovery words will be provided on the next screen. Always make sure to note them down and secure them.

6. As shown on the next page, add more accounts by clicking on the gray bar at the bottom. It will bring you back to the **Getting Started** page we saw previously.

7. Click on the account we just created, and then **Show Account QR Code**:

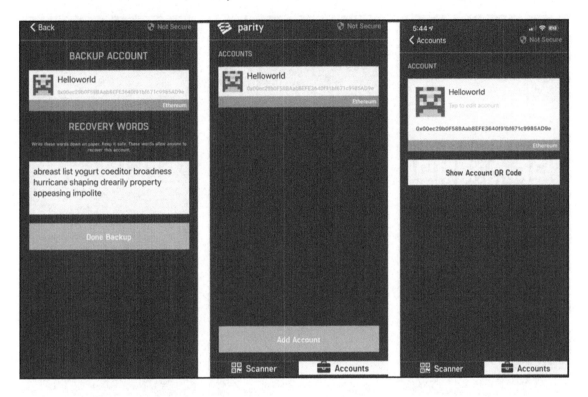

8. At the bottom of the screen, click on the **Scanner** bar. From here, you will be able to sign a new transaction.

Notice there is a red sign, **Not Secure**, in the top-right corner in the following screenshot. This is because I keep my internet connection on when I am using it. When I switch to airplane mode, it shows a green sign stating **Secure**:

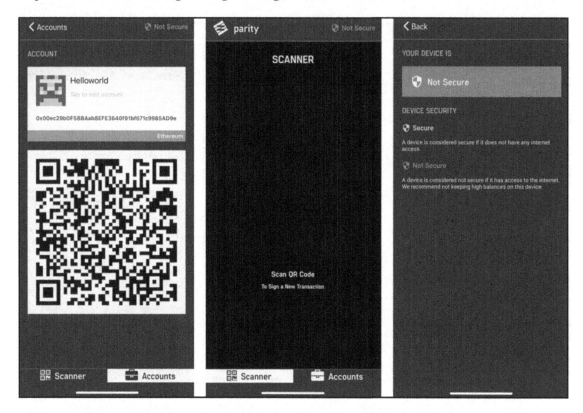

If you have created quite a few wallets at this point, you might want to transfer funds between accounts and see how the transactions work between them.

# Transferring funds between wallets

Let's go through an example of how to transfer ethers between accounts on the Ropsten Testnet:

1. Right now, I have 3.9705 ETH on the account with MetaMask. We are going to transfer 0.3 ETH from the account on MyEtherWallet to MetaMask, as shown here:

2. To log back in to the MEW, let's access the account via MEWconnect on our smartphone. Scan the QR code on MEWconnect, as shown here:

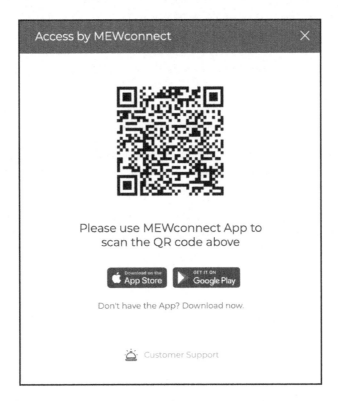

3. As shown in the following screenshot, I have under 0.5 ETH on this account with MEW. I will transfer 0.3 ETH to address 0x8a52f3242f1fA41Af5525315a5954406b5108A08. Copy the address into **To Address**:

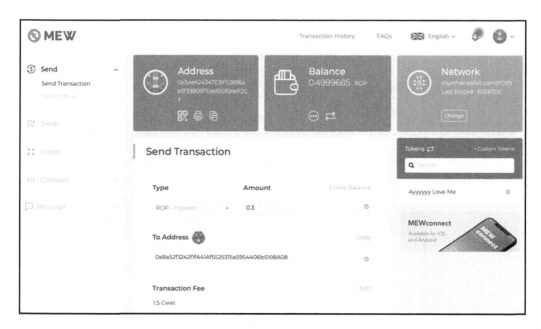

After submitting the transition on the web page, you will need to validate the transaction on the smartphone. Both the addresses that you are sending to and the amount of ether will need to be validated.

4. As shown in the following screenshot, confirm the transaction if it looks correct and return to the web page of MEW:

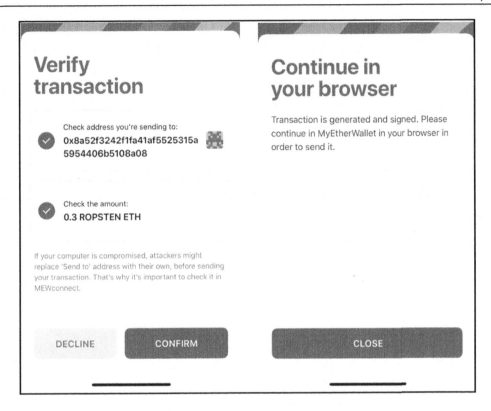

On the web version of MEW, as shown in the following screenshot, you will be able to see that the transaction went through successfully. MEW also provides a link to Etherscan:

5. As shown in the following screenshot, when we go back to MetaMask and check the balance of the account, it shows 4.2705, which is 0.3 ETH more than before the transaction was made:

The details of the transaction can be tracked on Etherscan. It shows the transaction hash, status, block, timestamp, accounts sent to and from, value, and transition fee, as shown in the following screenshot:

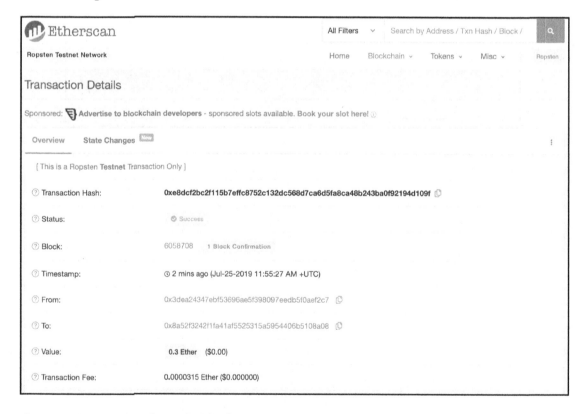

Congratulations! You have finished creating your wallet and using it to deploy your smart contract and transfer ethers into another wallet.

# Summary

In this chapter, we learned that Ethereum wallets make it easier for users to hold, send, and receive ether and to interact with applications on the Ethereum network. We saw how different types of wallets are created to achieve the respective goals. It's important to know that Ethereum wallets don't work the way the physical ones do. We learned that Ethereum wallets hold ether but that ether is not stored in the wallet. What is stored are collections of addresses and keys. Holding keys and addresses allows users to apply digital signatures and make transactions.

The next chapter is going to be the concluding one and will summarize the previous chapters, and will also provide an overview of the future of Ethereum.

# Section 5: Conclusion

This section provides a concluding chapter where we will briefly touch on a few fascinating areas, including cross-blockchain interoperability, technology fusion, and the convergence between blockchain, AI/ML, and IoT.

This section comprises of the following chapter:

- Chapter 12, *Conclusion*

# 12
## Conclusion

Throughout this book, you have looked at some key concepts in blockchain and Ethereum and learned how the Ethereum blockchain and cryptocurrency work. Through the examples that were given in each chapter, you also learned how to develop smart contracts and **decentralized applications (DApps)** step by step, as well as launch your own cryptocurrency. Starting as an innovative solution for solving electronic payment issues, blockchain has been quickly established as a new technology foundation for transforming the entire banking, finance, and payment industry. It is such a disruptive technology that almost all sectors have started to feel its impact. It is like a replay of the internet technology. Traditional business models and business processes are under tight scrutiny, and new business models have started to emerge. We are starting to see a parallel universe being built on the solid foundation of blockchain and cryptography – a digital and virtual world running on a decentralized network.

This doesn't mean cryptocurrencies won't be volatile, or that blockchain and Ethereum will sail through everything without challenges. As a matter of fact, there's a plethora of challenges, doubts, and uncertainties facing blockchain and Ethereum. At the same time, major cryptocurrencies, such as Bitcoin and ether, continue to ride high, or go low, and even crash. Before concluding this book, we will examine those challenges, discuss the major activities and players in the Ethereum ecosystem, and point out what we perceive as the future direction of Ethereum.

This chapter will cover the following topics:

- Facing the challenges of Ethereum and blockchain
- Glancing over the Ethereum ecosystem
- Emerging technology fusion – blockchain, AI, ML, and IoT
- Meeting the future of Ethereum

# Technical requirements

For all the source code of this book, please refer to the following GitHub link:

`https://github.com/PacktPublishing/Learn-Ethereum`

# Facing the challenges of Ethereum and blockchain

There are quite a few challenges that Ethereum and blockchain are facing. We will go through them in the following sections.

## Consensus protocol and scalability

As we discussed in `Chapter 3`, *Deep Research on Ethereum*, there are several active work and research streams in the Ethereum community racing to solve Ethereum's scalability issues. Obviously, the Ethereum ecosystem has evolved considerably since it was invented 4-5 years ago. However, for the mainstream adoption of Ethereum and blockchain technology in general, **scalability** is the most pressing issue. The solution to the scalability issue holds the key to making Ethereum sink or swim.

Let's recap on the current state of scalability challenges and analyze various approaches and activities in improving scalability in Ethereum:

- **Scalability issues in Ethereum**: In Ethereum and blockchain, scalability occurred because every transaction needs to be processed and verified by all the nodes in the decentralized network. For the network to agree on the true state of the blockchain network, there are consensus protocols involved which allow the network of untrusted nodes to reach consensus. In general, blockchain compromises scalability and throughput in favor of decentralization and the security of the network. In this section, we'll take a step back and discuss the common challenges that are faced in scaling Ethereum.

In the abstract sense, when a transaction happens, it is sent to the network and relayed to all the network nodes. It will be packaged into a block, which will be added to the blockchain by the mining node, and then verified by all the nodes. The whole process involves totally uncoordinated, but largely interdependent, activities to make a transaction recorded and secured in the network. It involves the communication of transactions and blocks, proof of the transaction's validity and verification of it, and an agreement on the finality of the transactions. Think of Ethereum as a heart valve. At its current capacity, transactions are pumped in and out at a slow and steady pace. The network is operating as expected. But as transaction volume picks up, or any part of the network becomes clogged, the system becomes inadequate for running critical business and finance operations.

Simply adding network nodes won't help at all. Solutions such as increasing block size or packaging more in a block have their limits. In Chapter 3, *Deep Research on Ethereum*, we discussed the block size increase solution. There are some proposals to reexamine the block structure and Merkle tree, with an intention to be able to effectively package more transactions in a block. It may be worth reading. Such solutions may help in the short term, but they alone won't fundamentally address these issues. There were solutions for increasing the block creation's frequency that didn't fly, simply due to the fact they may cause long finality and instability of the blockchain. That leaves most of the focus on proof, verification, and finality.

- **Sharding and Layer 1 solutions**: As we discussed in Chapter 3, *Deep Research on Ethereum*, the Ethereum community has settled into a multi-pronged strategy in addressing scalability through the Ethereum 2.0 roadmap. Shifting to a **proof-of-stake (PoS)** consensus with Casper CBC is the ultimate goal. In the short term and as a tactical step, Ethereum is moving to a hybrid PoS and **proof-of-work (PoW)** model which seems to be a practical and prudent approach.

Ethereum sharding is the audacious attempt to address the fundamental issues with blockchain scalability. It intends to find a scalable solution without compromising network security and decentralization, two tenets of blockchain technology. Sharding is not a new concept and has been proven effective in managing large distributed database systems. The success with sharding in the traditional world comes from two factors: one is that the solution itself typically involves a central mediator or intermediary to make sharding and aggregation coordination, while the other is that software vendors have a central authority or governance structure in making sharding solution decisions, and deciding where to compromise and what subset of the issues to address and where to market.

The complexity and risks in implementing Ethereum sharding increase immensely. Not only will the blockchain and world state be sharded, but the entire decentralized peer-to-peer network will be grouped into different shards as well. The complexity lies in enforcing data and network security while being able to coordinate those transaction activities and aggregate data and transactions across blockchain data and network segments. For that purpose, Ethereum Casper introduces the **beacon chain layer** as the decentralized alternative to the central mediator in the traditional sharding implementation. A mix of PoW and PoS consensus protocol, as well as the finality solution of Casper FFG, will certainly add to the complexity of sharding implementation. How it works is still largely a work in progress.

 Ethereum 2.0 spec is a masterpiece of the Ethereum architecture and design specifications for the sharding and beacon layer design. Those of you who are interested should check it out at the Ethereum site at `https://github.com/ethereum/eth2.0-specs`.

- **Off-chain computation with Zero-Knowledge Succinct Non-Interactive Argument of Knowledge and multiparty computation**: Ethereum is envisioned as the world computer, but people quickly realized that, in the Ethereum architecture's current form, there are huge expenses associated with that vision and the consequence in scalability and throughput this has caused. One of those is computations. Another one is on-chain storage. We talked a little about zk-SNARKs in `Chapter 3`, *Deep Research on Ethereum*. This is another promising strategy that offloads expensive encryption computation out of the **Ethereum Virtual Machine (EVM)** to third-party verifiers, without compromising privacy and security, to improve scalability and throughput in Ethereum. Vitalik thinks that, by using zk-SNARKs to mass-validate transactions, we can actually scale asset transfer transactions on Ethereum to about 500 transactions per second. We have seen such success in Zcash. It is one of the areas the Ethereum community is closely watching. More research and prototypes have yet to be seen before we can see a clear roadmap or a future implementation.

Multiparty computation (MPC) is another area that may have the potential for addressing privacy and scalability issues. In an MPC model, a set of participants, P1, P2, ..., Pn, are assigned a subset of private data, D1, D2, ..., Dn, respectively. The participants want to compute the value of a public function on that private data while keeping their own inputs secret. While pairing with blockchain, the subset of blockchain data (mainly the reference to the public blockchain), will be stored privately in some kind of **distributed hash table (DTH)** within each MPC node.

The following steps explain the process flow for some MPC blockchains such as Platon:

1. Deploy the smart contract to the blockchain.
2. Invoke the smart contract function by providing computation algorithm parameters.
3. The computation task will distribute the contract to an off-chain MPC network.
4. The MPC nodes will verify the computation and generate the required proof.
5. The on-chain nodes will broadcast the result and proof.
6. The block producers verify the proof.
7. The verified result will be returned to the user through a smart contract.
8. The miner will get coin as an economic reward.

The computation is offloaded and done securely through the coordination of all the MPC nodes, without anyone knowing anything from other MPC nodes. The idea behind this is that, by offloading computations out of the main chain, it will stay leaner and more scalable.

- **Layer 2 solutions**: There are discussions in the Ethereum community and Ethereum 2.0 roadmap about reexamining Ethereum's blockchain data structure, as well as the storage model. Hopefully, a solution will be created to make the Ethereum client stateless and leverage it more for enforcing security and integrity. A good compromise would be to offload those to Layer 2 or off-chain solutions.

We will continue to see Layer 2 scaling solutions take shape in Ethereum. We talked about state channel solutions with Raiden and side-chain solutions with Plasma in `Chapter 3`, *Deep Research on Ethereum*, and discussed how the Layer 2 solution would work. As the Ethereum ecosystem evolves, and more and more transactions need to be processed, it definitely makes much more sense to explore the Layer 2 solutions. Their purpose is to offload expensive computations and transaction processing out of Mainnet and leverage Ethereum as the root chain for security guarantees and enforcement. State channels, as the perfect solution for micropayments, will continue to flourish in the payment space. Plasma, as the side-chains for many different verticals, will probably be the main avenue for Ethereum to expand beyond the finance, banking, and payment industry.

# UI/UX, usability, and design thinking

This is a mouthful. The truth is, in order to gain widespread adoption of Ethereum and cryptocurrency, there's much to be done by the Ethereum and blockchain community to improve the usability of the technology, tools, and user experience of DApps. Cryptocurrency may be a hot topic in the blockchain community and crypto-investor circle, but to the average Joe, the concept of Bitcoin or crypto-token is too foreign to understand. What they heard or saw is a bunch of magic alphanumeric characters. Those characters seem to make no true connection to their own daily life. It is something like `1BQhEut2E4XmYm53Qt614NbrhBvuCoyxVc` in their crypto-wallets, with a final balance of 10.0005 BTC. It is hard to fathom how much I have actually owned, how much profit I gained from this trade, and how much I paid for a cup of coffee.

**User interface (UI)**, **user experience (UX)**, and usability is the collective name for the user experience design. It is an experience design process of taking a user-centric approach to products and services, with a focus on usability, accessibility, and desirability throughout the entire journey and interaction with end users. It intends to design a product with the goal of creating an attachment, satisfaction, and stickiness with end users.

The usability and UI/UX of DApps will greatly influence the adoption rates of Ethereum, blockchain, and cryptocurrency. The UI's design goal is to come up an intuitive and clean design to hide all the complexity of DApps. It needs to navigate the user through complex business processes and create trust and confidence between the machine and network. Typically, it also involves streamlining and redesigning the traditional business process and coming up with new digital experience processes.

One common technique that's used in user experience design is the design thinking process. It is a five-stage process that was developed by Stanford University, and is shown in the following diagram:

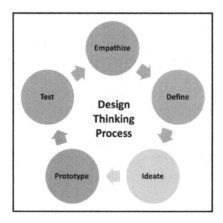

The preceding five-stage process is as follows:

1. Starting with empathy, it gets to know the users and understand their needs while gathering information about the targeted users.
2. It then comes up with a problem definition and tries to make sense of the user.
3. Once you have defined the problem statement, during stage 3, you can start to anticipate the user's expectation and come up with solutions and ideas.
4. The last two stages in the design thinking process are to come up with a prototype as a scaled-down version of the final design and test the new product and design with the users, and then refine and improve the design and user experience.

It has been an effective approach for defining innovative products and services. Those of you who are skeptical should try it out for yourself.

# Ethereum governance

Good governance is at the heart of any successful business or organization. A good governance framework defines the decision-making process upfront. It has a clear definition of roles and responsibilities in the decision process, defines what decision influences the common objectives, and specifies how the decision outcome is disseminated and tracked. Typically, in a well-run business entity, IT governance is one of the key components of enterprise governance, which governs IT decision-making and investment directions.

The governance process plays a key role in blockchain and Ethereum development. It has three aspects of the decision and governance process. One is like the IT governance process, that is, to have a process to define the future vision, goals, and objectives of the network. In particular, like Ethereum, it is still at the earlier stage of development and so it requires good governance and a decision process to define the future roadmap, as well as shepherd the community to the future. Another one is operations and economic governance, which governs the economic and monetary policies and decisions that are made on the Ethereum network. The third one is DApp and crypto-token governance, which are typically done by the owners themselves, but depends on the underlying platform governance from the other two.

In general, there are four types of governance that are applicable to the Blockchain network and community, as shown in the following diagram:

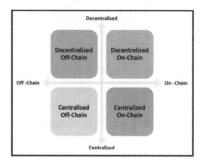

On-chain governance refers to the decision process that leverages the network and code for voting or decision-making. Off-chain governance refers to a blockchain improvement or operations decision that's made outside the network, usually manually. The decision can be made through a centralized decision authority or in a totally de-central approach.

Although it seems a bit nebulous, Ethereum employs a decentralized off-chain approach for Ethereum platform governance. It is quite effective, according to Vitalik. EIPs are the main avenue for anyone to propose the improvement proposal, and through community voting, they will be prioritized and get assigned to someone to implement. There is some undercurrent that may challenge the current governance model and quite a few contentions in certain Ethereum decisions, but largely, the community is aligned when it comes to major development decisions, especially when it comes to scaling solutions.

# Government regulations

Many observers of the cryptocurrency investment felt quite relieved after the United States **Securities and Exchange Commission (SEC)** issued a no-action letter on April 3, 2019, to confirm that the tokens that were issued during the startup's **initial coin offerings (ICOs)** are not securities. As a matter of fact, over 80% of ICOs are Ethereum backend tokens and run on the Ethereum blockchain network. Tightened government rules, policies, or regulations on ICO and cryptocurrency are always viewed as the headwind thought to pose huge challenges regarding the growth of Ethereum, blockchain, and cryptocurrency. It is always debatable. On one hand, it is an effective crowdfunding approach for startups so that they can raise funds for developing innovative products, services, and solutions. Any tight control may put a brake on the innovation and adoption in this space. On the other hand, many also welcome moderate regulations to these emerging investment instruments since it will raise the bar for ICO offering, and hence makes the Ethereum network and cryptocurrency market more robust and much healthier.

Stablecoins, which we discussed briefly in Chapter 3, *Deep Research on Ethereum*, may provide a much different perspective than ICOs for government regulators since they design the cryptocurrency governance and regulatory framework. Nothing extraordinary has come out of this yet. However, one thing is probably true, no matter which way the wind blows: solutions in compliance with existing KYC-AML rules, policies, and regulations are always worth investing in.

# Mainstream adoption

The Chinese proverb says, *"Not only can water float a boat, it can sink it also"*. That is probably the best way to describe the Ethereum platform and its widespread adoption. On one hand, Ethereum has a broad ecosystem for developing and implementing smart contracts and decentralized applications and is the most popular and ideal platform for launching ICOs and crypto-tokens. This has fueled the explosive growth of the Ethereum network over the last few years. On the other hand, the fundamental issue in Ethereum is its scalability, that is, its ability to scale up and handle a much larger volume of blockchain transactions. Some suggest that Ethereum is already at its maximum capacity at the moment. The truth is, scaling Ethereum is difficult and implementing a solution such as sharding, alongside Casper, is a daunting task. The road to Ethereum 2.0 may be much bumpier than anyone may expect.

# A few more words about privacy

Security, transparency, immutability, and transaction integrity are some of the most highly touted advantages blockchain has over traditional centralized applications. With blockchain, transactions are secured through the consensus protocol. Once the transaction is made, it is permanent and publicly accessible. There is no way to alter the records on the blockchain, tamper with records, or even deny the transaction happened.

However, increased transparency is a double-edged sword. The transaction records are linked to the public address of the account. If anyone knows the public address, they will know what you have traded and owned. If you lose your private keys, you may lose everything. Data that's been recorded on the blockchain may include private or confidential information, such as personal identification, or patient health and medical records. This may infringe the customer's privacy, especially in industries where privacy is protected by the law, rules, and regulations. In healthcare, patient privacy is protected by the HIPAA and minimal use rules. Europe has **general data protection rules (GDPR)**, which is the data privacy legislation that protects EU citizens from data breaches.

Earlier, we mentioned some solutions via the use of ZK-SNARKs and **Multiparty Computation** (**MPC**) to address privacy and scalability issues, though much still needs to be done for them to be compliant with existing privacy rules. One component of the privacy rules—consent management—provides a vehicle for sharing personal information with the user's consent or erasing the data when the consent is revoked. Such requirements may directly contradict blockchain design principles.

# Glancing over the Ethereum ecosystem

The biggest advantage the Ethereum community has is its large variety of DApp coding, testing, and deployment tools, which make it much easier to develop and run decentralized applications on the Ethereum blockchain.

# Tools and infrastructure

The Ethereum ecosystem distinguishes itself from other blockchain ecosystems with a wealth of development and infrastructure tools. Those development tools make the developer's life easier when it comes to developing sophisticated DApps. Infrastructure tools make it possible to deploy and run smart contracts on the decentralized network.

The following diagram shows a list of Ethereum DApp **software development life cycle** (**SDLC**) tools. We covered many of these tools in the previous chapters:

| IDE | Framework | Testing | Monitoring |
|---|---|---|---|
| • Remix | • Truffle | • Ganache | • Etherscan |
| • Eth Fiddle | • Embark | • getho | • Etherstat |
| • Superblocks Lab — Web IDE | • Waffle | • Cliquebait | • Chainlyt |
| • Atom | • ZeppelinOS | • Kaleido | • amberdata.io |
| • Vim solidity | • Dapp | • Pantheon Private Network | • Neufund |
| • Visual Studio Code | • Etherlime | • Private networks deployment scripts | • Scout |
| • Intellij Solidity Plugin | • Parasol | • Local Ethereum Network | • Tenderly |
| • YAKINDU Solidity Tools | • Oxcert | • Ethereum on Azure | • BlockScout |
| | | • Ethereum on Google Cloud | • Quickblock |

The following list further explains the tools:

- There are many popular IDEs available, and you can always choose something you are familiar with. Remix, Eth Fiddle, and Superblocks are the web IDEs that you can use with any browsers. The rest of the IDEs are popular plugins to different desktop IDEs. In `Chapter 4`, *Solidity Fundamentals*, and `Chapter 6`, *Smart Contract Development and Test Fundamentals*, we demonstrated how to use Remix to develop a smart contract.

- Common frameworks, usually offered as CLIs, allow you to quickly create, test, and deploy smart contracts. Popular ones include Truffle, Infura, Embark, and Waffle. ZeppelinOS provides a complete set of tools, too. We used the Truffle tool in our DApp examples in Chapters 5 through 8. By reading these chapters, you should feel comfortable about how to use Infura and ZeppelinOS.

- In terms of testing, you can use Ganache for local testing, or you can set up a private Ethereum network for testing your smart contract. Azure, Google Cloud, and Amazon AWS allow you to set up cloud Ethereum networks too. We discussed private Ethereum networks in `Chapter 9`, *Creating an Ethereum Private Chain*.

- We also looked at a couple of block explorer tools, which allow you to monitor the smart contracts that are deployed on an Ethereum network. We discussed these in `Chapter 10`, *Deployment of Your Smart Contract*.

The following diagram shows the full stack of a framework, along with the library, tools, and infrastructure you will need to develop your DApps. Many of these tools, frameworks, and infrastructures have been discussed in this book:

| Wallet | Frontend API | Smart Contract | Infrastructure | Storage Messaging |
|---|---|---|---|---|
| • Metamask | • Web3.js | • Solidity | • Geth | • IPFS |
| • Mist | • web3-react | • Bamboo | • Parity | • Swarm |
| • MyEtherWallet | • Eth.js | • Vyper | • Pyethapp | • BigchainDB |
| • MyCrypto | • Ethers.js | • LLL | • Harmony | • Whisper |
| • Arkane | • Web3Wrapper | • Flint | • Pantheon | • DEVp2p Wire Protocol |
| • Portis | • Ethereumjs | | • Aleth | • Pydevp2p |
| • Eth lightwallet | • Drizzle | | • Trinity | |
| • Coinbase Wallet | • Tasit SDK | | • Ethereumjs | |
| • Trust | | | • Ethereumj | |
| • Trezor | | | • Seth | |
| • Ledger | | | • Mustekala | |
| • KeepKey | | | • Exthereum | |
| | | | • EWF Parity | |
| | | | • Quorum | |
| | | | • Mana | |

The infrastructure is explained in further detail as follows:

- There are many types of wallets, including browser extensions, web wallets, mobile wallets, as well as hardware wallets. You can choose any wallet with your DApps, but using one that has compliance with ERC-20 is recommended. Some of the most popular wallets we discussed in Chapter 11, *Build Ethereum Wallets*.

- For the frontend API to connect your wallet and UI application to the Ethereum network, you need an API such as web3.js. For a reactive type single page application, you might want to use web3-react with your React JavaScript framework. In Chapter 7, *Writing UI for the DApps*, we developed an end-to-end DApp example using the Web3 API and React framework.

- In terms of smart contracts, there are a few choices, though the most popular one is Solidity.

- For Ethereum network clients, there are quite a few to choose from if you plan on running as the Ethereum client. Geth and Parity are a few that we mentioned in Chapter 2, *Ethereum Architecture and Ecosystem*.

- For DApps to access data or communicate with each other, we need to use a storage messager. IPFS, Swarm, and Whisper are a few that we can use. BigchainDB is a blockchain database that can be leveraged as data or file storage. Ethereum provides the Oraclize API for accessing external blockchain or non-blockchain data sources. Lower-level messaging APIs such as Devp2p, along with the RLPx protocol, allow P2P messaging between network nodes. IPFS, Swarm, and Whisper were mentioned in Chapter 8, *Ethereum Tools and Frameworks*.

# Decentralized applications

As we discussed in *Chapter 2, Ethereum Architecture and Ecosystem*, DApps are software applications that communicate with the blockchain network and run on the P2P network. The following diagram shows the top 100 DApps that are running on the Ethereum blockchain network, by ranking from the State of the DApps website (https://www.stateofthedapps.com).

| Exchange | Finance | Marketplace | Games | Media, Social, Gambling | Wallet, Governance, Security, Misc |
|---|---|---|---|---|---|
| •IDEX | •MakerDAO | •SingularityNET | •My Crypto Heroes | •FCK | •Golem |
| •0x | •OmiseGO | •Auctionity | •0xUniverse | •Playtowin | •Mycontract |
| •KyberNetwork | •Polymath | •OpenSea | •CryptoDozer | •Livepeer | •aelf |
| •Augur | •Compound | •Origin Protocol | •Chibi Fighters | •Refereum | •Enigma |
| •Bancor | •Synthetix | •CryptoKitties | •Axie Infinity | •AdEx | •MyWish |
| •Uniswap | •DigixGlobal | •CanWork | •Blockchain Cuties | •Theta Network | •Aragon |
| •AirSwap | •Genesis Vision | •Bounties Network | •ZED | •Upfiring | •Kleros |
| •ForkDelta | •Nexo | •SuperRare | •HyperDragons | •Lunyr | •Token-≤ Curated Registry |
| •LocalEthereum | •VeADIR | •district0x | •LORDLESS | •SpankChain | •BITNATION |
| •Ethfinex Trustless | •FriendsFingers | •Dether | •Gods Unchained | •Primas | •SelfKey |
| •Lescovex DEX | •InstaDApp | | •Etheremon | •Primas | •ENS Manager |
| •Raiden Network | •Simple Token | | •MegaCryptoPolis | •Cent | •Decentraland |
| •Switcheo | •Token BulkSender | | •CryptoRome | •Loom Network | •Ethereum Name Service |
| •Gnosis | | | •MLB Crypto Baseball | •Crowdholding | •FOAM |
| •Loopring | | | •World of Ether | •CITY | •Chainlink |
| •OasisDex | | | •First Blood | | •Storj |
| •The Token Store | | | •CryptantCrab | | •Status |
| •Saturn Network | | | •EthBattle | | •Ethos |
| •MetaMorph | | | •Dragonereum | | •Basic Attention Token |
| •PayFair | | | •BlockCities | | |
| •Stox | | | •Ether Kingdoms (IMPs) | | |
| | | | •Gittron | | |

About 43% are related to finance, exchange, or marketplace, which are collectively categorized as the **decentralized finance** (or **DeFi**) area, about 20% for games, 15% for social media and gambling, and 22% for the rest, including security, governance, wallet, and development and storage.

DeFi is a collection of traditional finance products, services, and tools running on Ethereum or some other blockchains. These digital native products are almost like the analogy twins of those traditional products from the finance, banking, and payment service industry. In almost all cases, business processes are digitized and streamlined to take advantage of digital and blockchain technology. They are redesigned and rebuilt with blockchain technology and offer products in lending, issuance platforms and investing, prediction markets, exchanges, and marketplace areas. One such example is the decentralized lending platform known as MakerDAO. Blockchain-enabled DeFi applications have been able to steadily encroach into the traditional markets in the last couple of years, following the surge in popularity of the Ethereum platform. The trend shall continue.

 Those of you who are curious should check out a more comprehensive list from ConsenSys' site (`https://media.consensys.net/the-100-projects-pioneering-decentralized-finance-717478ddcdf2`).

We provided a bird's-eye view of the economical aspect of the blockchain ecosystem in the *Making sense of crypto-economics* section of `Chapter 3`, *Deep Research on Ethereum*. With DeFi applications, it goes well beyond a self-sustaining and autonomous incentive-based blockchain ecosystem. We discussed the concept of stablecoin and explored the various types of stablecoins on the market. Maker DAO is one interesting and successful example of this. Essentially, the investor can stake a certain amount of ether as collateral to acquire dais and loan dais out as an investment to earn interest. This is also called staking.

You may also remember we discussed staking in the context of the PoS consensus algorithm. This is a consensus mechanism where the validators can stake coins to earn the opportunity to add new blocks to the blockchain and generate income that's been accrued from various sources such as transaction fees and new mint coins. In fact, staking is one of the most popular cryptocurrency investment vehicles. A crypto lending platform (such as MakerDAO or Nexo) is where you can borrow cryptocurrencies against collateral or lend them out and earn interest.

# AML and KYC

As DeFi applications become more and more mainstream, it certainly raises more and more regulation and compliance concerns from governments all over the world. The blockchain and cryptocurrency community should be prepared to work with financial regulators and develop solutions to address such thorny issues.

One that's close to watch is the **Anti-Money Laundering (AML)** law. According to Sec.gov (`https://www.sec.gov/about/offices/ocie/amlsourcetool.htm#3`), financial institutions are required to establish an AML program, which is a formal program within the institute that establishes reasonable policies, procedures, and internal controls to comply with Bank Secrecy Act rules. They also need to set up risk-based procedures to **know your customer (KYC)** and conduct due diligence throughout customer interaction with the institutions.

KYC is the ability to verify the identities of your customers, assess their suitability as a customer, and know about the potential risks of illegal intention toward the business relationship. The idea of knowing your customers throughout the time they are with you is to detect and deter any activities related to money laundering, terrorism financing, and more run-of-the-mill fraud schemes.

There are a lot of debates in the cryptocurrency community about compliance with AML and KYC rules and their impact on innovation and efficiency. Currently, only a small percentage—around 15%—of cryptocurrency institutes are establishing the program to tackle such issues. More rigorous solutions in distinguishing lawful and unlawful financial transactions in the virtual world have yet to come.

# Emerging technology fusion – blockchain, AI/ML, and IoT

So far, in most parts of this book, we've been talking about blockchain, Ethereum, and cryptocurrency. There are a few other areas worth mentioning as well. One is the integration of different blockchains, while another is about the intersection between blockchain and big data, **artificial intelligence (AI)**, and **machine learning (ML)**. The last one is to integrate **internet of things (IoT)** and smart devices with blockchain.

## Internet of blockchains

Unlike the electoral college system in the United States, where the winner takes all in the state, the future of blockchain's infrastructure will be an integration and coexistence of all major blockchain platforms. No matter how dominating Ethereum could become, it is not going to be the only platform running all DApps. New platforms, such as EOS or IOTA, will come up and fit into the space Bitcoin or Ethereum may have left. An integration of different blockchain technologies and a network of many independent blockchains are emerging trends in the Blockchain ecosystem.

In Chapter 3, Deep Research on Ethereum, we discussed Plasma, an organic multi-chain hierarchy and cross-chain integration concept from Ethereum. We briefly mentioned the Cosmos network too. Cosmos is intended to provide the network infrastructure of blockchains. It has its own consensus layer based on Tendermint Core, as well as a **Byzantine Fault-Tolerant (BFT)** blockchain consensus engine that's also leveraged by BigchainDB 2.0. Polkadot is another one in this space. It provides a composability framework to enable intercommunication between different blockchain platforms.

## Blockchain meets AI and ML

**Artificial intelligence (AI)** and **machine learning (ML)**, together with big data technologies, are another set of disruptive technologies that have a profound influence on business and technology advances in the world. Artificial intelligence has been around for many decades, but thanks to Google's AlphaGo, AI/ML has returned to the forefront of technological innovation and disruption. Businesses are rushing to leverage techniques from AI, ML, and data science to make sense of the myriad of data they have gathered over the years, and get business insights and drive informed business decisions.

Intersections between blockchain and AI/ML are often discussed. There are three ways this intersection may go. The most common one is to leverage blockchain, big data, AI, and ML together to address complex business issues. This approach takes advantage of each technology appropriately to solve any particular problem. However, as a whole, they are able to solve large fundamental issues in the business. For example, some large enterprises may use blockchain to streamline the cross-border payment process, and at the same time use big data, AI, and ML to find out about their customers and define intelligent and concierge customer engagement platforms.

The second one is to leverage AI/ML to solve problems with blockchain and cryptocurrency. There are lots of applications that have been developed in the blockchain community to leverage AI and ML to analyze data and transactions on the blockchains, usually via off-chain processes. AI/ML is an evolving technique that brings real-time trading insights to the trade table. In the same way, it applies to crypto trading on blockchain transactions too.

The last one is real-time on-chain analytic AI/ML capabilities. Some claim these to be the true benefits of bringing AI/ML capability to the blockchain, though they have yet to be seen. One that should be watched is SingularityNET, which provides an AI service marketplace and a decentralized AI network for blockchain. Another one in this space is DeepBrain Chain, which is more focused on a decentralized artificial intelligence computing network and platform for a variety of artificial intelligence products. Both intend to bring AI/ML capability to the blockchain and smart contracts.

# Smart things on a decentralized network

Speaking of smart things, this means that all the smart IoT devices are interconnected with each other and integrated with the IoT platform. They become new neurons of the enterprise in the digital world. They generate a large amount of real-time data through all kinds of sensors and communicate with each other through edge devices or IoT platforms to act or react to events they have seen, felt, or sensed. With the combination of big data, AI, and ML, it has become as sophisticated as an autonomous device. For example, a driverless car has the ability to sense its surroundings and take action accordingly. It can leverage AI/ML to make sense of the information at hand and make autonomous decisions.

There have been some attempts to connect IoT devices to the Ethereum blockchain, but blockchain may not be the right platform for collecting, processing, and transacting on such a large volume of real-time, low-level sensor data.

IOTA is an emerging and promising platform that's been designed as the transaction settlement and data transfer layer for IoT. It is envisioned to be the public and permissionless backbone protocol for IoT that enables true interoperability between all smart devices. It doesn't use blockchain technology; the sensor data is recorded as the distributed ledger using a **distributed ledger technology (DLT)** called Tangle. Instead of blocks in the blockchain, Tangle uses a **directed acyclic graph (DAG)** data structure to record all valid transactions. Each connected device in the IOTA network serves as a node and is active in the consensus and validation of transactions. By protocol, each node has to validate the two previous transactions on the network before making its own transaction. The current transaction, as well as the pointers to the previous two transactions, will piece together a directed acyclic graph.

IOTA is still in its early stages of development, but it is worth watching. At the same time, some Layer 2 solutions on the Ethereum blockchain may be a good choice for smart devices and IoT. To get there, Ethereum will need to address its pressing scalability issues with the Casper implementation and be able to scale up to the transaction volume like Visa and MasterCard did.

# Meeting the future of Ethereum

Ethereum is making inroads into the enterprise space too. Microsoft was a pioneer among large technology firms in offering Ethereum-based **blockchain as a service (BaaS)** on its Azure cloud platform, which was announced as early as Nov 2015. Late last year, during the re:Invent event in November 2018, **Amazon Web Services (AWS)** unveiled a new service that allows its clients to build Ethereum-based blockchain applications on the cloud. Using the AWS blockchain template for Ethereum, you can choose to run smart contracts on a private Ethereum network within AWS, or join the public Ethereum network. Earlier this year, it was rumored that JP Morgan is rolling out the first US bank-backed cryptocurrency, a digital US dollar, to transform its payments business. The blockchain technology they are using is called Quorum, the private version of Ethereum. Additionally, the Quorum network is partnering with Microsoft to integrate cloud-computing services. The social media giant Facebook unveiled its plans for a cryptocurrency called Libra, and its Calibra digital wallet on June 18, 2019. Libra will let you buy things or send money to people with nearly zero fees. With a 2.7 billion user base worldwide, Facebook has become a potential game-changer regarding the outlook for many existing crypto industry players. Similar to Facebook's Libra, the retail giant Walmart has also applied for a digital coin patent.

The "Walmart Coin", like Libra, will be a stablecoin. With over 265 million customers visiting Walmart's stores, across 27 countries, Walmart Coin will provide financing for all of them. These stablecoins are decentralized. The service will be available to anyone who connects to the blockchain, with low fees and costs. As such, we think the momentum in the enterprise space will continue.

This is an exciting time for Ethereum, as blockchain is still at the primordial stage of technology evolution we haven't seen for decades. The future of Ethereum is largely dependent on its ability to pull together and resolve the pressing scalability issues it currently has with its 2.0 roadmap. With a portfolio of scaling solutions, from state channel, Plasma, sharding, eWASM, to PoS, we see Ethereum on the way to becoming the backbone of the new internet infrastructure, and it may not be the only one. Blockchain and Ethereum are here to stay, and all that means is that there's a myriad of opportunities out there, now and in the future.

# Summary

In this final chapter, we explored the different challenges Ethereum is facing and took a quick peek at the tools, technologies, and DApps in the broad Ethereum ecosystem. We paid special attention to one very promising DApp category, DeFi, where we see the incoming players becoming the ones to disrupt the traditional ones. It is always fascinating to see the convergence and integration between blockchain, AI/ML, IoT, and other emerging technologies. Finally, we also provided our view of the future of Ethereum.

With that, we hope this book has helped you understand the ins and outs of blockchain and Ethereum, and equipped you with all you needed to get started with DApp development. We hope we have provided you with some insight into the future of the broad blockchain and cryptocurrency space.

# Other Books You May Enjoy

If you enjoyed this book, you may be interested in these other books by Packt:

**Mastering Ethereum**
Merunas Grincalaitis

ISBN: 978-1-78953-137-4

- Apply scalability solutions on dApps with Plasma and state channels
- Understand the important metrics of blockchain for analyzing and determining its state
- Develop a decentralized web application using React.js and Node.js
- Create oracles with Node.js to provide external data to smart contracts
- Get to grips with using Etherscan and block explorers for various transactions
- Explore web3.js, Solidity, and Vyper for dApps communication
- Deploy apps with multiple Ethereum instances including TestRPC, private chain, test chain, and mainnet

**Ethereum Cookbook**
Manoj P R

ISBN: 978-1-78913-399-8

- Efficiently write smart contracts in Ethereum
- Build scalable distributed applications and deploy them
- Use tools and frameworks to develop, deploy, and test your application
- Use block explorers such as Etherscan to find a specific transaction
- Create your own tokens, initial coin offerings (ICOs), and games
- Understand various security flaws in smart contracts in order to avoid them

# Leave a review - let other readers know what you think

Please share your thoughts on this book with others by leaving a review on the site that you bought it from. If you purchased the book from Amazon, please leave us an honest review on this book's Amazon page. This is vital so that other potential readers can see and use your unbiased opinion to make purchasing decisions, we can understand what our customers think about our products, and our authors can see your feedback on the title that they have worked with Packt to create. It will only take a few minutes of your time, but is valuable to other potential customers, our authors, and Packt. Thank you!

# Index

# D

# Z

Made in the USA
Middletown, DE
11 May 2021